THE DARK SIDE OF SOFTWARE ENGINEERING

THE DARK SIDE OF SOFTWARE ENGINEERING
Evil on Computing Projects

JOHANN ROST and ROBERT L. GLASS

A JOHN WILEY & SONS, INC., PUBLICATION

Published by John Wiley & Sons, Inc., Hoboken, New Jersey.
Published simultaneously in Canada.

For general information on our other products and services please contact our Customer Care
Department within the U.S. at 877-762-2974, outside the U.S. at 317-572-3993 or fax 317-572-4002.

Wiley also publishes its books in a variety of electronic formats. Some content that appears in print,
however, may not be available in electronic format.

Library of Congress Cataloging-in-Publication Data is available.

ISBN 978-0-470-59717-0

ePDF: 978-0-470-90994-2
oBook: 978-0-470-90995-9
ePub: 978-0-470-92287-3

10 9 8 7 6 5 4 3 2

CONTENTS

FOREWORD

Dr. Linda Rising

Robert Glass has always been one who "boldly goes" where the more cautious fear to tread. I have been a fan of his writing for, well, let's just say, a long time. I remember when he started telling the truth as he saw it about software development and was forced to change the names of the companies and products that he was discussing—he even changed his own name to conceal authorship of published accounts. I remember teaching a course on structured design (using the green book by Yourdon and Constantine—that's how long ago that was!) and if I finished a class early, I would say to my students, "You can go now or I can read another story by Robert Glass." No one ever left before the story was finished. "Cornbelt Shakedown" (from Glass and DeNim [1980]) was a favorite. Many of these stories are the kind of humor that leads you to wonder, "Why am I laughing? To keep from crying?"

Later, as I was working in the industry, I led a study group on *Software Runaways* (Glass 1997) and experienced the serious side of Robert Glass. Very little of the wry and witty here, but, instead, a lot of lessons for serious consideration.

Robert Glass, joined in this book with Johann Rost, is still at it. He continues to be (I can't resist) fearless! (The reference is to my own book, Manns and Rising [2005]). I don't know Johann except through his work on this book, which is excellent, and from what I've been told—that he's a German former IT consultant now living in beautiful Romania, the land of Transylvania, Dracula, and Ceaușescu … it's no wonder the book has a "dark side" theme! This book is also full of stories about real projects at real companies. Names are named. The result is a compelling look at the dark side of computer programming. We are all hardwired to learn from stories, especially when we can identify with the protagonists.

Hacking, espionage, sabotage, theft, whistle-blowing, subversion, disgruntled employees who want to get even—and, of course, the dance of deception. We've all seen it—where *we know* and *they know*, in fact, *everyone knows*—but we all smile and keep dancing as long as we can. The authors cut in on this charade and force us to wake up and take stock.

Robert and Johann also include the results of their serious research. They have certainly done their homework. There's an abundance of citations to back up their observations. The survey data on sabotage is fascinating!

This reporting is way out of the box; in fact, these authors are standing on the box and they share with us a good look at the terrain—something most of us just don't take the time to do; we prefer to rush ahead and ignore the lessons of the past.

So, take a moment. We need a breather now and then. We need to step back and retrospect on the history of our industry and think about a better way of working within it. Robert Glass and Johann Rost are offering us a chance to do just that. Stop. Listen. Think. Is this the road that will serve us best for the next part of our journey?

REFERENCES

Glass, Robert and DeNim, Sue. "The Second Coming: More Computing Projects Which Failed," *Computing Trends*, 1980.

Glass, Robert. *Software Runaways: Monumental Software Disasters*. Prentice-Hall, 1997.

Manns, Mary Lynn and Rising, Linda. *Fearless Change*. Addison Wesley, 2005.

INTRODUCTION

I.1 WHAT'S THE DARK SIDE?

The dictionary doesn't give a definition for "dark side." Not even my heavyweight dictionary that I can barely lift. Oh, it defines words such as "dark" ("secret, mysterious, evil," among other things), "darken" ("perplex, make foul, sully, cast a gloom upon") and "darksome" ("dark, dismal"). So you get the idea—things that are on the dark side tend to be evil, gloomy, dismal.

That's not a surprise to most of our readers, we suspect. The "dark side" has a sort of intuitive meaning that we all grasp and is (pretty much) in synch with those related dictionary definitions. Things that are on the dark side of the computing profession would be things that we wouldn't necessarily want to be a part of or approve of.

I, Robert, remember an incident from my days of child-raising, when one of my sons played on a little league baseball team. There was a pitcher on that team whose father, like me, attended nearly all of the games. When his son was pitching, the father would shout to his son, from time to time, "Throw the dark one." I never knew exactly what he meant by that cry. But I always assumed that it wasn't so much about a particular pitch his son could throw but about intimidating the opposing batter, who might become convinced that the pitch to come was somehow evil and be less likely to make contact with it because of that.

In any case, even on the baseball diamond, the words "dark" and therefore "dark side" have an intuitively universal meaning.

It's interesting that, if you know the software literature—be it the popular computing press, the academic journals, or even the general popular press—you would be aware that it doesn't say very much about dark side issues. Oh, it says a lot about project success and project failure but that's a different kettle of fish. Projects that fail may be in a sense "dark" but not in the sense of "evil." We tend to assume, without ever saying so, that even projects that fail, do so largely because of some kind of ineptitude, not because of some kind of evil.

Let me be perfectly clear about what we are doing here. This is NOT a book about software project failure, or about prescriptive thinking about how to build software better. This is a book about the EVIL THINGS that happen on computing and software projects—what the kinds of evil are, how they manifest themselves, and what we good guys can do about them. I emphasize this point because a lot of folks we've asked to review the book's material keep thinking that this is "Yet

Another Book About Project Failure" (YABAPF) or "Yet Another Book About Doing Software Engineering Right" (YABADSER)!

Where might we find discussions of dark side matters in the traditional software engineering literature? Look at the topics that literature on computing and software tend to be divided into. They are usually organized into these topics:

Problem-solving

Computer hardware

Systems/software

Data/information

Application problem domains

Systems/software management

Organizations

Society

Disciplinary issues

This list is derived from the computing research topics explored in the series of papers culminating in Glass, Ramesh, and Vessey (2004).

Where in that list of topics would you look to find "dark side" topics? Perhaps in "systems/software management." Perhaps in "disciplinary issues." It doesn't fit comfortably into either of those topics, but it could be forced to fit—inconveniently—into them. But the fact of the matter is, any taxonomy of computing topics you choose is unlikely to provide a convenient home for this issue of the dark side. It is, in other words, a topic that people writing about computing have not only avoided over time; they have avoided it because it doesn't fit nicely into any list of topics that describe the field.

And that brings us to the topic of the next section.

I.1.1 Why the Dark Side?

Both authors of this book have been intrigued by the lack of discussion of dark side issues in computing literature. We were both aware, from personal experience, that dark side things happened in the field. But hardly anyone seemed to be talking about them. Perhaps more importantly, hardly anyone was researching them. For example, how often did dark side matters affect computing and software projects?

I, Johann, had initially thought about exploring this issue. I knew from personal experience the effect of dark side behavior: For example, subversion on software projects, while it does not occur often, has serious repercussions when it does. Because of that, and because of the lack of any appearance whatsoever of "subversion" in computing literature, I conducted a study to determine its prevalence, its effects, and ways of overcoming it. That survey is presented as a chapter later in this book. It is a pioneering study in the software field; to this date, no one else has explored this topic.

My co-author, Robert, came at the subject from a different direction. He was surprised while presenting a topic at a software seminar; the seminar attendees hijacked the session and diverted it to talking about lying as a problem in the software project world. The attendees were vehement—lying was a big-time problem in the projects on which they had been involved. Because of that, and because—once again—of the lack of any significant appearance of the topic of "lying" in the computing literature—he began to explore that topic in more depth.

It was about then that we met one another. (It is interesting to note, in this day of electronic communication, that we have only met on the Web, never in person!) I was having trouble finding a leading journal willing to publish my subversion paper, that is, the one that resulted from his survey. I asked Robert for help, and—to make a long story shorter—the result became a co-authored paper that eventually was published in a leading journal.

Intrigued by the subversion study, Robert suggested that we conduct a similar study about lying. As we have said, neither topic was discussed much in any of the literatures surrounding the field. So the two of us, together with another contributor named Matthias Matook, performed a study in the form of a survey about the prevalence of lying, its effects, and ways of overcoming it. Eventually, to make this long story also shorter, that too was published. Variations and enhancements of the two published papers are presented later in this book.

By then, we had become thoroughly intrigued by these topics, and we began to see them as part of a broader issue: "dark side" issues on computing projects. We expanded the topic into more and more sub-topics, eventually identifying seven dark side matters that affected these projects: subversion, lying, hacking, theft of information, espionage, disgruntled employees and sabotage, and whistle-blowing. There is a chapter of this book devoted to each of those topics.

We considered doing thorough research into the latter five topics, but decided that there was sufficient material in the literature of those more-often covered topics; so we relied on already published case studies, not the survey research that we conducted about subversion and lying, to cover them. (To be honest, that research was extremely laborious and time-consuming, and we were reluctant to engage in it beyond what we had already done!)

And then there is another final fact that brought the interest in dark side matters to a head: Robert has published a number of books and articles on the subject of failed computing projects. (As we said earlier, there is not a direct link between failure and dark side matters, but the two are similar enough to draw the same kind of interest.) He had been intrigued by failure and became equally intrigued by dark side matters!

I.1.2   Who Cares About the Dark Side?

The short answer to this question, of course, is that we hope YOU do! We chose to write about the dark side because we were interested in the subject and because we felt we had some contributions to make on the subject. Our fervent hope is that you, our intended reader, will also be interested in what we have to say.

But that raises the question, "Exactly who is our intended reader"? Usually, both of us have a preferred reading audience, namely experienced software practitioners who have an interest in broadening their knowledge on the topic. And—we can't help it—that's who we've been thinking about as we did the research and the initial writing of this book.

But it would be disadvantageous and perhaps even disingenuous of us to leave it at that. There aren't that many experienced software practitioners in the broader world, and if we restrict our readership to those folks we won't sell very many copies of this book! So, as we developed our material, we increasingly began to think about others who might like to know about dark side matters in computing and software engineering.

For example:

- **Software managers.** When we started thinking about broadening our readership, we began by expanding the material to appeal to a management-focused audience. Certainly, if the problems of dark side matters in software engineering are ever to be addressed (and perhaps even solved!), managers will have to be involved. We have many reasons to wish that software managers become interested in reading this book. And the same goes for managers of those managers. And so on, on up the hierarchy!

- **Academics.** We believe that the same spirit of intellectual inquiry that prompted us to look into this topic in the first place will also engage academics. And we believe that, given the absence of this topic from the textbooks on computing and software subjects, there are some unique pieces of academic insight to be had in our book.

- **Researchers.** To be honest, we have some self-interest here. We discuss the absence of relevant research findings on matters dark side. We hope that this book will stimulate other computing researchers into delving more into this topic. We believe the field will be the richer for it.

- **Novice software practitioners.** The people most likely to be stunned by dark side matters are the field's "greenies," those who have no reason to believe—going in—that dealing with dark side matters is going to become part of their job description. So welcome, novices, to the word involving more evil than you might ever have considered being a part of!

- **Software engineering students.** If those greenies we discuss above need to be warned about dark side matters, so do students, who typically are greener than green. Both of us were students once, both of us have taught tons of students, and both of us realize that "dealing with the dark side" doesn't occur anywhere in an academic curriculum. We don't intend to scare you off, student—we both believe that software engineering is a career with its own many faceted rewards. But beware: You will run into evil, and evil folk, even in the otherwise wonderful world of computing and software.

- **The general public.** Now this one is tricky. When you're a professional in some subject matter, there's a tendency to write for readers who understand your lingo, and in the process of doing that you make your material inaccessible to a broader, non-computing, professional audience. And to overcome this limitation, you need to think carefully every time you put finger to keyboard. It's not at all a matter of "dumbing down" your material (that's a term I've always found to be particularly offensive); it's a matter of writing in such a way that you can be understood. And, to be honest, you the reader get to cast the final vote on how successful this particular quest has been. I believe that the general public will find our thoughts and research about the dark side in computing and software engineering interesting, but I don't know whether we have succeeded in working that particular problem successfully. We'd be interested in hearing from you on this: rlglass@acm.org.

So there you have it. We've defined "dark side," we've explained why we chose to write about it, and we've tried to introduce not only ourselves to you, our intended audience, but you to us. It's time to get specific about what all this dark side stuff is really about. For example, how often does it really happen?

I.1.3   How Dark is the Dark Side?

It would be nice if there were a clear-cut, straightforward answer to the question we just asked as we concluded the previous section of our book—how often do dark side matters arise? But the fact of the matter is this: The truthful answer is "it depends."

"It depends" is not a very satisfactory answer, especially to academics. For decades now the software engineering field has been hoping for a universal solution to the problems of building software. Each new methodology, invented by an academic, a guru, or a practitioner, is touted as the new be-all end-all for software. And, as we slowly begin to realize through the experience of using these methodologies, each of them has its own "sweet spot" of applicability and its own areas where applying it is an exercise in frustration. Structured programming was the "solution" for all applications in the 1980s; object-orientation in the 1990s; and Agile approaches more recently. There are those who still believe in the claims of universality for methodologies; most of us by now can see that each approach is wonderful in its proper context, but not so wonderful in others. We have arrived at the point where one software engineering expert says "anyone who believes in one-size-fits-all belongs in a pantyhose commercial." In other words, "it depends" is becoming the watch-phrase for such methodologies.

In order to talk about how often the dark side issues arise, we need to break the dark side topic down into its constituent elements. We have some fairly crisp and clear answers for each of the dark side topics that emerge as chapters later in this book—but as we will see in what follows, those answers don't spread well over the "dark side topic" as a whole.

So let's look at each dark side issue one at a time.

- **Subversion.** Here, our survey produced some nicely definitive numbers. Slightly over 50% of our survey responders had seen episodes of subversion, whereas 35% had not. Asked to estimate how often such subversion occurs, the predominant answer was "on 20% of projects." In other words, subversion is an occasional, not a frequent, problem on software projects.

- **Lying.** Again, we have some survey results that allow us to speak with some confidence on this matter. The results showed that 86% of survey responders said they had seen lying on software projects, on perhaps 50% of such projects. The majority of lying is about either cost/schedule estimation, status reporting, or is for political maneuvering (these causes of lying were nearly equivalent in their frequency; nearly all other causes lagged those numbers considerably). Based on these numbers, we feel we can say that lying is a common problem on software projects.

- **Hacking.** Here we enter into the dark side issues where we do not have any data on the frequency of occurrence. If you believe this figure can be judged by incidents reported in the popular press, then hacking is a very common problem. But if you ask questions of this kind to experts who specialize in studying hackers and hacking, you get a fairly strong "I have no idea." Such experts go on to say they have no idea, either, about what percentage of computer systems are hacked and what percentage of hacks go undetected, except for educated guesses such as "less than 50% of hacks go undetected (which tends to be immediately followed by its own kind of "it depends"—it depends on what kind of hack we're talking about).

- **Theft of information.** Like hacking, information theft is discussed somewhat often in the popular press, but we are not aware of any data on its frequency. There is a suspicion that most corporate employees who leave an enterprise, either under duress or otherwise, may take information (data or software code) with them, but again there is little data to support this belief. But see the discussion below about disgruntled employees and the frequency with which they take things. In any case, we suspect that there is a problem with theft of information, but it is not a very common one.

- **Espionage.** Stories on espionage in the computing field tend to splash in big headlines in the popular press. But it is important to remember that the press goes in for "exception reporting"—if something is common, it is covered with much less emphasis than if it seldom happens. That's why it is important to avoid an attempt to translate splashy headlines into frequency information. Here again, we have no data on the frequency of occurrence of espionage on computing projects, but we suspect it is uncommon.

- **Disgruntled employees and sabotage.** Although we have no survey data to rely on in this matter, the popular press has done a nice job of studying the frequency of this particular problem. For example, 60–70% of data theft is conducted by disgruntled employees, according to a recent study, and to make matters worse responders in that study believed that 82% of companies who had had such data stolen would not even realize it. Another study said that perhaps only 1 in 400 such data thefts get reported. Based on that data, we feel safe in saying that disgruntled employees cause mischief quite frequently. Sabotage, sometimes engaged in by disgruntled employees along with other dark side acts, is by contrast infrequent.

- **Whistle-blowing.** Whistle-blowing is an interesting topic in the context of this book. For one thing, it is not at all clear that whistle-blowing is a dark side activity. But it is certainly a reaction to a dark side activity, and that is why we include it. For another thing, there has been little research into whistle-blowing in the broader literature and none whatsoever in the software engineering field. We are happy to report that we include one of the few research surveys of whistle-blowing in general later in this book, but we have to admit that it doesn't help us in judging how often whistle-blowing occurs on software projects. For reasons that we will explain in the chapter on whistle-blowing, we suspect that it seldom if ever occurs on software projects.

There you have it. How often do dark side issues arise on software projects? Anywhere from "seldom if ever" to "quite frequently." If ever there was a case where "it depends" was the correct answer to the question, this is it!

It is interesting to compare this discussion of dark side matters with a comparable discussion of software project failures. Dark side discussions tend to occur, but only in a particular context (as we have seen, based on our chapter topics above). But with software project failure, it is common to see cries of "software crisis" as whoever is writing about the matter bemoans that software is always "behind schedule, over budget, and unreliable." The general belief is that software is a field with a big-time problem) at least based on such discussions of project failure). Robert believes that cries of "crisis" are bogus, and that the software field, which is the basis for the obvious success of the "computing age," is a field with far more spectacular successes than spectacular failures.

In any case, whereas software project failure gets enormous attention from the press, dark side matters slide under the press radar for the most part. What that means in practice is that there are few biases to overcome among you readers regarding how often dark side matters arise.

I.1.4 What Else is on the Dark Side?

When we first conceived of this section for our introductory chapter, we envisioned a small section with a discussion of those few other books and articles that pertained to dark side issues. Big hah!

If you Google "dark side," you are returned 620,000,000 results. With a number that big, we quickly gave up on even trying to categorize the uses of the term "dark side."

Note that when we first introduced the topic of the dark side, we noted that the dictionary didn't define the term per se. But we guessed that most people already had an idea of what it meant. Little did we know! You don't get 620,000,000 Google results for a term that people don't understand.

If you look up "dark side" on Amazon, you get another big number. Not as big as the one you get from Google. Still, 94,500 books with dark side or something related to it in the title?! (And that's not even counting ours, which Google doesn't know about as of this writing). Books on the dark side deal with topics ranging from religion to psychology to politics to dating to leadership (this one, interestingly, links the subject of failure to matters of the dark side, an issue we presented rather tenuously above!). Based on books people have written, you'd guess there is a dark side to nearly any subject you can think of—and someone has likely written a book about it!

Closer to home, in the software engineering and computing literature, the topic comes up far less often, as we have already mentioned. It does arise, of course, disguised under different terms. For example, consider the subject of "ethics."

I.1.5 Ethics and the Dark Side

Ethics is a topic that is explicitly addressed by almost all professional societies. For example, the IEEE, the ACM, and the German computing society all have codes of ethics, that is, relatively brief statements of how their members should behave. These codes tend to focus more on professionalism than outright misbehavior and overlap to a large extent. Here is an overview of those codes

- **Contribute to society and human well-being.** Avoid injuring others, their property, reputation, or employment by false or malicious action. Make decisions consistent with the safety, health and welfare of the public. Disclose factors that might endanger the public or the environment.
- **Be honest and trustworthy.** Give unbiased estimations, reject bribery. Undertake technological tasks for others only if qualified by training or experience. Seek out, accept, and offer honest criticism of technical work and acknowledge and correct errors. Honor confidentiality. Honor contracts, agreements, and assigned responsibilities.
- **Acquire and maintain professional competence.** This includes technological skills, legal skills, and communication skills.
- **Improve the IT understanding of others.** Train students to assist colleagues and coworkers in their professional development. Promote and strive for excellence. Improve public understanding of computing and its consequences. Accept and provide appropriate professional review.
- **Honor property rights including copyrights and patents, and credit properly the contributions of others.**
- **Be fair and take action not to discriminate.** Treat fairly all persons regardless of such factors as race, religion, gender, disability, age, or national origin.
- **Respect the privacy of others.** This includes the refusal to support the implementation of control and surveillance technology without informing the affected persons.
- **Access computing and communication resources only when authorized to do so.**

It is interesting to compare these codes with our dark side topics. There is barely any intersection between these codes and subversion and espionage, for example.

There is more of a link between lying, hacking, theft of information, and disgruntled employees and sabotage. For example, the material on injuring property, public welfare, honoring property rights, respecting privacy, and access authorization has a more or less direct relationship to our topics. Whistle-blowing, interestingly enough, has almost no linkage to these codes. Once again, although we see a deep societal concern for ethical behavior, we see an odd sort of mismatch between our topics—behaviors seen on actual computing projects—and the professional and philosophical content of these codes. Clearly, not only has research tended to ignore these topics, but so have the more ethical foci of our field.

Curiously, twice in the six months preceding the writing of this material, the societal journal *IEEE Computer* has done something on the subject of software engineering ethics. In the first such article ("Professional and Ethical Dilemmas in Software Engineering," by Brian Berenbach and Manfred Broy, published in the January 2009 issue) the key word from the title is "dilemmas." The article describes nine specific ethical and professional dilemmas for software engineers:

1. Mission impossible: accepting a schedule that is obviously impossible
2. Mea culpa: delivering a product that lacks key functionality
3. Rush job: being more concerned about product delivery than product quality
4. Not my Problem: showing no inclination to improve productivity or quality
5. Red lies:making statements about a project/product known to be untrue
6. Fictionware versus Vaporware: "fictionware" is signing up for features known to be infeasible; vaporware is announcing a product that does not exist
7. Nondiligence: failing to review key documentation
8. Canceled vacation: management overly pressuring employees to meet short-term deadlines
9. Swept under the rug: ignoring key issues in the hope that they will go away

Interestingly, and as we saw above in analyzing ethical codes, these ethical dilemmas do not overlap well with our dark side issues. Several of them are about lying, but most of our other dark side categories simply do not appear on this list. This serves to reinforce our belief that dark side matters appear all too seldom in the computing literature. There is little doubt in our minds that dark side issues are strongly related to ethical matters, and therefore should somehow appear in any discussions of ethical dilemmas in our field.

The second recent *IEEE Computer* coverage of software engineering ethics was actually a special issue devoted to the topic ("Software Engineering Ethics," edited by Awais Rashid, John Weckert, and Richard Lucas, published in the June 2009 issue). There were four articles and a point/counterpoint debate in the special issue. The articles dealt with items such as these:

- Addressing certain values in software applications, such as trust, privacy, identity, user content control, green technology, and public welfare

- Ways of discouraging harmful uses and encouraging beneficial uses of a software product
- The social impact of information systems failures (note that here, again, the topic of failure is coupled with the topic of ethics)
- How a code of ethics, such as that of the IEEE, can be used to aid decision making
- The point/counterpoint debate: whether and how software engineering and ethics can mix

Again, there is not much overlap with dark side topics.

The subject of ethics is one way that the software field explores matters of this kind. But often, humorous treatments of related subjects can be, in effect, discussions of ethical matters in disguise.

For example, years ago some philosophical readers of the humor publication *Mad* magazine noted that most of the material in *Mad*, although funny, was also moralistic. There were lessons to be learned and morals to be grasped in the madcap world of the pages of *Mad*.

But the Back Page section of *Computerworld* (June 27, 2005) contained something in the same vein but more specific to the computing field. While noting that lots of publications discussed the best places to work in the IT field, no one was talking about the worst places! To alleviate that problem, the Back Page article offered 10 ways to make the "worst places to work in IT list." The list, for all its humorous intentions, becomes a nice list of things not to do, a sort of ethical violations recap:

1. Hide information. Don't give employees the information they need to do their work.
2. Blame. Name and shame employees publicly when they do something wrong.
3. Go slow. Postpone anything that's postponeable.
4. Distrust. Make it clear that you don't trust your employees.
5. Reduce visibility. Don't share broader corporate information with IT employees.
6. Block opportunities. Don't reward successful employees.
7. Stifle arguments. Put a lid on discussions of relevant but controversial matters.
8. Outlaw play. Maintain discipline at all costs.
9. Discourage experiments. Don't allow failure of any form, even under carefully controlled circumstances.
10. Don't listen. If it's worth hearing, your boss will have said it to you.

Once again, there would seem to be little overlap between these discussions of software engineering ethics and our dark side issues. For whatever reason, the issues we raise are simply not yet on the radar of most authors of software engineering materials.

I.1.6 Personal Anecdotes About the Dark Side

We thought it would be relevant to share with you at this point in our book some incidents of dark side issues that have occurred to us authors personally. For one thing, the dark side—up to this point in our book—has been a sort of distant concept, not well fleshed out with actual anecdotal material to make it come alive. For another, as we describe our personal experiences with dark side matters, it may help you envision times when you, too, have been involved in such matters. So here we go. (Note: For certain purposes, the "I" in what follows refers (indiscriminately and ambiguously) to either of us authors!)

- **Subversion.** I don't really have a totally relevant subversion story to share. But I had a couple of episodes in my career where it felt like my work was being subverted.

  In the first, a manager for whom I worked but with whom I felt terribly uneasy because I couldn't figure out where I stood with him, eventually told me that he never gave me sufficient direction to do my work properly because he was afraid that if I performed well I might go after his job! I guess he was worried that I would subvert him, but in responding to that he actually subverted both me and the work I was supposed to be doing.

  In the second episode, I was given the task at a major research facility of writing a particular document, one for which I had a good background because what I was asked to write about was very similar to a book I had already written.

  When I had my first meeting with my colleagues on the project, it gradually emerged that they were totally opposed to what I proposed to do (or at least how I proposed to do it). Somehow I staggered to a completion of that work, in spite of the subversive road blocks they kept throwing up in my path. But when I left the facility, the first thing they did was throw out my work and redo as they had wanted it done all along.

- **Lying.** The subject of lying on software projects kind of snuck up on me. I was conducting a seminar on something or other (it doesn't matter much what it was, after all these years). I gave my seminar attendees a task to do: one with a deliberately impossible schedule. My intent at the time was to see what they would do if they could not finish their project by the scheduled completion time, Would they override the schedule and take whatever time it took, or would they short-circuit the project goals and try to finish on time?

  I think it is significant that those seminar attendees took the schedule as a requirement and downplayed quality in their rush to finish "on time." I think much of the evidence since then supports the notion that that's just the way it is on software projects, at least at this point in time. Schedule trumps quality, even if it shouldn't.

  But as the attendees and I discussed what had happened, they also quickly swung the conversation around to "lying on software projects." (My schedule requirement had been, in a very real sense, a lie). They said things such as "I have to lie 30–50% of the time to get my work done"; "I had to check my ethics at the door when I went to work here"; "I make wildly optimistic promises to get my management off my back"; and "managers who don't tolerate failure I especially lie to." Lying, as these seminar attendees saw it, was a conflagration destroying the profession of software engineering.

I have chosen to talk about the subject of lying rather than to cite personal examples of my lying on software projects. You didn't really think I would talk about lies I personally have told, did you?!

- **Hacking.** I have an account with a leading investment firm, one where I keep my retirement funds. It is, as you might imagine, ID and password protected.

  But, a couple of years ago, a hacker managed to steal my identity and begin performing transactions in my account. I noticed the sale of a big bundle of corporate stock and queried it to the investment company. They immediately froze my account; the stock had been sold, but the money had not yet been transferred out of my account.

  As we pursued this matter further, we could see that the hacker had provided an overriding address for the delivery of the check for his sale of my stock and a contact phone number. Fortunately, that was as far as he had gotten.

  There were two things to be done. The first was to change my ID and password, and I did that (even that kind of change is not simple when you are under attack). Then I needed to decide what legal steps to take.

  In the end, I notified the police department in the city whose address had been provided. The last I heard, the police were going to contact whoever lived at that address. But it is a characteristic of our legal system that there is no follow up; for a variety of reasons, you are never told what came of the matter. So although I would like to end my anecdote by talking about how the rotten character who did this to me got his comeuppance, I will never in fact know if that was the case(!).

- **Theft of information.** There was a time in my life when I supplemented my full-time income by doing legal consulting on the side regarding theft of software. In one case that I remember quite clearly, the situation was that one company had produced a software product and another had put a similar product on the air not long after hiring a former employee of the first company.

  In such cases, the legal system provides for the lawyers involved to get access to the listings of both products, and I in turn was given those listings to examine and analyze. I found that in some parts of both versions of the software product, the code was noticeably different but the design structure (as reflected in the product's call trees) was nearly the same. And, to make matters more interesting, there were a few places where marginally relevant comments included in the first company's product code showed up in the second company's version as well!

  Now at this point, I'd like to say that the second company was appropriately punished for taking the first company's code. But what actually happened was that the companies at that point settled out of court, with a provision in the settlement that the result could not be disclosed. As a result, I never knew what actually happened!

- **Espionage.** I have never really encountered espionage as such on any software projects I have been involved with. Or perhaps what is really true is that I never recognized any espionage that may have been going on around me!

- **Disgruntled employees and sabotage.** Probably the most disgruntled employee I ever worked with was a pacifist I'll call Harley Dove who for some reason I have never fathomed found himself working on military projects at an aerospace company.

    I was the project lead; Dove was one of my workers. And, as time passed, it became next to impossible to get any useful work out of Dove, whatsoever. Project due dates came and went, and Dove continued to do almost nothing, and nothing I could do would motivate him to do any work. If not contributing to a project is a special form of sabotage, then Dove was a (pacifist!) saboteur as well as a disgruntled employee!

    My own personnel review, at the end of that unfortunate period in my career, reflected my total failure to be able to get any work out of Dove. It's no wonder that this is a pretty memorable episode to me!

    I'd like to say that the company converted Dove into a disgruntled ex-employee, but to the best of my knowledge they never fired him. I sometimes wonder what he is doing today, and whom he is doing it to or for!

- **Whistle-blowing.** I once had a consulting contract with a leading banking company. I was invited to do the job by one of the bank's top technical people, whom I will call Top Tech, and at the end I was to present a report on my findings to the top manager, whom I will call Senior Manager. The problem that caused the bank to call me in was that they were falling badly behind on a key project.

    During the course of my information gathering, Top Tech told me that one of the problems they had was that they were paying bonuses for the fixing of key bugs, that their best programmers were hoarding those key bugs in order to achieve those bonuses, and that therefore the backlog of bugs to fix was huge and growing. And then, having told me that, Top Tech went on to ask me to keep that finding confidential!

    Time passed, and it came time for me to present my findings to Senior Manager. Top Tech attended that briefing with me. I had wrestled all along with the dilemma of reporting that key bug finding or suppressing it to keep my commitment to Top Tech. Going in to the meeting, I still wasn't sure what I was going to do. In the end, what I did was this: I hinted at the problem in my presentation, and Senior Manager picked up on the hint and asked me about it. I hesitated to see if Top Tech would speak up, and when he didn't, I glossed over the whole thing.

    Here is my conclusion from a whistle-blowing point of view: I had a golden opportunity to blow the whistle at a point that would have counted, and I failed to do it. Whistle-blowing, I have to conclude based on my own failings, is not an activity for the faint of heart!

REFERENCE

Glass, Ramesh, and Vessey. "An Analysis of Research in Computing Disciplines," *Communications of the ACM*, June 2004.

PART 1

DARK SIDE ISSUES

You have just finished reading our introduction to our dark side book. We have told you what we mean by the dark side, why we chose to write about it, how prevalent it is, and who else is talking about it. And we shared with you some personal anecdotes about our own experiences with dark side matters.

We also pointed out that, although we'd like to say some generic things about these dark side issues, in fact it is nearly impossible to do so. All these dark side issues have some things in common—they are all evil manifestations of computing behavior—but on the other hand, they differ enormously in how often they occur and what they are about.

It's high time, at this point in our book, that we stop waving our hands about these dark side issues, and get down to brass tacks about them. In the seven chapters that follow this introduction to Part 1 of our book we get very specific about each of these matters. Welcome to the many-faceted worlds of subversion, lying, hacking, theft of information, espionage, disgruntled employees and sabotage, and whistle-blowing. We hope you will find it as fascinating to learn about those issues as we did.

The Dark Side of Software Engineering, by Johann Rost and Robert L. Glass
Copyright © 2011 IEEE Computer Society

CHAPTER *1*

SUBVERSION

We use several approaches to explore subversion. The first section covers case studies and examples of subversion on software projects; the background information for the material is drawn from the computing and popular press. In the second, and longest, section of this chapter, we present the findings of our unique research survey, one in which we surveyed practitioners to determine how often subversion happened in the software world, and in what ways. We are particularly proud of this section, in that we present the results of exploring a major topic in the field of computing and software that no one else has explored. (An abbreviated version of this material was published earlier in a leading computing journal). Finally, in the third major section of the chapter, we present the hitherto unpublished results of a follow-up survey, one in which we asked responders to the first survey for additional input.

Now, on to the case studies.

1.1 INTRODUCTORY CASE STUDIES AND ANECDOTES

Some Motivational Examples. A sprinter is preparing to break a one-hundred-meter record. During the race someone on the edge of the track disturbs him by throwing pebbles at him and holding up funny pictures. The sprinter's chances of breaking the record are diminished because of the distractions. If the person who is causing the disturbances is an experienced sprinter himself, he might do it in a more sophisticated way—for example, tens of seconds before the official start he might imitate the sound of the starting signal. The sprinter is thus likely to fail in breaking the record and, what is more, he may even fail before the start of the race. The analysis of the failure of the project concludes the following: "Study after study reveals that sprinters have the most problems in the fractions of a second around the start, that is, at the very beginning of the race" (also known as the "requirements phase"!).

Such a situation in sports verges on the ridiculous. However, it happens quite frequently in software projects. A great number of software projects involve people who wish the project to fail. How is this possible?

The Dark Side of Software Engineering, by Johann Rost and Robert L. Glass
Copyright © 2011 IEEE Computer Society

1.1.1   A Faculty Feedback System

A college wanted to introduce an online system that allowed students to give anonymous feedback to their teachers. The feedback system was intended to provide an outlet for the evaluation of the quality of lectures and even reveal possible problems. It was hoped that, in the long run, the system would help to identify ways to improve the average quality of lectures.

A superficial analysis revealed three stakeholder groups: the students, the professors, and the college management. The students and the management supported the planned system for obvious reasons: The quality of the lectures and thus the reputation of the college were expected to improve through this project. In theory, both the students and the management would benefit from increased influence; the management would have gained access to additional ways of control. The students were concerned, however, that the anonymity could be broken one way or another, resulting in potential disadvantages for students who had given negative feedback.

A broad consensus of opinion indicated a concern that the feedback needed to be secured against potential manipulation. To prevent the possibility of results tampering by the students, each student was provided with only one opportunity to vote for each lecture. The chances for a very angry student to submit the same negative feedback more than once (thus dramatically lowering the average evaluation feedback for that particular lecture) were reduced. To prevent the possibility of a professor illicitly tampering with the system (for example, giving excellent feedback to his own lecture by pretending that he was a student), other safety measures were introduced. The system had to prevent all these kinds of potential manipulations of information. However, the aspect of protection against falsification required some authentication, which could be a conceptual conflict to the prerequisite of anonymity.

The professors' responses were multifaceted and therefore required further analysis. Some professors who were well known for their outstanding lectures welcomed the plans for the feedback system enthusiastically for quite obvious reasons: They expected excellent feedback for their lectures. Officially, there was no connection between the students' feedback and the career opportunities of the professors. It was obvious, however, that continuous good feedback would be taken into consideration if a higher position in the college management became vacant.

Other professors were more reluctant about the feedback system. Some teachers bore the responsibility of teaching difficult (and mandatory) lectures such as math. Since these lectures were known to be unpopular with many students, the teachers expected negative feedback: Even an excellent lecture of this type (for example, in statistics) would never get feedback as good as a "special interest group" lecture in which only students who are fascinated with the topic participate.

Additionally, some teachers, who were running a small consulting business in addition to their teaching duties, were concerned that the feedback system might force them to spend more time preparing the lectures, something that could eat into their time for professional engineering consulting. This college allowed additional consulting income as long as the teaching duties were not affected. However, this type of sideline was only tolerated but not fully accepted.

Other teachers had secret concerns that the feedback system could reveal deficiencies in their teaching abilities. These teachers feared they might be unable to solve the problems fast enough (or worse, might be unable to solve these problems at all); the teachers had serious concerns about the negative impact of the feedback system on their careers. Some teachers even advocated the cancellation of the project system plans due to the anticipated negative impact of the system on the working atmosphere among the professors, in addition to their concerns about possible data misuse. Most professors, however, kept their opposition secret, hoping that the project would fail or that the topic (an online feedback system) would simply disappear from the agenda one way or another.

After the project was under development, a growing discussion arose around the issue of who "owned" the data and what would be done with the results. The students were of the opinion that student representatives should administrate the data. They claimed that the feedback was given by students and that for this reason the students are the legitimate "owners" of the data. Moreover, the students suggested that all results should be made public automatically. The teachers were not particularly fond of this idea. Publishing the results in an automatic way implied certain risks, particularly if the results were very negative. (For example, if the system was manipulated, it would be difficult to completely rehabilitate the reputation of the [unjustly] denounced teacher.) The results could be borne out of methodical weaknesses—that is, if only one or a few students provided feedback for a certain lecture, these few opinions might be negative even if the lecture was, in reality, more or less okay. However, in certain cases where the lecture was really poor and the negative feedback was more than justified, the college management would have a more efficient way to solve the problem (rather than pillory the particular teacher). It became clear that negative results would need further analysis and that the decision to stop the automatic publishing if necessary should be placed under human authority.

Some teachers suggested that the results should be accessible only to the professor whose lecture was given feedback. Others suggested that the results should be accessible to a committee consisting of professors, management, and perhaps students. The committee would analyze the results and decide what should be done with them. But here were disadvantages to this solution. For example, if this committee had exclusive access to the data, some of the professors (i.e., the members of the committee) would have had access to very delicate information about other professors (i.e., their colleagues). This knowledge would give them additional influence and power. The shift of power might prove to be a disadvantage for the "group dynamic" of the college.

Then, a prototype of the system was presented publicly at the college. The meeting was meant to encourage decision making regarding the fate of the project and whether it should be continued or not. During the presentation, it became completely clear that a large group of professors were totally against the project and wanted it cancelled (perhaps even the majority of professors shared this sentiment). This group, however, did not have enough of an argument against the system. That is, they did not have enough of a legitimate argument. Of course the professors had more than enough (secret) reasons to wish for the cancellation of the project. Those reasons, however, could not be brought into discussion—the reasons had to do with the sideline consulting business.

So this group of opponents changed their strategy: They did not try to cancel the project anymore. Instead they tried to destroy it. Notice the subtle but important difference between "cancel" and "destroy." When a project is "canceled," an authority decides that the project will be discontinued. Usually this decision requires logical reasons that are considered legitimate in the particular group. When a project is going to be "destroyed," the project goes on—at least for the time being. The subversive stakeholders, however, try to influence the project in a way that finally leads to its failure (usually for "technical reasons"), thus enabling them to keep their true motivation secret. Unlike a "cancelled" project, a "destroyed" project (which "fails" for allegedly technical reasons) does not require any additional arguments to be discontinued.

The group of professors who were against the project followed the above-mentioned subversive strategy: When it became clear that they (the group of professors) could not bring the project to a halt by using political arguments, they apparently "accepted" that the project would continue. From this moment on, the political discussions seemed to fade away in the background. But by making various suggestions, they tried to influence the project in a way that would finally cause it to fail, that is, be terminated for technical reasons. The discussion was centered on purely technical decisions. (Nevertheless, the opposing group of professors never lost the desire to stop the project.)

The Achilles' heel of the project was the conceptual conflict between the anonymity of the feedback and the security against manipulation. The resolution of this problem would require non-technical processes (that is, processes that happen on paper, not in software) and trusted individuals who could mediate negotiation and compromise on the part of all responders. But the opposing group of professors rejected all possible solutions for various reasons. Officially, the reasons were based on purely technical arguments. Unofficially, the group of professors just did not want to proceed with the project, hence the rejection of all possible solutions.

Using entirely technical arguments to achieve a political goal is highly conspicuous in many projects. Subversive stakeholders sometimes use this strategy to block out senior management from making decisions. Note that senior managers usually cannot follow a purely technical discussion. This means that senior management cannot control the decision—they cannot control what they cannot understand. This specific project was particularly "lucky" because one of the managers had enough knowledge of software technology to see through the subversive strategy and save the project. But it was merely a lucky coincidence. Many projects lack such a member who has just the right combination of political instinct and software skills.

How would the post mortem report look if this project had failed? That depends on whether it is written by a software developer or by a manager.

An average software developer (without political instinct) might give the following feedback: "The clients and our superiors were constantly changing their opinions. It was simply impossible for us to find out what their expectations and plans concerning this project were. There was an endless back and forth of opinions. After a series of pointless meetings the project was finally cancelled."

An average manager (without skills in software technology) might write something similar to the following: "The software engineers did not understand the real needs of the users at all. They were completely lost in pros and cons over some technical decisions. When it became clear that this project would definitely not be completed and that we were beyond the point where we could expect any beneficial results, it had to be cancelled. Otherwise, even more money would have been invested on a hopeless project."

In this software project (and in many others), there is a wide rage of interests among various stakeholders. The range of separate interests might include some stakeholders' intentions to destroy the project. Such attempts may either be made out in the open or, more often than not, behind the curtain (depending on whether the reasons of the particular stakeholder are considered legitimate or illegitimate within the group). If the reasons are considered legitimate, they become a subject of open negotiation. If the reasons are considered illegitimate, however, they cannot be discussed openly; hence, they are not liable to negotiation. So the stakeholders would have to find other ways to reach their goals.

In the case study that was just discussed, some professors had motivations that were not considered legitimate in this group (such as maintaining the sideline consulting business or the fear that the teaching performance might turn out as unsatisfactory according to certain standards). Such motivations were against the true objectives of the project. So the professors had to find alternative ways to arrive at their goals without revealing their motivations—they used subversion.

1.1.2 An Unusual Cooperative Effort

A big organization and a small consulting company formed a consortium to develop a new software product. The partners agreed that they would equally share the efforts and benefit from the results together. For the small company the project was considered huge; it consumed the lion's share of their resources. For the big organization, however, the effort was somewhere between a small and medium project, compared to the size of the organization.

The project failed for technical reasons. Subsequent analysis revealed that most problems were within the big company's scope of responsibility. There was even suspicion that the big company had damaged the project deliberately.

That is the essential issue: Did the big company deliberately damage the project, and if so, why? Both companies suffered significant financial losses because they had to pay for their efforts, but did see any results to benefit from. The two companies, until the point of failure, apparently shared the same fate. But the effects due to the failure had completely different results on the two companies. The quarterly incomes of the big company were only slightly lower than expected. Conversely, the small company was almost ruined. The small company had to be sold. And—surprise, surprise—the big company became the new owner of the small company. The bigger company bought the smaller one at a rather cheap price because it (the small company) was in a difficult position. In hindsight, it became obvious that the big company had initiated the project from the very beginning with a view to ruin the small company—so that they could buy it... a strategy that turned out to be a complete success.

After the takeover was completed, the big company did not have any more reasons to obstruct the project. They restarted it, corrected their "mistakes" and finalized the project with moderate success. They even balanced most of their earlier losses by the profits made during the last part of the project.

1.1.3 Lack of Cooperation due to Self Interest

A German company with its own software development department decided to initiate cooperation with an "offshore" software company in Romania, where software engineers would not demand as high compensation as in Germany. In order to establish the basis of future cooperation, the German company first ordered a pilot— a rather small project of minor strategic importance.

The German software manager (middle management), however, refused to cooperate, providing information only when he was forced to do so by senior management. Even on such occasions the information was scarce and delivered at an extremely slow pace. His "official reason" for doing so was his demanding engagement in other tasks which were apparently too time consuming to allow him to contribute to the project. Nonetheless, the others suspected that he considered his job to be threatened by the software produced by Romanian engineers at lower costs. Due to the fact that the German software manager had considerable influence in his organization and his responsibility in other projects was far reaching, senior management did not want to put too much pressure on him to cooperate. But taking into account the promising economic prospects of the offshore cooperation, the German company decided to initiate the project, regardless of the lack of support on the part of the middle manager.

Eventually, the project failed. The final report analyzing the causes of failure concluded the following: "The project failed because of incomplete and inadequate requirements that did not meet the real needs of the client." On one hand, this statement is true because the requirements were indeed of unsatisfactory quality. On the other hand, the poor quality of the requirements was caused by the blockage of access to important information withheld by the uncooperative manager. At the beginning, the project team and the top management were unaware of the crucial nature of the manager's information. When this problem became apparent it was already too late.

1.1.4 An Evil Teammate

One responder of the survey that we will discuss later in this chapter related the following anecdote. This case study is of particular interest because it shows how the attacker uses technology to achieve a political goal. Usually these technical details are "below the radar" (and beyond the understanding) of top management. Thus they are not aware of the political dimension of the problem.

The attacker was a subordinate developer who was very keen on landing a position in higher management. First, he planned a subversive attack on the project lead and carried it out, step by step by using the bug tracking system in an interesting way.

In the beginning of the project, the bug-tracking system was applied only for its usual purpose—tracking bugs. The subversive developer was ceaselessly involved in the minutiae of the bug-tracking process and insisted that the bug-tracking system should be used as the adequate forum for various discussions—not only for the rather narrow purpose of reporting bugs and tracking bug fixes. This was a gradual process, starting with the forms of language used in problem descriptions, advancing to the definitions of problem categories, and finally gaining effective control over the policy settings for developers and projects leads in the configuration of the bug tracking service itself.

The project manager and the loyal colleagues were not aware of the danger of the attack and did not invest the necessary energy to stop this process early enough. That's how the subversive developer was able to defeat the utility of the tracking system for its intended function (measuring the change in quality of the software and charting the progress of the project). Instead, the bug tracking system supplanted e-mail, telephone, and verbal dialogue as the central messaging system for communicating deceptive information to the corporate directors about schedule, resource usage, and project status. Developers and project leads could no longer use it for tracking bugs without filling it with material that the subversive stakeholder could use to stir counterproductive controversy, which attracted negative attention from corporate directors and management.

The attacker used blind carbon-copy e-mails to management and clever PowerPoint® presentations to increase the social tensions and doubts of senior management regarding the project lead's qualifications. It didn't help that management gave the direction, in a doomed effort to stop the controversy from consuming project time, to start keeping double books of bugs rather than reckon with the subversive stakeholder's attacks. Then, when the project lead was replaced and the disloyal stakeholder assumed her position, he attacked the manager in a similar way.

The subversive stakeholder in question was not particularly technically skilled—but he was well versed in Machiavellian political strategy, and he exploited a weakness in the organization's defense mechanisms against such subversive attacks. They were utterly defeated by it.

Here is what they should have done: Recognize the methods employed by the subversive employee as those of a political attacker and respond accordingly. There is a large body of knowledge (which is hundreds of years old) about how to thwart the efforts of political tricksters. An effective defense would have first required learning some of it. The project lead, her peers, the management, and the other members of the technical staff were all ignorant of the patterns, ignorant of political attackers, or simply unaware of the attacks.

Here is what they did: The project lead had a nervous breakdown and hasn't recovered since; the manager quit in disgust and retired from the industry. The other project leads and members of the technical staff were mostly dumbfounded—they had never encountered this behavior before. The person who shared the anecdote reacted by learning about organizational psychology and political strategy.

1.1.5   Thwarting the Evil Union

The trade union wanted to delay (and finally destroy, perhaps) a project. They met once in two months to talk about new software, and no software could be installed without the union's "OK."

Here is what the contributor of this anecdote had to say:

"I had heard that they [the union] lacked information about the system and would not give their OK before they had this information. So I asked several people what kind of information it could be and when the meeting would take place. It was early on a Monday morning. I had been told not to contact them; they would contact me. They did not. The week before, I had gathered the addresses of the responsible people (the addresses were available on the company's Web site). I started writing e-mails to the union, but the e-mails were not answered. Then I called and tried to get someone on the phone, but they were constantly in meetings and they did not call back (although this was promised). But the union could not totally ignore my attempts to contact them—and on Friday afternoon at four o'clock, I got a phone call. The lady on the line was amazed that I still was in the office. I suppose she expected that I would already have started out for the weekend. She told me openly what information they needed from me. It was a lot! I asked for the details. After the phone call I wrote a protocol, sent it by e-mail, and promised to deliver the information by Monday morning, nine o'clock. It was not possible to gather all of the information, especially because it demanded the help of developers and others who were already in their well earned weekend. But I was prepared. I knew what information would be needed, and I had spent the last three weeks getting it from the different people. Now only some details were lacking. But I knew I could provide them myself, and at eight in the evening, everything was done. I could send the missing information to everyone who was involved. So it was official: I talked to the union and sent all the information they needed. And on Monday morning, they gave the 'OK.' How did I know that they were subversive at all? No one told me, but during the user training sessions, some of the union members were in my course, and I felt strong resistance. It was during the user training that I learned they had concerns about certain topics; therefore, I researched the topics."

As usual, subversive stakeholders cannot be subversive openly; one can use this against them. But it is very hard and one single error can spoil the whole fight.

1.2   THE SURVEY: IMPACT OF SUBVERSIVE STAKEHOLDERS ON SOFTWARE PROJECTS

"Subversive stakeholders" are software project stakeholders who want the project to fail. This section of our book discusses our survey which we designed and conducted to explore incidents of such activity—how frequently it occurs, why it happens, how such incidents are discovered, and what can be done about it.

The survey finds that the problem is widespread: Over 50% of responders have encountered the problem of subversive stakeholders on software projects, impacting about 20% of projects. The findings also suggest that the subversive stakeholder is successful or at least partially successful in a non-negligible number of cases.

To the best of our knowledge, this is the first formal survey of the problem.

1.2.1 Introduction

Studies of software project success and failure factors frequently appear in the software literature (some recent examples include Verner [2006], Jeffrey [2006], KPMG [2005], Nelson [2005], Ewusi-Mensah [2003], and Glass [1998]). Failure factors commonly include such things as unstable requirements and faulty (under-) estimation. It is also found that management problems cause failure more often than technical problems.

The literature in the field of software project management is particularly rich (some recent examples include Humphrey [1997], Morasco [2005], Glen [2003], Miller [2004], Boehm and Turner [2004], and Thomsett [2002]). These publications do an excellent job, in general, of identifying best practices in software project management and in providing treatments and cures for project difficulties. Failure and its causes are frequently topics of concern in this literature. Thus one could expect that, even though software project failure factors are frequently presented in the failure literature, the means of addressing those failures are well provided for in the management literature.

The risk literature in particular is a place where these concerns are often addressed, for example, Moynihan (2002), Jones (1994), Charette (2004), Charette (1997), Britcher (1999), Cockburn (1998), McConnell (1998), Ropponen and Lyytinen (2000). Project risks are identified in this literature, and means of addressing those risks are discussed. The second citation, Jones (1994), is a virtual medical handbook approach to software project problems and their solutions.

However, there is an interesting problem here. For all the discussion of failures, their causes and cures, mentioned above, there is one failure factor that is rarely included in any of these literatures: failure caused by subversive stakeholders. It is the purpose of this survey to identify this failure factor, to explain why the existing literature does not cover it, to discuss its prevalence, and to present ways of overcoming the problems it causes.

Here is our definition of that term: "Stakeholders" are people inside or outside the project who have any interest whatsoever in the software project and some influence over it. (That includes developers, project leads, architects, patrons, customers, consultants, and various user groups as well as managers outside the project). A "subversive stakeholder" is a person who wants the project to fail—that is, a stakeholder who wants to sabotage, to disturb, or to destroy the project. Only people who act intentionally to the detriment of the project are considered "subversive." Stakeholders who disturb the project due to incompetence or who are not aware of the consequences of their actions are NOT considered subversive in this survey.

Interestingly, while almost everyone in the software industry can share stories of projects that they have been involved with and which suffered from subversive activity, somehow that failure factor rarely, if ever, surfaces in the software literature. There are reasons for that, of course: There is something faintly embarrassing about failures that happen deliberately; there is usually lingering uncertainty as to whether the failure was deliberate or not.

We have encountered enough examples of such behavior that we believed it was important to explore its prevalence and frequently how such behavior served to the severe detriment of the project on which it occurs.

This is, so far as we know, the first formal survey of subversive software project stakeholders as failure factors (informal reports have appeared in such articles as Rost (2004), Rost and Glass (2005), Thibodeau (2005), and Nelson and Simek (2005); note that only the first two of these informal reports are specific to the field of software). An abbreviated version of this survey was published in the leading journal *Communications of the ACM* as Rost and Glass (2009).

1.2.2 The Survey

The survey involved contacting software practitioners and presenting them with a series of questions about their experiences with subversion.

Questionnaire

1. Have you ever encountered subversive stakeholders in software projects?
2. How frequently do projects include subversive stakeholders? That is, according to your experience, what is the percentage of software projects affected by the subversive interests of certain stakeholders?
3. What were the motivations and goals of the subversive stakeholders? Why did they do it?
4. What was the percentage of cases in which the subversive stakeholders finally achieved their goal (at least partially)? What fraction of the subversive attacks was finally

    4a. fully successful?

    4b. partially successful?

5. What role did the subversive stakeholders assume within the projects? (For example, developer, user, consultant, project lead, or manager).
6. How were the subversive attacks discovered? How did you find out that a subversive attack was being prepared?
7. How can projects be defended against subversive stakeholders? What did the project leads or the loyal stakeholders do against the sabotage?
8. How much experience do you have in industrial projects (outside of university)?

    • More than seven years

    • Between two years and seven years

- Less than two years
- Other pattern of experience (For example, three years fulltime plus ten years of occasional consulting). Please specify the pattern of experience.

9. Which role do *you* usually assume within software projects (For example, developer, user, consultant, project lead, manager).

10. Do you have any additional remarks left uncovered by the questions above but which might help to clarify the issue?

11. Do you want to receive a copy of the final report?

Development of the survey instrument went through two rounds of trial use, with feedback from 14 initial subjects resulting in instrument improvements.

The final instrument was then submitted to a broad population of computing professionals. Subjects were chosen from a variety of sources. Candidate responders were identified by using Google to search on such software-focused terms as "project manager" or "team lead." Following that, online bios were studied to determine potential responders. Authors of relevant papers, professors with practitioner experience, industry "gurus," and a large number of practitioners formed the chosen population. Attempts were made to have a wide geographic distribution, including the United States, western Europe, Russia, Romania, India, and China, and to have a wide variance in subject experience.

Identifying a sufficient number of responders and the responder response rate were both problems (see Section 1.2.7).

The questionnaires were distributed, and the responses were made by e-mail. Due to the use of this method, it was possible to link each set of answers to a certain responder and to ask for additional information where worthwhile. Consideration was given to collecting the data via a Web interface instead. However, during the pre-test, some "fierce" and very emotional answers were received, leading to the fear that some responders might want to sabotage the survey by abusing the Web interface and inputting "junk" data. Thus e-mail was used instead.

The result is a set of numeric findings, but, perhaps more importantly, a rich set of quotations and opinions from the responders. Both the quantitative and qualitative findings are presented below.

1.2.3 The Survey Findings

Ten questions were asked of the subjects of the survey. They involved the issues of the existence of subversive activity, the frequency with which it occurs, the motivations/goals of the subversive stakeholders who engage in such activities, the frequency of failures caused by such activity, the methods by which the subversion was detected, and approaches projects can use to defend themselves against subversive activity. Two of the questions resulted in primarily quantitative responses, and those responses are presented in Section 1.2.3.1. The other eight questions resulted in qualitative responses, and those are presented in Section 1.2.3.2. Finally, some responses to the questions revealed patterns of subversion; those are presented in Section 1.2.3.3.

1.2.3.1 Questions and Quantitative Responses   In this section, the core quantitative questions in the questionnaire are presented, followed by an analysis of the responses to that question.

Have You Ever Encountered Subversive Stakeholders in Software Projects? Fifty-four responders (a little over 50%) reported that they have encountered subversive behavior in software projects. Thirty-eight (35%) said they have never seen this problem. Fifteen (14%) responded but refused to answer the questionnaire (follow-ups suggest that some of them were precluded from doing so by corporate policy, and others felt they had insufficient experience for their input to have value). The findings are presented in total and broken down by experience level of the responders. See the table below for details.

The figures in the cells of the table are the number of responders in that respective group. (That is, 21 colleagues with more than seven years experience have never seen this problem). Note that years of experience tend to correlate with encountering the problem.

How Frequently Do Projects Include Subversive Stakeholders?   There are several interpretations of the responder answers to this question. The median of all responses is that 20% of projects involve subversion. However, many responders gave qualitative answers rather than a percentage—for example, "twice in ten years," "once or twice in ten years of experience," or "one out of seven projects."

The responses showed varying levels of frequency of subversive behavior: Sixteen responders are aware of subversive activities but consider them rare (≤5% of the projects); another 31 felt they were common (5%–80% of projects); and seven reported that this problem interferes with their projects rather frequently (>80%). Thus about 40% of the practitioners are acquainted with the problem of subversive stakeholders and have encountered it in a significant part of their projects (>5%) while the other 60% considers subversion a minor problem or one that has not confronted them at all.

In Table 1.2, the column "Number of responders" indicates how many responders gave the respective answer. The sum of $16 + 31 + 7 = 54$ matches the respective number in Table 1.1.

These results raised an interesting question: Why have a significant fraction of experienced responders never encountered subversive behavior, while others reported this problem as "rather frequent"? To clarify this issue, additional questions were sent to the responders who had never or rarely encountered subversive activity. Here are those follow-up responses:

- Some organizations are more "political" and therefore prone to subversive activity than others. Six responders considered their respective organization's well-defined processes to be an important reason why subversive behavior is at a minimum.

- Some people are more sensitive to political processes and subversion. Eight responders considered it somewhat paranoid to search for subversion behind behavior that might simply be the result of incompetence or mishap. Another

TABLE 1.1   Have you ever encountered subversive stakeholders in software projects?

Experience	0–2 years	2–7 years	7+ years	Other patterns	Unspecified Experience	Industry Gurus	Sum
Have encountered subversive stakeholders	0	6	37	3	3	5	54
Never seen subversive stakeholders	2	5	21	3	6	1	38
Answered but refused participation	0	0	2	1	7	5	15
Sum	2	11	60	7	16	11	107

TABLE 1.2   How frequently do projects include subversive stakeholders?

	Number of responders	Sum
Have never seen subversive stakeholders	38	38
Have encountered subversive stakeholders in at most 5% of the projects	16	
Have encountered subversive stakeholders in more than 5% but less than 80% of the projects	31	54
Have encountered subversive stakeholders in at least 80% of the projects	7	

responder, however, wrote: "One can choose to perceive or not to perceive subversive behavior, but if the behavior has a subversive effect, it really doesn't matter whether one chooses to perceive it or not. The effect is real." Increasing awareness of subversive activities requires a certain overview of the project's politics. Subversive activity is less conspicuous to those in certain roles (such as developers).

- Eight responders admitted that the reason for which they had never or rarely encountered subversive activities might be that they are lacking relevant experience or their projects had specific properties that make subversion very unlikely.

- Four seasoned project managers wrote that they know potential sources of subversion and they are aware of the symptoms of such an attack. If they notice mildly subversive behavior, they have enough influence and experience to fix the problem. Consequently they reported that subversive behavior is not a serious issue on their projects.

1.2.3.2   Questions and Qualitative Responses   The survey led to a number of qualitative, as opposed to quantitative, responses. In this section we present a summary of those results, which is derived from the remarks and anecdotes that we

received from the responders. In each case below, we provide the question that prompted the qualitative response, then a summary of these qualitative responses.

What Were the Motivations and Goals of the Subversive Stakeholders? Responses to this question were grouped informally into 11 classes (derived bottom-up from the responses). Under each class umbrella are some of the responses that caused that class to be invented. A more complete presentation of these responses is given in Section 1.3.1.

Egotistic Motivations Conflicting with Corporate Goals.   Often, individual project members thought that the project should be conducted in a different manner from the way in which it was actually conducted; alternately, the project members would have preferred project outcomes to be more in line with their own personal wishes. Responders noted concerns about things such as project success leading to more work, more (undesirable) accountability for the subject, or a personal preference for project failure over project success.

Job Security.   Defending one's own position was a motive for subversion. Responders noted concerns about things such as the successful project eliminating or drastically changing their job.

Revenge and Disgruntled Employees.   Getting even for some past occurrence was another motivation. Responders noted concerns about things such as disgruntled stakeholders seeking revenge for past problems or harming a project simply through a bad attitude.

Challenge of Authority and "Ego-Reasons."   For a variety of reasons, people lower in a hierarchy sometimes try to attack those above them. Responders noted concerns about people who sought to make themselves look especially good (for example, hiding incompetence), or making specific others look bad (for example, shifting rewards in their favor). Attempting to diminish the power base of someone else, or seeking more power for themselves, was another factor.

Competition Between Individuals, Rivalry, and Animosity.   The motivation was often at the individual level, a person-to-person kind of thing. Some example responses concerned battles over whose idea the project was, or conflict between backers of new ideas versus older ones.

Competition Between Departments and Organizations.   It is not unknown for the motivation to be organizational rather than personal. Some responses noted the seeking of benefits from competing incentive plans, pushing others toward being scapegoats if the project fails, or agitating control struggles.

Competition for Budget and Resources.   Organizational motivation might be about resources, budget, and time. Responses included the following: "There is a competitive world out there…. There will always be turf wars. Budget cutting caused by stakeholders outside the project (non-stakeholders) is probably the number one killer of good software."

Resistance to Change.   Some people are motivated by a wish to keep things as they are (such as wanting to keep the old product in order to avoid having to learn something new).

Disagreement on Some Major Architectural or Technological Choice. Some people are motivated by strong feelings about technical issues. Technical people, mainly programmers, sometimes become saboteurs when they want to use a different tool/technology/methodology than the one(s) mandated for their project, or they want to eliminate constraints/standards that they see as counterproductive.

Disloyal Partners.   Sometimes it is the people from outside the enterprise who are motivated to sabotage it (such as partner firms, contractors, and outsourcers who want to improve their contractual position, or who want to win a culture clash battle at all costs).

Split in Upper Management.   Sometimes it is the senior people in the enterprise itself (for example, the upper manager nurturing the project may have enemies who want the project to fail, sometimes simply because of who is nurturing it!).

What Was the Percentage of Cases in Which the Subversive Stakeholders Finally Achieved Their Goal (at Least Partially)?   Even though the subversive stakeholders constitute a small minority, they can make a lot of trouble, causing incredibly high costs for their organization. There is a broad consensus that most attacks are at least partially successful. A number of responders confirmed that the attack *always* causes delays, additional costs, and/or may motivate good people to leave. Most responders agreed that only a smaller fraction of subversive attacks are fully successful—that is, actually disastrous for the project.

Some responders reported that certain patterns of attacks are much more dangerous than others (such as a senior manager from outside derailing the project from a distance). Attacks on the part of management may be an indication of a split or political war at the level of higher management. This is frequently (or almost always) disastrous for the project. Attacks from below (such as one from a user base or from developers) can be efficient if they are coordinated.

How Were the Subversive Attacks Discovered?   Once again, there were several classes of responses, grouped in bottom-up chosen categories. A sampling of those responses is given below; a more complete presentation of these responses is given in Section 1.3.2.

Some Attacks Are Carried out Overtly.   Perhaps surprisingly, not all subversive activity is carried out in secret. Responders spoke of subversive activity being in the open, such as during meetings or via e-mail. Some reported subversive stakeholders even boasted openly of their success.

Informal Network.   Other subversive activity may be handled by a cadre of people (for example) via the exchange of faulty information or via groups intimidating those who might report the subversion.

It Is Not a Single Event—It Is a Process.   Sometimes it is hard to identify a single event that can be called subversive; the designation of some event as a "subversion" comes from patterns of behavior over time. Such subversion rarely rises to the level of project progress reports.

Case-Specific Discoveries.   Sometimes subversion is identified through things unique to the project: subversives withhold information, attack the project in status reviews, report progress where little or none is being made, or report none when the project is moving forward.

How Can the Projects Be Defended Against Subversive Stakeholders? Here we present the bottom line on the subject of subversion and ask the following question: "What can be done about it?" This sampling of responses is about solving the problem. A more complete presentation of these responses is given in Section 1.3.3.

Applying Quality Project Management Practices.   A nice and hopeful answer to the problem is that "good management will win out in the end." Techniques suggested include a robust development process, project audits, and the use of appropriate checks and balances. One responder noted that *"in a well- managed company this sort of political in-fighting does not happen."*

Quality Communication.   Another hopeful answer is that communication is the key. Such communication should be open, honest, inclusive, and focused. Methods include project reports, audits, and less formal involvement of all project players.

Psychology.   And then there's the hopeful answer that common sense, via psychology, will prevail. Improve the hiring/firing process, particularly focusing on psychological and not just technical factors. Make a priority of identifying/keeping cooperative and capable people.

Support from Senior Management.   Sometimes it's necessary to call in higher powers. Move up the management ladder when necessary to solve problems, involving senior management if the problem is sufficiently severe.

Taming.   At times, one can tame the savage subversive beast. Involve and include the subversives, seek their cooperation, convince them if possible, comfort them if they need help.

Or Fighting Back—If Taming Fails.   But in some cases, the opposite must be tried. Eliminate them, work around them, fire them if possible.

Pessimistic Opinions.   And, unfortunately, sometimes nothing will help—there are no hopeful, or common sense, or taming approaches. Responders provided the following statements: "You can't fully defend any project against sabotage, either from within or without"; "There was probably nothing I could have done, except perhaps to get all tasks to be performed and the reasons for performing them, in writing"; "If the subversive stakeholder is quite powerful, the project lead and loyal stakeholders may lack countervailing power"; "There is no solution, not in the environment I work in"; and "I have tried several defense alternatives. However, I must admit that they never worked thoroughly because the subversion was not evident enough to really fight against."

1.2.3.3 Patterns of Subversion   Our survey results have revealed a number of patterns of subversive activity. This section explains these patterns. It also includes anecdotes related to these patterns that provide a framework for structuring the anecdotes.

The patterns

1. Rivals and enemies of the project lead (inside or outside of the project). The project lead might have enemies within the organization, some of whom might be competing with him/her for positions in higher management or in order to assume his/her role as project lead (that is, a subversive insider). Others might even have a personal conflict with the project lead.

2. Subversive stakeholders within the project.

    2.1 Subversive project leads. Subversive project leads are people who are officially assigned the role of project leads and who act intentionally to the detriment of the project's success (that is, NOT out of incompetence).

    2.2 Subversive subordinated team members. This group consists of people who are part of the project team but who are not project leads (such as developers and testers).

    2.3 Disloyal consultants. Consultants can be subversive in a way similar to the subordinated team members. The difference, however, is that the consultant tries to interfere with the project in such a way that s/he can continue billing—or can even extend the billable time.

3. Customers and users

    3.1 Uncooperative users. Some users might be subversive because they reject the project for various reasons: They are concerned with keeping their jobs, they expect additional work, and they do not want to change established work processes.

    3.2 Other dysfunctional persons on the customer's side. Dysfunctional customers are subversive stakeholders on the customer's side apart from users (such as a customer representative or manager).

4. Subversive stakeholders outside the project

    4.1 Promoters of other projects who are competing for budget allotment. Subversive stakeholders can be motivated by the project budget. If the project is cancelled, the remaining project budget can be assigned to other projects. Thus the protagonists of other projects might gain an advantage from the project's failure.

4.2 Other subversive managers outside the project. This group consists of managers outside the project, who are NOT promoters of competing projects (see last item). The managers are not directly involved in the project's day-by-day business. They fire/launch missiles against the project from a safe distance. They do not have to "pay" in any way if the project fails.

4.3 Unfair partner companies. Unfair partner companies are legally and economically independent organizations who have some influence on the project's development and who behave subversively. The subversive behavior in this pattern is in fact a corporate decision

5. Other patterns of subversion.

5.1 Coordinated attacks. Several apparently independent stakeholders (for example, different user groups and/or developers) attack the project in a coordinated way (such the spreading of negative rumors about the project that reach senior management from apparently independent sources). Sometimes the coordinator is a manager from outside the project.

5.2 Split in higher management. The danger stems in fact from a split in higher management: Senior management is segregated into two or more factions that are at war with each other.

1.2.4 Conclusions

The strongest conclusion we draw from this survey is that incidents of subversive stakeholder activity on software projects are all too frequent. Over 50% of responders have encountered such activity. Unsurprisingly, such incidents have occurred most frequently among responders with more experience (presumably because they had had more years in which such incidents could arise).

There was an interesting disparity of findings in regard to the frequency of problems occurring. Some responders gave qualitative rather than quantitative responses to this question, but the median for all responders indicates that perhaps 20% of software projects are contaminated by subversive activity.

The remaining issues studied in the survey involved qualitative/opinion rather than quantitative responses. However, a strong and potentially useful collection of opinions were presented.

Eleven different categories (regarding the motivations of the subversive stakeholders themselves) were presented. The collected opinions noted that subversive stakeholders were motivated most frequently by ego (especially when it conflicted with corporate goals), intentional challenge of authority, and disagreement on major issues. Less significant were revenge and resistance to change. (A complete listing of specific answers to the survey question about motivation and goals is found in Section 1.3.1).

Four opinions were presented regarding how subversion was discovered. Perhaps surprisingly, the most common way the discovery happened was due to the fact that the subversive stakeholders were overt in their activity or because open rumors of such activity were pursued and found to be true! (A complete listing of specific answers to the survey question about discovery of subversion will be found in Section 1.3.2).

The (possibly) most important question in the survey ("What can be done to defend against this activity?") yielded five categories of responses. Several of them had to do with what would normally be considered good management practices, such as applying quality management approaches, keeping lines of communication open, seeking support from senior management, and the use of positive psychology. Some responders suggested what to do if all else failed (generate a work-around or dismiss the subversive person), and several responders expressed the belief that very little could be done. (A complete listing of specific answers to the survey question about what can be found about subversion is found in Section 1.3.3 of this chapter).

1.2.5 Impact on Practice

These survey results should be useful for several reasons:

1. They highlight a problem that is apparently very real and all too common.
2. They suggest ways that practitioners can discover the problem and suggest approaches that can be used to defend against it.
3. They present the motivations and goals of those who engage in subversion, which may make it easier to identify such patterns in advance.

1.2.6 Impact on Research

Researchers may find this survey interesting for several reasons:

1. It identifies an issue worthy of further survey, especially given this subject has not been studied before.
2. Although management problems have generally been seen as the most significant cause of software project failure, there has been little breakdown of "management problems" into more useful subcategories. There may very well be other subcategories of "management problems" besides subversion worthy of further survey.
3. Certainly this should not be the final survey of subversive stakeholders. Additional research and analysis of those results could explore the accuracy and usefulness of this first set of survey results; all of this gathered information can help to hone-in on causes and solutions to the problems.

1.2.7 Limitations

The biggest limitation of this survey pertains to the response rate of those contacted. As is typical with practitioner surveys, the response rate was disappointingly low, less than 5%. (Because the survey was announced in some mailing lists, it is impossible to give an accurate response rate). However, that rate is not the entire picture.

To achieve a richer set of responses, follow-ups were sent to some of the responders, wherein clarifications were sought and deeper discussions were initiated. Those responders who participated in this follow-up contact constituted both a significant number and contributed in large measure to the findings reported here.

A note regarding demographics: There is probably an over-proportional representation of industry "gurus." The majority of responders are from the United States and Germany. Interestingly, however, the subgroup did not seem to affect the responses—that is, results broken down by these subgroups tended to be the same as for responders as a whole, with the possible exception of "years of experience," a factor that did seem to affect the responses.

1.2.8   Challenges

All survey studies face certain challenges: Is the sample representative? Can the questions be misunderstood? Factors affecting software survey research are thoroughly discussed in Pfleeger and Kitchenham (2001).

Beyond these issues (which are common to all studies), our survey had its own specific challenges.

Recruiting Responders Is Difficult.   This happened for several reasons:

- One obstacle is common to all survey studies: It takes time to answer the questionnaire and the responders ask, "What's in it for me?"

- More important, however, was the fact that this is a very sensitive issue. Some organizations suspected that survey results could be used to their disadvantage. The promise that the results would be used anonymously was not always enough (some responders felt that the survey would collect "doubtful competitive information" about their company).

- It requires a certain degree of trust to answer such a questionnaire. This may contribute to the observation that many responses are from persons personally known to Johann.

- Many responses were very emotional—to both extremes. Some were very enthusiastic. Others deeply rejected the notion that such a survey was being done at all.

Perception of Subversion Is Subjective.   Some people choose to perceive its occurrence. Other people choose to ignore signs of possible subversion. For this reason, the results have a range of uncertainty. Another sample of responders or another setting for the survey might lead to different numbers.

There Is a Gray Borderline Between Subversion and Conflicting Interests. Many projects involve conflicting interests. It is not rare that project responders are somehow "forced" to contribute to a project. Alternately, they might experience advantages if the project fails or disadvantages if it is successful. It is difficult to identify all such responders as being subversive. They may not actively sabotage a project, but they behave in a subtle way to hinder its success. (For example, the project will need certain information, but they don't know it yet. Such a responder might think, "Well, they did not ask me and I'm not obliged to inform them." Other project responders might perceive this behavior as "subversive." The suspected "subversive" stakeholder, however, might perceive his or her behavior to be legitimate.

In other cases, the stakeholder might think that the project should not be carried through because it is contrary to the goals of the organization as a whole (or worse, contrary even to goals for human beings on this planet!). The project members who support the project will probably perceive this stakeholder to be subversive.

1.2.9 Acknowledgments

This survey was successful due to the contribution of the many practitioners who were kind enough to spend time filling in the questionnaire and share their valuable experience. Many of them gave extensive explanations and answered additional questions. Each of these contributers deserves inclusion on the list of references. However, promises of anonymity preclude that.

1.3 SELECTED RESPONSES

1.3.1 Sample Answers to the Question: "What Were the Motivations and Goals of the Subversive Stakeholders?"

The survey revealed a variety of reasons for subversion that can be roughly grouped into the categories below. (The categories were formed after we received the answers.) Thus the grouping of answers into categories is done by the authors—not by the responders—and might be considered subjective.

We have included some of the actual responses (provided in quotes). The selected responses may be considered representative. Nevertheless, the responses give a more "qualitative" impression. (Note that we do **not** think the number of contributions to a certain item allows a quantitative conclusion to be made, based on the frequency a reason occurs in practice.)

Egotistic Motivations Conflicting with Corporate Goals.   A key observation of subversion is that it occurs in environments dominated by conflicting interests. Conflicting interests are not new: The buyer wants a low price; the vendor wants a high price—that's just one example. The specific factor here, in relation to subversion, is that some of the interests are considered "illegitimate" in that environment. This observation blocks the solution via usual negotiations. You cannot negotiate something when you don't dare speak about this "something." Notice that the same interests could be considered completely legitimate in another context. For example: An employee who optimizes his own personal advantage at the expense of the employing organization would be considered "subversive." If an independent vendor did the same, it would be a very usual and completely accepted business practice. That is, if the independent vendor optimizes its own advantage, it could create a circumstance that is not necessarily to the advantage of the customer.

Two examples should illustrate this issue:

1. An employee goes to his boss and makes a suggestion: "Let's negotiate the technology that we will use for the next project. Some possible technologies are advantageous to me because the usage (that is, having the knowledge to use them) would allow me to apply for well paying jobs." This would be considered a ridiculous suggestion.

2. A partner company suggests the following: "Let's negotiate the technology that we will use for the next project. Some possible technologies have strategic advantages for us." This would be a perfectly legitimate suggestion.

The following statements by several responders of the survey shed light on the issue of conflicting interests:

- "Their interests are better met by the failure rather than by the success of the project."
- "Their motivation comes from something other than success in the project. It is not so much that they want the project to fail, but it is 'OK' with them if it fails because something else is going to succeed for them instead."
- "Some might consider personal profit ("What's in it for me?") [that] overrides the larger company motive."
- "There are considerations, such as strategically involving the firm in certain activities, to attract or forestall takeover considerations or company reorganizations."
- "The successful project would lead to additional work on the part of the subversive stakeholder."
- "It will introduce a [new] learning curve into a procedure that is comfortable as it is."
- "The new system might make people more accountable."

Variations on the theme of conflicting interests range from the subversive stakeholder expecting additional workload to—the other extreme—losing the job.

Job Security.   Many software projects need the cooperation and the constructive input of various groups of stakeholders in order to succeed. The persons who are performing the job at the moment are particularly important, especially at an early phase of the project. If they refuse positive cooperation, the project may run into serious trouble.

Quite a few software projects, however, make workers redundant. This is one way in which software projects can cut costs in the long run. In time, many of the dismissed workers find new job opportunities—perhaps even better than before. For the time in between, however, they are face trouble. Thus, it is more than understandable that people fight against a software project if the most likely result is that they will be fired.

- "Concern about job security is one of the most common reasons we have seen as newly introduced systems would have eliminated many of their duties."
- "People whose jobs will be affected by the new system sometimes prefer to continue as they are, especially if they will have to relocate or lose their jobs."
- "Either they're comfortable with how things work now, or they're afraid of not doing well in the new environment, or they're afraid the new system will cost them their job."

Additional Workload and Unpleasant Working Conditions.   Job security is only an issue for those who are affected. Others, however, might end up with a higher work load than before; this is a scenario that, in turn, might lead to overtime and worsened working conditions.

The following contributions provide some examples:

- "The successful project would lead to additional work for the subversive stakeholder."
- "Their goal was not to have much work with the project and not to take responsibility for something."
- "The software team had the goal to have everything with their technical platform. New service would disturb that easiness to maintain."
- "They have an economic interest in it (work shifts to them)."
- "It might introduce a learning curve into a procedure that's already comfortable."
- "They were scared and felt it would be too hard to be successful supporting the new system."
- "The stakeholders might see the project as being boring, causing them to work in a way they dislike (e.g., overtime) or working with parties they dislike."
- "Management's blind eye. If management is only paying attention to the dollars, and not the work environment, the workers themselves may determine their only way out is to cause the project to fail, losing the business, and thereby freeing them from the punishing environment."
- "They will not have to pay any cost for failure and may have no direct responsibility for the project, and yet the project might not succeed without their contribution. This can happen when individuals hold rare or poorly understood skills and management doesn't do 'capacity planning' for the person's time. Ultimately it leads to the person being overloaded when too many demands happen at the same time. This leads the person to flex their power to reduce the workload to a manageable level. The only problem is [that] this ends up undermining any projects that were overcommitted. Thus overwhelmed people with relatively unique skills can end up being subversive some of the time, especially around unexpected requests, or requests that show an utter lack of planning and foresight."

The last item gives an example of how difficult and how subjective the classification of "subversive behavior" can be. It might quite well happen that most team members regard one of their colleagues as "subversive" while this person himself might not have any bad intentions—he just does as much as he can do. For anything beyond his capacities he has no other choice but to say "No!" or delay tasks if a "No!" is not acceptable in this specific environment.

Resistance to Change.   Change may lead to better opportunities in the long run. We all know, however, that change also has its challenges, risks, and hazards—and humans tend to take the line of least resistance.

- "The stakeholders wanted to keep the old software. (We suppose their motivation was that they wanted to avoid working hard and learning new technology)."
- "They are fed up with new projects, as the last projects failed to bring the promised benefit."
- "The stakeholder wanted to hide his incompetence. The project would make the lack of competence obvious."
- "Ninety-nine out of 100 people prefer to cling to familiar things rather than to try something new. At least this is my experience. Thus it is obvious that software projects which rely on many stakeholders are openly or covertly attacked to various degrees."

Shift of Power.   Many software projects results in some persons are gaining power and others are losing power. The group which is about to lose power might try to disturb and subvert the project. Some responders reported such cases.

- "Why did they do it? Power."
- "They stand to lose (power/budget/money/pride) upon success."
- "The subversive stakeholder thought the outcome of the project might threaten their current standing in the organization."
- "The most heinous and explicitly identified acts of "sabotage" are performed by stakeholders who believe their position (viewpoint, opinion, pet feature) is at risk."
- "One memorable incident was [in relation to] a controller. My belief is that he saw how the financial system being implemented would reduce his power in the organization."
- "Loss of control over business processes which have been handled with own means so far. The project would result in dependency on third parties."
- "Before the project was developed the subversive stakeholder had exclusive access to certain resources within the organization. The new software makes these resources accessible for others."
- "The new project may diminish their importance or shift the power base."

The Project Entails Additional Control

- "A variation of losing power is that another gains additional control over my work."
- "The project would allow additional control of the stakeholders work."
- "The new system might make people more accountable."
- "The software would allow insight into project details and organizational structures."

Underdog Architects, Visionaries, and Prophets

- "They had proposed an alternative, which was rejected, and they believe that they will be exonerated at least or perhaps even gain praise or influence in the future. This is amplified if they were shamed or disturbed by how the decision was made."
- "Some stakeholders (e.g., functional departments or customers) have unclear or diverting visions [that] to satisfy [all] in one project is not easy and can result in damage. Mostly it's conflict of interest or conflicting objectives/ visions. Sometimes it's personal bias and the desire to prove a project will fail ('In half [of a] year we will see that this was the wrong approach.')."
- "The subversive stakeholders thought they should be more involved in certain aspects of the project and they didn't want it to succeed without their contribution."

Looking Good by Making Others Look Bad?

- "They want to create problems which only they can solve and gain importance."
- "A very power-hungry employee who had a mix of motivations wanted others to look bad [and] cared more about being 'proven right' on various points than about project success."
- "Mostly to demonstrate their personal superiority."
- "The stakeholders sought to increase their share of the rewards, though the illusion of brilliance or through extending the work needed."
- "The project involved someone who didn't want me to look good. The method was to withhold information."

Revenge and Disgruntled Employees. A widely agreed upon statement among many responders was the following: "The interests of the subversive stakeholders are better satisfied by the failure than by the success of the project." (See also the anecdote by Chapter 9).

Even though it seems that this statement forms a generic pattern, from which many other motivations can be derived, it is only one side of the coin. The other side is that destructive behavior can also be motivated by irrational reasons that do not lead to any obvious advantages for the subversive stakeholder.

- "We've seen disgruntled employees who passively damage a project through bad attitude."
- "A middle manager had to leave the project against his will. This former stakeholder sought revenge and failure of the project."

Unwanted Competition Between Departments and Organizations

- "The subversive stakeholders did not agree with the charter or mission of a department and they 'hung 'em out to dry' without management support. Why? Competing incentive plans for upper management."
- "It was motivated by scapegoat strategies, i.e., if marketing wants to eventually blame development for a failed project all they have to do is insist on more requirements than can possibly be built given the schedule constraints. We have not been involved in many projects where there was a typical 'loser user' as defined by Gause and Weinberg."
- "The subversive stakeholder was from another department within our organization. He wanted to keep information close to the vest and provide the project only what he wanted the team to know in order to control the process. It was his way of trying to maintain some measure of control since he was no longer project lead."
- "The attackers didn't want to see [the] success of a different group."
- "The projects that attracted the attention of political opponents were all new projects developing new technology. The people who became political opponents of the projects all had older projects that could potentially be displaced."
- "Their own organization wanted something similar to the service that was developed. ([That is, it was a] struggle for power to be the leading part.)"
- "The subversive stakeholder was a customer who wanted to weasel out of a contract (changed their mind after signing)."
- "Product management [and] marketing representatives within engineering were associated with feature areas. Each fought to have their feature area advanced in each release. even without any correlation with true customer priorities."

Competition Between Individuals, Rivalry and Animosity.   Whenever a project runs into a crisis, the position of project lead might become a subject of discussion. When the reputation of the project lead is destroyed the position may become vacant, hence opening new job opportunities for those who are not project leads at the moment.

- "The subversive stakeholder would like to be the project lead and gain total control."
- "The stakeholder had been passed over for a leadership role (in the project) in favor of an outside consultant."
- "The failure of one group may allow for new management to take over, and possibly change direction or do some empire building."

- "Personal animosity to the project leadership.*"*
- "They'd developed some antipathy towards the contractor due to misunderstandings about the business arrangements made over their head and some unfortunate personality conflicts."
- "The project involved someone who didn't want me to look good. The method was to withhold information."

The following statements show that there is no clear-cut dividing line between uncalled for competition between individuals and competition between organizational units.

- "It was because the project was not 'theirs.' In other words, the project was created and motivated by somebody else in the company, someone whom they did not particularly wish to support."
- "Subversive people wanted the project manager on either the supplier's side or the client's side to have a failure. They would have sacrificed the project success for their own intrigues."
- "We have encountered managers of other projects who wanted a project to fail because they viewed it as competition."

Competition for Budget and Resources.   A failed project is not necessarily a bad thing—at least not for everybody in the organization. When the project is cancelled, the budget that was allotted to a project becomes available and liable to a new allotment. Others in the organization, those who have not been officially involved in the project (and who do not have to pay for its failure) might be interested in that budget.

- "Internal budget competition."
- "There is a competitive world out there. There will always be competitive priorities and projects. There will always be turf wars. Budget cutting caused by stakeholders outside the project ('non-stakeholders') is probably the number one killer of good software."
- "Sometimes it happens in dysfunctional organizations (e.g., a line organization is not suitable for projects), where such subversion occurs with resource availability to projects."

Disagreement on Some Major Architectural or Technological Choice. This motivation has been reported in the context of the pattern of subversive subordinate team members and developers. Sometimes developers have a strong vision of what the "best" technical solution for a given problem looks like. The reasons for this suggestion may or may not be valid. They might be biased by lack of experience, by lack of relevant experience, by lack of overview of the political and financial background of the project, and—last but not least—by marketing efforts of technology providers. Nonetheless it is sometimes emotionally difficult for technologists to give up their vision (or parts of it) and yield to the decisions of bosses and bozos—decisions that they consider simply wrong.

- "We work with a lot of technical people, mainly programmers, and usually they become saboteurs when they do not want to work to some constraint, technical or otherwise, that has been imposed on the project. It may be something like he/she reads about a new piece of technology or software that he/she really wants to work on or it may be the desire to work to a different methodology than the rest of the team."
- "The stakeholder does not buy the idea."
- "Team members are forced to do a project they do not want to do, or they are forced to do it in a way they dislike to do it (e.g., using a certain technology)."
- "Developers whose ideas have been overruled will sometimes hope that the project fails, so they can feel they were proved right."
- "Ideological differences ([and] in [the]case of technical people, technical ideological differences)."
- "One possible case is where a developer or other staffer is ordered to do a project that for whatever reason they do not want to do. These projects are usually doomed to failure. Apprentice managers learn that you cannot order staff to do things they don't want to do."
- "Technical people, mainly programmers, become saboteurs when they do not want to work to some constraints, technical or otherwise, that have been imposed on the project. It may be something like this: He/she reads about a new piece of technology or software that he/she really wants to work on; or it may be the desire to work according to a different methodology than the rest of the team."
- "The subversive stakeholder wanted to come up with his own solution instead of buying one. So he fought against merely buying the-solution."

Disloyal Partners

- "Third parties are stakeholders, such as partner firms, clients, suppliers, vendors, and a host of others. They typically want a project to fail because it doesn't match their own objectives, or it depletes their resources, or they are not convinced of the benefits of the project. Other reasons can include misunderstanding of the project's objectives. Partner firms are the most common source of subversive elements in a project, in my opinion, because they are likely to resent the loss of their resources, will not likely see as many direct benefits as the party that initiated the project, will have a different culture and will likely not appreciate the project initiator's environment, for example."
- "The most serious examples we have encountered involved our customer's organization: Often there was a "make versus buy" decision. The customer decided to buy our product instead of letting its staff create an in-house solution. So they did it because they hoped our implementation would fail and they could build their own system instead of learning our system. One customer had a hostile IT group. They just didn't [want] to maintain another system. They looked for excuse after excuse to unplug our system. In the end

the customer moved the maintenance of the system from one group to another internally. It seems like the hostile IT group got what it wanted: less work. Internally, product releases were a very political process with competing stakeholders."

- "Sometimes the customer consultant or product management or even individual engineers would blow requirements out of proportion. This also led to skewed priorities with too much time being spent on minor features. Or sometimes, [a major issue was that the project] could not adequately be staffed. Customer consultants would do this sometimes to try to make us fail, either so they could run their own internal project or sometimes just because they refused to compromise on changing existing internal practices."

- "In my opinion, partner firms are the most common source of subversive elements in a project. They are likely to resent the loss of their resources or they may not see as many direct benefits as the party that initiated the project. They may have a different culture and will not appreciate the project initiator's environment."

- "External consultants have changed scope needlessly in order to maximize their billable hours."

- "We have seen subversion in projects between companies. The motivation was that their own company could advance their own solutions without competition."

Split in Upper Management.   The tale in Section 9.5 by Anonymous shows that subversive attacks are particularly dangerous if the attacker is a senior manager. According to the opinion of the responders, such attacks are frequently "successful"— that is, [they] end in disaster for the project. This pattern can occur in a context in which the senior management is split in two or more factions [and] are "at war with each other."

- "It can happen that senior managers have competing goals."

- "Senior management may work to discredit a project or remove its funding in an attempt to damage it for political reasons."

- "Management understaffing or underestimating—individual managers would intentionally underestimate work so they could understaff projects they didn't consider important. Again this was a way of undermining agreed upon priorities. Sometimes in collusion with product management. Sometimes they would commit adequate resources in planning but divert them after the project started."

- "They want to deliver a message only failure can achieve."

1.3.2   Sample Answers to the Question "How Were the Subversive Attacks Discovered?"

Here are sample answers to the question "How were the subversive attacks discovered?"

Some Attacks Are Carried out Overtly.   Surprisingly enough some attacks are not secret: even persons who are not involved in the conspiracy know of the attacks. It may happen that the entire development team is aware of the subversion and know that the project is doomed to fail. However, the loyal stakeholders are unable to find a way to solve this problem. They might be lacking countervailing power, or the evidence might not be clear enough to address senior management.

- "None of the reported attacks were behind the scenes. The confrontation was out in the open, at least at my level. Not everyone in my organization had knowledge of the confrontation."

- "Attacks were done in the open via e-mail and forums (meetings) and in other private conversations, as we later found out."

- "They were pretty much in the open. [The] project was vulnerable to attacks due to scope-creep enlarging [the] project beyond performance capabilities. Client failed to transfer data correctly and needed a scapegoat, so the new system was identified as the problem; the contractor was paid, but ultimately twenty million dollars was wasted when entire venture was cancelled."

- "Since we was once part of the IT group and knew their procedures, it was very obvious to me that the reasons/causes of delays was abnormal; believable not to raise 'red flags' but very apparent to me."

- "Working with them we heard them expressing their resistance to the project quite openly."

- "They were pretty obvious about wanting it to fail. The attack wasn't all that hidden. Their agenda was well known."

We Found It out Later.   In some cases, subversion could be fathomed to a certain extent; however, there was no clear evidence. Later it was indeed found out that the disturbance was in fact a deliberate and well planed action.

- "First we did not know if he did it due to incompetence or on purpose. Later it became clear that he did it deliberately, because he boasted about his tactic in private conversations."

- "It took time to discover what was going on. It was a pattern of behavior that identified the developer's issues. When the business lead was replaced, and the new person did not have [that agenda], ... what had happened became apparent."

- "It started with unimportant decisions and rumors about negative talking of a certain person. But we [weren't] sure about the [subversion] before an important decision was delayed and negative."

Social Skills.   Many responders to the survey reported that they rely on informal channels of information: friends among their colleagues and careful observation of behavior patterns. Many details are like the pieces of a puzzle: Each single piece of information does not say much; but several pieces come together to form a complete picture.

- "Subversive people rarely put their plans in writing; it's not like you can sneak into their cubicle, look under their keyboard, and find a mastermind plan written in crayon. Such plans are usually uncovered by bringing together data-points from various groups—getting the whole picture, but from different perspectives."
- "First, the loyal stakeholders become suspicious as a consequence of rumors. Although rumors and doubts are not very reliable indicators of subversive attacks they give an indication that it might be worthwhile to have a closer look to this issue: You hear rumors—they are usually wrong but they indicate where you have to search."

Other responders however warned against an intensified feeling of distrust:

- "We think the project manager is in the best place to see subversion, but actively looking for it is likely to sow seeds of the subversion anyway."

Informal Network

- "We found it out by friendly talking to some reliable people who might have smelled trouble, but were frightened to report it on their own."
- "Among the most important sources are: word-of mouth, informal networks and hallway discussions outside team meetings."
- "The stakeholder will give trusted people a piece of information, and then they will pass it along to those who might be affected."
- "The attacker spread disinformation and negative stories about the project. These rumors finally reached the project team."
- "Finally asked a colleague who, it turned out, knew what was going on."
- "By speaking with other stakeholders. People are naturally sensitive to other stakeholders doing nonsensical or counteractive things. And they naturally compare notes. Such subversive elements **always** come out."

Careful Observation of Behavior

- "You know you've been subverted when…
  - You're given difficult goals by upper management and no way to accomplish them.
  - You're set up to fail in any of countless ways.
  - You don't find out about key objections by the stakeholder until it is too late to do anything about them.
  - There is a credibility gap with the stakeholder, with them denying verbal agreements that were made, or imagining different details in a conversation.
  - The stakeholder continues to change their mind, or delays providing their feedback at every stage.
  - The stakeholder speaks pleasantly to you, but when you aren't there they speak poorly of you or your project to influence others.

- ○ The stakeholder omits crucial information that might have saved a lot of time and effort.
  - ○ The stakeholder lurks in the shadows until the project reaches a weak point, perhaps right after a bug has been found or there has been a delay in the schedule, and then unleashes an onslaught of negative criticism in the form of rants sent via private e-mails that end up in everybody's inbox."
- "Body language and other social hints given by the saboteur during meetings which gives me the idea to follow this suspicion more carefully."
- "A deliberate or accidental discovery while going though code repository in detail."
- "The person does not participate or provide relevant information when asked to."
- "At meetings in which decisions that had been made without full group participation are uncovered, or via other communications that reveal these prior decisions."
- "Letter sent a few levels above; clash during a meeting; attempt to hire project members."
- "People became unreasonable sticklers, rejecting solutions that were clearly superior to the ones that had been planned earlier in the project. They began to define "success" not in terms of the original project goals, but in terms of (often irrelevant) details. One person was doing incredible damage to morale: getting information from people, then using it to harm them; saying hurtful things to people in project meetings."
- "The subversive worked for me and we found out his feelings in personal conversations and meetings we conducted."
- "Information wasn't distributed by those subjects."
- "We became suspicious because of the project tracking. Late response; rejected product; withdrawn support."
- "The attacks were all political. For example, the opposing manager would attend design reviews and attack the design. They would attend management reviews and attack the product and its implementation."

It Is Not a Single Event; It Is a Process

- "It's rarely obvious. Most of the time you notice that things aren't going right but don't know why. Tasks aren't completed as planned. Quality of work is poor. Deliverables are not signed off by outside stakeholders. There are a lot of minor changes demanded continually."
- "Many small details form together a picture. In time, a pattern of behavior becomes more obvious."
- "You can notice the way people act. Project managers are not at all naive and know it. Of course, subversion is rarely written down in project reports."
- "Implicit conclusion during the attack (usually during meetings and presentations) and later on confirmation via informal network or background details (who is connected to who—the corporate social network)."

- "Personality conflicts are generally visible to people who pay attention in meetings."

- "For instance, does the subversive element say one thing and do another? Does the subversive element tell you one thing and tell someone else something different? Can you find out how well the subversive element knows their domain, or is it an excuse to hide ignorance? Is there a power grab going on? Where do political winds blow? Is there a promotion, bonus, or performance numbers that make a nonsuccessful outcome more profitable? Is there retribution for some prior act? The rumor mills usually are wrong, but they are often right about where you should go to seek answers. Find out who is in the fold and who is excluded."

- "It took time to discover what was going on. It was a pattern of behavior that identified the developer's issues. When the business lead was replaced, and the new person did not have those agendas, then what had happened became apparent."

Intervention of Senior Management.   The first thing that springs to one's mind is that senior management has to stop such processes. This however is not easily put into practice: frequently enough senior management is not even aware of the problems. Who should inform senior management and based on what kind of evidence? Subversive stakeholders generally use informal channels of information, which do not leave traces. What is more, stakeholders can easily present righteous and honorable justifications for their actions, apparently exonerating them from any feeling of distrust concerning their participation in a conspiracy.

Nevertheless the responders reported some cases where the way to senior management was the key to the solution.

- "The subversive manager had said there was no product, that the project was just wasting money on something that could never ship. Upper management at corporate HQ sent a fact-finding team to see whether there was an actual product. …They fired him."

Project Audits

- "We think the best solution is a project audit. For large implementations across multiple divisions, implementation team members may make comparisons to determine if stakeholders are being 'subversive'."

Case-Specific Discoveries

- "The attacks were all political. For example, the opposing manager would attend design reviews and attack the design. They would attend management reviews and attack the product and its implementation."

1.3.3   Sample Answers to the Question "How Can Projects be Defended Against Subversive Stakeholders?"

Here are sample answers to the question, "How can projects be defended against subversive stakeholders?"

Applying Quality Project Management Practices

- "The problem is in the definition—malicious sabotage is very rare. In those rare cases where an individual maliciously goes out to sabotage a project, a robust development process will self-correct and the individual is put in line. In fact, a robust development process keeps the potential for sabotage at a minimum. If a stakeholder is hell-bent on driving their agenda, a well defined development process has sufficient checks and balances to make sure this attempt is a) either unsuccessful or b) that the very real and appropriate stakeholder concerns are taken into consideration."
- "In a well managed company this sort of political in-fighting does not happen."
- "I think the project manager is in the best place to see subversion, but actively looking for it is likely to sow seeds of the subversion anyway."
- "Increased ability of project manager to understand situations end to end."
- "Acknowledge it and treat it as a real risk, then use risk analysis techniques to deal with it."
- "Better up front stakeholder analysis, casting a larger net to identify stakeholders, more responsive to stakeholder concerns, early and visible risk management, be more proactive in identifying stakeholder concerns as risks, client leadership taking more responsibility for project success."
- "Don't use system developments projects to solve management problems; the projects just magnify the management problems."
- "Choose the initial course of action very carefully, considering the why, what and how. Don't get locked into paths from which you can't recover from problems predictable from the outset. What is the organization's previous history? Count on it happening again."
- "Develop your team once you have the right people on board. This is a lot of work. It means making sure people are agreeing to all major decisions about the project all the time and communicating well. For instance, don't be surprised if you have a whole band of saboteurs when a major architectural decision is made without the team's entire consent. [Provide incentive.] Usually this is not material or monetary. Instead, give all the members of the team a chance to breath and enjoy their successes. Provide an environment of trust. Positive feedback is never a bad idea."
- "I have never seen measures taken specifically for the purpose of detecting project subversion. I believe that carefully designed project auditing procedures would be effective."
- "It depends on the power structure within the organization. If the subversive stakeholder is quite powerful, the project lead and loyal stakeholders may lack couter-vailing power. My experience is that project audits are especially useful in this situation, as they provide an objective, independent report to the project sponsor, along with findings and recommendations."
- "Strengthen relationships with party that paid for the project, a very influential party. Gain support from people that can influence the subversive stakeholder (in)directly."

- "Again, in a well managed company this sort of political infighting does not happen."
- "Write good specifications for the project and involve the users/customers in writing the specifications. I use the ivy hooks method of writing specs which means for every specification there is a rationale for the spec and a way to verify the spec was met. I have found that involving subversives in the spec writing process, especially having them provide the rationale for a spec both captures, expert's knowledge and reduces the resistance to change from the subversive."
- "Involve users—including subversives—in the software development process. Have them critique screens you develop and make them test users of the new system."
- "Adopt the Six Sigma team approach to projects. A black belt (project leader) sets up a team including users/customers and they follow a set of steps in doing the project. These steps include define (define the project and determine the risks to the business), measure (set goals for the project and permanent methods to measure the results of the project), analyze (study to find best solution for the project), improve (implement the project), control (make sure the gains made by the project are maintained over time). GE and Caterpillar [are] the two most famous companies I am aware of that successfully utilize 6 Sigma methodology. Motorola initiated 6 Sigma but dropped it I believe due to company financial difficulties."
- "Against subversive project leads only a new project team can help. Against persons in 'lower' position a project team can build collateral structures by setting up information correspondingly."
- "Expect it and set up processes to protect yourself against it. For example, I had one senior manager who didn't think a project owned by another senior manager was important, but he needed to sign off on the deliverables. Knowing this ahead of time, I inserted a statement in the management kickoff meeting that unless a deliverable is approved or rejected by management within three days, it is assumed to be approved."
- "A clear project plan with roles and responsibility is needed to define who does what. Without this, there may be no difference between subversion and misguided efforts. I think the project manager is in the best place to see subversion, but actively looking for it is likely to sow seeds of the subversion anyway. Probably regular one-on-one meetings between the [project manager] and each stakeholder to allow stakeholder concerns/problems to be voiced will prevent passive subversion and should allow the [project manager] to find active subversion over time."
- "By routine examination of work and peer review. The more that someone tries to shield their work from such examinations the harder everyone else should push to expose that work. Secrecy is rarely in the public good."
- "Leadership. Open communication of goals and progress. Welcome other people's ideas and discuss them fully. Manage the impact on affected staff sensitively and openly and generously."

- "Better integration of all user requirements. Tighter, centralized project management."
- "Awareness. People need to be aware it can happen, so they are on guard and recognize the symptoms."
- "The project lead must immediately deal with developers and other contributing elements to keep them producing, and be prepared to replace any element that is not functioning as it should. Loyal management must use the political environment to manipulate the situation when other subversive management peers are identified. Management and developers must be vigilant against anything less than excellence from the project lead. Management in particular must make the project and project lead synonymous within the corporate environment to ensure that the project lead is inexorably tied to the project's success."

Quality Communication

- "Communication is the key to reducing people's feelings of disenfranchisement and alienation. If an individual does not believe s/he has a voice in the decision making process, s/he will find subversive ways to get their agenda pushed. If the development environment does not provide a relatively risk-free context in which people are allowed to express their convictions, then "sabotage" is only one of the probable outcomes."
- "I think a healthy and open team atmosphere is the best way to avoid subversion and sabotage."
- "Provide for full visibility within the project."
- "My experience is that project audits are especially useful in this situation, as they provide an objective, independent report to the project sponsor, along with findings and recommendations."
- "Inform stakeholders about real events / status / results of the project to tackle misinformation. Strengthen relationships with the party that paid for the project, a very influential party. Gain support from people who can influence the subversive stakeholder (in)directly."
- "Expose some of the subversive actions. This, however, is not always easy to do—depending on the respective relationship between stakeholders."
- "Communicate the project progress and minor successes. Install a project leading committee which involves important managers with power. Talk to the subversive stakeholders openly.
  - Escalation 1: Discuss[ing], expression of empathy and searching together for solutions.
  - Escalation 2: Project lead submits clear statement regarding the goals and the importance of the project.
  - Escalation 3: Senior management or steering committee submits a statement regarding the goals and the importance of the project.
  - Escalation 4: Overt statement of the steering committe/senior management: The success of the project is more important for us than your contribution.

○ Escalation 5: Replace the stakeholder. (This I have seen only once because Escalation 4 usually performs miracles.)"

- "Keep IT and process control individuals together in groups (as much as possible). This gives ownership to all involved and everyone has a stake in the success, or failure, of the project."

- "In the case of coding sabotage, by having individuals 'overlap' module responsibility will help prevent deliberate sabotage, as well as inadvertent bugs."

- "Do your requirements analysis. Also, figure out who the stakeholders are and map out whether they are positively or negatively disposed to the project. Work to influence negative stakeholders by getting their peers and others around them to influence the negative stakeholder. Turn negative stakeholders into positive stakeholders by making sure their needs are accounted for. Also, let some of the ideas be theirs so they feel like they have made a contribution and are invested, at least psychologically, in the success of the project."

- "Give always full visibility."

- "Portfolio management on high level, combined teams with different stakeholders aligned on a shared vision; balanced scorecard approach."

- "Facilitated workshops to charter the project at the beginning.

  ○ Creating role 'pointers' which each person creates and discusses as a group stating what their role is, what they expect and need from others, how they will interact with others who depend on their work.

  ○ Creating team working agreements at the start, and periodically checking on how they are working and what could be revised.

  ○ Creating sponsorship agreements (for how sponsors will actually sponsor the project)

  ○ Daily scrum meetings for status stuff.

  ○ Having a well-planned, collaborative requirements process which uses early and continual direct involvement from users and subject matter experts.

  ○ Ongoing use of well-run inspections and reviews of key deliverables beginning with plans and requirements (so defects can be surfaced early with the right people).

  ○ Ongoing use of well-run interim project retrospectives (at the end of each iteration, release, period of time or milestone).

  ○ Frequently social activities whereby the team—customer and IT—share food together (onsite and offsite) to build trust and genuine caring."

- "Work to transparency; when everything is transparent, it is harder to hide."

- "Inform stakeholders about real events / status/ results of the project to tackle misinformation."

- "Encourage active involvement, get them to feel a true sense of 'ownership', both by being financially involved in the company and by having an element to be proud of their work. Also, encourage better communication skills."

- ○ Escalation 1. Convince the stakeholder (if ideological or technical based)
- ○ Escalation 2. Comfort the stakeholder (if economic or power based) or offer pacifiers
- ○ Escalation 3. Eliminate the stakeholder
- ○ Escalation 4. Bring in an external mediator—mostly pre-emptive (assuming that we know about the attack)
- ○ Escalation 5. Die together—kill the entire initiative and wait for the corporate dynamics to change before bringing it back again.

Psychology

- "A certain amount of prevention of employee subversion can be accomplished by making sure the hiring process is as concerned with personalities as with technical skills."
- "Have some psychological savvy into picking team members. If two plus two don't add up: what a person says and how they perform, then be suspect and follow up on those concerns."
- "Awareness—people need to be aware it can happen, so they are on guard and recognize the symptoms."
- "Very, very, very carefully screen technical people when you hire them. You must not overlook the social and personal traits of a person in this position (a typical mistake for people doing hiring in my field). Some people are absolutely brilliant technicians on the surface but are extremely selfish primadonnas underneath and this is the most common style of subversion in an IT project."

Support from Senior Management

- "Get support/action from as higher in the organization as possible."
- "In my case senior management intervened and changed the responsibilities"

Taming …

- "Thorough inclusion of the potential subversive stakeholders."
- "It is important to work with them and not against them. To make them see how they can contribute to the project, and how they may benefit from it. In many cases the right approach may change their attitude."
- "Convince the stakeholder (if ideological or technical based)."
- "Comfort the stakeholder (if economic or power based) or offer pacifiers."
- "At least early information, yet better is early and thorough inclusion of the potential subversive stakeholders."
- "Make the subversive the project leader. The subversive won't be able to complain about the project after it is completed since they were in charge of the project."

... Or Fighting Back—If Taming Fails

- "Work around that person. Continue not to involve him or eliminate the stakeholder."
- "Proof destructive nature of attack."
- "Expose some of the subversive actions. This, however, is not always easy to do depending on the respective relationship between stakeholders."
- "Every stakeholder should be given ownership (from the sponsor down to the developer)—and by ownership, have a reward for success and a punishment for failure. This keeps the group's vested interest focused on the success of the project. If someone starts to subversion practices, it will be noticed sooner and called out. The subversive element should be dismissed from the project and management made aware of what and why."
- "The division president fired him."
- "Get support/action from higher in the organization if possible."

Pessimistic Opinions

- "You can't fully defend any project against sabotage, whether from within or without. You can pay attention to the issues that arise as the project progresses. You can keep in mind the simple maxim: A projects greatest challenge is too much success. Successful project teams behave a lot like successful rock bands. Everyone gets an ego. Everyone falls victim to the fundamental attribution error and assumes that everything that goes right on the project was a result of their work; that everything that goes wrong on a project is somebody else's fault. I see more problems with personality conflicts and self-promotion on successful projects than on others. The best thing you can do to fight this is to work constantly to create and maintain a sense of the team and of team accomplishment while keeping a lookout for personality issues. Bring in the psychologists and team motivators while things are going well. If they go badly it is often too late."
- "It's really hard to know how to deal with this. In my case, there was probably nothing I could have done, except perhaps to get all tasks to be performed and the reasons for performing them in writing."
- "If the subversive stakeholder is quite powerful, the project lead and loyal stakeholders may lack countervailing power."
- "There is no general protection of the project. If the attack is based on disinformation and bad stories some protection is possible if all information is shared project-wide."
- "There is no solution, not in the environment I work in."
- "Communicate the project progress and minor successes. Install a project leading committee which involves important managers with power. Talk to the subversive stakeholders openly. But in fact I must admit that all this never worked thoroughly because the subversion was not evident enough to really fight against or to exchange the subversive stakeholder against a more positive one."

- "In that scenario, the problem was essentially resource acquisition. It failed because no stakeholder had authority or inclination to compel."

- "I have tried several defense-alternatives. However, I must admit that they never worked thoroughly because the subversion was not evident enough to really fight against."

1.4 A FOLLOW-UP TO THE SURVEY: SOME HYPOTHESES AND RELATED SURVEY FINDINGS

How Did This Material Come Into Existence?   When studying the first set of responses (summarized in Section 1.2), we noticed that certain statements appeared time and time again in the answers. These statements formed a starting point for what we thought should finally be a kind of "quantified consensus" among the responders of the survey. So we decided to conduct a second-round survey regarding the perceived validity of those statements. We present those statements below as hypotheses, each with the second-round survey responses regarding their validity.

Some hypotheses (such as Number 1 and 2, below) appeared in some of the responses. Some responders emphasized their confidence in the validity of the hypothesis enthusiastically, while others did not mention this hypothesis at all, or they even expressed their doubts. So we included these statements to get a hard number regarding what we had here: a consensus, a controversy—or a fallacy?

A few hypotheses appeared only in a single response (for example, Number 8, below). However, the responders included interesting anecdotes or other thoughts that convinced us that it was worthwhile to have a closer look.

We added another few hypotheses from our own experience. However, the vast majority of them were extracted from the contributions of responders (although we had to change the wording in most cases). These considerations led to a set of 22 hypotheses that we sent back to the responders, asking them to assess the hypotheses. The rating for each hypothesis is a number between 0 and 10. In this range, "0" means completely wrong, and "10" means completely true. The responders left questions unanswered if they did not have an opinion or had no relevant experience.

We calculated the median as the center of the random distribution. The median is a number chosen in a way that half of the responders' ratings are equal or higher than the median and the other half of the ratings are equal or lower than the median. In statistics, it is known that the median is more robust against outliers (that is, values far away from the ordinary) than the arithmetic average. Since we do not have a reliable hypothesis regarding the random distribution of the ratings, the median seemed to be more suitable than the arithmetic average.

The ratings for each hypothesis are summarized in the tables, below. The second line of the table shows the number of responders who gave the corresponding rating (shown in the first line.) For example, in Hypothesis 1, four responders gave the rating "7." The lower half of the table summarizes the results of the upper half. The fourth line shows the number of responders who gave a rating in the interval indicated on the third line. For example, in Hypothesis 1, eight responders gave a rating in the interval "0" to "3" (that is, they expressed their doubts regarding this hypothesis).

Some responders included additional explanations in their responses. If we encountered an opinion that was out of the ordinary, we asked for confirmation and more explanations (to exclude the possibility of a typo). We allowed more space for these opinions, which were somehow different from the ordinary, for the following reasons:

- These opinions might give some insight of issues the majority is not aware of.
- Hypotheses which are supported by the majority of responders are quite likely to also be acceptable for many readers. The interesting point is: what objections are there against these (apparently) obvious statements.

Hypothesis 1—Median Rating: 8   Subversive behavior happens mainly in a dysfunctional environment, that is, when the management processes of the organizational unit are somehow wrongly defined. A robust development process keeps the potential for sabotage to a minimum.

TABLE 1.3

Rating	0	1	2	3	4	5	6	7	8	9	10	?
Num Part.	4	1	1	2	1	2	1	4	11	2	7	1
Rating		0–3				4–6			7–10			?
Num Part.		8				4			24			1

Responder's Rating [0]:   "According to my experience, subversive behavior is more likely to be successful in a dysfunctional organization because there is no strong process to prevent it. However, it is just as likely to be attempted in even the most functional organizations. Subversive behaviors take place among individuals, and you are likely to find them anyplace.

The most dysfunctional organization I've ever worked with is a California Life Insurance Company, where I created their program technology office. The CIO created an atmosphere of finger-pointing and blaming other people for problems by screaming at them in public meetings. I saw more than one long-time employee leave a meeting in tears after being screamed at. Subversive activities were normal, so that people could avoid blame. But everyone knew this was going on, and expected it.

One of the most functional organizations I worked at was financial services department of a large car producer. I developed the PMO for them and organized their project management processes. But even there, I could see a couple of mid-level functional managers who would agree with people in project meetings but then go around afterwards and criticize the project. This was more subtle and difficult to counteract. Company cultures don't create sabotage, people do. And you find these people in every type of company."

Responder's Rating [0]:   "Let's first define a dysfunctional environment. A broad definition would be an environment that lacks leadership and direction, lack of specific functionality specifications, and a lack of (programming and analysis) standards.

The 'leadership and direction' can be lacking and still have a good deliverable if the staff is good. So, let's examine the remaining two elements.

1. Lack of specific functionality specs. Of course and obviously, if the programmer instruction is ambiguous he may interpret the functionality in many (of his own) ways, and if his intent is detrimental to the cause, much complicated code can be created to easily mask intentional and harmful code. Which leads to the next and most important element.

2. Lack of standards. One of the most important features given to us by language developers (VB, C, etc.) is the ability to insert comments in the code. Good code standards require heavy commenting by the code developers. I personally have little use for hard-copy flow charts (except during system design). After the coding starts, I demand pseudo-flow comments in every routine. Basically, this means that the coder first enters comments describing every intimate step of the routine. When finished, the code is entered following each comment. This ensures anybody reading the routines can quickly understand the coder's intent and recognize 'unusual' entries.

   Also, I tend to restrict the overuse of called functions. If a function is to be used again, then it's necessary. But many programmers (especially the old C programmers) design all code in functions, whether or not is used again. In turn, many of these functions call other 'single-use' functions, and so on. This makes the code incredibly hard to follow and thus makes it easier to make mistakes (?). KISS is the rule here (Keep It Simple, Stupid)

   So far, this brief describes what a programmer can do to harm the project. You could substitute 'programmer' with 'business analyst' and change 'code' to 'functional specs.' Again, if no standards are available (or strong leadership), all sorts of 'misinterpretations' can be generated.

   Weak leadership is similar to weak parenting. If a staffer thinks they can get away with their agenda, they may try. Not that I condone 'Gestapo' tactics, but a firm hand on the wheel can prevent accidents."

Responder's Rating [0]:   "It strongly depends on the definition of 'dysfunctional environment' that people have in mind. Wrongly defined management processes are a potential part of the problem. I think if you would do a root-cause analysis of the problem you get a picture that is something like this:

- Ingredients that are a must for subversive stakeholders to appear: environment that allows this kind of behavior. This has to do with a combination of unclear or wrong policies or management processes, less attention of people in charge, need for people to derail a project.
- [A] must is also a person or group of people that have a somewhat lower ethical standard 'winning at all costs.'
- Also a kind of stick to hit the project is necessary."

Responder's Rating [0]:   "Obviously not true. Not all dysfunctional environments have subversive elements, consider the case of two business partners who don't know jack, but want very badly to succeed. Or, consider the environment which is not dysfunctional but filled with talented individuals; as such, I rewarded them with a $100 bonus for every bug they fix: what happens? They get sloppy, introducing bugs so they can fix them and write themselves bonuses. It is the incentive that caused the problem, not a dysfunctional environment. Is it easier to hide subversive behavior in a dysfunctional environment? Absolutely, but that isn't what was asked."

Responder's Rating [1]:   "I do agree that a robust development process keeps the 'potential' for sabotage (I would add 'potentially' here as well) at a minimum. In this case 'development process' means a 'standardized' system/application development life cycle that is integrated with a quality assurance process.

However, I still believe that sabotage of varying levels happens in any environment. I was not clear what you meant by 'dysfunctional'—if that meant not having standards and regulated processes, or if it was referring to a human level of interaction based upon some organizational disparities that creates a higher potential for a 'breeding ground,' if you will, [for] the sabotage.

In either case, I feel that the human element in projects and the smooth accomplishment of processes, with or without standards is so huge that I was unable to narrow its potential to that one view or definition. Hence, the number '1.'

In my view, sabotage can be passive or active. For example, if you ask a developer for an intermediate progress report and they tell you that they will not give you that information: i.e., don't worry about it, I'll have it done by the (final) due date. I view that as passive sabotage. It blocks the project manager's ability to correctly, let alone accurately, track progress.

So, without knowing more of the definition of 'dysfunctional' I would stay with my number (not a typo) because of that human element and the existence of both passive and active sabotage."

Responder's Rating [2]:   "Sabotage is at different levels—ideation and project initiation stage, and project execution stage. At the ideation and project initiation stage there are a lot more political impacts than technical impacts. Development processes have less influence on pre-'go-no-go' stage of the project."

Responder's Rating [4]:   "I'm willing to grant that a dysfunctional environment may encourage subversive acts, so I won't say the hypothesis is wrong, but I object strenuously to the inclusion of the word "mainly". Subversion, as you appear to define it, can happen anywhere. Sometimes, moreover, it is a good thing. Some ideas are zealously pursued even though they are inherently bad, unethical, or dangerous to a business.

Subverting those projects is probably a good thing, and is more likely in a particular kind of dysfunctional environment: one that stifles disagreement and the presentation of alternatives. One notes again the fine line between subversion and conscientious disagreement. The managers who create this kind of dysfunctional environment would not, in general, regard it as dysfunctional. Indeed, they would regard an environment that encourages conscientious disagreement as dysfunctional because, among other things, decisions take too long (which is the nice way of saying 'my opinion is right and any discussion that might show that my opinion is not right is dysfunctional'). Employees whose disagreement is stifled, by contrast, are likely to regard this kind of environment as dysfunctional, and if they can leave they will."

Responder's Rating [6]: "When subversive behavior happens in a functional environment, it can make the environment dysfunctional very quickly."

Responder's Rating [7]: "Yes...but the minimum is still quite a bit."

Responder's Rating [8]: "—although this may be a truism."

Responder's Rating [10]: "Right on! '10.' I completely agree, and this is a strong thesis point! I cannot emphasize it enough: subversive behavior is one of the unhealthy coping mechanisms of people caught in unhealthy environments. Healthy people in healthy environments are too busy being creative and getting work done to bother with subversion."

Hypothesis 2—Median Rating: 7 The organization can be structured in a way so that subversive stakeholders are not tolerated.

TABLE 1.4

Rating	0	1	2	3	4	5	6	7	8	9	10	?
Num Part.	3	2	2	1	1	8	0	3	5	4	6	2
Rating	0–3				4–6			7–10				?
Num Part.	8				9			18				2

Responder's Rating [0]: "There is always a subversive behavior from one perspective or another."

Responder's Rating [0]: "Some subversive stakeholders may take the company in new positive and productive directions that were never originally conceived, just like beneficial mutations, evolutions in biology. Nature abhors a dogma."

Responder's Rating [1]: "There are many ways in which people can subvert projects. I have never seen any effective protection against all possible subversions, especially those by managers."

Responder's Rating [2]: "Not the structure, but the coherence of the management as a group can make them responsive to subversion."

Responder's Rating [9]: "I agree mostly. The reason it doesn't get a '10' is that even in very open organizations, some areas are more transparent than others.

Influence can still be gamed, and there are still personal reasons for opposition, such as ownership, control, and who has to rewrite their stuff."

Responder's Rating [9]:   "Absolutely. If you don't reward subversive behavior, which means getting rid of performance evaluations and rewarding based upon when the whole is delivered, you make everyone accountable and they police themselves. Will corporations do this? Often not. The subversive element realizes this takes money from their pocket, so if you have a subversive element in upper management, you can't get the change through."

Responder's Rating [10]:   "This is absolutely correct, but there is a huge danger in at least some approaches to doing so. The line between conscientious disagreement and subversion can be largely a matter of perception. If one is intolerant of disagreement, one can easily create an environment of groupthink and make huge mistakes as a result. One might easily argue that recent NASA space shuttle disasters are the direct result of an inattention to subversive stakeholders."

Responder's Rating [10]:   "Completely true. Subversive stakeholders are rare enough that they can be eliminated in a process that makes an example of them to other potential subversives."

Hypothesis 3—Median Rating: 6   The size of the organization has a strong influence on the frequency of subversive behavior.

TABLE 1.5

Rating	0	1	2	3	4	5	6	7	8	9	10	?
Num Part.	3	1	1	1	2	3	7	3	7	1	3	5
Rating		0–3				4–6			7–10			?
Num Part.		6				12			14			5

Responder's Rating [0]:   "The two most subversion-attracting organizations I can think of immediately are marriage and the telephone company, particularly before the breakup. Perhaps the CIA, or any other agency of enforcement, has a few less subversive stakeholders than the phone company."

Responder's Rating [4]:   "I agree only somewhat. Small organizations can become very unhealthy, in ways a larger organization would have a hard time sustaining. So, small orgs can be more vulnerable because they may be more unhealthy. A large enough organization has a hard time staying healthy, especially if there is stagnation in the business. A thriving business gets to create new parts of the organization, which is easier than transforming an existing organization into something different. So a stagnant org has an increasing chance of becoming unhealthy during stagnant times. And, since 'what goes up must come down,' there must necessarily be a plateau or decline for any company. Honestly though, any company that big is bound to have pockets of unhealthiness which could stimulate subversive behavior."

Responder's Rating [6]: "It is certainly the case that the likelihood of subversive acts increases as the number of stakeholders who are invested in other solutions increases, but the kind of subversion that is presented in these questions can happen in any organization."

Responder's Rating [6]: "Subversive behavior correlates with number of concurrent but not coincident projects."

Responder's Rating [8]: "Clearly. The more people in the mix, the greater the statistical likelihood you'll encounter a subversive person. The more people in the organization, the more you get people who don't have jobs producing, but who are being measured on some other criteria. I wonder if people aren't malicious, but greedy."

Responder's Rating [8]: "The larger the organization, the more people are treated by rules, the more lower level management there is that wants to get higher up and the less control by senior management there is over these lower level managers. The lower level manager has a sense of 'power' and will use that to get up higher."

Hypothesis 4—Median Rating: 6.5 Subversive behavior happens more frequently in large organizations

TABLE 1.6

Rating	0	1	2	3	4	5	6	7	8	9	10	?
Num Part.	3	1	1	4	0	4	4	3	7	3	4	3
Rating		0–3				4–6			7–10			?
Num Part.		9				8			17			3

Responder's Rating [3]: "I agree only somewhat. There are factors that lead a small org to suffer subversive behavior, and other factors that lead a large org to suffer subversive behavior."

Responder's Rating [3]: "I don't think so. Large organizations don't get to be large organizations without finding ways to inoculate themselves against internal threats."

Responder's Rating [5]: "More likely due to numbers, but I suspect it is more a matter of complexity and rewards, than sheer volume. One needs to ask, if this person were to over-achieve in the areas he's being rewarded for, does his success put him at odds with the company goal or hurt the company overall?"

Responder's Rating [10]: "Large organizations are bad. Even worse are multi-part organizations, such as where one firm is in charge of the project and other firms are involved (e.g., closely-allied partners or other firms that share some or all of the project owner's ownership)."

Hypothesis 5—Median Rating: 7   Subversive behavior is rare and unlikely to succeed if the project lead is "strong" (such as professionally qualified, strong personality, trusted by the top management).

TABLE 1.7

Rating	0	1	2	3	4	5	6	7	8	9	10	?
Num Part.	1	3	2	2	0	7	2	4	6	4	4	2
Rating		0–3				4–6			7–10			?
Num Part.		8				9			18			2

Responder's Rating [2]:   "It is less likely, but as a whole you're only going to focus on a localized group within the process. The best development efforts can be entirely undone by upper management shuffling a budget. How many great products can you think of that totally died because the CEO suddenly decided to liquidate and get out?"

Responder's Rating [5]:   "I don't know how I feel about this one. I guess a lot depends on how you define 'strong'. Strong leadership that is intolerant of disagreement risks groupthink and backchannel subversion. Strong leadership that treats programming teams like 'mushrooms,' gives employees little ability to either exercise or perceive disagreement, pretty much takes subversion out of the equation (along with creativity or the power to identify and proactively fix problems). Strong leadership that facilitates discussion of the problem, the requirements, and the solution such that it creates team buy in is probably the most likely to avoid real subversion, but 'strong,' in this case, is a set of people skills rather than a set of powers."

Responder's Rating [7]:   "I agree. There are many factors that may be out of the control or influence of the project lead. However, if you extend that to mean all management from the project lead up to the CEO, then I'd give it a '9.' The only reason it can't get a '10' is that personal issues can still lead to internal business conflict. People have their own personal motivations and interests that are oblique to everyone else and the company."

Responder's Rating [7]:   "It is rare. It can sometimes succeed if the subversive is stronger. Trust by top management is irrelevant."

Responder's Rating [8]:   "This is largely correct. These traits (especially the last) are important in minimizing/mitigating subversive behavior."

Responder's Rating [9]: "If the project lead is openly trusted by top management there is much less likely to be subversion. Much subversive behavior is decreased or eliminated when the subversive stakeholder knows that there may be negative consequences of subverting someone in management's favor."

Hypothesis 6—Median Rating: 5 Female project leads are more frequently attacked than their male colleagues.

TABLE 1.8

Rating	0	1	2	3	4	5	6	7	8	9	10	?
Num Part.	2	0	3	4	2	6	0	5	3	1	0	11
Rating		0–3				4–6			7–10			?
Num Part.		9				8			9			11

This statement has been included because a certain responder of the survey was rather convinced that in her case the gender had a strong influence. The results, however, do not indicate a compelling conclusion. Some few responders confirmed the hypothesis while others expressed their doubts. The high number of responders who abstained is particularly striking.

This issue might need another setting to be analyzed thoroughly.

Male Responder's Rating [?]: "Females often believe they have to prove themselves more/harder than their male colleagues. That may or may not be true, I don't know but this in itself makes them less respected. Personally, I believe a project can be run [in a maternal or paternal manner] with equal results, but 'ma' wanting to be 'pa' doesn't work."

Male Responder's Rating [0]: "I don't see gender as playing a role at all, and have had quite a number of very competent and talented female project leads. There are two possibilities that might be worth exploring: 1) Is this a self persecution complex? Every group feels that it is at the disadvantaged state because the grass always looks greener. Stating the same statement, but substituting in skin color, age, political belief, or religion would most likely get the same degree of passion from the speaker. 2) I have noticed that with some number of women they think in order to complete in a 'man's' world of business that they need to act like a bitch to get respect. Obviously, any inappropriate and unprofessional behavior isn't supportive and will generate ill-will and conflict. True, men can compartmentalize; Bob can tell Dave that he's not carrying his load and is being laid off, Dave gets it without insult, both opt for going out to lunch, and Dave buys Bob a beer. Working relationships are different from friendship ones. I've had a number of women admit to me their gender just can't do that well. It's foreign to them."

Male Responder's Rating [3]: "I can see how this could be a factor, but I cannot say 'more frequently.'"

Female Responder's Rating [5]: "This is valid only in cultures where being male presents a clear and effective leadership advantage."

Male Responder's Rating [7]:   "This is a gut feeling on my part."

Male Responder's Rating [7]:   "I agree. Some men can be such pigs… Successful female managers can be extremely competent communicators, and have their own arsenal of techniques for dealing with people who cross boundaries. But these kinds of subversive behavior are incredibly costly for the company, because it can lead to lawsuits. It may be easy to show in a court of law that it was sexual harassment. Therefore, in an otherwise healthy organization, this kind of subversive behavior is inherently weak, because if it is exposed the full weight of the company must necessarily side with the female employee, or the company may suffer even worse consequences. Thus, it is weak sabotage, destined to fail, and a strong female manager knows that as long as she sticks to the facts and is competent, the weak subversions will fall by the wayside. So, there is an odd twist to some degree with female managers in some situations, it can also be used to an advantage, as a kind of hysteresis. In other words, it might be easier to launch a subversive attack, but it is inherently weaker. It kinda caps your risk because if the female manager is obviously subverted, she probably will raise the issue with her management, and the subversion will end. Also, some women are naturally collaborative, and that tends to play against subversion in general. That said, some males interact in ways that are more aligned with how females are described above. Similarly, some women interact in ways that are more typically male. Rather than pin behavior to specific body configurations, I prefer to consider how individual personality traits induce or reduce subversion. For example, anyone using an emotional basis for influence is likely to induce subversion. Whereas, using a transparent, logical basis for influence is more likely to reduce subversion. However, someone who is aggressive or strong willed may engender subversion because people are afraid to confront the person directly."

Female Responder's Rating [7]:   "This is an interesting question. And a difficult one as well. My gut-feeling is that this hypothesis deserves a '10.' However I can speak only from my own personal experience and do not have an overview of the situation. For this reason I only gave here a '7.'

It is quite possible that women just perceive subversion more intensely because they are more sensitive and they have higher standards of collaboration. In some organizations the subordinates accept only a tough, almost brutal, leadership style. Since I'm not a manager of this kind they interpreted my management style as 'weakness.' So I had to adopt a tough style to get things done.

In addition I'm not even sure that women are more frequently attacked by subversive stakeholders. Anyway, this is certainly not a strict rule—perhaps on an average.

However, I think that persons with a female style of leadership encounter more problems of this kind."

Male Responder's Rating [7]:   "This may be true to some extent, but even if it isn't, it is likely to be perceived to be true, especially by female project leads. This is far from a universal truth, but I have certainly encountered female managers and project leads that viewed any disagreement to be an attack, not just on their leadership capabilities, but on the notion that women can be effective managers.

I don't want to oversimplify here. I have encountered many female project leads and promoted a few myself. Most simply did their job. A few were very sensitive to anything that they perceived as undermining their authority. That's true of men as well, but men never attributed the attacks to their being male. They usually attributed it to a lack of loyalty or an inability to be a team player. My point, I guess, is that this may be more a matter of perception than reality. On the other hand, there are some genuinely sexist guys out there."

Male Responder's Rating [9]: "IT is, unfortunately, still sexist. I have no doubt that this leads to **more** subversion of females than of males, even if the difference is small."

Hypothesis 7—Median Rating: 5 Subversive behavior is usually against people, not against projects.

TABLE 1.9

Rating	0	1	2	3	4	5	6	7	8	9	10	?
Num Part.	6	0	3	3	1	13	2	2	3	2	1	1
Rating		0–3				4–6			7–10			?
Num Part.		12				16			8			1

Responder's Rating [0]: "No. By definition. We are talking about subversion of the projects. The methods employed may include attacks on the personnel involved in the project. It may frequently include that, for all I know."

Responder's Rating [3]: "Often it is about job security and others."

Responder's Rating [5]: "I agree somewhat. Actually, projects are quite crucial. If a project decides to go in one direction, that may orphan or obsolete someone's primary responsibilities and software. There are often two ways that will both work. So the decision gets made on other factors. Then it can get really nasty..."

Responder's Rating [5]: "Equal."

Responder's Rating [5]: "Both. I've seen projects suffer because of someone's personal gain. I've seen a director set up and attack a subordinate in a public meeting because at some point in the past he accidentally surfaced some material that she didn't know the answer to (that she should have)."

Responder's Rating [5]: "It is often the case but not 'usually'."

Responder's Rating [10]: "I was at least one of the people who suggested this, and I still agree, but I start from a perspective, which I don't see reflected in your questions, that there is a difference between subversion and disagreement. When we disagree with people, it is most often because we disagree with them about an issue that relates to the project. When we subvert them, it is because we don't like them. When we disagree about a project, it is generally because we have the ability to do so in an environment where our disagreements will be considered. It is only when we are unable to have our disagreements with a project considered that people subvert projects."

Hypothesis 8—Median Rating: 9   Attacks from a user base or a client can be very effective if coordinated.

TABLE 1.10

Rating	0	1	2	3	4	5	6	7	8	9	10	?
Num Part.	0	0	0	0	0	1	0	3	8	5	14	6
Rating			0–3			4–6			7–10			?
Num Part.			0			1			30			6

Responder's Rating [7]:   "Company XYZ wants to revamp its internal software, so it contracts out to have some new software made which will keep track and make people more accountable. Employees at XYZ either perceive or learn through the grape vine that the new software will require them to work harder and be more accountable. So there is an instant disposition not to want to use it. The contracting company delivers the perfect software on time and under budget, it does everything right. Users at XYZ make up complaints that the new software isn't like the old software, and within 72 hours refuse to use it. The users are the subversive element. Company XYZ now has a choice. Mandate that the users will use it (and start firing those who don't). Or, cancel the follow on development contract. Note: the subversive element is affecting the development but is not engaged in the process at all."

Responder's Rating [8]:   "Yes, but it should be considered that the most fundamental act of any subversion that has any hope of working is some level of coordination. It is usually the person who is trying to subvert the project that is coordinating things. The people coordinated may well be unwilling dupes who have no idea how they are being used. This is fairly true, but it may not be terribly relevant."

Responder's Rating [9]:   "Any coordinated attacks are much, much, much more effective."

Responder's Rating [10]:   "I totally agree. But, then, I think I wrote that. ;-) Yes, that's true. Thank you. Johann"

Hypothesis 9—Median Rating: 9   All subversive attacks disturb the project to some extent.

TABLE 1.11

Rating	0	1	2	3	4	5	6	7	8	9	10	?
Num Part.	0	0	1	2	0	3	2	3	4	5	15	2
Rating		0–3				4–6				7–10		?
Num Part.		3				5				27		2

Responder's Rating [3]: "Many subversive attacks have little impact on the project at all. Others ultimately kill the project."

Responder's Rating [8]: "Hard to imagine how they couldn't."

Responder's Rating [10]: "I totally agree. If nothing more measurable, then at the least it deflates the enthusiasm that makes people want to keep looking for a creative answer to their business problems."

Responder's Rating [10]: "Yep. Life disturbs the force of universal stasis. In fact, at many levels, growth and development can be equated with disruption."

Responder's Rating [10]: "Absolutely, because it's just one more thing that needs to be dealt with by someone who could be doing something else more productive."

Hypothesis 10—Median Rating: 4.5 Carefully screening of people when they are hired is an efficient defense against subversive behavior. The personalities, the social and personal traits of a person, are equally important to the technical skills.

TABLE 1.12

Rating	0	1	2	3	4	5	6	7	8	9	10	?
Num Part.	4	2	6	5	1	5	2	5	0	2	4	1
Rating		0–3				4–6				7–10		?
Num Part.		17				8				11		1

Responder's Rating [0]: "Yes. You can screen for and against social and personal traits as well as technical skills, but that's like getting people to pee in a cup for drug screening. The act of peeing in a cup does not guarantee consciousness and consciousness is what is required on the job."

Responder's Rating [0]: "Most subversive behavior I have seen comes from outside the project. Often from functional managers who believe they are negatively impacted by the project."

Responder's Rating [0]: "You can't screen for these people in a job interview."

Responder's Rating [3]:   "This only brings you so far. It's required for the staff you bring onto the project, but does nothing about outside parties who have influence on the project."

Responder's Rating [3]:   "While it is certainly true that 'social and personal traits' are as important as technical skills, at least at the level where people get to participate in decision making processes, I don't think that this is true at all. The skills that are most desirable for avoiding the problems that lead to subversive behavior are the same skills that would make someone effective in organizing and coordinating a subversive attack. People skills are important to both endeavors."

Responder's Rating [6]:   "Most of your people need decent people skills. But a lack of 'people skills' absolutely does not equate to subversive behavior. Some 'quirky' engineers are fastidiously dedicated to the company's success. Factoring them out of an organization suggests an expectation of producing an 'also ran' product line in a rigid engineering environment where innovation is not necessarily encouraged except within narrow boundaries."

Responder's Rating [7]:   "While possible, in small groups, it is unlikely you'll find any filtering criteria that will catch them with any reliability. What one wants is to make subversive behavior have no reward. However, this will not eliminate subversive behavior caused by personal grievances."

Responder's Rating [7]:   "… it can help … a bit."

Hypothesis 11—Median Rating: 10   Refusing to give information is a method frequently applied by subversive stakeholders.

TABLE 1.13

Rating	0	1	2	3	4	5	6	7	8	9	10	?
Num Part.	0	0	1	0	0	1	2	3	7	2	21	0
Rating	0–3				4–6			7–10				?
Num Part.	1				3			33				0

Responder's Rating [2]:   "This is IMHO 'subconscious' most of the time and therefore not 'subversive' in the sense of your definition."

Responder's Rating [5]:   "Or giving misinformation, or putting a spin. News teams, media analysts, networks and people who produce documentaries, can all be subversive stakeholders about the state of our environment/political world."

Responder's Rating [8]:   "Either as the primary attack (40%) or to cover the attack (99%)."

Responder's Rating [9]:   "Withholding crucial information means the system will miss certain capabilities or qualities."

Responder's Rating [10]: "I agree strongly. It takes the form of omission most often. They know what you need to know, but you don't know that you need it yet. And 'it's not their job to tell you.'"

Responder's Rating [10]: "Yes. It can send people down the wrong path. It introduces unnecessary risk to a project. It burns time from the development cycles."

Hypothesis 12—Median Rating: 7 For an experienced software manager inside the project, it is usually rather easy to recognize the existence of subversive stakeholders.

TABLE 1.14

Rating	0	1	2	3	4	5	6	7	8	9	10	?
Num Part.	0	0	2	0	2	5	4	8	7	3	6	0
Rating		0–3				4–6			7–10			?
Num Part.		2				11			24			0

Responder's Rating [2]: "There is a know-how and perspective distance between a manager and [for example] a technician. So a subversive technician can do sabotage which that not be recognizable to the manager. At least, not without the help of another (non-subversive) technician. [That is,] sometimes 'doing what is specified' instead of 'doing what is actually required' can stop progress on a project that starts with poor specifications and subversive technicians. Afterwards, it's tough arguing 'who is guilty', though both the spec writer and the developer can interact in intentionally subversive ways."

Responder's Rating [5]: "It's also easy for an experienced software manager inside the project to misperceive conscientious disagreement as subversion."

Responder's Rating [6]: "The biggest obstacle to recognition is the failure to even consider it."

Responder's Rating [7]: "I should think so. Identifying who is the subversive might be more difficult."

Responder's Rating [8]: "This is usually the point where the company goals, the project goals, and the personal goals are all visible and available for comparison. When someone starts acting counter to the primary objectives, it stands out."

Responder's Rating [8]: "From below, '9.' From above, '7.' From below, you can still be blindsided if you didn't cover your bases when figuring out who is a stakeholder. But from above—you actually might not have enough information. Your project may be subverted from above in ways that may well doom the project.

Um. Ford just destroyed their battery powered trucks. You think the experienced project managers running the experimental truck project saw that one coming? ;-)"

Hypothesis 13—Median Rating: 8   Informal networks are very important for discovering subversive attacks.

TABLE 1.15

Rating	0	1	2	3	4	5	6	7	8	9	10	?
Num Part.	0	0	1	0	0	1	2	4	11	3	14	1
Rating		0–3				4–6			7–10			?
Num Part.		1				3			32			1

Responder's Rating [8]:   "This is pretty true. Most coordinated attacks from the inside are likely to result in related grapevine chatter."

Responder's Rating [8]:   "In that case, there will be someone who informs you of a hidden agenda."

Responder's Rating [8]:   "Information is very important. Diverse information comes from informal networks."

Responder's Rating [10]:   "I'd say they are very important for discovery. Particularly the smoking-room group—cigarette smokers usually find they have a broader range of contacts :)."

Responder's Rating [10]:   "I agree. This is sometimes the only way in which enough perspective can be gained to infer the presence an invisible subversive attack, or to raise the flag about the nature of the subversion, and even to mediate the situation."

Hypothesis 14—Median Rating: 8   Understanding subversive mechanisms and awareness of the symptoms are important prerequisites when defending against subversive attacks.

TABLE 1.16

Rating	0	1	2	3	4	5	6	7	8	9	10	?
Num Part.	0	0	1	0	0	3	1	3	11	3	15	0
Rating		0–3				4–6			7–10			?
Num Part.		1				4			32			0

Responder's Rating [5]:   "They are important to recognize attacks; and only then it helps in defending against it."

Responder's Rating [7]:   "I don't think you have to be aware of these mechanisms to avoid attacks. I think simple observance of the principles of human relations management will do a pretty good job of preempting most subversion. Subversion is much less likely to occur when everyone feels they have had a chance to evaluate the proposal and contribute to the final solution; when they have had a chance to disagree and have their disagreement considered and addressed. Subversion is more likely to occur when people feel they are being coerced into doing something they feel is wrong, whether for political or other reasons. The human relations approach deals with this. Several well understood methods of problem solving make this an explicit element of their method.

On the other hand, awareness of where problems are likely to come from, and how they happen, can be helpful in understanding the importance of using these kinds of preemptive methods."

Responder's Rating [10]:   "Naturally. But the better technique is to avoid them to begin with by using collaborative techniques that engage stakeholders in a way that they share the ownership of success with everyone else, and so no stakeholder is incentivized to subvert the project."

Responder's Rating [10]:   "Yes. Experience will often let you see the consequences of actions. Let's face it, developers think in terms of code, not dollars. A budgetary attack will be effective against them. Upper management think in terms of dollars, and information attack will be effective against them."

Hypothesis 15—Median Rating: 5   Project members in the role of developer or technical lead are frequently not aware of subversive activities of managers

TABLE 1.17

Rating	0	1	2	3	4	5	6	7	8	9	10	?
Num Part.	0	1	2	3	4	9	4	5	3	0	4	2
Rating		0–3				4–6			7–10			?
Num Part.		6				17			12			2

Responder's Rating [4]:   "If the subversion is from their own management, they can usually be fed a line about why the change in activity is necessary. If the subversion is from external management, it might not be on the radar. This, however, is more apt to happen with less experienced personal. The more experienced developer/lead will engage with other groups downstream and upstream and ask how the activities are affecting them, and are there any feedback loops or advanced warnings that would be beneficial to all?"

Responder's Rating [6]:   "… may be aware but unable to respond."

Responder's Rating [6]:   "This is particularly true of developers in 'mushroom' environments. It should be less true of technical leads, even in 'mushroom' environments. It is generally not true in rapid development environments in which the whole team has a role in evaluating the problem, generating the solution, and making project related decisions. Indeed, I have occasionally found project members to be aware of problems (via the grapevine of chatter with people on other projects) before anyone in the management or technical leadership of a project was aware of those problems. If this happens, by the way, the damage is probably already done and may be irreversible."

Responder's Rating [8]:   "… they are kept in the dark on purpose…"

Responder's Rating [10]:   "I agree strongly. '10.' Techies get set up and hung out to dry regularly. We call it a 'change of priorities.'"

Responder's Rating [10]:   "Yes. Yes yes yes."

Hypothesis 16—Median Rating: 8   Defending the project against a subversive attack requires at least one loyal person with end-to-end understanding of the project and influence in the organization.

TABLE 1.18

Rating	0	1	2	3	4	5	6	7	8	9	10	?
Num Part.	1	0	2	2	2	4	0	2	7	5	11	1
Rating		0–3				4–6			7–10			?
Num Part.		5				6			25			1

Responder's Rating [2]:   "I'd say that the people with the broadest knowledge tend to be found towards the less-influential end of the power spectrum, and that 'higher-ups' with a higher-altitude less-detailed view would have more influence. Perhaps more in the case of subversion-from-above, a higher-up ally would be important. But in the cases of same-hierarchical-level competition, higher-ups might be disinterested in taking sides of contests at that level. Having said that, contest-by-proxy would involve the higher manipulating the lower. In that case, one's project would be a proxy target for some other higher-up project stakeholder. Attack deflection in such a case might, for example, be helped by shifting the attacked stakeholder laterally away from one's project so as to terminate the attack. Such a shift would need the cooperation of a higher-up, whatever their motivation, with or without knowledge of one's project. But this all reflects my cynicism in supposing that an organization would not in general try to eliminate such interference at all levels; in several places I've worked, this kind of thing is very much a part of the business process. Some organizations seem to encourage this so as to have an atmosphere of competition and consequent supposed enhancement of performance. This apparently is the case where I am currently, but there is an excellent ring-fencing of development away from such turf-wars, so at least on my floor, there is a very cooperative collegiate atmosphere.

But I've no experience with such politicking; I keep my head down and get my invoices in on time. :),"

Responder's Rating [4]: "This can help, but it is no panacea."

Responder's Rating [7]: "Agree somewhat. You can do it without that, but that would be pretty useful. Actually, without that, you have to work the wheels of direct and indirect influence. In the worst cases, going public with an accusation of subversion could have devastating consequences. If there isn't a clear line of inter-ested authorities up to the level where budgetary decisions are made for both parties involved in the conflict, then there is no guarantee of a resolution, and the situation could fester. If it festers the cost in terms of lost time and productivity naturally increases, perhaps dramatically. It may also be harder to resolve as time goes on, since decisions will have been made in the mean time which perhaps should have been made differently had the subversion not been in effect. Still, an experienced person who witnesses a subversion can in some cases bring this to the attention of multiple people who can act together to accomplish the same thing that a single person with end-to-end understanding of the project might accomplish."

Responder's Rating [8]: "Influence in the organization, yes. End-to-end understanding of the project, not really."

Responder's Rating [8]: "Either loyal or someone who is compensated to having the thing succeed. However, all you may get is detection. Defense requires resolving the problem or neutralizing it."

Responder's Rating [8]: "… at the very least.."

Hypothesis 17—Median Rating: 3 Change projects are more prone to subversive attacks than new projects.

TABLE 1.19

Rating	0	1	2	3	4	5	6	7	8	9	10	?
Num Part.	8	1	5	5	1	4	1	1	1	0	4	6
Rating		0–3				4–6			7–10			?
Num Part.		19				6			6			6

Responder's Rating [0]: "They are subject to different kinds of attacks and can be defended on very different grounds, but new projects are certainly much more vulnerable to subversion than projects that have an established business value based on existing products and processes. Change projects can find an opposition that new projects won't have in those who would prefer the status quo, but new projects face a constant uphill battle of maintaining the case for building something that has no established business case (known market, established customer set, necessary process). The accountants are more likely to subvert new projects. The old guard is more likely to subvert change projects. The old guard, at least, can be brought into and given a stake in the success of, change projects."

Responder's Rating [0]:   "It's not the kind of project, but who gets what if things win, fail, or drag on."

Responder's Rating [2]:   "Also new projects imply change."

Responder's Rating [3]:   "Not really."

Responder's Rating [3]:   "I disagree. There are factors that affect both. Change projects suffer from stagnation in unhealthy organizations; whereas, new projects are like 'fresh meat' and people want to carve out their territory."

Hypothesis 18—Median Rating: 8   Projects which will change the structure of the organization are particularly prone to subversive attacks.

TABLE 1.20

Rating	0	1	2	3	4	5	6	7	8	9	10	?
Num Part.	0	0	0	0	2	1	1	2	14	4	9	4
Rating		0–3				4–6			7–10			?
Num Part.		0				4			29			4

Responder's Rating [4]:   "I'm not sure that there is any project that cannot be attacked from some direction, but projects that change the structure of the orga-nization and raise the possibility that people will lose their jobs and/or power as a result of the change are certainly likely to be resisted. Getting buy in from stakehold-ers that are likely to be effected this way will be particularly difficult. I think, however, that the most likely projects to be successfully subverted are new projects that are predicated on an imagined business case rather than a real market, customer set, or process."

Responder's Rating [4]:   "Rather, these projects are more likely to have vested interests opposed to them."

Responder's Rating [8]:   "They imply insecurity about one's job, unless the future is clearly communicated."

Responder's Rating [8]:   "This kind of project generates more resistance."

Responder's Rating [10]:   "I agree. If this won't prod a subversive attack out of your organization, nothing will. ;-)"

Hypothesis 19—Median Rating: 7   Subversive stakeholders are frequently experienced managers with a lot of political understanding.

TABLE 1.21

Rating	0	1	2	3	4	5	6	7	8	9	10	?
Num Part.	2	0	1	2	2	4	4	4	8	4	3	3
Rating		0–3				4–6			7–10			?
Num Part.		5				10			19			3

Responder's Rating [4]:   "I have seen more engineers as subversives."

Responder's Rating [6]:   "From their political understanding of what is achievable; they can make a good judgment about the foundation for the project. I do not find this subversive, as killing an unsupported project early may be better for the organization."

Responder's Rating [7]:   "I agree. The rest are for personal reasons. But, if the organization is changing, and there are people who 'aren't keeping up' (either in management or otherwise), then those people are more vulnerable to exhibiting subversive behavior as a result of the inherent conflict of interest they are experiencing. On one hand, they are expected to make rational decisions. On the other, their livelihood, or at least the comfort of understanding what their job is and how to do it, may be at stake."

Responder's Rating [7]:   "In my case, it was a developer with little management experience, but lots of political understanding. I have no other points to compare."

Responder's Rating [8]:   "Certainly the most successful ones are."

Responder's Rating [8]:   "**Effective** subversive stakeholders are."

Responder's Rating [9]:   "These guys are more dangerous and capable of manipulating the system, but it isn't wholly limited to them."

Hypothesis 20—Median Rating: 6   Managers outside of the project who shoot missiles against the project from a safe distance are a frequent pattern of subversive attacks.

TABLE 1.22

Rating	0	1	2	3	4	5	6	7	8	9	10	?
Num Part.	0	0	1	2	3	8	2	4	6	1	4	6
Rating		0–3				4–6			7–10			?
Num Part.		3				13			15			6

Responder's Rating [?]:   "Are those managers really 'stakeholders?' Or are they just bystanders?"

Responder's Rating [5]:   "… or they are desirable critical thinkers whose input can temper the project output."

Responder's Rating [6]:   "Though, less effective. Ask what they have to gain by doing so."

Responder's Rating [7]:   "e.g., from competing project and affected teams and so on."

Responder's Rating [8]:   "I agree. That is how they are perceived. The connotation of a missile is that is has a big impact and is unexpected. That is exactly what it is like to have a VP from another part of your company say in a public meeting that they see no point in your project and they think it should be cancelled and the people assigned to other projects. That's a missile. It can hardly be viewed as any way but subversive to the people in the project. However, it may very well be exactly the right thing for that VP to be thinking. If it is the right thing to be thinking, it is incumbent upon the VP to communicate this through appropriate channels and not just to lob a missile. But, some people who are VPs are VPs because they have connections [and] not because they are particularly good at healthy techniques for influence and governance."

Responder's Rating [8]:   "Yes, especially when their project or power is at risk or they see the principles in the project they are attacking as competitors or enemies."

Hypothesis 21—Median Rating: 8   "Attacks from above" are frequently successful. That means if the subversive stakeholder is a senior manager, the attacker is likely to succeed.

TABLE 1.23

Rating	0	1	2	3	4	5	6	7	8	9	10	?
Num Part.	0	0	1	2	3	8	2	4	6	1	4	6
Rating		0–3				4–6			7–10			?
Num Part.		3				13			15			6

Responder's Rating [?]:   "I have no idea. It strikes me as odd to imagine a senior manager engaging in subversion of a project. Why not just kill the project openly?"

Responder's Rating [5]:   "It depends on the projects support."

Responder's Rating [7]:   "… unless stopped by peer senior managers."

Responder's Rating [8]:   "I agree mostly. It isn't a guarantee of success, but unlike other kinds of subversion, attacks from above can be 100% effective sometimes. A strong attack from above is likely to succeed unless there is a yet stronger supporter above."

Responder's Rating [9]:   "Very likely. No amount of process or talent can defend against he who holds the purse strings."

Responder's Rating [10]:   "Of course."

Hypothesis 22—Median Rating: 8   The interests of the subversive stakeholder are met better by failure of the project than by success.

TABLE 1.24

Rating	0	1	2	3	4	5	6	7	8	9	10	?
Num Part.	1	0	0	1	1	6	2	2	6	2	12	4
Rating		0–3				4–6			7–10			?
Num Part.		2				9			22			4

Some responders criticized me for including this hypothesis in the first place: "This is a truism. It is so obvious that you should not bother us with asking such questions". The high number of "10" ratings indicates that many responders were completely convinced of the validity of these statements. Nevertheless, other contributors expressed their doubts and gave extensive explanations for their reasons.

Responder's Rating [0]:   "Not true. The stakeholder may be interested in just dragging it out, getting more resources, calling attention to himself as a hero, or be manipulating the circumstances to financial gain—in some cases the project must still succeed. Failure is not always the goal."

Responder's Rating [3]:   "I'm aware that my rating might be out of the ordinary. But here [are] some explanations.

1. For certain categories of subversive stakeholders, yes the project's failure is directly better for them (managers who will lose influence, staff who will lose their jobs, suppliers who will lose a customer, customers who will wind up paying more—to mention just a few).

2. But for a great number of subversive elements (mostly employees and certain "caretaker" managers), the success or failure is immaterial, it's "change" that they oppose.

3. Then there are the consultants, staff, project managers, and outsourced parties or suppliers who want to see the project's implementation grow or be delayed

so that they can continue riding the gravy train. The ultimate success of the project is important to them, but if it can come now or in six month's time at $120/hr, let it be in six months time.

4. And lastly, it is my impression that a variety of subversive stakeholders are in most cases pursuing a strategy of competition with the project's stakeholders, and though the project's success might very well be a direct benefit to them, they would rather see it fail than see the rival behind the project succeed. That is, the subversive element sees the failure of the project's **stakeholders** as being in their interest, not the failure of the project."

Responder's Rating [4]: "Let's say there was a project that could save the company a lot of money. Everybody wants to see it succeed, except Fred. Fred sabotages the project. When the president finds out what happened, that Fred screwed it up, Fred is fired. I would say that Fred's interests were not very well met. ;o)

Even if you are not fired, you are known as a foot-dragger this can impair your career path in many other subtle ways."

Responder's Rating [5]: "I'm guessing sometimes yes, sometimes no. Sometimes, the interests of the stakeholder are met simply by engaging the project in subversion. The success or failure of the project is irrelevant—it's the effect of the subversion that the subversive is trying to produce."

Responder's Rating [5]: "If we all could foresee the future... One man's effective strategic defense against subversive attacks is another man's buggy whip company."

Responder's Rating [6]: "I agree somewhat. Often this is true, especially when a crucial decision between alternative approaches or technologies is at stake. It can be a zero sum game. However, when the subversion is for human reasons (as mentioned in answers above) there are several other possible outcomes, including:

- The subversive person changes stripes and supports the project once their human needs have been met (such as recognition or the respect of being asked for their opinion before decisions are made).
- The subversive person relinquishes once it is revealed that they are doing it for personal reasons.
- The subversive person rethinks their behavior and changes their behavior.
- The subversive person is themselves the target of effective influence and they elect to subdue their subversive behavior.
- The subversive person is put on report and has to fight to keep their job."

Responder's Rating [9]: "... almost by definition."

Responder's Rating [10]: "That is, at the very least, their perception."

REFERENCES

Boehm, Barry and Turner, Richard. *Balancing Agility and Discipline*, Addison-Wesley, 2004.

Britcher, Robert N. *The Limits of Software*, Addison-Wesley, 1999.

Charette, Robert N. "The Rise of Enterprise Risk Management and Governance," *Executive Report*, Cutter Corp., Nov. 2004.

Charette, Robert N. "Managing the Risks in Information Systems and Technology," *Advances in Computing* 44:1–58, 1997.

Cockburn, Alistair. *Surviving Object-Oriented Projects*, Addison-Wesley, 1998.

Ewusi-Mensah, Eweku. *Software Development Failures*, MIT Press, 2003.

Glass, Robert L. *Software Runaways*, Prentice-Hall, 1998.

Glen, Paul. *Leading Geeks*, Jossey-Bass, 2003.

Humphrey, Watts S. *Managing Technical People*, Addison-Wesley, 1997.

Jeffrey, Joel. "A Data-Driven Analysis of What Goes Wrong in IT Projects," *The Software Practitioner*, July 2006.

Jones, Capers. *Assessment and Control of Software Risks*, Yourdon Press, 1994.

"Global Management Survey," KPMG, 2005.

McConnell, Steve. *Software Project Survival Guide*, Microsoft Press, 1998.

Miller, Roy. *Managing Software for Growth*, Addison-Wesley, 2004.

Morasco, Joe. *The Software Development Edge*, Addison-Wesley, 2005.

Moynihan, Tony. *Coping With IS/IT Risk*, Springer-Verlag, 2002.

Nelson, R Ryan, "Project Retrospectives: Evaluating Project Success, Failure, and Everything in Between," *Management Information Systems Quarterly Executive*, Sept. 2005.

Nelson, Sharon D., and Simek, John W. "Disgruntled Employees in Your Law Firm: The Enemy Within," http://www.senseient.com, 2005.

Pfleeger, Shari Lawrence and Kitchenham, Barbara A. "Principles of Survey Research," *ACM SIGSOFT Software Engineering Notes*, Nov., 2001.

Ropponen, J. and Lyytinen, K. "Components of Software Development Risk: How to Address Them. A Project Manager Survey," *IEEE Transactions on Software Engineering*, 26(2), Feb., 2000.

Rost, Johann. "Political Reasons for Failed Software Projects," *IEEE Software Loyal Opposition* column, Nov. 2004.

Rost, Johann and Glass, Robert L. "Subversion and Lying: the Dark Side of IT Politics," *Cutter IT Journal*, April 2005.

Rost, Johann and Glass, Robert L. "The Impact of Subversive Stakeholders on Software Projects," *Communications of the ACM*, July 2009.

Thibodeau, Patrick. "Firms in India Seek Better Background-Check System," *Computerworld*, April 18, 2005.

Thomsett, Rob. *Radical Project Management*, Prentice-Hall, 2002.

Verner, June. "A Study by the National Information and Communication Technology Institute of Australia (NICTA), *Software Practitioner Newsletter*, July 2006.

CHAPTER 2

LYING

Subversion, we have just seen, happens on occasion on software projects, enough so that it can cause major problems if allowed to go unchecked. We were concerned enough with learning more about this problem that we conducted some original research on the subject, research into the who/what/when/where/why/how of subversion, and that research study made up the bulk of the material in our previous chapter.

Here, we take a similar approach with respect to the subject of lying on software projects. We introduce the subject with some anecdotes and case studies, below, but we quickly move into a discussion of our research study, one similar to the one on subversion.

Here, we discovered that lying is quite ubiquitous on software projects. Those lies may vary in outcome from minor white lies to serious project-killing ones, but it is nevertheless a chillingly common software project phenomenon.

First, we will start with some anecdotes.

2.1 INTRODUCTORY CASE STUDIES AND ANECDOTES

A Motivating Example. The management of a software project has a problem. They have committed to a schedule that may well be impossible to achieve (Lie #1). They ask their employees to buy into that schedule anyway, and the workers, afraid to say "no" to management, agree to the commitment (Lie #2).

One manager realizes that a certain "breakthrough" software development approach could conceivably result in accomplishing the impossible, and completing the project on time. (Note that this is not a lie; the manager simply doesn't know whether this will work or not). The manager asks one of his staff specialists to explore the use of the breakthrough technology by using it on this project, and the specialist, convinced that the breakthrough cannot possibly accomplish what it promises, agrees to try (Lie #3).

Time passes, and the project does indeed fail to meet its schedule. As the end of the scheduled time approaches, the project lead continues to tell management that the schedule will be met (Lie #4). When it becomes obvious that it cannot be met (because the schedule date has passed), the entire project team expresses surprise and says it will try harder as the project continues (Lie #5 is the expression of surprise; Lie #6 is the statement that trying harder will allow the project to finish respectably).

Finally, the project staggers to a halt, having completed most of the desired functionality, albeit several months later than the original schedule. The project lead gives the project manager, and the project manager gives his boss, an essentially phony reason for their inability to meet schedule (Lies #7 and #8). No one on the project tells anyone, except among each other at the worker level, that the problem was that the original schedule never was achievable and that they have done the best they could under impossible circumstances, which means that the same problem will occur on future such projects (Lie #9, a communal lie).

Management spreads the word that the software project team was the problem, and notes that they shouldn't have been surprised, because this kind of thing happens all the time on software projects (Lie #10, the most damaging lie of all).

(Our "motivating" example of lying is, as a matter of fact, a very de-motivating example! It is de-motivating because it paints a picture of rampant lying. It is also de-motivating because it describes a not-uncommon software project scenario).

What Is Lying?   For the purposes of this study, lying is defined as "intentionally distorting the truth" (that matches the dictionary definition). We specifically did not consider accidental or inadvertent lying. Lying is not a new phenomenon. People have been lying to other people as long as there have been people. There is reason to believe, however, that the number of incidents of lying is increasing. For example, in the popular psychology magazine *Psychology Today*, an article by Allison Kornet (1997) took the position that "the quintessential sin of the 1990s might just have been lying." (Kornet came to that conclusion after noting the "cliché" that "the 1980s was the decade of greed"). The article went on to say that "until recently lying was entirely ignored by psychologists, leaving serious discussion of the topic in the hands of ethicists and theologians." The article reasonably reflects the more theoretical literature of the various fields that study lying.

Regarding the amount of lying and the increase of incidents of lying Charles Ford (1996), a cognitive psychologist, reports on a poll that shows that 54% of people say dishonesty is more common now than a decade ago. (That book goes on to say that lying is "ubiquitous," that "our society is permeated with deceit," notes study results that say that 90% of people lie, and even contains a chapter entitled "Everybody Lies"). Similarly, philosopher and psychoanalyst David Smith (2004) says "Nature is awash with deceit."

Regarding the ignoring of the subject, Ford (1996) takes the position that "lying ... [is] neither inherently moral or immoral," adding that it is the kind of lie told that determines the wrongness of it. For example, many authors say "white lies," whose intention is to help and not harm, are not morally wrong. Similarly, human relations specialist Schein (2004) says "lying is not per se a moral issue," and goes on to take what he calls a "moral relativism" position on the issue. And Smith (2004) says that "deceit is normal, natural, and pervasive." However, many philosophers (such as Thomas Aquinas and Immanuel Kant) condemn lying in all its forms, as do many religions. (It is interesting to note, however, that Christianity's Ten Commandments single out "Thou shalt not bear false witness against they neighbor" as the only kind of lie specifically condemned.) And in a political sense, it is certainly true that in the case studies reported in Ford (1996), telling lies leads the liars into lots of trouble! Finally, philosopher and ethical theorist Sissela Bok (1999) comes down firmly on the side that says lying is largely wrong, noting "truth and integrity are a precious resource, easily squandered, hard to regain."

In this discussion, we are specifically interested in the phenomenon of lying as it occurs in the computing profession, more specifically in the software field. There have been many anecdotal reports of the prevalence of lying in the field. Here are some examples.

- Robert Sutton (2002) tells several stories of incidents of lying to computing managers involving Atari (where "many Atari engineers pretended" that things were all right when they were not), and Hewlett-Packard (where the book reports on surprising incidents of lying in a company better known for its truthful engineering-driven culture).

- One of us, Robert, notes in Glass (1993) that "lying to management is a con-flagration , one that threatens to consume our field," based on the results of a seminar that explored the topic of lying among a dozen practitioner attendees.

- Regarding the well known CONFIRM project failure story, an article in *Computerworld* (1992) reported that one of the key contentions in the lawsuit that was filed was that "some people who have been part of the CONFIRM RS management did not disclose the true status of the project in a timely manner."

- In the perhaps better-known NASA space shuttle Challenger disaster story, an article in *IEEE Transactions on Professional Communication* (1988) found what it called "miscommunication" as the key cause of the problem, resulting partly from this fact: "Thiokol engineers concluded that the O-Ring problems were serious before their management did. However, in their written com-munication, they varied the extent to which they voiced that seriousness, depending on whether the audience was internal or external."

- In an analysis of the level of trust between CEOs and CIOs, an article in *Information Week* (1992) noted that "IT executives offer up fictitious benefits simply to gain approval for systems … And the culture gap grows wider."

In fact, it is not unknown in the computing and software field to find support for the notion of lying. For example, Alan Davis (1995) identifies as one of his 201 prin-ciples of software engineering the recommendation that "Minor underestimates (in software project estimation) are not always bad." Glass (1993) reports that some of his seminar attendees concluded "I had to check my ethics at the door when I went to work here" and "lying gets me resources I wouldn't otherwise get."

However, it is also not uncommon in the software field to find an ethical and pragmatic concern over lying. For example, Sutton (2002) takes the position that "Lying is a sleazy thing to do."

Anecdotal and pop psych findings aside, there is a need for objective research on this subject. It is the intention of our study survey reported here to supply that need. We conducted it during the year 2006; to the best our knowledge, there had been no prior study on the prevalence of incidents of lying in the software field. Before we present the results of our study survey, we will review several additional case studies about lying in the software and computing fields. These case studies are drawn from real projects, as reported in such books as *Software Runaways* (Glass 1998) and *Computing Calamities* (Glass 1999) (books that, in turn, reprint stories drawn from the computing and popular press).

CONFIRM.   Above we alluded to CONFIRM as a software project on which lying apparently occurred. (We use the word "apparently" advisedly, since people on one side of the complex issues involved in the demise of the project said that lying was involved, and those on the other side said it did not [not an unusual situation in the real case study world of software projects and lying!].)

At any rate, the article "When Professional Standards Are Lax: The Confirm Story and Its Lessons" by Effy Oz, originally published in the professional journal *Communications of the ACM* in 1994 and reprinted in (Glass 1998), says: "In 1998, a consortium comprised of Hilton Hotels Corp., Marriott Corp., and Budget Rent-a-Car Corp. subcontracted a large-scale project to AMR Information Services, Inc., a subsidiary of American Airlines Corp. The consulting firm was to develop a new information system (IS) called CONFIRM, which was supposed to be a leading-edge comprehensive travel industry reservation program combining airline, rental car, and hotel information. A new organization, Intrico, was especially established for running the new system. The consortium had grand plans to market the service to other companies, but major problems surfaced when Hilton tested the system. The problems could not be resolved, however, and three-and-a-half years after the project had begun and a total of $125 million had been invested, the project was cancelled."

A fertile field for lying, you may be thinking. And, sure enough, it was. In fact, charges of lying hit the press, and soon everyone knew that lying may have been a part of the project's demise. One of the company principles in the case sent a letter to employees, saying among other things, "Our CONFIRM problem has many roots—one more serous than the others. Some people did not disclose the true status of the project in a timely manner. This has created more difficult problems—of both business ethics and finance—than would have existed if those people had come forwards with accurate information."

(Note the polite euphemisms chosen to avoid using the confrontational term "lying"; even when people are visibly angry, they really work hard to avoid using the "L-word.")

There was, as we previously mentioned, some debate about whether lying had really happened. One letter to the editor, written in response to stories claiming that lying had occurred, "objected strenuously to statements that there was a cover-up," said that "CONFIRM customers had changed requirements and sought individual competitive advantage," and called an article mentioning that lying had occurred "a flawed and distorted supermarket tabloid view of what happened."

At the very least, then, unpleasant charges flew thick and fast after the demise of CONFIRM. However you feel about lying on software projects, I suspect that you don't want to be involved in any project, involving lying or not, where that much rancor is produced!

Wang Labs.   Wang Labs is a fascinating "riches to rags" story, one that, I suppose, is not that uncommon in the computing and software field. Not only was Wang the leading provider of word processing systems to the business world a couple of decades ago (back when "word processing" was not just a software concept but a hardware one as well), but out of that dramatic success came the even more unique concept of establishing an educational institute for teaching software engineering. Wang Institute was one of two prominent software engineering academic programs established some 25 years ago (the other was at a more traditional academic institution, Seattle University), and for a number of years it was known as a successful example of industry and academia cooperating.

Wang Institute died, unfortunately, a victim of the financial disaster that befell its parent institution, Wang Labs. The story of the demise of Wang Institute is told in Glass (1999); here we are more interested in the Wang Labs story because as the financial axe fell, the company engaged in what can only be described as corporate lying. As Wang slipped beneath the waves, its management began to move toward desperate measures to try to keep it afloat. As told in the article "What Went Wrong at Wang," by Joseph Nocera and originally published in the *Wall Street Journal* in 1992 (and reprinted in Glass [1999]), the company began to report new products for sale that simply did not exist! (The article from which this information was gleaned said only slightly tongue-in-cheek, "When you make product announcements, it helps to have products.") One day the new management at Wang "simply announced a series of 14 products, most of which were dazzlingly innovative. It turned out, however, that many of them existed only on paper. The event was madness."

Lying, we see here, can take many forms in the computing and software fields. One of those forms is simply claiming to have done something that you haven't, in fact, done.

Miniscribe.   The preceding two stories of lying were fairly visible cases, reported originally in such highly rated international outlets as *Communications of the ACM* and the *Wall Street Journal*. The story of Miniscribe is, by contrast, a much more localized story. The information sources we use, for example, are not from the international press, but from Los Angeles and Denver daily newspapers. (Although both articles are included in Glass (1999), the first article here, "Why the 'Dr. Fix-It' of High-Tech Firms Failed to Save Miniscribe," by Patrice Apodaca was originally published in the *LA Times* in 1989, and the second, "Computer Chief Will Face Trial," by Peter G. Chronis, is originally from the *Denver Post*, published 1993).

The "Dr. Fix-It" referred to in the first story headline was a well-known rescuer of troubled high-tech firms. He was brought in to the troubled company Miniscribe to perform a similar act of salvation. But somehow, at Miniscribe it all went wrong. In fact, according to the charges filed against Dr. Fix-It, there was lying on a massive scale as the good doctor tried to make Miniscribe appear to be successful. The *LA Times* story referred to this as a "Greek tragedy" emerging from an "outrageous" (and later, "massive") "fraud," noting that the company's reported sales for the last three years were "inflated," and saying "things were so out of control that at one point bricks were packaged as finished disk drives and sent off to customers to temporarily boost sales and inventory numbers."

The *Denver Post* report, written at the time Dr. Fix-It went to trial, added a few other claims:

- Two company officers were ordered to break into locked trunks in order to alter financial record paperwork.
- A memorandum detailing corporate losses was destroyed.

The story about bricks shipped as disk drives was repeated in the *Post* story as well.

While some of the case studies reported above were somewhat narrow in scope, the last one is a story of massive lying, completely out of control. It is interesting that the smaller cases of lying made the international press, whereas the massive cases of lying didn't get further than the local press. We're not sure what the message here is, except that lying—of any scope—will perhaps get you more attention than you ever wanted!

An Anonymous Tale. All of the above case studies involved serious lying with serious consequences. By contrast, let us tell a story where not lying resulted in positive consequences!

This particular case study is from a short item called "The Truth Helps" in Glass (1999). (This story is from a newsletter produced by David Schmaltz, president of True North PGS, Inc., a project management consulting firm in Portland, Oregon.) Here, the story is told of a manufacturing firm that gave IS an "impossible" deadline (sound familiar?!). Usually, IS would have just gone ahead as if it could make the deadline and then, at a really inconvenient time, the truth would be disclosed (again, sound familiar?). In this case study, the IS group decided it would speak the truth. Top management didn't want to hear it, but eventually a compromise was reached. A series of milestones were set so any slip-ups would be revealed earlier rather than later. "They still have an impossible date," but they have a process where they can talk about the truth as their experience tells them what's really going to happen. The end result: No one got hurt as a result of failing to meet the original deadline.

In other words, there is a way to avoid lying and convert a Greek tragedy into a happy ending!

2.2 INCIDENTS OF LYING: THE SURVEY

To explore the issue of lying on software projects, we decided to conduct a study in the form of a survey about the prevalence of such lying; we, Johann and Robert, joined together with a third computer software author and consultant named Matthias Matook for the effort.

We set out to conduct the lying survey among active software practitioners and those closely connected with software practice. The survey was conducted using a structured questionnaire (see Section 2.5) which was both specific and open-ended;

the questions asked were structured and specific, but there were opportunities provided for the responders to provide further details of what they reported.

The questionnaire was distributed to potential responders in several ways:

1. Each of the authors of this book (and survey) maintains contact lists of software professionals; the questionnaire was e-mailed to them.

2. The questionnaire was posted on a Web site, and responders were encouraged to go to the Web site and fill out and e-mail in the questionnaire.

3. At least one professional journal publically noted the existence of the survey; that journal published the questionnaire, encouraging journal readers to fill it out and e-mail it in.

There were 62 responses, all of which were used. Geographically, responses were nicely distributed across Europe, the United States, and Australia.

There were advantages and disadvantages to this distribution method, which will be further discussed in Section 2.2.7. The distribution approach was clearly an opportunistic one, not necessarily the best survey approach (as noted, for example, in Pfleeger and Kitchenham [1995]). But we felt that both our contacts and approaches were as optimal as could be obtained, given the nature of the survey and noting that the most common (and huge) problem in such surveys is the extremely low response rate typically obtained.

Responses were, of course, about responder perceptions of lying. It is difficult, on software projects or elsewhere in life, to distinguish accusations of lying from actual occurrences of lying.

The questionnaire itself is included as Section 2.5 of this chapter.

2.2.1   The Survey Results

As previously stated, the intent of the survey was to determine the nature and prevalence of lying on software projects. Questions were asked around the following:

- who the responders were
- what their experience with lying had been
- how often they had encountered lying
- what the motivations for the lying were
- who (organizationally) had been involved in the lying
- what they perceived to be the solutions to the problems of lying

The survey results showed that there are apparently four generally common activities that result in lying: estimation, status reporting, political maneuvering, and hype.

2.2.2   General Scope

The general questions asked concerned the demographics of the responders and an overview of the problem of lying.

2.2.2.1 Demographics Regarding the background of the responders, most of them were senior people in the field:

- 48% had greater than 15 years experience.
- 6% had less than two years.
- The remainder had varying degrees of experience in the range of 2 to 15 years.

Regarding age, here are the results:

- 37% were 21–35 years old.
- 35% were 35–50.
- 26% were older than 50 years old.

Job titles varied considerably, ranging between the following titles:

- 35% software engineer, programmer, application developer
- 22% software consultant
- 7% systems analyst/engineer
- 7% academic faculty
- 5% project manager
- 5% software architect
- 3% software QA, testing

Other exotica listed were "epidemiologist" and "scrum master."

2.2.3 An Overview of the Problem

Regarding the prevalence of lying, fully 86% of the responders said that they had, indeed, encountered incidents of lying on the software projects on which they participated. When given a structured set of options for why the lying had occurred, here is what they said:

- 66% said the lying was about project cost and schedule estimation.
- 65% said it had to do with status reporting.
- 58% said it was about political maneuvering.
- 32% said it was about some form of hype.
- 27% said there was some other reason for the lying. (Other reasons included "seeking CMM certification" and "the results of an unforgiving 'can-do' culture.") Grouping these "other" responses, we find 16% were about increasing sales;11% were about lying being more advantageous than telling the truth; 10% were about looking good in the eyes of bosses or customers; 8% were about overconfidence; and 2% were about hiding mistakes, while another 2% were about trying to get workload decreased. A complete set of these answers is found in Section 2.3.

TABLE 2.1 Lying frequency

Lying category	Responders who experienced lying (%)	Number of projects on which lying occurred (%)*
Cost or schedule estimation	66	50
Status reporting	65	50
Political maneuvering	58	10
Hype	**32**	**30**

*The percentage chosen by the most responders.

Note: Explanations for the terms will be provided in the sections that follow. Also note that here and throughout this survey, multiple answers were allowed, so percentages do not necessarily add up to 100%.

Given that most responders had experienced lying, we also asked, "How often did that lying occur?" Responders were given the choice of specifying 0–100%, in 10% increments. The largest number, 18%, said it happened on 50% of projects, and a further 14% encountered it on 100% of projects.

Fully 86% of the responders said that they had encountered incidents of lying in the software projects on which they had participated.

We also gave participants a structured set of options to describe the type of lying that had occurred. Table 2.1 summarizes the data.

To determine how often lying occurred, we gave responders the choice of specifying 0–100%, in 10% increments. The largest subset, 18%, said it happened on 50% of projects. However, 14% encountered it on 100% of projects.

We asked three "who" questions regarding each category of lying: "Who lied?"; "Who knew?"; "To whom was the lie told?." Table 2.2 summarizes those responses. Responses to the "to whom" question were problematic, so we omitted them from the table.

2.2.4 Clarification of Terms

2.2.4.1 Estimation (Providing Cost and Schedule Estimates Early in a Project) As noted above, the most predominant form of lying on software projects was (by a tiny margin) estimation. Seventy-two percent of those responding to the survey, when asked, specifically about estimation lying said they had experienced such lying. Interestingly, 15% reported "too large" estimates, while many more, 34%, reported "too small." (Another 34% reported both "too large" and "too small").

How large was the typical estimation lie? Again, responders were given the choice of specifying 0-100%, and the largest number 18%, said the lie was 50% off.

With regard to the frequency of estimation lying, 18% said it had happened on 50% of the projects they were familiar with, while another 10% saw it happening on 100%. The remaining percentages were spread fairly evenly among the 0–90% range. (The fact that 18% of responders both experienced lying on 50% of projects. Check and estimation lying on 50% of projects is interesting but largely coincidental).

TABLE 2.2

Lying category	Management	Project lead	Developer	Marketing	Customer or user
Cost or schedule estimation					
Who lied	53	48	45	40	11
Who knew	47	60	66	36	13
Status reporting					
Who lied	49	54	30	20	12
Who knew	43	59	59	23	16
Political maneuvering					
Who lied	44	34	19	26	13
Who knew	42	45	48	29	16
Hype					
Who lied	31	32	29	36	16
Who knew	31	36	44	34	19

There were several "who" questions regarding this estimation lying:

- Regarding who made the (deliberately wrong) estimate, 53% said management, 48% said the project lead, 45% said the developer, 40% said marketing, and 11% said the customer/user.

- Regarding who knew the estimate was wrong, the "who" were interestingly different, whereby 66% said the developer, 60% said the project lead, 47% said the manager, 36% said marketing, and 13% said the customer/user. (Apparently management makes estimates, but knows less than the people under them about their validity!)

- A question about "to whom" the lie was told was apparently not understood or not of interest to the responders; the answers to this question were not meaningful.

Why were these lies told? The "motivation" answers were particularly interesting as we see here:

- 42% said the estimates were a cave-in to people with more power (31% said that happened on 50% of projects).

- 42% said it was to win via a low estimate (28% said that happened on 50% of projects).

- 40% said it was padding with a high estimate to hold back reserves (23% said this happened on 10% of projects).

Responders were also asked what could be done to minimize or eliminate such lying. This was an open-ended question, and there was a huge variety of answers (note that responders to the survey were strongly motivated to respond even when there was no structured question). The complete set of responses on this matter is found in Table 2.1.

In terms of the responses, 21% were about improved management techniques (e.g., better time tracking, better control); 18% were about changing the "who" (that is, who did the estimation) (e.g., involve the developers); 15% were about improved estimation process (e.g., use independent estimators); 10% were about better communication (e.g., don't "shoot the messenger"); and 10% constituted a kind of "miscellany," ranging from "wrong estimates are not always bad" to "it is not possible to fight human nature."

2.2.4.2 Status Reporting (Providing Progress Reports As a Project Proceeds)   The second most predominant form of lying was during status reporting.

Seventy-seven percent of those who responded to the survey said they had experienced status reporting lying. Note that more people in the general results reported experiencing estimation lying than status report lying (66% versus 65%); however, the answer to the specific question about status report lying resulted with more people reported such an experience (77% versus 72%). Fifty-two percent reported overly optimistic reporting, while only 2% reported overly pessimistic.

With regard to the frequency of status report lying, 21% said it happened on 50% of projects (no other percentage of projects drew a significant response).

Again, there were "who questions":

- Who made the (deliberately wrong) status report? Fifty-four percent said the project lead, 49% said the manager, 30% said the developer, 20% said marketing, and 12% said the customer/user.

- Who knew the report was wrong? Fifty-nine percent said the project lead, 59% said the developer, 43% said the manager, 23% said marketing, and 16% said the customer/user. Note that the key player for status reporting is the project lead. This is not, of course, surprising. Also note also that the developer once more knows more than the manager about the telling of lies.

- The same problem reported above applies to the "to whom did they lie" question. There were no meaningful answers.

Regarding motivation, here are the results:

- 66% said they lied in order to tell management what it wanted to hear (19% said this happened on 100% of projects, and 15% said it happened on 50%).

- 44% said it was to hide bad work (21% said this happened on 20% of projects, 16% said it happened on 50%).

Responders were also asked what could be done to minimize or eliminate such lying. The complete set of responses on this matter is found in Section 2.4.

Thirty-one percent of the responses were about management techniques (e.g., change management incentives, have interim retrospectives); 10% were about better communication (e.g., encourage openness and honesty); 11% were simply pessimistic in nature (e.g., "I don't really have a constructive suggestion," "punish the guilty").

2.2.4.3 Political Maneuvering (Any Activity Wherein Positions Are Taken to Improve a Political Stance)

The third most frequent form of lying reported was for political maneuvering. Sixty-five percent had encountered this form of lying, 24% saying they had encountered it on 10% of projects. (Note that the occurrence of this form of lying is apparently infrequent; that 10% is the lowest figure for any of the reasons for lying reported here).

Regarding the "who" questions, here are the results:

- 44% said the manager did the lying; 34% said the project lead; 26% said marketing; 19% said the developer; and 13% the customer/user. It is apparent that lying for political advantage happens at the top, not the bottom, of the management ladder (again, this is not a surprise).

- 48% said the developer knew about the lying; 45% said the project lead; 42% said the manager; 29% said marketing; and 16% said the customer/user. The indication here is that, although management tends to tell lies for political advantage, those lower down the management ladder are pretty aware of those lies.

- 21% said the lies were told to the manager; 13% to the project lead; 10% to the customer/user; 7% to the developer; and 7% to marketing. Note that in this case the responders did answer the question about to whom the lies were told, but even here the answers look suspicious, since they do not come close to totaling 100%.

There was no question asked about the motivation for lying as a form of political maneuvering. The expectation was that an explanation is fairly obvious.

Responders were also asked what could be done to minimize or eliminate such lying. The complete set of responses on this matter is found in Section 2.4. 22% were about management approaches (e.g., focus on problem-solving, not blaming; make reporting verifiable); 10% were about communication (e.g., keep reporting data open and transparent); and 10% were pessimistic (e.g., "it's the same all the time," "you're asking for a solution to combat human nature").

2.2.4.4 Hype (Exaggeration for Effect)

The final and least frequent form of lying was "hype." Fifty-seven percent reported they had encountered this, 16% seeing it on 30% of projects, with the other percentages of projects fairly evenly spread.

Who employed hype? 36% said marketing, 32% said the project lead, 31% said the manager, 29% said the developer, and 16% said the customer/user.

Who knew that hype was being employed? Forty-four percent said the developer, 36% said the project lead, 34% said marketing, 31% said the manager, and

19% said the customer/user. It is apparent that the best defense against hype is to listen to those at the technical levels of the organization (again, this is not a surprise).

To whom was the hype told? Eighteen percent said management, 18% the project lead, 15% said the customer/user, 13% the developer, and 10% marketing.

Once again, no question was asked about the motivation for employing hype.

Responders were also asked what could be done to minimize or eliminate such lying. The complete set of responses on this matter is found in Section 2.4. 13% were about management techniques (e.g., flatten the management structure; involve the customer); 10% were about communication (e.g., have a tolerant corporate culture); and 8% were pessimistic (e.g., "I have absolutely no idea").

2.2.5   Discussion

In the view of other disciplines, lying in the general populace occurs frequently and increasingly. Yet, researchers in those fields tell us that most researchers ignore lying. (Those views were consistent across such disciplines as psychology and psychiatry, human relations, philosophy and ethics, and even international relations). Perhaps, then, the fact that lying is also prevalent and understudied on software projects isn't a surprise.

In those other disciplines, we also found mixed feelings about whether lying was morally wrong, with most experts agreeing that certain kinds of lies aren't but that others are. In this survey, we sought to study lies that are fairly clearly morally wrong, such as intentionally wrong project estimates and status reports, because those lies will likely most significantly impact software projects. We chose not to address the issue, except in passing, about whether software project lying could under some circumstances be benign.

We believe we chose the proper audience to query about the prevalence of lying in the field: software practitioners, mostly senior technical specialists.

In every case, the developers on a project knew more often than anyone else that a lie was being told. But who told the lie was a bit more varied—estimation and political-maneuvering lies came most often from management, status-report lies came most often from project leads, and hype came most often from marketing.

Responders were quite willing to share their perceptions about lying. Many questions were open-ended and qualitative; nearly all responders provided lengthy, insightful responses to those questions, especially those relating to ways to minimize or eliminate lying. (Interestingly, as one reviewer of this article pointed out, most responders suggested accomplishing this by increasing control, but some experts suggest this can't help, and instead recommend finding ways to increase trust.) The full set of responses is at http://smartconsultant.de/survey.html.

2.2.6   Conclusions

We believe that our findings paint a reasonably accurate picture of the nature and prevalence of lying on software projects. Specifically and most importantly, they learned that:

- An impressive 86% of responders had encountered such lying; apparently, lying is a common software problem.

- The leading activities on which lying occurred were in estimation and status reporting, with those forms of lying happening on 50% of projects, some saying even 100%.

- When lying happens, developers at the bottom level of the management hierarchy are most aware of the lying; they often know it is happening even where their management does not.

- Activities to minimize such lying are quite varied, but most responders suggested several such approaches.

2.2.7 Limitations

The most serious limitation encountered in doing this research was in getting a practitioner audience to respond to our inquiries. This is, of course, a problem with all surveys, especially surveys of practitioners. But it was worse in this case because we were asking our target audience to talk about situations of some delicacy. We offered anonymity to all our responders, but nevertheless we are sure some people did not respond due to the possibility of personal compromise.

It is not possible to discuss the response rate for this survey. There were 62 responders, out of hundreds of contacts made. Normal response rates for this kind of survey run in the 5–15% range, and we have every reason to believe ours would have been in that range. But our questionnaire was both distributed directly to potential responders and published in print or posted on Web sites, and those responders could opt in as opposed to responding to an inquiry. One of the editorial boards of *IEEE Software Magazine* was also invited to respond on an opt-in basis; that is, we asked first whether any board members wanted to opt in. *ACM SIGSOFT* published the questionnaire and invited readers to opt in; so, once again, "response rate" becomes somewhat meaningless.

The question remains, of course, given the opportunistic nature of the responses: Did our approach reach the kind of audience we were hoping for? The demographic data reported above gives us great confidence that we did. Responders were typically senior people (48% had over 15 years experience and 61% were over 35-years old), with suitable technical job titles (all but 7% were software professionals, and most [64%] were at the programmer/consultant/systems analyst level, which we consider the correct level for questions of the type we were asking).

However, the heavy concentration of responders at the technical level no doubt means that the findings are biased by that viewpoint.

Many of the direct inquiry responses resulted from the use of our contact lists which we mentioned above. Robert is a long-term U.S. software practitioner (largely in the aerospace industry) with more recent academic affiliations; Johann is a former European software professional now affiliated with a university in Romania; Mattias is a software consultant with a strong European background. Two of us currently live in Australia. We believe that the use of these lists is justified by the demographic findings mentioned above. Note that, from an international viewpoint, the findings are centric to the United States, Europe, and Australia.

There was also a small but predictable problem regarding the answers to questions "On what percentage of projects did this kind of lying occur?". Responders were given the full choice of 10% increments from 0% to 100%, but most answers came back clustered at 50% or (less often) 100%. This likely means that the answers were educated guesses rather than the reporting of accurate data. Another problem arose with responses to questions "To whom were the lies told?". We are perplexed by this problem, and have no reasonable explanation for it.

2.3 QUALITATIVE SURVEY RESPONSES ON LYING

What follows are verbatim responses from the survey. These qualitative results underlie the quantitative study findings presented in the preceding section. We categorized the according to motivations seen by the survey responders for the lying behavior.

1. Increasing sales
   - "Wanted to sell the software, so he hyped it up so they couldn't refuse."
   - "From a sales/management perspective, to sell the software."
   - "Sales and to win a contract."
   - "Selling, whether internally or externally. People want their project/product to sound exciting and important. Who is going to say (to their boss or their customer): 'It's just a maintenance release. There are a few new features, but they aren't important.'"
   - "Sales/Manager might want to increase sales."
   - "To get a 'leg-up' on the competition and win bids."
   - "In the case of sales/marketing, for money."
   - "Mostly 'marketing' (these are rather straw fires than longer-term lies)."
   - "Desire for resources/money."
   - "Political and monetary gains."
2. Telling them what they want to hear
   - "To please the recipient."
3. Decreasing workload
   - "Being overworked. By exaggerating problems, the developer tried to rid himself of some of his tasks."
4. Understanding why in some cases, lying has more advantages than telling the truth.
   - "Generally speaking I expect that it was to gain some sort of advantage in terms of budget, resources, career development or any of the usual reasons people have for hyperbole."
   - "They thought that they could get away with it I guess."
   - "People, I think, exaggerate or hype [up] to cover an insecurity or to seek favor."

- "To generate a feeling of optimism when someone takes over a project that hasn't been going too well."
- "I currently work in an academic environment where there is a lot of emphasis on who did what first and the importance of such work. So there is a lot of hyperbole and exaggeration, even in (especially in) externally published works."
- "Customers sometimes lie in order to get developers or helpdesk support to solve their problem."
- "I think this type of lying would be present in projects where the customer lacks confidence in the result they will be getting from the development team. I would see this as the project manager/director overselling a particular point or status to make things better than they really are: team output more functional than exists, team progress better than it is, that kind of thing. I haven't seen this on any of my projects."

5. Looking good in the eyes of the bosses and or customers
   - "Impress marketing or customers; fool the competition into believing you are further advanced than you are; fool the industry analysts."
   - "To maintain their own jobs or to get promotions."
   - "To be the 'star' developer/project manager."
   - "To be the hero."
   - "From a developer perspective, to earn a reputation and to avoid doing tasks that he/she didn't like."
6. Hiding mistakes
   - "To cover up for poor management."
7. Addressing over-confidence
   - "Most often, irrational exuberance and lack of an understanding of the capability of the team, the forces that weighed upon the project, and the fickle nature of the market."
   - "Over-confidence."
   - "Wishful thinking."
   - "Dedication to a vision without regard to reality."
   - "Pride in what had been created, but out of proportion to its value."

2.4   WHAT CAN BE DONE ABOUT LYING?

Here are verbatim responses to the survey regarding qualitative input to supplement the quantitative findings presented above. They are presented grouped by the kind of lie told and suggestions about what can be done about that specific kind of lie:

1. Estimation
   1.1. Estimation process

1.1.1. Score estimation precision

- "Institutionally, place the responsibility for estimating in the hands of someone with no other stake in the matter. Reward them, over time, for the accuracy of their estimates rather than for the success/failure of the projects. In an extreme example, if an estimator says, 'This will be an unmitigated disaster and will never deliver,' that estimator has succeeded if that is, indeed, what happens. Needless to say, this will never be called success if that is the same person required to deliver the project. (This, of course, assumes that institutionally you WANT accurate estimates.)"

- "I don't know if it works for everyone, [but] we are scored as a contractor on how close we come to the actual estimate. Bonuses are shared with amounts based on score, so you can earn more from being accurate and truthful."

1.1.2. Transparency of the estimation process

- "Transparency to the forces that led to those estimates."

1.1.3. Improved estimation techniques

- "Do not estimate whole projects, but work packages or components of a handy size (not more than 20 man days at a time); write down the work packages/components and estimates and do a review on it."

- "As a manager or project lead, know the people you are working with. Know that developer A always thinks things will take him half as long as they really will, while developer B always pads her schedule. Know that your boss or your subordinate has a track record of saying contradictory things to different people, and try (if possible) to find out what version of the story someone else heard."

- "Demand detailed explanations on how the estimate was obtained. Doing estimation repetitively (at each iteration). Having some company standard on estimation. Keeping metrics on past project estimates and actuals."

1.1.4. Independent estimators

- "Consult several technical experts, individually or in a group."

- "Get a second opinion."

- "Have a third party involved in the estimation process."

- "From my experience, the best way a customer can protect itself is to involve a second software engineering company which has no share in the project. Instead the second company's expertise is used to check the estimates and proposals of the main contractor."

1.2. Management techniques

    1.2.1. Project management

- "Agile techniques seem to be the most effective; also in general early prototyping before estimating."

- "At my corporate job, managers and project leads typically did review revision history and bug tracking to see what work was really done and what areas were problems."

- "Demand traceability of the estimation from the needs/ requirements to the way it will be implemented."

- "Better time tracking and using this information for future projects."

- "Better tracking of time, so everyone can learn from their mistakes. Better tools for tracking time to simplify the process. Better archiving of data and sharing of data so comparisons can be made. A means to document efficiency so productivity of a developer or other technology person can be visible."

- "Tighter control of the process."

- "Hold people accountable. Clear process and ownership—he who owns must deliver. Have the counter power that will challenge the owner of the estimation."

- "Set testable benchmarks so that schedule progress is less easily fudged; try to make sure these benchmarks correlate meaningfully to actual progress in the tough areas of the project; be aware that, inevitably, benchmarks set in advance are not quite the right ones, but make sure that the modification of benchmark criteria is itself a transparent process."

    1.2.2. Understanding behind the reasons why wrong estimates came into existence in the past and resolve these issues

- "I say I will take one month, the [project manager] reports it will 'conservatively' take three weeks and then the customer goes crazy saying it must be done in one week. … They fight it out for a couple of hours and then we are hung out to dry on a two-week deadline! I'm pretty sure a lot of this is bravado on the part of the customer to see how far they can push it. This mixed with a [project manager] who is not usually a 'developer' means they will almost always submit. Why don't people take the developer to these meetings (just for their specific discussion point) to give a 'technical' reason why it takes one month. We are not sitting around drinking coffee; we all want to deliver strong, efficient solutions and sometimes it really does take that long!"

- "Management always wants something at the last minute. Usually something that has to be done 'now' and we can test it later. My management has to have several additional things done after the feature set is coded."

1.2.3. Attention to hidden agendas

- "Customers should pay special attention to the hidden agendas of the involved parties. From my experience the consulting company's primary concern is never the customer's well-being. Instead it is its own well-being because it needs to earn profits for its shareholders and has to pay its employees. Therefore it will always try to cut development times by cutting down the number of features or trying to find an easy way to implement things."

1.2.4. Balance of power: sales versus technological people

- "Balance sales needs against what can be accomplished by IT."

- "For example, development provides an estimate, Sales challenges that estimation. Have product management with dual objectives—sales target + technical accuracy."

1.3. Communication

1.3.1. Provide quality communication

- "Managers should be open to listening."

- "Circulate information more freely, take the time to judge yourself by managers."

- "Explicit assumptions, teamwork, open communications."

1.3.2. Encourage truthfulness

- "As a developer: Have the nerve to say to your boss who tries to negotiate down your honest estimate something to the effect of, 'If you make it a condition of my job, I'll give you a smaller number, but it isn't going to make the project go any faster. If you need to lie to upper management or the customer as a political necessity, of course it is your prerogative, but please don't delude yourself or ask me to assure you that, unlike all other projects, this one will magically go perfectly.' In [terms of] sales/marketing: Don't over-promise. And if that's not possible, don't be surprised when over-promising leads to inability to deliver. Don't get angry at your co-workers when the results are what you really knew they would be all along, because it just means that next time they will do their best to leave you truly in the dark. In any role: When asking someone else for their estimate, if you want their best guess, don't tell them in advance what you want to hear."

- "Encourage truthfulness. Not shoot the messenger who told the truth. No unreasonable pressure to lower estimates without reducing requirements."

- "The project manager should allow the developers to make realistic estimates without demanding that they change it if it is not in line with what they want."

1.4. Optimize know-how of the people who are doing the estimates

1.4.1. Include developers

- "Involve the ones that are going to develop the software in the estimation process."
- "Ask the technical person directly."
- "Check information with developers."

1.4.2. Provide (technical) training of managers/people who do the estimation

- "Better top executives are well informed (and interested to know) about the work of project mangers and the activity of many other levels of managers between developers and high executives."
- "Better technical education and involvement of those in management positions."
- "The developers and engineers that do the work and have a better understanding of the environment, need to be consulted prior to any contract bid."

1.4.3. Eliminate the chance for the estimates to be done by the wrong people

- "Although salesman might bid low to get a job (the Big Dig is a classic), this is lesser seen on the [project management] side."
- "Fire the consultant and pay more attention to the people who do the work."

1.4.4. Educate customers and managers

- "The two situations I have been witness to for lying were [these]:
  - The marketing person for the project was also the project manager. He committed us to eight weeks for something we'd never done before, only to win the project from the customer. The only suggestion I can think of to prevent this type of behavior in the future, is for his/her boss to discourage inaccurate estimation. This isn't as practical because the same boss is putting pressure to win more contracts.
  - The other situation is where the project manager caves in to the customer's demands. This can be prevented by the project manager actively working with the customer to make sure that they understand what the project entails and how many people are working on the project. This is something that requires a large amount of patience, and [it] only works when the customer is interested in understanding the development process, rather than just demanding a delivery."
- "Educate managers (including customers) about the true cost of developing quality software. You get what you pay for, and

nickeling and diming at the outset often pushes the real cost up, not down. (Not that this would be easy.)"

- "Managers, sales reps and project managers need to have a better understanding of the work required to implement a project."

1.5. Optimistic and pessimistic opinions

1.5.1. Wrong estimates are not always bad

- "Note, however, that wrong estimates are a tool for adding flexibility to a project; they act like shock absorbers. (A car's shock absorbers lie to the car body regarding the condition of the road.)"
- "It is natural, and it is not always bad."

1.5.2. It is not possible to fight against human nature

- "Change human nature? Seriously, I am not sure there is any obvious way to change this because 'everybody lies' one way or another."
- "I don't know. People lie. Sometimes for good reason, often for not-so-good reason[s]."
- "Nothing. Because it is all about humanity! But at least estimations should be high. Because no one will say no to an early completed project)"
- "Nothing: you're fighting human nature which will not change. You have to learn to work around these problems."
- "Change the nature of business and politics? :-)."

1.5.3. Suggestions that are interesting but not an answer to our question

- "Management incentives have to change to reward for the big picture, not optimize for tiny pockets of projects and time. We've all had to work weekends to rush out a project to meet an artificial deadline and then discovered that no one looked at the delivery. Why? So someone, somewhere, who was usually at their summer home that weekend, can tell their boss the delivery happened as planned, thereby securing a personal bonus. Was it the right thing for the company? No. Does it have a damaging impact? Absolutely. Does he care? No, that's tomorrow's problem."
- "Metrics, the real kind, not just measurements. Leadership is critical."
  - ○ See the following references for more information:
    Wess, Roberts, Ph.D., *Leadership Secrets of Attila the Hun*, Warner Books, New York, 1985
    Weinberg, Gerald, *The Psychology of Computer Programming*, Van Nostrand Reinhold, New York, 1971.

Shneiderman, Ben, *Software Psychology*, Winthrop Publishers, Inc., Cambridge, Massachusetts, 1980.

2. Status reporting

2.1. Management techniques

2.1.1. Independent people who are responsible for project tracking; score report precision

- "Management incentives have to change. If you want an honest report, I must be completely free from consequences; if you don't like the message that's being reported. In short, long term guarantees you (or others) won't shoot the messenger."

- "Simply having capable project managers. Again, it can help to have a division of responsibility, where people responsible for tracking progress of a project are not the same ones responsible for making it succeed. For example, this is one of the many reasons for keeping QA/test as independent of development as possible."

- "Make experts evaluate the report. Also make the report writer feel confident and comfortable that no action will taken against him/her because of the additional work etc."

2.1.2. Improved processes

- "Interim retrospectives, iterative development, daily stand-ups."

- "Reviews."

- "Work on instituting [a] problem-solving culture rather than blaming. (A 'can-do' culture is a blaming culture too, because management won't let people be honest about what is really feasible.) Teach everyone, from senior managers on down to the lowliest tester and developer, real risk management principles and techniques. (Genuine project risk isn't something you manage down to zero by next report.)"

- "[Implement] simple process rules such as 'the work is not done until it's checked in' or perhaps additionally passed regression or unit testing. Basically convert reporting into something measurable or independently verifiable."

- "Appropriate project controls. Just because a status report exists and is filed does not mean project controls are in place and working properly. Project audits and reviews can protect against this occurrence if it is done during the earlier stages and not after the project has gotten into trouble."

- "It is too easy to fudge on progress reports when 1) no detailed plan exists in the first place and 2) there is no clear meaning of 'progress' when it comes to problem solving."

- "Break projects into smaller tasks (two to three days max). A task is either done or not done."

- "Code reviews."
- "Audits, automation, traceability, different type of reviews that can be compared."

2.1.3. Understanding of the reasons why wrong reports came into existence in the past and resolve these issues

- "More realistic deadlines."
- "I am not sure whether it is a problem. Everyone is responsible for his/ her information tactics. In the end, the facts will speak for themselves and reveal each major lie. But what makes people lie more, is intolerance against errors. To err is human. So, if the company culture allows people to err, they will more easily report problems early. When a problem is reported, the first question should not be 'Who will we have to punish?' but 'How can we solve the problem?' I, personally, do not think that employees need to be punished for errors. Usually, they are ashamed of it, and this is punishment enough."
- "Be honest about how long it would take to complete the project."
- "Most of our customers seem to be resistant against consultation. Therefore, they set a number of mandatory features and an impossible timeline in the beginning to keep the pressure in the project. However, as almost everybody involved knew about the mission impossible nobody really cares about delays and other problems. Consequently the customer is still told what he/she wants to hear. However, the real state is much different. The issue can be improved by customers listening to their contractors. The latter should have the chance to propose a possible schedule (from the contractor's point of view). Afterwards this schedule should be fixed and any delays be punished (e.g., in monetary terms) unless well reasoned."

2.1.4. More qualified management

- "Better management and fewer positions for managers that are not interested in the success of the company and skilled for such businesses"
- "Educate business managers on the nature of software development"
- "Get managers that have the domain knowledge to begin with and not just someone that came in off the street."

2.2. Communication

2.2.1. Quality communication and transparency

- "An "open door" policy would help. That company was all political and somewhat corrupt. They really frowned upon stepping over your manager. Meaning if you went to discuss an issue with another high level person or VP level without your VP involved they got very upset. It is that sort of bull shit that causes corruption, problems and lying."

- "Transparency of the data and process... e.g., if all project data and history are in a collaborative Web site, it makes it much harder to hide from reality"

2.2.2. Encouragement of truthfulness

- "Interview junior staff, anonymously."

- "Accurate and deliverable time and cost estimates that remove the political and monetary motivation to make project progress seem better that it really is. Customers are just as motivated to show less than optimum progress in order to get the concessions associated with missed deadlines, etc. I think that we need to find a way to build a 'true' partnership with our customers, something that most situations do not promote. It's a 'two-way street,' with the consultants/contractors caught in the middle and, unfortunately, too often a poor end result."

- "In my opinion, if the project manager is actively working together with the customer, there is no need to make the status reports, project plans, etc. look better. When there is good communication and management of expectations, the customer won't need to see anything other than an honest statement of the work being done."

2.3. Pessimistic Opinions

- "I don't really have a constructive suggestion."

2.3.1. It is not possible to fight against human nature

- "Change human nature."

- "Not a lot. Manage expectations!"

- "People will always do whatever they need to do to protect their position."

2.3.2. Other suggestions

- "Work on volunteer projects. Assume that there will be drop off so projects are set up with long-term direction and acknowledgment of potential for changes in emphasis and direction based on what we learn about degree of difficulty and workload of volunteers."

- "Punish the guilty. Metrics, the real kind, not just measurements."

3. Political maneuvering

3.1. Management techniques

- "Establish clear value system; avoid wrong type of pressure; review assumptions and promises periodically versus the reality; ask external audits."

- "360 [degree] performance assessment; regular project 'audit' in person (face to face); rotate people across projects."

- "Better project management practices that define specific guidelines for project scope and managers that can keep 'scope creep' out of the project. If a project is well defined with set limits and agreements as to time lines and deliverables there is less need for exaggeration and political maneuvering."

- "Get a second opinion; trust your staff but all of them not just your prodigies."

- "Doing chartering and requirements workshops."

- "Externally visible deadlines to customers, not vague promises of future deliverables. As above, independently verifiable metrics such as check-ins and testing for status."

- "[Upper] management needs to make their direct reports accountable, and not let the blame roll too many levels downhill."

- "Fire the culprit once the truth comes out, as a matter of declared company policy."

3.2. Understand the reasons why lies came into existence in the past

- "Nowadays, every software project seems to be very expensive. Once a customer representative is set as the project lead his/her performance assessment will include the progress and/or success of this particular project. However, most of the time the customer representative has no real influence on the project's progress. As the project contractor would like to stay in the contract he/she will always assure the customer's representative that things will improve and that the schedule will be met. Consequently, the customer's representative is sitting between all chairs. He/she knows that not everything is going alright. On the other hand his performance assessment depends on the project's success. There he/she is easily tempted to readjust status reports."

3.3. Communication

- "Shall I say it again? Transparency…"

- "Better communication."

- "Intensive questioning of specific plans, assumptions, staffing, etc."

3.4. Understand the politics of the project

- "Understand the political dynamics of the organization if you are a permanent employee. Have strong sponsorship of the project so that the [project manager] or the project lead can elevate the issues."

3.5. Pessimistic and optimistic opinions

- "Again, I am not sure much of anything can be 'done' about it. Politics is the second oldest profession and it appears in any group of three or more. The software field is full of it."

- "You can have a staff composed entirely of angels instead of human beings (although Milton's *Paradise Lost* serves to remind us that this is not sufficient). Or you can expect it and deal with it."
- "Besides 'watch your back' and be straightforward yourself? Not a lot."
- "Beginning to be stupid question... you're asking for a solution to combat human nature."
- "It is not [that] the people to lie, but it is the boss [who] believes in lying."

4. Hype

   4.1. Management techniques

- "A flatter management structure with less delegation, more accountability."

   4.1.1. Improved processes

- "Workshops on debunking results. Independent replication of results. Citations (people actually using results)."
- "I am a big fan of having the customer involved with all key decisions, and actually be part of the team to get projects working. When this happens, there isn't any overt lying or trying to make things better or worse than they are because everyone is on the same page. In the case where the customer relies on the consultant(s) to provide the end result with no partnership work done, it's up to the consultant to be ethical in practice and be an educator to the customer. When the customer isn't interested in the 'how,' but the 'when,' the consultant needs to be patient and not just lie to make things look better than they really are in order to appease the customer—the truth will always come out when the software product is delivered."

   4.1.2. Understanding of the reasons why wrong reports came into existence in the past and resolve these issues

- "Safer jobs and better secured contracts."
- "Often following the money or seeing who has what to gain or lose will expose if there's motivation for stretching the truth."

   4.1.3. More qualified management and/or customers

- "In these cases, have more qualified people on the customer side."

   4.2. Communication

- "Technically, keep historical data and learn what each person's slush factor is so you can recognize when estimates are actually wild guesses or straightforward lies."

   4.2.1. Quality communication and transparency

- "Greater transparency in the deliverables of a project (in theory)."

4.2.2. Encouragement of truthfulness

- "If the company culture is tolerant and one can talk about everything, people will more easily tell the truth. An intolerant and rigid environment forces them to lie."

- "Again, reality checks. If you don't want hype, don't reward it. Don't favor the manager who toots his own horn, don't buy from the company with lots of 'check-the-box' features on their low-quality product, don't worry about whether the consulting team bidding for the job sends a team that strokes your ego, etc., etc., etc."

- "Punish the guilty."

- "What can be done to protect against this problem? Encourage healthy cultures where it's okay to tell the unvarnished truth; when it happens with sales and marketing people, that can be connected to ethical issues, and getting a new salesperson might be the only way [of resolve]."

4.3. Pessimistic Opinions

- "I have absolutely no idea."

- "Not much."

- "Don't know. I think overall the industry (and business in general) lacks a culture that values honesty in the face of unpleasant truth."

- "Not a lot actually … some people just like to blow their own trumpet!"

- "It is nature. If people always tell the truth, many companies will go bankrupt."

2.5 THE QUESTIONNAIRE USED IN THE SURVEY

Dear Software Person: The purpose of this e-mail is to ask you to complete a questionnaire on the subject of incidents of lying on software projects. We know you are busy; all of us software folks are! This questionnaire should take less than 15 minutes to complete, so we hope you will take the time to respond.

This request is being made by Robert L. Glass (who writes several practice-focused columns that are published in the IEEE journal *Software and Communications of the ACM*), Johann Rost (a visiting professor at a technical university in Romania), and Matthias Matook (a German software consultant presently living in Australia). Our goal in conducting this study is to

- supplement a book we are writing entitled *The Dark Side of Software Engineering*

- publish the results in one or more journals, both practitioner and academic

- learn a lot more about a subject that fascinates us—and, we suspect, you as well!

If you return the completed questionnaire, we will send you a copy of the findings of the study. Rest assured that your response will be anonymous.

And if you'd care to add an anecdote or three about your own experiences with lying on software projects (you can use fake names for the players and institutions), we'd be delighted! Feel free, in fact, to expand on any of your responses (below) beyond the space allocated.

Questionnaire About Lying on Software Projects (Lying is defined as intentionally distorting the truth.)

Your Background

1. What is your current job title?
2. How much industry software experience do you have?
   • More than 15 years
   • 7–15 years
   • 2–7 years
   • Less than 2 years
3. What is your age?
   • Over 50
   • 35–50
   • 21–35
   • Under 21

General

1. Have you encountered lying on software projects?
   • Yes
   • No
2. If so, for what reason(s)? (Check all that apply.)
   • Estimation
   • Status Reporting
   • Political Maneuvering
   • Hype
   • Other (What?)
3. Who did the lying? (Check all that apply.)
   • Developer
   • Project Lead
   • Manager
   • Sales/marketing

- Customers/users
- Others (who?)

4. To whom did they lie? (Check all that apply.)
   - Developer
   - Project Lead
   - Manager
   - Sales/marketing
   - Customers/users
   - Others (who?)

5. What percentage of projects have you experienced this on?

Estimation

1. Have you encountered deliberately wrong estimates?
   - Too large?
   - Too small?

2. What percentage of projects?

   2a. By what percentage are the estimates wrong? (*)

3. Who made the estimate? (Check all that apply.)
   - Developer
   - Project Lead
   - Manager
   - Sales/marketing
   - Customers/users
   - Others (who?)

4. Who knew that the estimate was wrong? (Check all that apply.)
   - Developer
   - Project Lead
   - Manager
   - Sales/marketing
   - Customers/users
   - Others (who?)

5. What do you think was the motivation for lying? (Respond with a percentage.)
   - Padding with a high estimate to hold back reserves?
   - Price to win" low estimate?
   - Cave-in estimates to people with more power?
   - Other?

6. What can be done to protect against this problem?
   - Think primarily about your most recent three projects.

Status Reporting

1. Have you encountered deliberately wrong reports?
   - Too optimistic?
   - Too pessimistic?
2. What percentage of projects?
   2a. By what percentage are the reports wrong? (*)
3. Who made the report? (Check all that apply.)
   - Developer
   - Project Lead
   - Manager
   - Sales/marketing
   - Customers/users
   - Others (who?)
4. Who knew that the report was wrong? (Check all that apply.)
   - Developer
   - Project Lead
   - Manager
   - Sales/marketing
   - Customers/users
   - Others (who?)
5. What do you think was the motivation for lying? (Respond with a percentage.)
   - Relieve pressure from higher ranks
   - Hide bad work
   - Tell them what they want to hear
   - Other
6. What can be done to protect against this problem?
   - Think primarily about your most recent three projects

Political Maneuvering.   (struggles for personal or organizational gain)

1. Have you encountered lying for political gain or position?
2. What percentage of projects?
3. Who did the lying? (Check all that apply.)
   - Developer
   - Project Lead

- Manager
- Sales/marketing
- Customers/users
- Others (who?)

4. Who knew it was a lie? (Check all that apply.)

- Developer
- Project Lead
- Manager
- Sales/marketing
- Customers/users
- Others (who?)

5. To whom did they lie? (Check all that apply.)

- Developer
- Project Lead
- Manager
- Sales/marketing
- Customers/users
- Others (who?)

6. What can be done to protect against this problem?

Hype (Exaggeration for Effect)

1. Have you encountered such lying?
2. What percentage of projects?
3. Who did the lying? (Check all that apply.)

- Developer
- Project Lead
- Manager
- Sales/marketing
- Customers/users
- Others (who?)

4. Who knew about the lying? (Check all that apply.)

- Developer
- Project Lead
- Manager
- Sales/marketing
- Customers/users
- Others (who?)

5. To whom did they lie? (Check all that apply.)
   - Developer
   - Project Lead
   - Manager
   - Sales/marketing
   - Customers/users
   - Others (who?)
6. What do you think was the motivation?
7. What can be done to protect against this problem?

Yes, I'd like to receive a copy of the study findings.

REFERENCES

"Communication Failures Contributing to the Challenger Accident: An Example for Technical Communicators," IEEE Transactions on Professional Communication, Sept., 1988.

"IS Cover Up Charged in System Kill," *Computerworld*, Aug. 10, 1992.

"Plenty of Mutual Mistrust," *InformationWeek*, July 27, 1992.

Bok, Sissela. *Lying: Moral Choice in Public and Private Life*, Vintage Books, 1999.

Davis, Alan M. *201 Principles of Software Development*, McGraw-Hill, 1995.

Ford, Charles V. *Lies! Lies! Lies! The Psychology of Deceit*, American Psychiatric Press, 1996.

Glass, Robert L. Special Issue on Lying to Management, *The Software Practitioner*, March 1993.

Glass, Robert L. *Software Runaways*, Prentice-Hall, 1998.

Glass, Robert L. *Computing Calamities*, Prentice-Hall, 1999.

Kornet, Allison. "The Truth About Lying," *Psychology Today*, May/June 1997.

Pfleeger, Shari Lawrence, and Kitchenham, Barbara A. "Principles of Survey Research," *ACM Software Engineering Notes*, Dec. 1995 and subsequent issues.

Schein, E. H., "Learning When and How to Lie: A Neglected Aspect of Organizational and Occupational Socialization," *Human Relations*, March 2004, pp. 260–273.

Smith, David Livingstone. *Why We Lie*, St. Martin's Griffin, 2004.

Sutton, Robert I. *Weird Ideas that Work*, The Free Press, 2002.

CHAPTER **3**

HACKING

The preceding two chapters are the "research-y" part of our dark side material. As you have seen, we studied subversion and lying on software projects via case studies and (in some depth) research surveys into the occurrence of such issues.

From here on in this book, we stick to a case study approach. That is partly because case studies are commonly available and provide a rich source of understanding for our subsequent subjects. And it is partly because such research is laborious and time-consuming; we couldn't see how much that work would contribute to these other more-commonly-studied-elsewhere subjects.

This chapter is a perfect case in point. The rich lore of information from case studies that we discussed earlier is perhaps at its richest for the subject of hacking. Hardly a day goes by in the popular and the computing press when some hacking story doesn't appear in print, often with large headlines on a fairly prominent page! The work of hackers impacts not only software projects but the computing public at large; therefore, much attention is paid to the issue in the popular press.

3.1 CASE STUDIES OF ATTACKS AND BIOGRAPHIES OF HACKERS

Gabriel Bogdan Ionescu, Genius by Trade.   Gabriel Bogdan Ionescu is a young Romanian hacker. At age 20 he was involved in a phishing scheme (phishing is explained later in this chapter) against some Italian banks. He was captured at his parents' home in Craiova, Romania. In 2009 he was sentenced in Italy to a three-year, one-month prison term.

The case received a lot of coverage from the Romanian and Italian mass media. Phishing was not new at that time; Ionescu and the other members of his gang had modified some technical details of the classical scheme, but this does not really explain the high interest of the media. That's because Ionescu is not the typical hacker. He was trained in the Romanian system for outstanding talents and won the gold medal at the Balcanian Olympics of Informatics (see sidebar).

After his arrest the Italian authorities allowed Ionescu to participate in the admission test of the respected Politechnica University at Milan; they knew little of the surprise that awaited them. Ionescu finished the test in the record time (1 hour 20 minutes with 97 out of 100 points) and with the best result in the history of the

The Dark Side of Software Engineering, by Johann Rost and Robert L. Glass
Copyright © 2011 IEEE Computer Society

faculty. He was admitted to the university but was not allowed to attend lecture. During his trial, Ionescu was held in a kind of monestary, not a security prison, which he was allowed to leave for exams only. He finished and passed exams such as "mathematical analysis" and "elements of informatics" in significantly less time than what it normally took—and with the maximum possible score. After the exams he commented: "I am prepared to take any exam at any time." One of his professors made the following statement to local media: "He's not just the best in his generation. He's probably the best on the planet."

The impressive results further raised the interest of the media. Italian media reported on Ionescu with a lot of admiration. The Italian public, deep in their hearts, forgave Ionescu for the "sins of his teenage years." The Romanian media reported with sympathy and pride. One TV station mocked the Romanian authorities, saying they were fools to extradite their best genius to the Italian police. The tone in the media was more similar to a report about a local sports man who became famous with a foreign team than about a thief.

Sidebar: The Romanian Talent Education System

Romania has a long tradition in talent education. This program, stemming from the old communist elite training structures, exists even after the breakdown of the political ideology.

The first round of this competition is usually at the level of a single school. The winners qualify to participate at the regional then national and international levels.

Such systems of competition are established in many countries all over the world. However, the Romanian and the other former communist-country systems are significantly different from the corresponding systems (such as the German one). Many families take the terms much more seriously than the average family in western countries. There are trainers who specialize in preparing children and teenagers for such competition. The atmosphere in such training lessons is unlike the noisy distraction of a school class; it resembles instead the concentrated working style of a professional sports team. It could be compared with children who receive individual lessons in, say, tennis or golf. The decision to pursue such a course is not cheap for their parents, and the investment is justified only for particularly talented and motivated children.

The trainers are in high demand because there are fewer successful teachers/trainers than potentially talented children. It rarely happens that one of the students forgets the teacher's birthday: They show up with candies and flowers, of course.

There is also a keen awareness of talent education among parents. It is a frequent discussion topic at the playground: Which kindergarten offers what foreign languages (notice the plural)? And quite a few families use the maximum of their available resources to provide their children with the best possible kindergarten experience. The authors do not remember having heard such discussions in the United States or Germany.

Last but not least: Many of the children in these programs take things quite seriously. They do not have many other hobbies or occupations in their free time; they prepare only for these competitions. So, the excellent results do not come as a surprise.

American elite universities screen this pool of talent, and quite a few of these students are offered scholarships at many high ranking schools, including Princeton, Stanford, and Massachusetts Institute of Technology (MIT).

Romania was a poor country and, even if things are changing, is still. For many years and for quite a few Romanian families talent education was among the best ways out of poverty, If the child progressed and managed to graduate from a high ranking American university, or even become professor there, the next generation lived in a completely different world—unlike the parents who worried if they had enough food in the house.

Reformed Hacker Kevin Mitnick. Kevin Mitnick was arrested twice and sentenced to prison for computer fraud and manipulation of the telephone system: the first time in the late 1980s, the second time between 1995 and 1999. He was and is still one of the most famous hackers. His popularity stems to some extent from the extensive coverage of his arrest and trial in the American mass media.

From a technological point of view, Mitnick did not invent particularly sophisticated hacks. Instead, he used a technique called social engineering, which includes more psychology than technology, to carry out his attacks. The title of one of Mitnick's books is *The Art of Deception*: *Controlling the Human Element of Security*. (We'll explain social engineering later in this chapter.)

But now, Mitnick is reformed and runs a consulting business that advises companies on network security. In addition, he writes books and has the reputation of being an excellent speaker.

Über-Hacker Gary McKinnon. Gary McKinnon (also known as SOLO) is a Scotland born, 42-year-old former system administrator who attended secondary school in London.

In 2001 and 2002 McKinnon allegedly hacked into 97 U.S. military and NASA computers. According to his own statement he tried to find evidence for unidentified flying objects (UFOs). Due to the high number of compromised systems, U.S. authorities called the case the "biggest military" computer hack ever. They described McKinnon as an über-hacker who posed a threat to national security.

McKinnon said he did not do any damage to the cracked computer systems. U.S. authorities, however, claim damages worth about $700,000—which is in large part the amount of money it cost to track him down and close the security gaps.

An interesting detail about McKinnon's attacks is the technology—or should we say "the non-existing technology." In fact, McKinnon used a Perl script to try computer systems for default passwords. (A system which still has its default password is at best "poorly protected." Many of our colleagues say it should be considered "unprotected.")

The case received a lot of coverage in the media because of its legal processes. The U.S. authorities requested McKinnon be extradited to the United States and judged there. McKinnon's lawyers again and again contested this request. McKinnon wanted to be judged in the United Kingdom for several reasons. He was concerned that he would be brought to the infamous prison camp Guantanamo Bay. In the United States, McKinnon could be sentenced for up to 70 years in prison. But the legal procedure was further complicated by the fact that McKinnon had also been diagnosed with Asperger's syndrome. On January 14, 2010, *The Guardian* (a leading U.K. newspaper) quoted a High Court judge as saying that the extradition of McKinnon was illegal because of his medical condition. At the time of writing this book, the legal procedure was still pending.

The case caused considerable public interest. Some known rock bands announced benefit concerts to support McKinnon's struggle to avoid extradition.

(One further note: Later, a rap sheet (record of arrest and publication) of the case was published. The IP addresses of the attacked systems were masked in the PDF file. However, when you copy-and-paste the text from the PDF into a usual text editor, the IP addresses are unmasked and very much readable.)

Mathew Bevan: One of Two Hackers Who Almost Caused a Third World War.   In the 1990s, Matthew Bevan had a difficult time at school and turned to the online world as an escape. One of his first hacks was the penetration of the telephone charging system. This gave him the possibility of making phone calls everywhere in the world without charge.

Later, he hacked into sensitive systems of the U.S. Air Force, NATO, and NASA. His alleged partner, Richard Pryce, then 16-years old, hacked into the systems of the Korean Atomic Research Program and copied its files onto computers of the U.S. Air Force. This could be considered an incident of espionage with serious repercussions in the current world. But the files, as it turned out, were not those of the North Korean government as expected—they came from South Korea and were of significantly less interest internationally!

In November 1997, 18 months after the arrest, a court decided that pursuing the case was no longer in the public interest.

Bevan has said that McKinnon's case is very similar to his own. The comparison of the two cases reflects the changed political assessment of the danger caused by hackers and hacking.

TJX Hacker.   In 2005, a gang of hackers broke into the networks of the retail company TJX and stole the details of 47.5 million (!) credit cards. Later, the gang stole details of another 130,000 cards from the same network. The gang consisted of 11 members from various countries, including Ukraine, Estonia, Belarus, China and the United States. The U.S. arm of the gang drove its way in by exploiting poorly secured wireless access to the network.

The hackers used the stolen credit card details for charging prepaid cards and taking large amounts of money from ATMs using the prepaid cards. Because TJX is responsible for the server that held the credit card data, it was held liable for the damage done. According to an estimate, the expected damage will be at least $118 million.

One of the key members of the gang, Ukrainian citizen Maksym Yastremskiy, was captured outside of a Turkish nightclub in 2008. He was sentenced to 30 years in prison. Many experts in computer security industry welcomed the sentence and commented that the severe punishment provides a deterrent for other hackers in the hope that they will think quite carefully whether it is really worthwhile to take such risks.

The high number of stolen credit card details made it the biggest commercial hack ever discovered (at that time). However between 2008 and 2009 another attack was discovered: the Heartland hacker. During this attack, at least the same number of credit card details was stolen (according to all known evidence). At the time of this writing, the case was only partially solved; we can expect new information in the months and years to come.

These case studies illustrate some features of famous and typical hacker attacks. In quite a few of these cases, the hackers did not need special technical knowledge at all: the über-hacker McKinnon tried default passwords. The TJX hackers penetrated a network which was as some authors say "poorly protected"; others say it should be considered "unprotected." Both of these attacks did not require much technical knowledge—certainly no more than what you can find in best selling books on computer security at the introductory to intermediate level, under something like "Hacking Exposed." Remember that Mitnick applied social engineering, which requires more psychology then technology.

Yu Hua.   In 2005 the Chinese hacker alias Yu Hua (his real name has not been released) posted the names of 11 websites that he was targeting and said that he could make those sites collapse within ten minutes. He posted this note together with his instant messenger details to contact him. Ten minutes later the websites were down. The police used the contact details to identify him and captured him at the Wuhan hotel where he was working.

Quite a few hackers are identified because they announce, and in fact boast about, their activities, as did Yu Hua. One of the reasons that so many hackers are identified in this way is logistics: It might be that tracking down a hacker by pure electronic means requires large teams, international cooperation of law enforcement authorities and—more often than not—many months, or even years. This effort is justified only for big fishes, that is, not for occasional hackers who have only compromised a few Web sites.

The eBay Hacker Vladuz.   In the years between 2005 and 2007, the Romanian hacker Vlad Constantin Duiculescu (alias Vladuz, the Romanian word for "little Vlad") compromised the networks of the auction giant eBay. The authorities, as well as eBay itself, have avoided publishing too many technical details about the case. For this reason it is not very clear how Vladuz cracked the networks, how deep he hacked into eBay, and to what extent he endangered the integrity of the system of buying and selling at eBay. At any rate, he managed to pose as an eBay employee and posted messages on the eBay message board in the name of this employee.

Cooperation of international law enforcement authorities managed to identify Vladuz as Duiculescu based on the IP address of the computer he was using. In 2009 he was captured in a raid at an apartment in Bucharest, Romania. At six o'clock in the morning, a police SWAT team entered his apartment by force. Vladuz threw his three laptops from the fifth-floor apartment window. The police took the debris for further forensic analysis.

Further investigation of Vladuz's history revealed that he had abandoned school after eight classes (years) because "school did not offer him anything worth learning."

Fighter Jet F-35 Lightning II.   On April 29, 2009, the *Wall Street Journal* reported that attackers had broken into the Pentagon's $300 billion Joint Strike Fighter Program project database. They were able to download several terabytes (!) of data related to the fighter. However, they could not access the most sensitive part of the data because it resided on a network that is disconnected from the Internet.

While the exact identity of the attacker could not be found, the attack was traced back "with a high level of certainty to known Chinese Internet protocol, or IP, addresses and digital fingerprints that had been used for attacks in the past" (*Wall Street Journal*).

According to the Chinese Embassy, China "opposes and forbids all forms of cyber crimes." China considers the Pentagon's report "a product of the Cold War mentality," and said the allegations of cyber espionage are "intentionally fabricated to fan up China threat sensations."

Theft of Oil Exploration Data.   In January 2010, *The Christian Science Monitor* reported that major oil companies have been victims of a cyber attack. According to the report, Marathon Oil, ExxonMobil, and ConocoPhillips lost valuable "bid data."

Before an oil company submits a bid for an oil field, they prepare a careful analysis as to how much oil and of what quality they can expect from this oil field. This analysis is very expensive to conduct. According to *The Christian Science Monitor*, the value of the stolen data is hundreds of millions of dollars.

3.2 CYBER TERRORISM AND GOVERNMENT-SPONSORED HACKING

Trans-Siberian Pipeline Explosion.   In 1982, the Trans-Siberian pipeline exploded. The explosion was observed by infrared satellites which reported a bizarre event in a remote area of the then Union of Soviet Socialist Republics (USSR). At first, the explosion was confused with the firing of a nuclear missile. With an equivalent to 3 kilotons of trinitrotoluene (more commonly known as TNT), it was the most violent non-nuclear explosion ever observed by a satellite.

The system of the Trans-Siberian Pipeline is complex enough that it requires special control software that runs the pumps, valves, and turbines. The explosion was traced back to a logic bomb in this control software. Important details of this explosion still remain secret. However, some authors are of the opinion that the CIA directly caused this explosion by inserting the logic bomb.

The story starts with a "shopping list" of western technology that the USSR considered of strategic importance and hence tried to buy—or, in times of cold war to steal. The CIA obtained this list from someone in the Russian secret service (the infamous KGB). The pipeline control system, produced by a Canadian firm, was included on the list.

The U.S. Reagan administration expressed that it "felt a bit disturbed" by this unwanted intended technology transfer to its Soviet enemies. In addition, the Trans-Siberian Pipeline was a crucial cornerstone for the export of natural gas to Western Europe. For the USSR, this export constituted an important source of urgently needed foreign currency. That's why, according to this story, the United States tried to block these exports.

According to the published material, it appears that the CIA inserted the logic bomb into the pipeline control software before it "allowed" the KGB to "steal" it. This logic bomb caused the explosion by changing the settings of the pumps and valves. It caused pressure far beyond the normal limits.

Because the explosion happened in a remote area, no human casualties happened.

His Holiness the Dalai Lama—Hacked.   In March 2009, Canadian researchers discovered GhostNet, a huge cyber espionage network that had infected at least 1295 systems in 103 countries.

The research started due to a request by the Dalai Lama. The spiritual leader of the exiled Tibetan government asked the researchers to see if his systems were infected. The researchers found malware on the systems in the Dalai Lama's offices in India, Brussels, London, and New York. Further research revealed that this virus also affected a large number of other systems all over the world, many of which were run by governments and embassies of south Asian and southeast Asian countries.

The malware was highly specialized. It did not target for random consumer information such as credit card details. Instead it focused exclusively on particularly important targets. The virus was able to retrieve documents and send them to its owner(s), but it also allowed more advanced functions—such as the turning on of microphones and cameras at the infected computers—Web cams and microphones for VoIP telephone installed by the legitimate users of the computers. In the case of the Tibetans, the virus also controlled the mail server.

The servers that controlled the spy network were almost exclusively based in China. The researchers, however, could not conclude that the Chinese government was behind the operation. The Chinese government denies having anything to do with this case.

In at least two cases, however, cyber espionage activity had some impact in the real world. On March 29, 2009, the *New York Times* reported about this case:

"... after an e-mail invitation was sent by the Dalai Lama's office to a foreign diplomat, the Chinese government made a call to the diplomat discouraging a visit. And a woman working for a group making Internet contacts between Tibetan exiles and Chinese citizens was stopped by Chinese intelligence officers on her way back to Tibet, shown transcripts of her online conversations, and warned to stop her political activities."

U.S. Electricity Grid Under Attack.   In the spring of 2009, U.S. intelligence agencies discovered spyware and hacker tools on systems used for controlling the electrical grids in the United States. According to the *Wall Street Journal*, which was among the first media outlet to publish the story on April, 8 2009, there were one or more attacks coordinated by foreign governments such as China, Russia, and other countries. The spies did not do damage in the real world, but they had attempted to map infrastructure and had also left behind some tools. In case of crisis or war, these tools could be turned on in order to disrupt the supply of electricity in the United States.

The published material mentions that "China, Russia and other countries" are suspected of having coordinated the attack. However, a cooperation between China, Russia, and other countries against civil facilities in the United States would appear to be unlikely. If such a country decided to attempt such an activity, it would be unlikely that a discussion among the governments would occur. If any of this is true, then we are speaking of a series of attacks—not of a single incident. This observation is supported by the statement of an admin of such a system who mentioned "many attacks" during the last year.

According to the published material, the hacker toolkits were discovered by an audit of the US authorities in the weeks and month before the case was published. They were not discovered by the electricity company that was running the systems.

A few days after the report about the incident was published, the US administration launched a new program for cyber defense. This program requires resources and budget, of course. The coincidence in timing suggests that we should see the audit and the publication of the incident in the context of the cyber defense program and the resources necessary for this program.

Irhabi 007.   The Morocco-born U.K. resident Younes Tsouli belongs to the Al-Qaeda network. "Irhabi" is the Arabic word for terrorist and 007 is a reference to the British fictional agent James Bond. Tsouli appeared in terrorism-related Web forums around 2003. At first, he seemed to be a typical agitator with little dangerous potential. But later, it turned out, that he had advanced skills in computer security systems and knew how to break into Web sites. He used his skills to hide conspiracy material on Web sites and distribute it to other terrorists within the framework of Al-Qaeda.

Authorities and intelligence services tried for almost two years to track him down. On October 17, 2005, in an apparently unrelated incident, the 18-year-old Swedish citizen Mirsad Bektašević was arrested because he was involved in a declaration that announced the intention to attack sites in Europe to punish nations with forces in Iraq and Afghanistan. Analysis of Bektašević's laptop computer revealed links to Tsouli. His mobile phone records showed he had recently called Tsouli. These indications led to Tsouli's arrest on October 21, 2005, in a raid on a house in London.

At first, Tsouli was suspected only of participation in the alleged bomb plot. At that time the authorities did not know of his second identity (Irhabi 007). However, immediately after the arrest the postings of Irhabi 007 disappeared from the message boards. This observation gave the authorities the clue to further investigate the matter.

In December 2007, Tsouli was sentenced to 16 years prison. At the time, he was 23 years old. Despite almost two years of effort by international police and intelligence agencies, he had not been tracked down in cyberspace. One blogger commented that "if he had remained strictly in his hacker functionality he might still be out there."

This case shows how difficult it is for the authorities to trace down a hacker— unless he or she is involved in "stupidities" such as posting his phone number in mailing lists or boasting in public about his illegal online activities.

KGB Agent Markus Hess.   Markus Hess is a German citizen who worked for the KGB in the 1980s. He was a particularly efficient hacker and managed to compromise 400 U.S. military computers.

He was finally identified when Clifford Stoll, a system administrator for the Lawrence Berkeley Laboratory (LBL), analyzed an accounting problem on one of their systems. Stoll became aware that a hacker had compromised the computer.

Stoll trapped Hess by creating a series of bogus military projects on the compromised computers. While this information was convincing, these "honey pots" had the single purpose of keeping the hacker long enough online so that he could be tracked.

In a cooperation of FBI, German police, and the involved telephone companies, Hess was identified and captured. In 1990 he was sent to trial. Eventually, he was released on probation.

3.3   THE HACKER SUBCULTURE

3.3.1   Why They Are Called "Hackers"

In mainstream language, the word "hacker" refers to a person who gets illegitimate access to computer systems and data. This usage of the word is rather new, however.

In its short history, the word "hacker" has experienced a remarkable change of meaning. It was used initially at MIT around 1960. The legendary MIT Tech Model Railroad Club conducted experiments regarding the control of a large model railroad. Whenever a participant found a particularly smart or surprisingly easy solution for a technical problem at hand they would call it a "hack," and the inventor was called a "hacker."

Later, the word "hacker" entered in general tech slang and changed its meaning: an excellent programmer, a person who writes programs because he or she likes programming in itself or a person who is delighted by the intimate understanding of a complex system. In certain hacker circles this meaning is still in use. In mainstream language, however, "hacker" means a technically savvy cyber criminal. We, the authors, believe that it is more exact to name a cyber criminal "a cracker."

3.3.2   Motivation of Hackers

When the first generation of computer viruses became known to a broader public (some 20 years ago), they showed a behavior which some teenagers considered somehow "funny"—so long as they were not affected by the virus.

One of those early viruses displayed the command "Give me a cookie." You would have to key in the word "cookie" or the computer would be blocked.

Many of our colleagues asked this question: Who is stupid enough to do such annoying nonsense? Quite a few of these first generation hackers were just brattish teenagers. By means of a virus they tried to become famous—make the headlines, if possible. Others pulled monkeyshines and polluted places (such as the computer lab in their school).

This kind of "nostalgic" hacking still exists. The motivation may be that the hacker wants to gain some "hacker reputation" that would provide him or her with access to hacker communities and chats. Another reason might be that the hacker wants to develop necessary know-how so he can later apply for a regular job as security consultant.

However, the motivation among the vast majority of modern hackers is different. Modern hackers want to steal money. There is a black market for all kinds of products and services of cyber crime. Depending on the quality of stolen credit card details, such information can be sold for a few bucks, even up to several hundreds of dollars. Compromised computers—so called botnets—are offered for rent. Virtually everything (including mother's maiden names and driver's license numbers) is offered for sale.

The motivation to earn money explains why modern malware does not disturb the victim's usual work flow; these types of attacks are as stealthy as possible. So, the spyware can harvest data for a longer time, that is, retrieve data that the hacker can sell afterwards on the black market.

The black market of cyber crime can be compared with illegal drug dealing. There is a number of various roles in this market: cultivation, manufacturing, distribution, and sales. For each of these tasks, there are established prices on the black market. And the drug cartel gets its profit from all of these roles. In modern hacking there are similar roles: malware authors, persons who find vulnerabilities, carders who sell stolen credit card data, and others.

3.3.3   Hacker Slang

Hackers developed an underground culture with their own language, a more or less distant relative of English. Some of the modifications are rather obvious respelling of English words—"Windoz" instead of "Windows." Other respelling are more creative. The suffix "–er" is frequently replaced by "–xor." In this way, "hacker" becomes "haxor" or "haxxor." The word "suxor" is derived from the English slang word "sucks" and has the same meaning.

Some of the changes are based on replacing letters by other characters or sequences that look somehow similar. If these replacements are rare, the meaning can easily be guessed, such as "8ob" or "Joh@nn." The resulting language—or should we say "code"—is called "leet." It has its own grammar and diction rules; Wikipedia dedicated an article to "leet."

If the replacements are more frequent or more creative, it gets increasingly more difficult for uninformed readers to guess the meaning: "4 1 /-\ l3 /-\ [V] @" instead of "ALABAMA"; "1337" means "leet"; "s&ndbox" means "sandbox." The "&" symbol is frequently used in phrases such as "you have been b&."

Leet has been used as a kind of cryptology to hide forbidden content on message boards and to circumvent Internet filters. Additionally, it is used to mock "newbies" in hacker chat rooms.

Some of the vocabulary of leet-speak has become part of general Internet slang. One example is the term "pwned." "Pwn" is derived from the verb "to own, to get ownership, to conquer." It is used in the Internet gaming culture where it has a connotation of defeating the rival and frequently used in a humiliating way: "You just get 'pwned.'"

There is also a *"New Hacker's Dictionary"* maintained by Eric Raymond on the Internet. This document is carefully managed, with version numbers and a revision history that counts in decades. It explains the meaning and the correct usage of various terms of hacker jargon.

3.3.4   Hacker Ethics

Mass media portray hackers as quite negative. The hackers themselves claim to be the good guys—not according to written laws, of course, but from a "moral point of view." Who is right?

Even hackers have their ethics. Well, the truth is that each hacker has his or her own ethics. However, these private ethical systems overlap to the necessary extent; they form something like a professional codex, even if the borders are not perfectly precise.

The ethics of the first generation hackers, borne in the atmosphere of the MIT Tech Model Railroad Club, are even coded. Steven Levy outlined in his 1984 book *Hackers: Heroes of the Computer Revolution* some principles of hacker ethics:

- Access to computers—and anything which might teach you something about the way the world works—should be unlimited and total. Always yield to the Hands-On Imperative!
- All information should be free.
- Mistrust authority—promote decentralization.
- Hackers should be judged by their hacking, not criteria such as degrees, age, race, or position.
- You can create art and beauty on a computer.
- Computers can change your life for the better.

(The above list is extracted from Chapter 2 of Levy's book.)

At the first glance these principles do not sound unreasonable.

This code is usually referred to as the "the ethics of the hackers of the 1980s." It is, to a large extent, still valid for certain modern-day hacker groups that continue this tradition. The hacker ethics of the 1980s have an extension in the ideas of the GNU/open source movement—a movement that stems from these roots.

Levy and other authors bemoan the fact that people in the modern-day computer underground should not be called "hackers" because they do not live according to these principles. According to these authors, the new hackers should be called "computer terrorists" or simply "juvenile delinquents," not "hackers."

Other authors claim that modern hackers have their own ethics: "the ethics of the hackers of the 1990s." These authors claim that the code of ethics has changed, adapting to the new environment, one that is very different from the atmosphere of the Tech Model Railroad Club.

Some of the elements of the 1980s hacker ethics exist also in the 1990s ethics; they are somehow "universal hacker principles." Among these principles is the belief that all information should be free. Everyone should have access to computers and communication facilities. And everyone should strive for hands-on experience with the free information and hardware resources. If the resources are access-protected, the ends justify the means of breaking the access protection or working around it.

Notice that this allowance of breaking access protection was already part of the culture of the very first generation of hackers at MIT, though the "moral permission" was restricted to some extent: The intruder must take care not to damage anything. Nevertheless, hackers didn't like (and still don't like) any kind of "fence." From the very beginning, the hacker movement included a touch of anarchism, distrust of authorities, and (strong) preference for decentralization.

At first glance, the principle of "free flow of information" sounds reasonable. Immanuel Kant (an influential German philosopher who lived from 1724–1804) wrote about the "categorical imperative" which forms the philosophical foundation of many modern—written and unwritten—moral systems. His principle states the following:

"Act only according to that maxim whereby you can at the same time will that it should become a universal law."

So, what does it mean if we make this hacker principle an official, written law, valid for everyone in a certain country—or even worldwide?

One consequence is that the owner of confidential material has no protection from law enforcement authorities against disclosure of the secrets: If he or she has technical and administrative facilities to keep the material confidential, it will remain confidential. If they don't have the necessary resources to protect it—bad luck! In this scenario, the police wouldn't help because all information should be free. The end justifies the work around security mechanisms.

Perhaps the implications of this principle can go further. Perhaps the principle includes the notion that nobody should be allowed to keep technical know-how confidential. If someone finds out that there is confidential material (e.g., source code) he can file a law suit and request the publication of this material because all information should flow freely. The law would probably depend a lot on the exact wording to structure how its implications in practice might look.

This vision is certainly not recommended for managers of Microsoft and Oracle after six o'clock in the evening—otherwise healthy sleep might be at stake. But for most of us who are born into and have grown up in the Western system of intellectual property, these ideas sound quite odd even if we are not mangers of large software companies. Can such a system really work?

Surprisingly enough there is no obvious and undisputed answer to this question.

We have to remember that intellectual property (IP) is a rather new concept in our history. The idea of copyright came into existence in the eighteenth century when London's booksellers lobbied the authorities to issue this law.

But interestingly enough, the first generation of IP laws in Europe was not issued to protect the legitimate income of authors, inventors, and other creators of intellectual properties. There were other reasons for these laws.

In early English copyright law, for example, it was allowed to print a book only if the book was registered at the copyright office. This registration was possible only if the book did not contain forbidden content. So, the so-called "copyright law" was in fact a mechanism of censorship.

Here are some more historical examples of free and protected intellectual property and technical know-how.

Guilds in the Middle Ages.   Young craftsmen who finished their apprenticeship were encouraged to travel from workshop to workshop for several years. During this time, they were not allowed to practice in a workshop closer than a certain distance to the town where they were born (for example, less than 50 km). In this way the guild encouraged—even enforced—the free flow of technology and know-how within the community.

Well, some workshops or regions that developed groundbreaking technology protected their economic interests, of course, and tried to keep their know-how secret for as long as possible. Venice, Italy is an example (see below). But the vast majority of smaller inventions that constituted the gradual development of technology was somehow considered the property of the entire community.

The tradition of sharing know-how is still widespread even among modern-day craftsmen. Many of us have seen the pleasure of a craftsman who gets the appreciation from his peers when he demonstrates a particularly smart solution to a well known problem. Similarly, scientists who enjoy appreciation from colleagues for their speeches at conferences are not much different.

Notice that the owners of professional secrets did not enjoy much protection from the guild or from the authorities. If somebody stole their "business secret"— bad luck. This is valid unless the "intruder" was not involved in other forbidden things, such as breaking down a locked door. But if the spy managed to find out the secret in another way—by listening to a confidential discussion—he did not do anything forbidden. The general policy of the guild was to support free flow of information, which is a policy very close to the hacker's principles.

Notice that this practice is different from what we experience in the modern day (proprietary) software industry. Even if there is a large body of knowledge that is considered free, software companies have many more legal ways to protect "business secrets." They are supported by the legislation of their country and they have non-disclosure and non-compete contracts with their employees. Anyway, modern software business is far removed from the free flow of technological know-how in medieval guilds.

Glass and Mirrors in Venice.   Medieval Venice, Italy was one of the most developed regions in the world. It was particularly famous for the skill of processing glass and mirrors. This technology was not available outside of Venice at such a level of sophistication. This technology was freely circulated within the professional community of Venice. However, there was a death penalty for craftsmen who practiced their art outside of Venice.

In this way the authorities of Venice guaranteed the wealth of the town in the long run. They sold their products at good prices but they did not allow a few crafts-men to become rich abroad by training future competitors. They simply considered anything related to offshore and outsourcing "the wrong way."

England responded to this situation with an early version of a patent law. At the time, England was among the lesser developed regions in Europe. Its introduc-tion of a patent law accelerated the absorption of technology from other more developed regions, for example, glass technology from Venice. The basic motivation of the creation of patent law was not the protection of the legitimate economic interests of the inventors but the accelerated absorption of technology: The English authorities granted the Venetian artists a certain amount of time to retain a monopoly on their technology. When the patent expired, the technology became available to English craftsmen too. This way of absorbing technology was much faster than developing this technology "from scratch."

Pre-Modern China.   Many authors are of the opinion that pre-modern China did not have any kind of protection of intellectual properties. This is not different from the reality in other pre-modern societies: They simply did not have the need for a strict protection of intellectual property. In some cases too much protection of intellectual property might even be an obstacle for the development of these pre-modern societies.

But even pre-modern China *did* have some technology protection in place. The production and manufacturing of silk is one example. The imperial family care-fully controlled anything related to silk. The base of silk is fibers that are produced by certain silk worms. There was a death penalty for anybody who tried to bring the worms or the eggs of these worms abroad. That's how China managed a monopoly on the production of silk for many centuries. In that time, the silk monopoly brought wealth and fame to China. It was only after about one millennium(!) that a Japanese expedition managed to bring some eggs of silk worms abroad. They took also four Chinese girls with them and forced the girls to teach the Japanese the production of silk.

Another example of protection of intellectual property in pre-modern China is the idea of "family secrets." If a craftsman developed a new technology, his family tried to keep this technology secret as long as possible—sometimes generations. It was in this way that they profited from the technological advantage for as long as possible.

On a contemporary note, there is a heated dispute between the United States and China regarding copyright infringement and Chinese copyright tradition. This might add to the reason why it is difficult (at least for non-Chinese speakers) to find out really reliable facts about Chinese IP tradition. It is hard to say to what extent technology was protected by family secrets. The economic and technological context in pre-modern China was similar to medieval European guilds. So the resulting situation might have been similar as well. We authors imagine that the vast majority of technical know-how was freely circulated in the professional com-munities while other outstanding ideas were occasionally protected by family secrets.

A family secret has an effect similar to a patent: only the inventor can use it, or persons to whom the inventor tells the secret can use it. The protection of a technology by a family secret might have been more or less efficient than a patent—depending on how carefully the secret was managed. Anyway, the Chinese silk monopoly was valid for many centuries and could not be broken even by the Roman Empire. In this way, the silk monopoly was surrounded by one of the most successful technology protection mechanisms of all times.

According to published material, it appears that most pre-modern Chinese authorities did not implement much protection of intellectual property. Still, for centuries, China was at the world's leading edge in mathematics, in technology, and arts. Then they lost some important wars; they were colonized and exploited. That's the reason why they lost their leading position; it was due to technology or lack of IP protection.

To some extent pre-modern China implemented something that is quite close to the hacker's principle of free flow of information. It was only in 1984 that China introduced a patent law (and did so due to pressure from the United States). Before 1984, it was not possible to register patents in China. Still, the country reported an impressive development: In a few decades it developed from a country where people die of hunger and hunger-related diseases to one of the most powerful nations in the world.

These examples show that there are a wide variety of successful ways to deal with IP—not just by copyright, trademark, and patent. Even in pre-modern societies, where IP protection was not as sophisticated as we know it today, the creators of intellectual property found one way or another to protect their advantages (through family secrets in China or the professional code in Venice).

The open source community and the medieval guilds show examples of communities that implement—and even enforce—the free flow of information. Some of these communities have been economically successful and stood the test of time. And even if the vision of a world with a completely free flow of information might sound strange to most of us, there are counter examples where this principle worked (such as guilds in the Middle Ages, pre-modern China, and the open source movement).

The discussion shows that there is no obvious answer to the question of whether a system based on this principle of free flow of information can or cannot work. In particular, there is no obvious proof that a system based on hacker ethics will certainly fail. This means we are still lacking the proof that hacker ethics is simply wrong.

It seems that both approaches are tolerable: The free flow of information is okay and protection of know-how as business secrets is okay as well. Then what is the problem with the confrontation pro and contra the free flow of information—the confrontation of hacker ethics and proprietary code? Why don't we just say, "You are okay and I am okay. Let's go our separate ways"?

One observation is that the comparison is not completely symmetric: A system that protects confidential information can also integrate "open or free" information. We know from modern-day operating systems that this coexistence is possible: There is proprietary software, which is protected, but there is also open source, which is not. The marketing departments of the proprietary software companies might feel somehow "disturbed" by open source, but open source is not considered illegitimate.

On the other hand, a legal system based on the hacker's principle of free flow of information cannot integrate closed source, that is, proprietary code, because the principle states that all information should be available freely. To enable this free flow of information it is allowed—and even encouraged—to circumvent access protection. This tiny asymmetry makes the hackers who stole Cisco's and Windows's source code criminals in one world and heroes in the other.

Conclusion. Hacker ethics and the intellectual property laws as we know them are two different legal systems. It is not completely clear if hacker ethics can or cannot work if implemented as a valid legal system for a modern country. But the discussion shows that there is no evidence that hacker ethics will certainly fail. It is not even clear if our usual IP laws are really better, more efficient in the long run, than a written law based on hacker ethics.

However, these two legal systems—hacker ethics and written IP law—have tiny instances of "incompatibility" and asymmetry. These "incompatibilities" have the effect that the two legal systems cannot coexist in the same community. Hence a person who is living according to the hacker ethics will suffer criminal persecution, even if he can give sound arguments for his "hacker ethics." But, for example, the medieval craftsmen, who implemented something very similar to the hacker's principle of free flow of information, were not at all outsiders in their community. On the contrary, they constituted a well established and prestigious class in their town.

Let's imagine a craftsman in the Middle Ages who carefully keeps his tricks secret. The community is one that encourages free flow of know-how and might feel somehow "disturbed" or "offended" by this loner. After all, he did not start from scratch; he got almost all of his knowledge from the community. If somebody manages to steal the "business secrets" of this loner, it is quite possible that the professional community would react positively. This is what happens in the hacker community if stolen source appears on the message boards.

This example demonstrates how it looks when hacker ethics is the official law of the majority and not the rules of an underground community.

> **Sidebar: Traditional Gypsy Law**
>
> A similar scenario that illustrates conflicting legal systems is the traditional law of the Gypsys in Romania. Many of the rules of Gypsy law refer to marriage, sexual life, and what is considered an "affront." The rules are interesting but beyond the scope of this book.
>
> There are also other groups of laws that deal with issues of everyday life (for example, one should not steal). Despite the fact that many Gypsys keep with their traditional rules, they are involved in large number of property-related crimes. For a long time I (Johann) did not understand how this could be: They take a lot of care in their traditional rules (which forbid stealing) and still they are responsible for the majority of thefts in Romania. How is this possible? It sounds as odd as having a traditional Native American shaman who runs a steel factory (?!).
>
> Once I was waiting at the railway station when a Gypsy beggar asked the passengers for money. Some gave a small coin, others didn't. Then she asked an older Gypsy gentlemen

who was waiting next to me. Without much discussion he gave her something like $10. At that time the per capita income in Romania was around $100 per month. So, $10 is a quite generous hand-out—it was 10% of the usual monthly salary in that country. The beggar did not even address particularly friendly to the gentleman; she just said what she wanted. Well, the gentlemen did not look like he had to worry about $10. Even though most of us would not notice if $10 disappears from the wallet one way or another, we rarely give $10 to a beggar.

I watched that scene and tried to understand what I was seeing. Later, someone explained it to me. The Gypsy law says: "You should not steal. If you don't have what you need you should ask someone who has more than he needs. If he does not give you, despite the fact that he has more than he needs, you are allowed to steal from him." The law does not specify exactly how much the poorer person is allowed to steal in such a case.

The details are crucial. Some Christian teachings and modern legal systems allow stealing but in rare cases. I cannot imagine that someone would be brought to court in the United States or Europe if he or she steals food when there is an imminent danger of death of hunger. Usually this exception, however, is interpreted extremely narrowly; that is, in cases where the life is *really* in danger. It is not enough that the person "is just poor" or feels "poor enough that stealing is justified." And it is not so easy in the United States or Europe to become so poor that you are in danger of dying of hunger.

The traditional Gypsy law interprets this exception much more broadly: If the rich person does not give anything, the poor are allowed to steal. There is even logic in this broad interpretation: Most of the time, a large fraction of the Gypsys were vagabonds; many of them still are. These vagabonds have no regular income and virtually no properties other than an old horse, a carriage, and a few things of daily use. And still they live in an industrialized nation. (Well, Romania is a poor country but it *is* also industrialized.) The capital Bucharest, home of two million people, has a subway and buildings of 20 or more floors. Bucharest is perhaps one of the most condensed cities in the world; there are 9000 inhabitants per square km (compared to Chicago, which has 4800 inhabitants per square km). How is it possible that vagabonds can survive in a densely populated, industrialized country? After all, Romania is not Morocco.

In this context the rule of (generous) hand-outs to the poor is at the core of the economic system of the traditional Gypsys. They do not get a fortune, but they get a reasonable amount. And they get these hand-outs without humiliation (at least, if they receive them from other Gypsys). Without this rule their vagabond culture would lose its economic base. Additionally, the rule provides a system of social assurance: No matter what bad luck a Gypsy has in business and no matter what else happens, he cannot fall deeper than the vagabonds; this means he will continue the life of his grandparents and of some of his cousins. Additionally, their children are more healthy than the children of the non-Gypsy majority.

That's why they consider it a serious offence if a rich person breaks this rule. It is not about $10; it is about their cultural identity.

Many of the Romanian non-Gypsy majority are considered "rich" from the point of view of vagabonds. However, many of this majority are not aware of this rule. If they do not give from their own free will, it will be stolen. This is perfectly okay from the point of view of Gipsy law, but it is a crime according to official Romanian law.

This sidebar outlines an additional example of conflicting legal systems. Notice that both legal systems (that of the Gypsys and that of hackers) have a lot in common: Both forbid stealing in general, and both of the allow stealing in exceptional situations of urgent need. The formal difference may be only a tiny detail and depends upon how broadly this exception is interpreted. But the difference has a dramatic effect in practice.

Each of these two systems (or interpretations) is perfectly okay. Both have their advantages and disadvantages. It is not even clear which of them turns out better in the long run. However if both systems are integrated in the same society, one group will be criminalized. That's why Gypsys contribute far more than half of the thefts—even if they constitute a small minority of the population in Romania.

3.3.5   Public Opinion about Hackers

It is a strange thing with these hackers. Virtually everyone disagrees with what hackers are doing, but still there is a surprising paradox in the public opinion about them: Many convicted hackers have received a lot of sympathy in the mass media (such as Romanian hacker Ionescu who was extradited to Italy and became famous due to his performance on the admission exam at Milan University). There is Mitnick, a reformed hacker, who is now an established security consultant and requested speaker. And don't forget Scottish hacker McKinnon, who received support from well known rock bands that supported his fight against extradition to the United States.

This paradox reminds us of legendary figures such as Billy the Kid and Jesse James: Almost everyone agrees that people who kill others should be severely punished. Still, Billy the Kid and Jesse James became some of the most famous personalities of the American Old West, and beloved folk heroes. (Ned Kelly in Australian folklore plays the same role).

To some extent the sympathy in public opinion is based on the personalities of the hackers: Mitnick, Ionescu, McKinnon, and others may appear attractive or somehow interesting for quite a number of persons.

However the sympathy in public opinion is not just about a certain hacker; it is somehow about the entire movement. The captured and convicted individuals are just representatives of a computing subculture. Part of the reason for their admiration is that hackers are assumed to be superior computing experts, even if this image is largely a myth: Most persons involved in illegal computing activities do not have skills far beyond the level that is necessary for using office software. But this fact is not very widely known, and it seems that it is not too important. After all, if teenagers are able to defeat armies of well paid security experts—and defeat them in a humiliating way—they must know *something*. At least this is what the average consumer of mass media might think.

It is not only the admiration for technical skills of hackers (which may or may not be based on reality); it is also the support for the hackers strong preference of decentralization and suspicion against authority as the following two case studies show.

The Swedish Pirate Party.   The Pirate Party ("Piratpartiet" in Swedish) strives to reform laws regarding copyright and patent. In the public opinion the party is closely related to the Web site "The Pirate Bay" that provides the infrastructure for downloading software, music, films, and other content using the BitTorrent protocol (which is in most cases illegal).

In 2006, when the party was founded, it received 0.63% of the vote—a tiny minority. But the party slowly and steadily grew until April 2009; then came the trial and the famous guilty verdict in the case of The Pirate Bay.

From a common sense point of view, it is an outcome that we should expect: The Pirate Bay was one of the largest Internet hubs that supported distribution of stolen (pirated) content—that's why they called themselves "Pirates." From a legal point of view things were not so easy: In fact, The Pirate Bay did not host the stolen content. It simply hosted links from Web sites where visitors could download material according to the BitTorrent protocol. If the owners of these linked Web sites upload stolen material, it is not the responsibility of The Pirate Bay—that is what the defendants said. The legal details are beyond the scope of this book, but the main conclusion remains valid: The Pirate Bay lost.

This trial had a tremendous political effect, one that was unforeseen by the authorities. In a few weeks time, the Pirate Party received tens of thousands of new members. One week later, it had grown to 40,000 members—compared to 15,000 before the verdict. Now it is the third strongest party in Sweden. In the 2009 European Parliament elections, the Pirate Party received 7.13% of the total Swedish votes.

The change in circumstance is the result across all ages of voters. A closer look at the younger generations shows that things are even more extreme: The Young Pirates, the youth organization of the Pirate Party, is the strongest political youth organization in Sweden in terms of number of members. What is happening here? A significant part of the Swedish population—7.13%—support ideas that are illegal according to existing law; that premise is at the core of the hacker subculture: "Get rid of the existing copyright laws." By measure of the younger generation, the numbers are even more impressive.

Since reform of the copyright law is one of the main targets of the Pirate Party, the conclusion is that a significant part of the Swedish population considers this topic more important than all other intensively discussed political issues, including global warming, recession, and financial crisis.

Germany Blocks Web Sites with Child Pornography.   In April 2009, the German government passed a law to the effect that Internet service providers (ISP) must block Web sites that contain child pornography. This decision caused a heated public controversy. How is this possible? Is there a significant part of the German population that supports child pornography?

The truth is that almost all Germans condemn child pornography (as most other people in the world do). But the discussion was not just about the 100 or so sites that distribute child pornography; it was about Internet censorship. The blocking of the sites is done based on lists provided by the German Federal Police (BKA). These lists are not published and they are not subject to public control. Many citizens were concerned that that this is how the technological and legal basis for extensive Internet censorship would be implemented. Some people who objected to the law noted that at a later point in time, and without much public attention, the lists can easily be extended to other sites (for example, those which criticize the government).

Free access to information and rejection of any kind of censorship are goals that lie at the core of hacker philosophy. This anecdote shows that significant portions of the public in Germany—and probably in other industrialized countries as well—support ideas that are promoted by hackers.

3.4 HOW A HACKER IS IDENTIFIED

In some cases, it is quite easy for law enforcement authorities to identify a cyber criminal: Some hackers boast of their "daring actions" on message boards and chat rooms. Occasionally, they even add some contact details. The hacker with pseudonym Yu Hua, for example, exposed his instant messenger details before he was captured.

Another great help for the police are so-called "handles," that is, a pseudonym the hacker uses consistently over a long period of time. This handle is his identity; it is the name by which he is known in the hacker community. There were cases in which the police found old postings that included the handle and other contact details (such as phone numbers). Even though these postings were written before the hacker began criminal activities, the identity of the hacker was not very carefully obscured.

But what happens in other cases, the ones where hackers do not make such obvious mistakes? The sad truth is that it is anything but easy to track a hacker by purely electronic means. The most obvious idea is this: If suspicious or malignant traffic arrives at server X, we should look where this traffic came from. The last hop on the way to server X can be identified with reasonable reliability. Working backward to the source of the suspicious traffic gets increasingly more difficult. In many cases it requires the cooperation of the administrator of the last hop to go one step backward and identify the last but one hop—and so on.

This method requires close cooperation of ISPs and international law enforcement authorities. Though it is not easy, there have been cases where the hackers have been identified in this way.

In many of these cases, the cyber criminals applied similar patterns of attack again and again over a long period of time. This allowed the law enforcement authorities to work their way backward and to install additional logfiles and recording facilities closer and closer to the source.

However, some of the famous cases which made the headlines show us how difficult this way is. Let's have another look at the eBay hacker Vladutz and the TJX hacker. More than 100 people were involved in solving these cases. And they still needed years to capture them.

One specific feature of a hacker attack explains why it is particularly difficult to trace back a cyber criminal: Hackers do not use their own computer to launch an attack; instead, they launch the attack from a so-called "reflection site." This is a compromised computer under control of the hacker. (In the 2002 book, *Know Your Enemy: Revealing the Security Tools, Tactics, and Motives of the Blackhat Community*, by the Honeynet Project, this technology is explained. The researchers in that book learned about it when they studied the tactics of hackers [see sidebar].)

Usually a hacker does not control a single compromised computer; they control so-called botnets of many compromised systems—sometimes hundreds of thousands of compromised computers. In this case the reflection site is controlled by another reflection site which is controlled by one more reflection site and so on. Some newer versions of malware have been distributed using peer-to-peer technology of the botnet. This makes it more difficult to trace back the malware to the source, especially if the communication between the bots is encrypted.

Most of the modern attacks are automated. That means at the time when the attack happens the cyber criminal is not necessarily at his computer. Instead he previously produced malware and placed it on the Web well before the attack. This malware attacks the targeted systems. And this malware is launched on reflection sites and botnets—not on the hacker's PC, of course.

This explanation adds to the reasons why it is so difficult for law enforcement authorities to identify a hacker, why large teams are necessary, and why they are kept busy for years to identify a single hacker.

In some cases the technical details of how the hacker is identified are not published. In other cases, it seems that the police had quite a bit of "good luck" that they captured the hacker at all. It is obvious that this massive investment of resources is possible only for the "big fish" of cyber crime such as hackers who stole hundreds of thousands or even millions of credit card numbers.

But how are the small "casual" hackers captured? They are captured, for example, because they say compromising things on message boards—things like contact details. Or they are not captured at all.

What about organized crime and government-sponsored hacking? These people do not post to hacker forums; they do not use pseudonyms; they do not boast of their actions in public. And, in the end, few of them have been captured.

The case of Irhabi 007 shows how difficult it can be to identify a hacker who avoids such obvious "mistakes." Irhabi 007 was considered part of the Al Qaeda network. So we can assume that the United States, NATO, and European authorities invested a reasonable amount of resources to identify him. But he was captured because one of his buddies was involved in a bomb plot. Only then, when his postings disappeared from the message boards, did they suspect that the suspected terrorist might be Irhabi 007.

Sidebar: Honeypot

The press is full of stories about hacking. There is lots of research on the subject as well. But there is one public report that stands head and shoulders above all the others. It is a book entitled *Know Your Enemy: Learning about Security Threats* and reports on a research investigation of the characteristics of hackers.

A growing team of researchers set out, back in 1999, to try to characterize who hackers were and why they did what they did. That team grew to 30 researchers as the group conducting the research came to realize that more and more kinds of expertise was needed to digest the data.

To gather this data, the team used a "honeynet" approach by setting attractive systems that could be easily hacked. And when the hacking inevitably occurred, they recorded and analyzed what the hackers did.

These researchers chose not to use the word "hacker" or its sometime-alternative "cracker," but instead they called their targets "blackhats." This is, of course, a judgmental name. Was that judgment reasonable?

You don't have to read very far into the book to begin to agree with them. The "good guys" (members of the Honeynet Project) are tracking down some colossally awful behavior by the "bad guys," those blackhats.

Perhaps the most interesting part of the book occurs near its end, when the researchers present verbatim transcripts of the blackhat community interacting with each other (online, as in a chat room). The chatting participants have each penetrated and nested in someone else's computer, and they are using that base as a platform for (among other things) bragging to each other about their exploits in other blackhat penetrations.

One of the most interesting things about these conversations is that many of the black-hats spoke Urdu, the official language of Pakistan. As with many blackhats, these Pakistanis espouse a cause as the reason for their activities. (In this case, they are pro-Pakistani regarding the Kashmir/Pakistan border dispute with India, and there is no hint of anti-American sentiment!).

The Honeynet Project authors, however, are dubious about this cause being the true reason for the blackhat behaviors, saying "These justifications tend to be nothing more than conjured-up reasons for the blackhats to satisfy their own personal motives." In the blackhat conversations, one of them speaks about "taking out India" (by denial of service attacks), but much more of the conversation seems to be about internecine warfare within the blackhat community itself, which appears to consist of feuding gangs who raid each other's captured territories (that would, of course, be someone else's computer!).

The book is intended for an audience of security professionals and spends early chapters talking about how to set and work with honeynets; much of this material is difficult for the non-security professional to read. In general, however, the book is quite readable.

The book's authors are totally convinced that attacks will continue and intensify. In one of their honeynets, during its first 30 days of being on the air, there were 524 scans seeking to penetrate the system. Blackhats attempt to penetrate any system they can, and honeynets were established for Red Hat Linux, two flavors of Windows, and Solaris. In fact, in the conversations in the back of the book, one blackhat specifically speaks of trying to crack Linux .edu systems, a chilling thought for most academics.

Is there any way to hide from blackhat attacks? The authors are convinced there is not, short of explicit security defense mechanisms (the book does not discuss that topic). Specifically, they say "you can't hide" and "security through obscurity will not work." (The reason why obscurity [being little-known] will not work is that most attacks are random searches of huge numbers of systems that seek to exploit specific known operating system security weaknesses. The authors say nothing about whether any operating system is more or less secure than any other; by implication, all were relatively equally vulnerable.

The question arose as to how sophisticated the attacks were, and the answer to that question is surprising—a "yes and no" kind of thing. The tools hackers use are, in fact, super-sophisticated (most are available on the Internet!). But their programming knowledge is not. From the conversations in the back of the book, it is obvious that these blackhats lacked rudimentary knowledge of how to write programs. Some of them apparently could not program at all!

The Honeynet Project began in 1999 and continued at the time the book was published (in 2002). The book ends with a description of the kinds of adaptations they found the blackhat community using, saying "as the enemy continues to adapt and change, so will we." How are the blackhats adapting? The book specifically mentions the increasing use of aggressive scanning, encryption (to hide their tracks), sophisticated "rootkit" tools, and worms (attacks that self-replicate).

The net effect of reading this book is (a) chilling, and (b) convincing that blackhats are really "the enemy."

Information Source: (Spitzer, Lance. "Know Your Enemy: Revealing the Security Tools, Tactics, and Motives of the Blackhat Community." *Honeypot Project*, Addison-Wesley, 2002.)

3.5   TIME LINE OF A TYPICAL MALWARE ATTACK

A "vulnerability" is a specific fault in computer software (in jargon, a "bug"). This bug affects the security of the system that runs the software. Malware uses the knowledge of this bug to break into the vulnerable system. The malware is called an exploit of the vulnerability. A vulnerability which been unknown so far (to the producer of the vulnerable software) is called a zero-day vulnerability.

A typical malware attack starts with a zero-day vulnerability. Finding such a vulnerability requires a savvy programmer with technological knowledge on a high level. Hackers who are able to find zero-day exploits constitute only a tiny fraction of the population of cyber criminals. We do not have exact numbers—our subjective "guesstimate" is below 1%, perhaps below 0.1%. Note: Simply finding a vulnerability is usually not illegal. Everyone is free to test existing software for bugs.

Once the hacker has found a zero-day vulnerability, he or she is free to decide what to do with it. For modern hackers the main motivation is making money. The black market pays somewhere between $10,000 and $30,000 for a zero-day vulnerability—perhaps even more. The "clients" are organized criminals who abuse the vulnerability for illegal purposes.

Some software producers buy the zero-day vulnerabilities of their own software at prices that are competitive to the black market: "The producer of software XY offers $20,000 for someone who is able to crack XY and explains to the producer how he did it." So, the hacker can also sell the zero-day vulnerabilities to the producer of the software—completely legal—a practice that is called "white hat" hacking.

Nostalgic "white hat" hackers do not hack for the sake of money, but for the reputation they achieve by finding vulnerabilities. The white hat hacker reports the vulnerability to the producer of the buggy XY software. Then the hacker allows some time to pass which he considers "fair and adequate"—perhaps something between a day and three weeks. In this time the producer can fix the problem and provide a patch for download. Users who have installed the patch are protected against exploits of this vulnerability. Or should we say "these and only these users are protected"? Because all others, who have not installed the patch, still have a buggy version installed and are hence vulnerable.

In the next step the white hat hacker publishes the vulnerability on the Internet such as on message boards for hackers. In many cases the published vulnerability comes with a "proof of concept"—documentation or a program which demonstrates the vulnerability. The proof of concept, however, is not usually a functional virus but instead something like a proof that the vulnerability really exists. In this way, the zero-day vulnerability becomes a known vulnerability, which can be accessed by a much larger number of people.

Finding vulnerabilities is not a rare event by any standards. There are lists of thousands of vulnerabilities in Internet software. All known software products are affected. It doesn't matter if the vulnerability has been published on the Internet or has been sold to a single customer: The vulnerability is used to generate malware such as viruses, worms, and/or spyware. This malware "exploits" the vulnerability. In many cases it takes only a few hours after publishing the vulnerability until an exploit of this vulnerability appears on the Internet.

Generating malware based on a known vulnerability still requires profound programming skills. There is, however, a larger number of malware authors than the narrow elite of hackers who are able to find zero-day vulnerabilities.

As soon as an exploit is published, anybody can download it and use it for attack. This does not require particularly strong technical knowledge. There is even hacker software available that integrates a large number of exploits in a graphical user interface. An attack based on such software does not require more technical skills than, say, applying office software. People who use such software packages are sometimes called "script kiddies." This name is used because many of them are rather young (hence "kiddies"). They are assembling existing malware to "scripts" that are used to launch an attack. This requires little or no technological knowledge.

Contrary to widespread opinion, only a small fraction of cyber criminals is technologically savvy. The others are script kiddies or other kinds of criminals who, for example, buy stolen credit card details and use them in fraudulent transactions.

3.6 HACKER ECONOMY: HOW DOES A HACKER MAKE MONEY?

Credit Card Fraud.   Many fraud schemes on the Internet involve stolen credit card details or online banking passwords. This raises three questions: How do the hackers gain access to that data? How it is abused? How does the hacker finally get the money? The answer is by accessing stolen credit card details and online banking accounts.

Cracking a Server.   In some cases, the fraudster gets access to credit card details by breaking into servers of large e-commerce sites or providers of online payment services. Since these servers store a large number of credit card details, a single successful attack can lead to the theft of tens of millions of credit card details (as we learned from the cases of TJX and Heartland).

Phishing.   The word "phishing" is a respelling of "fishing." In a phishing scheme, the attacker sends e-mails to potential victims and tries to lure them to cloned Web sites. The e-mail appears to come from the victim's bank and might read something like this: "There is a problem with your online banking account. Please login to your account to solve the problem. Otherwise your account will be blocked." The e-mail includes a link which appears to lead to the bank's Web site. When the victim clicks the link, a cloned Web page opens and looks exactly like the page of the bank. The cloned site, however, is controlled by the fraudster. If the victim completed login details or credit card data on this bogus site the attacker would reply with a message such as "Thank you, everything is okay now." But the access details or credit card data, however, are in the hands of the fraudster.

Spear Phishing and Whaling.   The phrase "spear phishing" is a reference to a traditional hunting method of catching a single fish with a spear. In early phishing schemes, the scammer would send a large number of epam e-mails containing the phishing message. Some of the addressees of these e-mails are lured into the trap and disclose passwords and/or access data to the scammer. Due to the large number of e-mails, however, these early attacks were surprisingly successful: Even if a tiny fraction of the addressees answered to the e-mail, the attackers could harvest quite a few passwords.

In time the filters in the Internet became more and more successful in spotting such messages due to the large number of identical or almost identical messages, which included key words like "account" and suspicious links.

The spear phishing scheme is a reaction to the increased efficiency of filters and addresses only a small number of carefully selected targets, such as the employees of a certain department. While classical phishing attacks try to harvest passwords, the spear phishing attack has the additional potential that the attacker might gain control of the entire network of the targeted department.

In extreme cases the scammer attacks only a single, particularly attractive target. Some authors call these very focused attacks "whaling" in reference to the hunt of a single, particularly large fish (a whale). In spear phishing and whaling attacks, the background of the potential victim is carefully researched using social engineering techniques. The following fictitious example is meant to explain the method: The attacker targets Jim Brown, research director at XY Solar Energy. The "clients" of the attacker are of the opinion that it would not hurt to have a closer look at the files on Jim's hard disk. From the Internet the attacker knows that Jim will speak on June 23 on the International Conference on Solar Energy (ICSol) in Paris. Due to this announcement the attacker knows also the complete name of XY Solar Energy's research director, the title of the speech, e-mail address, job title, and so on. All this data is precious to the attacker because it helps fabricate an e-mail which looks authentic.

Based on this information the attacker writes a mail which appears to come from the ICSol organization team. The faked "from" address can be done via e-mail spoofing which is technologically very easy. The e-mail may read like this:

Subject: Your speech at ICSol

Dear Professor Jim Brown,

We confirm that your speech with title "Modern installation of solar panels in the Sahara Desert" is scheduled on Wednesday, June 23 at 10:00 A.M. in Session M3, room R22.91.

Please verify the attached official announcement of your speech and confirm your participation using the following link.

It is quite likely that Jim will receive and read the e-mail. It is also possible that Jim will open the attachment which contains allegedly the announcement of his speech and visit the link given in the mail.

How the attack goes on depends on countless details such as which version and service pack of what operating system and Web browser he has installed and the like. All these details are beyond the scope of this book. However, it is a widely known fact that many attacks were successful because the victim opened attachments or was lured to infected Web sites. There have been attacks where simply reading the e-mail was enough to get a computer infected.

Anyway, it is clear that this e-mail brings the attacker a big, perhaps decisive step ahead.

And it is very difficult to protect against it. The spam filters in the Internet are unlikely to spot this message as "dangerous" because it is a single message that does not contain any suspicious key words. The firewall of XY Solar Energy will let is pass—otherwise, what will pass the firewall if this message is blocked? Jim has already received many messages of this kind—whenever he speaks at a conference. He will not be particularly suspicious. What should stop the attacker?

We authors have heard that some companies have decided to implement rather radical measures to prevent against cyber attacks: Each employee has two computers on his desk; one of them is connected to the Internet for e-mail and Web use and the other is connected to the internal network.

Pharming.   Pharming is another fraud scheme that includes cloned Web sites. The difference with regard to phishing, however, is that no suspicious e-mails are sent. Instead the attack is based on a compromised domain name system (DNS).

Before we study pharming, let's recall what happens when we type in the browser window something such as "www.my_bank.com."

The browser has to find out the IP address of the Web server that hosts "my_bank.com." This can be done in various ways. Perhaps the user has visited "my_bank.com" recently. In this case, the IP address is saved on the user's computer in a structure called "hosts file." As soon as the user keys in the first few characters of "my_bank.com," the browser completes the request. We can understand this as a suggestion: "Perhaps you want to go to "my_bank.com" where you went yesterday?". In this case the browser knows the IP address based on its own records.

If the browser does not find the address in the hosts file, it requests the IP address from a so-called DNS server which hosts a lengthy list of domain names and IP addresses. The user gets the IP address of the DNS server from the router. Most likely the server is managed by the ISP. In almost all cases the request can be resolved by this DNS server.

However, there are, on occasion, rarely requested domain names that are not on the list of an ISP's DNS server. In these cases, the network of DNS servers in the Internet maintains an updating protocol which allows the DNS server at the site of the ISP to get the IP address of "my_bank.com" from other DNS servers.

The final effect of this DNS system is that the browser gets the IP address from the Web host of any registered domain name. So, the domain name system provides for a mapping between domain name and IP address.

Pharming is based on an attack which compromises the domain name system. The attacker can compromise the host's file. In this case, a request to the host's file results in a wrong IP address. Another alternative is that the attacker compromises the router. This has the effect that the user accesses a bogus DNS server, which responds with a wrong IP address. There are even more variations of this attack. The attacker compromises the DNS server (DNS poisoning). Or he compromises the exchange protocol between DNS servers. All these attacks have the effect that the attacker somehow controls which IP address the user gets back when he keys in something such as "www.my_bank.com."

In the end the user gets an IP address that leads to a server controlled by the attacker. This server hosts a cloned Web site which looks exactly like the Web site of "www.my_bank.com." Then the fraud scheme continues like the phishing attack. The victim keys in credit card numbers or passwords at this bogus Web site. The fraudster saves and abuses them.

Notice that pharming does not include any e-mails or links. Even if the user keys in the domain name at his or her web browser, the attack will be successful. The user does not have to open suspicious e-mails or click on fraudulent links.

Spyware. Spyware is a kind of malware, that is, illegitimate software which is transported (for example) by viruses and worms. Spyware has the effect that the attacker has access to confidential information on the victim's computer—that's why it is called spyware.

A special kind of spyware is the so-called keyboard locker. A keyboard locker records all keystrokes on a certain computer and reports them back to its owner. In this way, the fraudster gets access to passwords and/or credit card details.

Black Market. Hacking is not a kid's game anymore—it has become big business. There is a black market which offers the exchange of virtually all kinds of products and services from and for cyber criminals (such as stolen credit card details).

The people who steal credit card numbers call themselves "carders." They offer the compromised card information on the black market (such as in Web forums). After the first contact between buyer and seller is established, the rest of the transaction is frequently conducted via encrypted peer-to-peer communication.

The prices on the black market for credit card details range between about $5 for the credit card number to several hundreds of dollars, depending on how many details the carder found out as well as the quality of the card and permissions the fraudster can get (for example, if the permissions include opening new lines of credit). Some company credit cards allow payment patterns abroad, a practice that could allow fraudsters to remain undetected and abuse the stolen card for a longer time.

How Does the Fraudster Use the Stolen Credit Card Numbers? The most obvious way is to use the card for buying goods on the Internet. Notice, however, that the hacker cannot easily ask for delivery of the goods to his real address—otherwise law enforcement authorities could identify and capture him or her immediately. So, hackers need a more elaborate scheme—something like freight forwarding.

Freight Forwarding.   In this Internet fraud scheme, the fraudster is based in a country with unreliable jurisdiction regarding Internet crimes—for example, Nigeria. Also, China and some Eastern European countries have been "en vogue" for this purpose.

Since Internet retailers know of these problems, they hesitate to deliver goods to these countries. So, the fraudster uses a middle-person who lives in an industrialized nation, preferably the United States or western Europe. This person receives the fraudulent ordered goods and forwards them to the fraudster's real address (such as Nigeria).

Usually this person-in-the-middle is not aware of being involved in a fraudulent scheme, and in fact he or she does not earn any money for it. And in many cases the person-in-the-middle even has to pay the FedEx transport from his or her own pocket.

When we recently explained this scheme, we asked the audience if they knew someone—or have heard of a person—who lives in the United States and is fool enough to take the role of this person-in-the-middle. Nobody in the audience had ever heard of such a person (except perhaps someone who is not allowed to do business because of mental diseases).

Well, it's not that simple. The following fictional case presents the features of a typical freight forwarding scheme: The fraudster poses as a major Russian company that allegedly wants to open an office in Boston, Massachusetts. In preparation for this project, they post a well-paying job on the Web, something like Senior Office Manager or CEO. The fraudster even prepares a bogus Web site of the fictitious Russian company. The fraudster agrees to any requested salary the candidate wants (anyway, he will never see a paycheck).

One of the tasks of the "future CEO" is the establishment of the office in Boston. For this reason, the fraudster orders 150 notebook computers. Since the new company is still to be established and does not yet have an office address, the "future CEO" can hardly refuse to receive the notebooks at his or her private address, in particular, if the computers are already paid for.

The computers are delivered to the home of the "future CEO," and everything looks fine. Then something very surprising happens: For one reason or another, the admin who was to come to Boston to install very important software on the computers cannot come. Something very unexpected has happened. And the Russian bogus company asks for the computers to be shipped to Russia *urgently*. This is no problem however. The "future CEO" receives a bunch of address labels from an express transportation company. All he has to do is stick the labels on the boxes of the computers and give them to the FedEx driver who comes to the door the next day. Then the contact to the Russian company is obliterated.

A few weeks later, the police show up at the door of the "future CEO" and ask about these computers because they were paid for with stolen credit cards. Later, the transportation company asks for money for the express shipping of 150 parcels to Russia.

What has happened? The fraudster had enough data of the "future CEO"—the man-in-the-middle—for an identity theft. After all, the "future CEO" considered the fraudster to be his future boss and felt obliged to provide him a correct name, address and social security number. So the fraudster could easily close a contract with the transportation company with the name of the future "CEO". The man-in-the-middle can hardly say that he did not know of anything. After all, the freight was taken from his real address, he was personally at the door, and he gave the parcels to the driver; the name, phone number, and all the other data are correct. How can he say he was not involved?

Well, the victim, that is, the man-in-the-middle, still has the address in Russia and could try to file suit against the person mentioned in this address. The Russian police may or may not find someone at this address. Perhaps they will find a drug addict who allowed the use of his address in exchange for a "shot of heroin."

Anyway, the typical result is that the notebooks disappear, the man-in-the-middle never gets back the transportation fees, and the police never find the fraudster.

A variation of this theme is via international marriage advertisements. In another fictional example, a man from Nigeria meets a woman from Germany on the Web: The online relationship evolves and the future couple decides to marry in Germany. The man seems to be quite well off, a kind of Nigerian prince. He is going to prepare for a generous wedding party and honeymoon. For this reason, he wants to order some goods on the Internet, such as expensive camcorders. The goods should be there for him by the time he arrives in Germany. So, he asks the woman to receive them at her private address. This should not be a problem, however, because all the goods including transportation fees are already paid in advance. Then, again, something happens: For unexpected reasons the Nigerian prince cannot come. Perhaps he caught a serious flu. So he asks for the parcels to be forwarded to Nigeria.

The story continues in a similar vein to the Russian case. The contact is obliterated, the German woman has to justify what happened with the parcels delivered at her address, and she (most likely) has to pay the international shipping fees.

How Does the Cyber Criminal Get the Money Out of the Internet?   Sooner or later the hacker wants to "harvest the fruits of his work" and get some money.

Banks, however, usually maintain records of all transactions. So the hacker risks being identified when he finally moves money to his own account or takes cash. This is especially true if larger amounts of money are involved. In this case, the financial service providers may have additional obligations of keeping records and/or reporting transactions to the authorities. This is necessary according to the laws against money laundering. This raises the question: How does the hacker finally get the money?

Some hackers accept payment in big plasma TVs, laptop computers, large numbers of Apple iTunes, or ink cartridges for printers—things which can easily be sold on a gray market. There are also cases where the hackers moved the money to counterfeit debit cards or prepaid cards. These cards were used to take large amounts of money from ATM cash machines. Some hackers were captured when they received money via Western Union wire transfer.

Cyber Criminals and Blackmailing Schemes. The hacker encrypts the data on the victim's hard disk and offers the key for decryption in exchange for money. A Web site for online sports betting was blackmailed with a distributed denial of service attack (DDoS) immediately before an important sports event.

Those blackmailing schemes are relatively rare, however, because the necessary direct contact to the victim makes them risky for the criminals. The following anecdote shows a case when scammers try to transfer significant amounts of money abroad.

Nigerian Scammers Try to Wire $27 Million. On February 20, 2009, the *New York Times* reported the case that Nigerian scammers tried to steal $27 million from an account at Citibank in New York. The account was held by the National Bank of Ethiopia, the country's central bank.

A gang of scammers involved with Paul Gabriel Amos, aged 37 and a Nigerian citizen who lived in Singapore, applied an advanced fraud schema. First they created official looking documents that instructed Citibank to accept transactions by fax. These documents contained a list of Ethiopian bank officials' names and phone numbers who are authorized to confirm such changes. The names in the list matched the names in the records of Citibank and the signatures seemed to be okay.

After this account change was completed, the fraudsters sent two dozen fax instructions to transfer in total $27 million to accounts controlled by the fraudsters in Japan, South Korea, Australia, China, Cyprus, and the United States, the complaint says.

With a lot of good luck things went well: The receiving banks returned the money because they could not process the transaction. In this way, Citibank became aware that something was wrong with these transactions and the company started an investigation. It turned out that the names of the bank officials who confirmed the instruction to accept faxes were correct—the phone numbers, however, were to cell phones in Nigeria, South Africa, and Britain that were controlled by the fraudsters. Also, the documents had come via courier from Lagos, Nigeria, rather than from the offices of the National Bank of Ethiopia.

Amos was arrested when he tried to enter the United States in Los Angeles. He claimed to be not guilty. The legal procedure is still pending.

3.7 SOCIAL ENGINEERING

According to Wikipedia, social engineering "is the act of manipulating people into performing actions or divulging confidential information. While similar to a confidence trick or simple fraud, the term typically applies to trickery or deception for the purpose of information gathering, fraud, or computer system access; in most cases the attacker never comes face-to-face with the victim."

Reformed hacker Mitnick was among the first who used the term "social engineering." He said "it is much easier to trick someone into giving a password for a system than to spend the effort to hack into the system." Social engineering was the single most effective method in his arsenal.

3.7.1 Social Engineering Examples and Case Studies

Want to Know the Password? Simply Ask for It.   The following example shows how a dialog between an attacker posing as technical support and a victim might look like. It is not a real story but it is derived from real stories and the dialogues that really happen. It explains the basic idea of "social engineering."

MR. JONES: Hello?

ATTACKER: Hello Mr. Jones, this is Mike Davis from technical support. We have to restructure the network tonight at 10 P.M. and your account will be moved to another hard disk. For this reason it will be unavailable for an hour or so.

MR. JONES: Oh? Okay. Anyway I won't be in the office at that time.

ATTACKER: Please take care to log off before you leave. We have to check a few things. What was your user name again? "jones"?

MR. JONES: Yes "jones." I hope my files won't be lost during these changes …

ATTACKER: No. Nothing will be deleted and nothing will be changed. We just have to move them to another disk. But I'll check your account just to make sure. What is the password on this account so that I can check the files?

MR. JONES: The password is "jennY" with capital "Y."

ATTACKER: Thank you, bye.

Diamonds Worth £14 in Exchange for Chocolates.   On March 18, 2007, the *Independent* (a leading U.K. newspaper) reported on a social engineering fraud that resulted in the theft of diamonds worth £14 million (€16 million; $21 million) from safety deposit boxes at an ABN Amro bank in the gem quarter in Antwerp, Belgium. The robbery of gems weighing 120,000 carats made it one of the biggest thefts ever committed by a single person.

In fact, the thief used an easy "no-tech" approach to circumvent the expensive security system, a weapon rarely applied to bank employees: personal charm. He posed as a successful business man who frequently visited the bank. During these visits he made friends with the employees and security staff. He even brought them chocolates.

The con-man gave his name as Carlos Hector Flomenbaum from Argentina. (It turned out that a passport in that name had been stolen in Israel several years ago.) Even though this person was not known to local diamond dealers, he became one of the trusted persons who received an electronic access card to the vault.

In Antwerp, more than half of the worlds diamonds are traded. For this reason the banks accommodate clients—diamond dealers—who want to store diamonds overnight and withdraw them during the day. The special clients who need frequent access to the vaults receive an electronic access card.

Mr. Claes, spokesman for the Diamond High Council in Antwerp, said of the thief and situation: "He used no violence. He used one weapon—and that is his charm—to gain confidence. He bought chocolates for the personnel, he was a nice guy, he charmed them, got the original of keys to make copies and got information on where the diamonds were ... You can have all the safety and security you want, but if someone uses their charm to mislead people it won't help."

Day of Open Doors at Large Financial Firm.   Colin Greenless, a security consultant at Siemens Enterprise Communications, was called to a client company, a FTSE-listed financial firm for a week of penetration tests based on social engineering. The name of the client is kept confidential, of course. The penetration test has been done under more "controlled" conditions than the diamond theft in the anecdote above. Nevertheless, the results are quite similar.

Greenless posed as an IT worker. Without being challenged by security personnel, he entered the office building. He based himself in a meeting room, where he worked for several days. During the exercise, Greenless could freely access data rooms, filing cabinets, telephones, and the IT center. He circulated on different floors of the office building and read confidential material left unprotected on desks. Greenless used the internal telephone system to call employees and to ask for additional information. Seventeen out of 20 persons gave their username and password when asked—allowing Greenless access to confidential data.

"The scary thing is, it's all simple stuff. It's just confidence, looking the part, and basic trickery such as 'tailgating' people through swipe card operated doors or, if you're really going for it, carrying two cups of coffee and waiting for people to hold doors open for you," said Greenless.

During this week, Greenless made friends with a number of employees of the financial firm. He was on first-name terms with the foyer security guard and even brought in a second Siemens consultant who was able to perform further analysis of the network.

Similar cases of inefficient access protection have been reported repeatedly by other security companies that conduct penetration tests at clients' sites.

The Paris Hilton Hack.   On May 19, 2005, The *Washington Post* reported that the mobile phone of TV star Paris Hilton had been hacked. The attackers downloaded embarrassing photographs and messages, as well as the personal contact information of several music and Hollywood celebrities. They published the material on well known hacker Web sites and waited for the thunderstorm in mass media to follow.

There is no completely published and confirmed report about the technical background of the attack. The *Washington Post*, however, published an analysis of that case which is technically sound and appears to be carefully researched.

According to this report the attack was done by a loosely organized group of 8 to 12 hackers who ranged in age from their mid-teens to early 20s. They called themselves "Defonic Team Screen Name Club." Four of the members of the group had met face-to-face. However, the vast majority of their day-by-day communication was online, a practice that is usual in hacker circles.

Several months before the Paris Hilton incident, the hackers had discovered a glitch in the Web site of T-Mobile—the wireless provider of Paris Hilton's phone. The group found a way to reset the passwords of T-Mobile users. By exploiting this programming flaw, the hackers could gain access to the account of any T-Mobile subscriber who used "Sidekick," a pricey device that stores videos, photos, and other data on T-Mobile's central servers. However, the hackers could use their exploit only if they knew the phone number of a Sidekick user. After a while, the group got bored with using this feature to toy with friends who used Sidekick. They decided to look for a real high profile victim. Finally the group settled on Paris Hilton because they knew she has Sidekick—she had previously starred in an advertisement for this device.

The breakthrough came on February 19 when a 16-year-old group member managed to trick a T-Mobile employee into a social engineering scam. The hacker posed as a member of T-Mobile technical support who was investigating reports on slowness on the internal network. The following dialogue was reported by the *Washington Post* (and sounds plausible to the authors) though it has not been confirmed by T-Mobile:

THE HACKER: This is [an invented name] from T-Mobile headquarters in Washington. We heard you've been having problems with your customer account tools?

THE SALES REPRESENTATIVE: No, we haven't had any problems really, just a couple slow-downs. That's about it.

PREPARED FOR THIS RESPONSE, THE HACKER PRESSED ON: Yes, that's what is described here in the report. We're going to have to look into this for a quick second.

THE SALES REP ACQUIESCED: All right, what do you need?

The hacker asked for the internet address, a username, and password of the site the sales representative of this shop used to manage user accounts. The shop assistant gave him this information. Game over.

The hacker browsed the database for name and phone number of some celebrities, among them Paris Hilton. They applied the exploit which they developed months before and reset Hilton's password, practically locking her out of the account. Then they downloaded the data from her account.

It seems that the T-mobile Web site was poorly secured in general. Jack Koziol, program manager with Infosec Institute, Inc., said in an interview with *Infoworld*, "I was amazed that a year after this kid did that, there were all sorts of Web security problems prevalent throughout their Web site. For example, T-Mobile still uses outdated server software with known Java vulnerabilities," he said. "The exact same Web hack that those kids used has been fixed, but the global issues are still there."

T-Mobile—just like all major wireless carriers—is a popular target for attacks. If the site had really known about vulnerabilities, it is unlikely that the first successful attack needs more than, say, a few hours, given the frequency of attacks against these targets. So, the authors suspect, that many hackers have "visited" the site.

This attack, however, was different. The group had the idea to combine the already successful technological attack with social engineering to get the "missing link"—Paris Hilton's phone number.

According to published material, social engineering attacks against phone companies seem to be quite frequent. Mitnick, the reformed hacker and social engineering guru, has mentioned that he knows private investigators who routinely obtain phone records of people they are investigating by calling a sales office at the target's wireless carrier and pretending to be an employee from another sales office. The investigators may say they urgently need data of this customer but cannot access their own computer. The investigators would ask the sales rep for data such as an account number, password, and perhaps social security number. Using this, a fraudster can retrieve the target's phone records.

Lexis Nexis.   Seisint is a Florida-based subsidiary of Lexis Nexis, a unit of Reed Elsevier's business branch. Seisint runs a service named Accurint: This service includes a database with names, addresses, Social Security numbers, and driver's license information of hundreds of thousands of people.

In March 2005, reports appeerted that stated this database has been breached; through numerous name searches, the intruders obtained the data of 310,000 people.

The breach started as a cyber joy-ride. A teenage hacker engaged a Florida police officer in a chat session by posing as a 14-year-old girl. The hacker sent the officer an attachment that allegedly contained a slide show of nude pictures of her. The officer opened the attachment which installed malware—a Trojan horse—on his computer. Using this backdoor the hackers gained access to the officer's system. Only then they found out of the existence of Accurint. It seems that the attackers have never heard before about Lexis Nexis and Seisint.

They used the account of the Florida police officer to search the database for personal data of celebrities. Allegedly, the hackers did it for pure curiosity and neither sold the data nor committed an identity theft.

Later, other hackers entered the game. They found an account named "Null" which belonged to a Texas police department. One of the hackers called Seisint, posing as a member of this department who wanted to run a performance test. Finally, he convinced Seisint to reset the password. Using this access, the hackers created new accounts which they then sold to other hackers. This is how the scheme got out of hand. A hacker stated: "A whole bunch of usernames were made and people were trading them and passing them around like candy."

Mitnick Hacks Motorola.   We have previously encountered Mitnick in several places in this chapter, especially in Section 3.1. Here, we find him involved in another case study.

This intrusion of Mitnick at Motorola was based on a combination of technical hacking and social engineering. At the time of the incident, Mitnick was already an experienced phone phreak and had a lot of experience in the manipulation of telecommunication networks. This knowledge helped him to make his access from outside the campus appear like calls from inside.

Motorola had their entire campus secured using SecurID. So Mitnick still needed an RSA SecurID code to complete his hack. In an interview Kevin explained:

I was able to convince one of the IT managers in the computer operations department to give me the PIN of the SecurID token used in the operations department (which was shared through the people in that department), and any time I needed access to the corporate network they would simply read off the token code, over the telephone.

During this attack Kevin managed to get remote access to Motorola's network and computing resources for about one week. Kevin explained the social engineering schema that was the core of the attack:

How hard is that going to be to do if someone called up a user that's gullible, claiming they're from the IT department, saying they're trying to synchronize the token, that they're trying to resolve a problem, and would you please read off your information? I think there's a high majority of people that will do it, if they really believe that the caller is legitimate and if they have some level of gullibility.

Finally, Mitrick managed to get the code for the MicroTAC Ultra Lite phone. He said he did not want to sell the code or do anything with it. He was just curious about the inner working of the phone.

Notice the shadows of the language: Mitrick does not say "I called up a user." Instead he says "How hard is that going to be to do if someone called up a user?" This tiny shadow makes a huge difference in front of the court.

Mortgage Fraud.   On November 28, 2008, the *Washington Post* reported that U.S. authorities "announced a series of arrests and convictions in connection with a global identity theft ring that stole millions of dollars by hijacking home-equity lines of credit issued to thousands of consumers." The estimate for the amount of money stolen is between $2 million and more than $10 million. The fraudsters face charges of wire fraud, which carries a penalty of five to 50 years.

The fraudsters targeted persons with large, untapped home-equity lines of credit. They found the victims by browsing through public records such as property deeds and mortgages, as well as other databases available on the Internet. The criminals used fee-based Web databases to find documents that included names, birth dates, and Social Security numbers of their victims The authorities suspect that the group used also other databases to find out the answers to common security questions such as a mother's maiden name. Armed with this combined information, the fraudsters ordered credit reports in the victim's name to verify account balances.

The gang used this information to transfer large amounts of money to accounts abroad, for example, in Asia. Most banks have additional security mechanisms in place before they transfer large amounts of money. They call back the owner of the account using a phone number which the bank knows already.

The investigations are still underway. However, in at least one case, a member of the group called the phone company of the victim, posing as the victim and complained about problems with his phone. The scammer asked to redirect all calls to a separate phone number which he controlled. The phone company asked some security questions, such as the amount of the last bill and the amount of the customer's last payment, but the fraudster was prepared to answer them.

In this way the call-back from the bank arrived at a phone of one of the fraudsters—who confirmed, of course, that the transfer of $675,000 to an account in Tokyo, Japan was perfectly okay.

The law enforcement authorities have some security measures in place to make this kind of fraud more difficult. Usually, the owner of a phone number or an IP address can be located. So it should not be too difficult to identify the persons who ordered the transfer and confirmed the phone call from the bank.

In this case, the scammers were particularly careful by obscuring their identity: They used prepaid cell phones and free Web e-mail accounts. They accessed the Internet via wireless public networks and wireless cards that had been bought using billing information of other victims.

"Ad-man"—Stealing Checks and Identities.   Loquann Johnson, a 53-year-old Baltimore, Maryland man, led a group of identity thieves. The fraudsters posed as ad-men and pretended to distribute advertising fliers. The group targeted victims in neighborhoods with outdoor mailboxes in Baltimore. Instead of putting something in the mailbox, they pulled mail out: credit cards, checks, and letters from the bank, for example. Using various costumes they cashed the checks. The information from the letters helped them to commit identity thefts.

With hindsight, seeing these case studies—and knowing how they ended—the reader may ask: How could the targets be so naive and give important, security-relevant information to fraudsters? However, we have also to understand the point of view of the targets.

Motorola's employees felt rather secure. They had two identification factors in place. Their entire campus was protected by securID. All these features are not quite cheap and were state of the art in security technology—at least at that time. What could go wrong there? From the point of view of the target, one could ask: "What should an IT employee do if he really has to analyze and fix a problem in the network? He will have to do some tests which will most likely require occasional cooperation with users." The targeted colleague at Motorola might have thought this: "A colleague from the internal IT department has called and asked to verify the mechanism for checking the security key. This mechanism seems to have some problems. The top modern and highly secure communication system reports that the call *is* really from inside the campus *and* comes from the IT department."

Is the colleague supposed to refuse the help? Well, the security policy could request that these "occasional cooperations" must be announced and verified by a kind of security council. This might be a solution from the point of security. How will this policy most likely look in practice? The IT employee does not know in advance what tests exactly are necessary. He still has to analyze and understand the problem. Anybody who has ever analyzed a tricky problem in a network will confirm that this "secure solution" will certainly be a long and stoney way.

Let's look again at the case of T-Mobile and Paris Hilton. It happens inevitably that a sales representative has occasional problems with her computer system or database access. What should be done if she needs urgently some customer data in this time of breakdown? Well, the security policy might require that the helping colleague calls back instead of helping immediately. This would make things much more difficult for the attackers—at least in this specific case. However, it is not clear if such a change in the security policy would also make Mitnicks's attack against Motorola fail because he had already compromised the phone system. He might have been able to forward the call back to a phone outside the campus. Even in the case of the mortgage fraud, this security policy was already in place, but the fraudsters managed to circumvent it.

Each problem has its solutions. And after carefully mulling over the problems outlined in the case studies, security experts will certainly be able to suggest changes in the policy so that something like this cannot happen anymore. This solution, however, will involve additional steps and probably more bureaucracy. It is quite possible that the secure alternative of "just calling a colleague and ask for the data" becomes a project in its own right which consumes more time than just waiting idle until the system breakdown is over.

This raises the question: What should the targets have done to make the attack fail? And it raises another question: If the targets behave in a secure way, do they still have time to get some work done?

Sarah Palin's Yahoo E-Mail Account Hacked.   During the 2008 U.S. election campaign, a hacker managed to crack the Yahoo Mail account of Alaska governor and vice president-candidate Sarah Palin. The hacker was the then 20-year-old David Kernell, son of Mike Kernell, a Democrat state-level representative in Tennessee. David exploited Yahoo's "forgot my password" feature to find out Sarah Palin's password. He posted his "victory" on a well-known hacker forum.

After the password recovery was re-enabled, it took (seriously) 45 minutes on Wikipedia and Google to find the information. Birthday? Found after 15 seconds on Wikipedia. Zip code? Well, she had was from Wasilla, Alaska—a town with two zip codes (thanks online postal service!). The second question was somewhat harder—"Where did you meet your spouse?"

Kernell did some research; apparently, she had eloped with Mr. Palin after college. The hacker adds the following:

> "If you look at some of the screenshots that I took and other fellow anon have so graciously put on photobucket, you will see the Google search for "palin eloped" or some such in one of the tabs. I found out later though more research that they met at high school, so I did variations of that (high, high school) [and] eventually hit on "Wasilla high." I promptly changed the password to "popcorn" and took a cold shower.

After a day or two, the attacker was identified because he made some mistakes. Kernell used a proxy service to obscure his identity—a method frequently used by hackers. The proxy service forwards the commands from the hacker using the IP address of the proxy server. In this way the hacker's IP address remains undisclosed; at least, that's how it's supposed to be. Kernell also made the mistake of including screen shots in his confession posts which showed the browser line with the complete URL. The URL allowed the identification of the proxy service. Consquentially, law enforcement authorities contacted the owner of the proxy service and asked for the server logs which contained the real IP address of the attacker. Another mistake was that Kernell used only one proxy server, not a chain of proxy servers. Lastly, to sign the confession posts, he used his e-mail address: rubico10@yahoo.com. Authorities identified Kernell as the person behind this e-mail address by means of Yahoo's internal records and server logs.

It seems that it was a battle between a weak attacker and a weak defender: It took only a few minutes to crack the account, and it took only a few more days to capture the attacker. In this case, the attacker took advantage of the fact that Sarah Palin is quite prominent and a lot of personal details about her are widely known.

However, even for the more typical person, many things can be found out from the Internet. Among the sources of information are profiles of users of social networking sites. The information on these profiles can come into the hands of hackers in various ways. The most obvious is a phishing scheme: The attackers lures the victims onto a bogus Web site that appears to be the log-in page of the social networking site. In fact, this bogus site is under control of the attacker. The victim inputs his or her password on the bogus site which then becomes available to the attacker.

Another attack vector is used on computers that are available to the public or to a larger number of users. Some careless users who log in to their Twitter account on these computers click the "keep me logged in" check box. The next person who uses this computer has access to the account of the careless user.

A more sophisticated way is used by attackers who manage somehow to hack into the administration tools of the social networking site. In January 2009, an attacker gained control of tools on Twitter's website. These tools are used by Twitter employees to manage the site (such as for changing e-mail addresses if a user forgot his password). The attacker, who has not been identified at the time of this writing, used these tools to change some high profile accounts including Bill O'Reilly, Britney Spears, and Barack Obama.

Anyway, user profiles of social networking sites are widely available on the black market. The price is usually below $1. The clients are curious persons such as hackers who try to use this information for a social engineering attack and spammers who buy valid e-mail addresses that are connected with additional personal data (name, birth date, and other data). There are also rumors of cases where the information on user profiles has been used to answer security questions (for example, for banks).

The Palin hack caused an interesting dialogue. Bill O'Reilly, one of the pioneers and master minds of the World Wide Web, commented on the air that the Web sites that published the e-mails stolen from Palin's account did something, not only immoral, but also illegal and should be punished. The reporter agreed with him and said publishing such information was "complicit" in the hack of Palin's e-mail account. However, the lawyer Megyn Kelly rejected this argument and explained why the First Amendment provides protection: Media organizations are generally allowed to publish newsworthy information.

In response to O'Reilly's comments, some hacker claimed to have hacked O'Reilly's Web site and published the e-mail addresses found there. Bloggers however questioned if the e-mail list was authentic; they tried some of the addresses and found them not valid.

3.7.2   Tactics of Social Engineering

Pretexting.   Pretexting is a special technique of social engineering that is frequently used to trick businesses into disclosing customer information. Usually the attacker already has done some prior research and found out data about the victim (such as Social Security number, mother's maiden name, or the amount of the last bill).

Here is a fictional scenario: A private investigator tries to get a detailed telephone record of the victim. He calls a junior service representative of the telephone company and impersonates the victim. The private investigator uses this information to establish even grater legitimacy when he calls a more senior manager to get certain documents where tougher questioning can be expected.

The pretexter may impersonate tax authorities, police, co-workers, bosses, or any other person who is somehow entitled to get the requested information. All that must be done is that the pretexter must have prepared answers to predictable security questions.

An efficient protection against pretexting is questioning of the caller who asks for the information; give a phone number and offer to call him back in a while. In general, pretexters avoid giving phone numbers and getting called back.

In another fictional example of social engineering, the fraudster calls arbitrary numbers at a certain company and pretends he is from technical support. With a bit of good luck and after several trials the attacker encounters a victim who really has a technical problem and who is happy that the alleged "technical support" calls and helps him. The fraudster lures the victim into a dialogue where the victim gives his password. Or the fraudster suggests starting some scripts which allegedly solve the problem; in reality, the script installs a backdoor that allows the attacker access to the victim's system. In another possible variation of this example, the attacker calls a junior database operator pretending to be a top executive of the company who asks urgently for some details from the database while using a firm voice.

Some scientists conducted a survey. The participants received a cheap pen in exchange for participating in the survey. During the survey they asked the participants for their password. Almost all participants disclosed their passwords. Similar results have been confirmed by other studies. For example, attractive women offered a chocolate bar in exchange for a short interview. In the course of the interview, the targets were asked for their password. Many of them disclosed it.

In most cases, the goal of social engineering is to get sensitive information or to get access to the system. If the attacker has access, even only with a "guest account" it is frequently rather easy to elevate the access rights, gain more privileges, launch new attacks, and hide the traces.

Intelligence Gathering.   Collecting information on the targeted company can be done in various ways. The easiest is probably by searching the Web. In particular, the home page of the targeted company contains countless details: structure of the company, projects which are currently under way, names and job-titles of employees, and the like. Another way is searching the garbage of that company; in jargon it is called "dumpster diving." Almost any small note, thrown away, may contain interesting information such as names of business partners, remarks about defective parts, and problems with guarantees. All these details are helpful for motivating the reason for a call and to make the discussion sound more plausible, credible, and authentic.

Most companies routinely shred documents before they are thrown away. Notice, however, that strip shredders are not very efficient. The document can be reconstructed because the strips are in close proximity in the trash.

Another source of precious information is "broken" CDs. Occasionally, the burn process fails and the CD is unusable, that is, "broken." A determined hacker may be able to recover the partial information already written on the CD. Experiments have shown that information could be retrieved even if the CD appeared to be broken.

Last but not least the attacker can try to call junior staff, that is, persons who are not the target of the real attack but can provide the fraudster with additional details such as the names and phone numbers of management assistants and of responsible persons. All names of employees are interesting for a social engineering attack because this information can be used for "name dropping"—just mentioning names—which makes the attacker appear to be an "insider."

It is quite possible that the attacker has not done anything illegal so far. Is it illegal to study a Web site carefully or to search garbage?

Targets of Social Engineering.   Among the most frequent victims of social engineering are help desk personnel and management assistants.

Help desk personnel are trained to help callers. Frequently, they can reset passwords, create new accounts, and perform other security sensitive activities—all of which are interesting for attackers. In addition, many organizations outsource the help desk to other specialized companies that have limited connection to the actual organization. In such a context it is easier for the attacker to impersonate a legitimate caller because the help desk personnel do not personally know most of the employees of the actual company.

Administrative assistants are another attractive target; they frequently have access to a large amount of sensitive information. They also have a good overview of their company and most communication between senior members of the organization passes over their desks. It is not rare that the assistant knows the passwords of the manager; it is necessary for routine activities such as booking appointments in electronic calendars. Approaching a management assistant can have two different purposes: launching the attack or gaining additional information for an attack against an even more highly valued target.

Psychology of the Attack.   Many social engineering attacks follow one of the following three patterns.

- The attacker addresses the ego of the target. In this pattern, the fraudster may look for people who feel under-appreciated in their organization and/or who have a position below their talent. The attacker may tell them how intelligent they are and how well they know how to solve the real problems. The attacker may try several potential targets until he finds one who is receptive for this kind of attack. A skilled attacker can sense this "weakness" usually after a brief discussion.

- The attacker pretends to be an influential person in the company or a law enforcement authority. In many cases, the fraudster invents a plausible situation which justifies the request of confidential information or security relevant activities (such as a password reset). Frequently, the attacker creates a sense of urgency.

In other cases the attacker may pretend to be a representative of law enforcement authorities (for example, a tax investigator or police).

- The attacker pretends to be a newly hired fellow worker, a customer, or a business partner who is in real trouble *right now* and needs to be helped immediately. Mitnick explained in his book *The Art of Deception* that people inherently want to be helpful and therefore are easily duped.

Social engineering, as we have seen, is far more about sociology and psychology than it is about technology. But that does not make it any less effective!

3.8   A LINGERING QUESTION

That brings us to the conclusion of material we wanted to present you on the subject of hacking in our book. But we can't resist adding one more thought. Or, actually, asking one more question.

Johann has been puzzling during its entire creation over this question, and so far he has not come up with an answer (nor, for that matter, has Robert!). The question is this:

Why is it that rank computing novices can interact with (or work against) the highest level professionals in our field to cause the kind of mischief that they do?

Elaborating that question, we then ask: How can teenagers without formal computing training outperform, at least in some ways, the top professionals of our field? For example, a Swedish teenager steals and makes mischief with the source code of Cisco. How can this happen? What is there about the field of computing and software security that makes the playing field so level?

It's not that computing and software are simplistic fields. We the authors deeply believe that writing software, for example, is one of the most complex tasks known to humankind.

Does this sort of thing happen in other fields? Can engineers specializing in bridge design, for example, find that their bridge designs have been hijacked and made weaker or otherwise harmed by novice bridge-focused non-engineers? We don't think so.

We could have concluded this material on hacking without asking this question and making this confession. But we couldn't resist giving you, the reader of our book, the opportunity to respond. What is so unique about the computing and software fields that allows them to be subjected to the kinds of hacker attacks we see here? We'd love to hear from you. E-mail us: Johann (Johann_Rost@yahoo.com); Robert (rlglass@acm.org).

3.9 LATE-BREAKING NEWS

Operation Aurora: Google Hacked by China? In January 2010, a few days before we had to send our final manuscript to the publisher, Google and other well known companies were successfully targeted by a cyber attack. If the circumstances of the attack were not so extraordinarily interesting we would probably have decided that the material was too premature to be included in our book. However, since the case includes so many new and important details, we include here our current understanding of the case—even if we expect more details to appear in the near future.

Many experts suspect that the attack came from China. And quite a few of them expressed their opinion that most likely the Chinese government is behind this attack. The Chinese government promptly denied having anything to do with the case and blamed an American conspiracy instead. Nevertheless, the attack caused an intensified public discussion and tensions in the international relations between the United States and China.

Note that we, the authors, are computing practitioners by profession and choose not to participate in this political and moral discussion. We simply will report the known facts and offer some explanations, leaving it to the reader to form his or her own opinion.

What Happened? The attack started in December 2009 and was publicly disclosed by Google on January 12, 2010. The cyber security company McAfee was among the first who published technical details of the attack (a few days later).

The attack was based on a zero-day vulnerability of Internet Explorer—i.e., a bug of Internet Explorer that affects its security (a vulnerability) but has not been published (or is not known) so far ("zero day"). This is what happened, according to our current knowledge.

The attack was classified as an "advanced persistent threat" (APT). Let's define the term by breaking it down into parts.

Advanced: The attacker applies state-of-the-art cyber war technology and usually one or more zero-day exploits. This makes it different from the more frequent "usual" attacks which apply (mildly adapted) technology readily available on Web sites visited by hackers.

Persistent: The attack works toward a strategic goal specified in advance. Unlike opportunistic cyber criminals who try to steal "everything what can be made into money," a "persistent" attacker ignores temptations such as credit cards. He might have the goal of capturing the source code of a certain system, for example. He will try his best to deliver this source code and will not risk his mission by being caught (for example, with a stolen credit card).

Threat: Usually there are people, real humans, behind the attack to control and guide it—not just a piece of software, such as a virus, that blindly infects all systems of a certain profile (that is, a certain version of the operating system). Usually these people are highly trained, motivated, and well funded.

An APT is usually, therefore, highly focused. The target is specified in advance. More often than not the attack is preceded by an elaborate social engineering scheme, which lures a victim into a trap. Then the computer of the target is infected by malware tailor-made for this one specific attack. (Since the malware is completely new and has not been used before, it cannot be discovered by antivirus programs If it is used only in a single case, it is quite possible that it might take quite a while before the providers of antivirus software learn about its existence. And perhaps they never find it out.)

The malware connects to a remote server and installs other illegitimate software on the target's system. The technical details are different among various attacks; the final result, however, is almost always that the attacker has something like system administrator privileges on the targeted computer. So the attacker is in position to steal intellectual property like source code repositories. (Given all of this, some experts call an APT the cyber war analogy for a drone in conventional warfare.)

Once the victim is lured into the social engineering trap at the beginning of the attack, things unfold with clockwork like precision and almost certainly end with the desired result (such as system administrator privileges for the attacker). Remember, previously in this hacking chapter, we provided explanations and examples of social engineering. The infected system can be used as a springboard to infect other systems of the victim's network.

These explanations show that APTs are not simple hacker attacks of teenagers, nor are they the activities of organized gangs of cyber criminals. They are nothing less than professional intelligence gathering. And many experts suspect that most (if not all) APTs are sponsored by governments. This also explains why most of the APTs that we have seen so far were against systems used for military purposes. In fact, APTs are often spying activities of one military organization against another. This might add to the reasons why so far few technical details of these attacks are known outside of the cyber security community. Operation Aurora was one of the first APTs that attacked companies outside of the military industrial complex.

Internet Explorer's Vulnerability. The Operation Aurora incident includes a number of nontechnical aspects that are worth a closer look.

- The attack was based on a zero-day vulnerability in Microsoft's Internet Explorer. Virtually all versions currently in use were affected. It is said that Microsoft had known of this vulnerability since September 2009, but they apparently decided that the development of new features had priority over fixing this problem. This might add to the reasons why the German government declared all versions of Internet Explorer—patched or unpatched—as potentially vulnerable, and discouraged its use. (Reported by BBC on Jan. 16, 2010)

- Many APTs seen so far were based on a cocktail of multiple zero-day exploits.

It is quite possible that we will learn about other vectors of this attack as our understanding of the incident matures.

Google's Communication Strategy.   Google was not the only company affected by this incident. In fact, several dozen large organizations from a variety of fields were targeted and learned that their intellectual property was misappropriated—Adobe, for example. A number of these companies have confirmed the attack. Some experts also mention Yahoo and Symantec in the context of the incident, although these companies have not, as of this writing, confirmed the attack.

Be that as it may, at this point something unexpected occurred: While the other victims kept the incident low-key, Google published the case in their blog and raised the interest of the mass media. Note that we, the authors, believe that the entire case would have otherwise passed unnoticed by the broader public. It would have turned out similar to previous APTs: Some researchers in the cyber security industry would discuss the technical aspects of the problem, exchange their hex-dumps, and post technical details and recommendations to platforms visited by professionals in that industry. And no one else would have heard anything about the incident.

But Google took a different course of action and came out with a big bang: Google believes that one of the goals of the attack might have been the ability to access e-mail accounts of Chinese humans right activists. As a consequence, Google announced that that they will reconsider the January 2006 agreement with the Chinese government, wherein the search findings of Google.cn are censored to conform to the restrictions imposed by Chinese law.

"We have decided we are no longer willing to continue censoring our results on Google.com, and so over the next few weeks we will be discussing with the Chinese government the basis on which we could operate an unfiltered search engine within the law, if at all. We recognize that this may well mean having to shut down Google.cn and potentially our offices in China." (Retrieved from the Official Google Blog on Feb. 1 2010)

For the purpose of this book, the technical description of the attack will end here, even though we expect more details to show up in the weeks and months to come. For an update, the interested reader may want to search Google or Wikipedia for the keywords "Operation Aurora exploit."

CHAPTER 4

THEFT OF INFORMATION

Here, we enter rather different waters from our previous chapters. Subversion and lying, we have already seen, happen often enough on software projects that they are worth paying attention to. Hacking isn't so much a software project phenomenon as it is a computing work phenomenon; it is glaringly apparent to anyone following the computing field that hacking is a problem with major consequences.

This chapter is about theft of information. Theft of information can range from subtle to blatant. We are about to learn that sometimes information is stolen without anyone knowing it. Equally often, information is stolen in order to make something else happen—a payoff, an embarrassment, revenge—and under those circumstances knowledge of the theft is quickly broadcast and made public.

As we explore information theft further together in this chapter, we soon come to realize that in opening this door we are opening the door to another and even more complex and controversial topic, intellectual property protection. In some ways, an in-depth treatment of that topic, with all its legal manifestations, is at the limit of the scope of this book. But because it is nearly impossible to have a meaningful discussion of information theft without considering intellectual property protection, we will take a stab at some superficial material on that topic!

Now, on to some introductory case study material about information theft.

4.1 INTRODUCTION

The Chinese Silk Monopoly: An Ancient Example.   We previously encountered the story of the Chinese silk monopoly in our chapter on hacking, where we used it as an example of early intellectual property protection. Here, we see it as an example of something slightly different: ancient theft of information.

According to the writings of Confucius and Chinese traditional accounts, the production of silk dates back to the twenty-seventh century BC. The legends say that a silk worm fell into the tea cup of princess Leizu. When she tried to remove the worm from her drink, she unrolled the cocoon of fibers that surrounded the worm. This gave her the idea to weave them.

In the beginning, the use of silk was limited to the imperial family. It was given as a present to other kings and as a kind of payment to high officials of the imperial administration. Later, silk was traded; it became a symbol of luxury in the

---

ancient world and brought wealth and fame to China. Even though silk was known in most parts of Asia and Europe, China managed to keep a monopoly on its manufacture for many centuries. A cornerstone of this monopoly was the imperial decree that condemned to death anyone who tried to export silkworms or their eggs.

Around the year 300 B.C. a Japanese expedition managed to bring some eggs of silk worms to their country. They also took four Chinese girls and forced them to teach the Japanese the production of silk.

A second successful attack against the silk monopoly dates to the year 552 AD, when the Byzantine emperor Justinian sent two monks on a mission to central Asia. The monks managed to smuggle eggs of silkworms, hidden in rods of bamboo, out of China.

These events constitute probably the earliest records of theft of information.

Information.   Information can come in many forms. In this chapter, we will speak of information as data as well as source code. Both kinds of information are, and have frequently been in the past, tempting targets for theft. This chapter will focus first on case studies of such theft; then, we will delve more deeply into causes, results, and defenses against such theft.

Information can be stolen in various ways:

- Information is available on a server and the thief gains unauthorized access to this server. This attack is a variation of hacking and was analyzed in more detail in that chapter.

- The people who normally process this data are disloyal or become disloyal. This problem appears frequently if former employees steal data that they processed while employed.

A specific problem with stolen data appears in the regulated industries such as health care, finance, or military contracting.

4.2   CASE STUDIES

4.2.1   Data Theft

Lubna Baloch from Karachi.   On October 7, 2003, the highly prestigious University of California, San Francisco (UCSF) Medical Center in San Francisco received an e-mail from a woman named Lubna Baloch who lived in Karachi, Pakistan. In this e-mail, Baloch described herself as "a medical doctor by profession." She said a Texan named Tom Spires owed her a certain sum (around $500) for transcribing UCSF voice files. She demanded that the medical center find Spires and remedy the situation. Otherwise, she would release the hospital's confidential patient files on the Internet: "Your patient records are out in the open, so you'd better track that person and make him pay me or otherwise I will expose all the voice files and patient records." To prove that she was not joking, she attached two authentic files to the e-mail.

At that time, the hospital did not know anything about the existence of either Baloch or Spires. So, how could such confidential files be in the hands of this person in far-off Karachi? Investigation revealed that patient records were based on voice files that had been outsourced for transcription to Sausalito, California-based Transcription Stat, a well-established company that specializes in transcribing medical records from voice files.

The practice of outsourcing transcription work is widely used in hospitals. The medical staff records the patient information on voice files, relating all aspects of health care from routine exams to surgical procedures. Later these files are transcribed into patient records by specialized companies. Insiders estimate this business amounts to $20 billion per year, and almost all large health care providers outsource at least part of their transcription work. It is not unusual for the entire medical history of a patient to be recorded in voice files.

The health center knew that Transcription Stat maintained a network of about 15 subcontractors throughout the country to handle the hundreds of files received by their office every day, but the health center assumed that was as far as it went. One of these subcontractors was the Florida-based woman Sonya Newburn. She typically handled about 30 UCSF files per day and had been steadily working with Transcription Stat for about one and a half years. Newburn out-contracted some of her work to the Texas man Spires, who in turn subcontracted the work to Baloch in Pakistan—even though the agreement with Newburn excluded outsourcing outside the borders of the United States.

The hospital paid about 18 cents per line to Transcription Stat. Out of this, about 3 cents reached Baloch in Karachi. In the beginning, Baloch was paid in due course. In time, however payment became more and more delayed. Thus, an increasing amount of debt accumulated. Finally, Baloch asked Spires to stop sending her work and to pay all outstanding debts, so she could deal with the problem. In response, Spires blocked her address on his e-mail and instant messenger lists. From the very beginning, Spires had refused to give Baloch any phone number or postal address, so there was no way for her to contact him. Her only possibility was to write to the hospital, and that is what she did.

Finally, things went well: Baloch received her money and then retracted her previous threats. She allegedly destroyed all confidential data from the hospital. Nevertheless, the case stirred up considerable public interest—even a hearing in Congress. But what happened afterwards? A few weeks later, Baloch was still in Karachi, still free and —to top it all—still working for doctors in the United States. In fact, one doctor in California, who was not aware of the details of the case, was still sending her work.

Let's take a closer look to this case from various points of view.

The Daisy-Chain.   The business model that includes a chain of outsourcing relationships—in jargon, a "daisy-chain"—is quite common in outsourcing relations. At the top of the chain, there are large companies, high prices, and polished manners. At the bottom, as prices decrease, the organizations get smaller and less reliable.

Most participants of the daisy chain are not aware of all these levels: Frequently, they only know one level above and one level below themselves—i.e., the contact(s) who send work and their own subcontractors who perform it. It would not have come as a surprise if, for example, as in the UCSF case, Baloch had maintained her own network of subcontractors in Karachi. We could imagine some medical students with fluency in English and quick fingers at the keyboard working for Baloch.

The Medical Center.   According to Tomi Ryba, Chief Operating Officer of UCSF Medical Center, "This was an egregious breach." We can imagine that the hospital considered the case somewhere between a crime and a terrorist action. Only the rather modest sum of $500 might justify doubts that the threatening e-mail was not part of a criminal blackmailing scheme.

Before this happened, the hospital did not see any reason to worry: They were working with well established partners within the borders of the United States. For decades, they had maintained steady relationships and paid fair prices. They had a contract that met the conditions of the relevant United States legislation, which is rather strict regarding confidentiality of medical records. So, what could go wrong in this scenario?

Tom Spires from Texas.   Tom was a kind of outsourcing agent. His business requires very limited capital and not much subject matter expertise. It is not so difficult to establish the business relationships, and once the ball is rolling he is hardly doing more than forwarding files and managing contracts (i.e., writing invoices). The prices are low, but it's a volume business. So, a person with very limited professional skills can earn an per-working-hour income that is not much lower than the salary of managers of a mid-size company—a prospect that is quite attractive for business agents.

From the very beginning, Tom operated his business so that there was little risk his offshore partners might start litigation against him: He refused to give phone numbers and postal addresses. He might have foreseen that his Pakistanian business partner(s) might consider filing a law suit against him sooner or later, but this should have been kept a remote possibility. Or his Pakistanian partner(s) might become so angry and desperate that she (or they) might consider other actions—worse than a lawsuit—against him. In such a case, it might be good not to be findable.

In the beginning, Tom paid on time to establish some trust. In time, however, he accumulated more and more debts. This brought the Pakistanian woman into a dilemma: If she went on she risked a growing stake of outstanding payment. If she dared to insist on timely payment, she ran the risk of making her Texas partner cancel the agreement and not pay the already accumulated debts. In fact, this is what eventually happened.

Notice the number of carefully prepared defense lines: First the Pakistanian woman had to have "the courage" to insist on a timely payment, risking the accumulated debts and the allegedly "precious" business contact in the United States. Then she had to find the owner—the real person—of an e-mail address which is not quite easy to do. Once she found him, she would have to file a lawsuit against him. The act of filing a lawsuit abroad on another continent in another legal culture requires know-how and funding. Last but not least she had to win the lawsuit— a feat that might turn out to be difficult if the entire business was based on e-mails, that is, without any "real paper." A "business architecture" that includes such fully conceived defense perimeters against partners who "might feel cheated" is probably based on some experience with this kind of "business model." For this reason, we suspect that Tom might not have been doing this kind of monkey business for the first time.

This time, however, a "shop accident" happened: Somehow Baloch knew the name of the hospital where the files came from. Otherwise, where would she have sent her e-mail?

Back to Lubna Baloch.   While $500 is a rather modest amount in the day-to-day business of an American health center, it is a large sum for a private person in Karachi. In 2004, the per capita income in Pakistan was around $700 per year. If somebody is cheated of $500, energetic steps of defense might be considered necessary. Baloch might not have foreseen the scandal she stirred up with her threat. Later she said that she "was the real victim in this case," and she had never really intended to make the records public—she was just asking for due payment in order to pay her debts. At least, that was what she declared afterwards.

If Baloch had been aware of what would happen, she might have considered other steps first: She could have sent an e-mail to the hospital in which she explained her situation and asked for help. If this failed, she could have proceeded to a harsher course of action. Perhaps some of her colleagues in Karachi were not even able to understand all this excitement: Rich clients in a rich country who did not want to pay their debts—$500 might be a small amount for the rich clients, but it was a lot of money for Baloch. So, she "scared them a bit." "Much ado about nothing," she might have thought. Or, perhaps that is what some of her colleagues in Karachi thought.

Anyway, two weeks after all this happened she was still free. It seems that Pakistanian law enforcement authorities did not share the American's excitement.

The Patients.   The medical center already had a number of security mechanisms in place, even before this happened. For this reason, the voice files did not contain real names of patients. Instead they included a "patient ID": a number that has meaning only within the records of UCSF. Even if the voice files had been made public, it would not be easy to trace them back to the real patients without access to other UCSF data. For this reason, the patients would not have faced too much inconvenience. They would just have gone on with their lives. Perhaps some of them would have never even heard of the case.

4.2.2 Source Code Theft

Let us now move from the subject of data theft to that of source code theft.

The fact that source code is accessed illegitimately should really be called "misappropriated source code" instead of "stolen source code" because the owners still have their source code; they might not even have noticed the misappropriation. When speaking in a legal context, the correct "misappropriated" expression is usually applied. In mainstream language, however, we hear more frequently of "stolen" source code.

Facebook Based on Stolen Code?   In 2004, Harvard students launched a project for a social networking site named ConnectU. The start-up included Divya Narendra, the twins Cameron and Tyler Winklevoss and Facebook founder Mark Zuckerberg, then 20 years old. The ConnectU team found out about Zuckerberg's own social networking project from a Harvard Newsletter. They then removed him from their project. But Zuckerberg allegedly had already stolen the material he wanted. Facebook quickly amassed 32 million users and an estimated value of $10 billion.

The case went through a lengthy legal procedure and was finally settled in February 2009 by a confidential agreement. According to unconfirmed rumors, Zuckerberg paid the Winklevoss twins (and presumably also the other ConnectU shareholders) $65 million. (Ironically, the news leaked out through a brochure of a law firm that was advertising its money-winning ability!)

Microsoft Windows Misappropriated.   In February 2004, Microsoft learned that significant portions of the source code for both Windows NT 4.0 and Windows 2000 were misappropriated and unlawfully released onto (and distributed over) the Internet without authorization. It never became completely clear how the code leaked out, but it was widely distributed in hacker circles. In time, the alarm in the Windows community relaxed and the hype among the hackers died down when it turned out that the code was incomplete and did not contain anything from Windows XP.

Many hackers had a look at the code just to be able to say they saw it. A man from Connecticut named William P. Genovese, Jr (a.k.a. "illwill," a.k.a. "xillwillx@ yahoo.com") ran the popular hacking site illmob.org. He posted the code to a password protected ftp site and wrote on his web page the following text:

> "win2000 source code jacked … and illmob.org got a copy of it … im sure if you look hard you can find it or if you wanna buy it ill give you a password to my ftp."

An investigator from an online security firm hired by Microsoft downloaded the code after sending online payment of $20 to Genovese. They then informed law enforcement authorities (who had an FBI agent doing the same).

On November 9, 2004, Genovese—then 28-years old—was arrested and charged in connection with his sale of the source code. He argued that such restriction on publishing trade secrets was a violation of his First Amendment right to free speech. He also claimed that since he had found the code on the Internet, he could not possibly have known that it was still a trade secret. The judge did not agree with this argument and said the posting on his Web site proved that he knew such material was not freely available to the public. In January 2006, the judge sentenced Genovese to two years of jail time, followed by three years of court supervision, during which Genovese's computer use would also be monitored.

Earlier, in March 2003, Genovese had been convicted of hacking and sentenced to two years of probation. This conviction, coupled with a longer string of petty crimes (spray painting a bridge, multiple thefts), certainly did not help his case and may explain some of the reasons for the harsh sentence: two years of prison for two illegal deals of $20 each. Remember, he had not stolen the code; he just sold what he found on the Internet.

Even before this happened, Genovese's Web site illmob.org had been involved in a number of, well, what some say are "colorful hacker events" while others call them simply "illegal activities." The Web site published, for example, the material stolen from Paris Hilton's mobile phone. Such a history adds to the reasons why the authorities might have felt that it is not a bad idea to teach him a lesson.

Cisco Source Code Out in the Open.   In May 2004, it was reported that up to 800 MB of source code for the Cisco Internet operating system (IOS) was stolen. On message boards, the attacker boasted of what he had achieved and posted 2.5 MB snippets on a Russian server. It was through these postings that Cisco found out that their source code was stolen; otherwise, they might not ever have known.

One year later, on May, 9 2005, the *New York Times* reported that this incident was part of a larger scheme which also included penetrating the systems of American military, NASA, and research laboratories. International law enforcement authorities conducted a one-year-long investigation and eventually identifed and captured the then 16-year-old Philip Gabriel Pettersson in Uppsala, Sweden. Within the hacker community, he was known as "Stakkato."

The authorities identified him because he had applied a similar scheme of attack again and again. Stakkato was already known to the Swedish authorities because they captured him when he broke into networks of Swedish universities. This fact helped the investigators; once they knew that the attacks had something to do with Uppsala, they took a closer look at the "bad guys" there.

It is unclear if the authorities would have captured him if he had stolen only the Cisco source code and then disappeared from the Web. Anyway, even though he used the same scheme again and again, it was difficult enough to identify him—it took one year and coordinated actions of local and international law enforcement authorities.

The Cisco source code was stolen from a Sun computer at a Cisco site; that is, it was not stolen from a developer laptop that may or may not have been secured with appropriate care but from a server inside of Cisco's office building and inside of Cisco's firewalls.

The attack was based on a Trojan-horse-infected version of SSH (a frequently used tool for remote administration of a computer).

Sidebar: Trojan Horse

A Trojan horse is a malignant version of a legitimate program. In the case of Stakkato, it was a malignant version of SSH. The Trojan-horse-infected version behaves exactly like the legitimate program it replaces, except that in addition it executes some illegitimate functions that give the attacker unauthorized access to the targeted computer. If the legitimate user tries to use the infected SSH, the malignant part would further abuse the access rights of the legitimate user and install more malignant software on the computer. In this way, the attacker "escalates" his access rights on the infected computer.

The name is derived from the ancient Greek myth of Troja. In this story, the Greek attackers placed a wooden horse at the doors of Troja. The Trojan defenders did not know that Greek soldiers were hidden inside the horse and brought it into their town as a kind of trophy. In the middle of the night, the soldiers came out of the horse and opened the city's doors for the Greek army that was ready to attack.

By exploiting the infected version of SSH, the attacker could take advantage of trusted connections between secure research servers and less secure computers at the borderline of the network. In this way, the attacker could steal passwords of legitimate users.

Legal proceedings in this matter are still pending as of the writing of this book. Sweden does not extradite its own citizens, so Pettersson will not be judged in the United States. In Sweden, the matter is treated as a juvenile case. After his capture, Pettersson was released to the care of his parents.

By using Trojan horse technology, the attacker captures passwords from compromised systems. The way these passwords were sent back to the attacker (Pettersson) used some technological elements that were new at that time. This may explain why the attacks were undetected for such a long time. However, the attack was based on elements that were already known in the hacker and defender communities.

It is interesting to stand back and put this case in some perspective. On the attacking side, there is a cheeky boy. On the defending side stands Cisco, a world renowned high tech company specializing in computer security; it is a company that provides many, if not most, of the routers on the Internet. Cisco has sufficient resources and reputation to attract some of the best security experts in the world (some of them with strong academic credentials, others with decades of hacking experience, that is, white hat hacking, of course). And now comes a teenager who steals their crown jewels—their source code. If he had not told them, they might not have found out.

Those readers who have ever worked through a technical book on computer security will confirm the following: It's not easy stuff, not at all. There are thousands, perhaps tens of thousands, of details: details about protocols, security equipment, tools from the Internet, hacker tactics, and others. These details are interrelated and all of them are important. Anyway, it is not easy stuff.

Petterson did not receive significant formal training in computing and computer security. Basically he was an autodidact. At the time of the attack, he was 16-years old. How many years of "experience in computing business" should we estimate for him if we ignore the times of kindergarten and early years in school? In fact, he was little more than a boy. But he launched long lasting attacks against Cisco and other highly secured networks.

For us authors, this all sounds like "A group of Swedish children challenged the Harlem Globetrotters in basketball. The children won 118-32."

4.3 HOW DO THE VICTIMS FIND OUT THAT THEIR SECRETS ARE STOLEN?

What would have happened if the targeted side had not been Cisco but, say, X Powertools (not a real name)? Does X Powertools have a defense that could be compared to that of Cisco? What would be true if the attacking side was sponsored by the government of country Y that is doing business with X Powertools? The government of Y might think that it wouldn't hurt to have a closer look at the accounting records of X Powertools before the next round of negotiations. What would happen in this case?

One thing is certain: The professional spies would definitely not boast on the Internet about how successful their attack was!

Frequently, hackers boast in public about what they did. In other cases, the victims find out when the stolen data is found in places where it is not supposed to be—on the computer of a captured hacker, message boards, or the black market. In even more cases, they will never find out. Many experts suspect there may be a high number of unreported cases.

There have been, however, some cases where the victims found out about the theft without the "help" of the attacker. The following anecdote gives an example.

AltaVista.   In Summer 2004, American authorities captured the former AltaVista Employee Laurent Chavet in Redmond, Washington. The French national was charged with having accessed the AltaVista networks illegitimately after he left the company in 2002. In those sessions, he had downloaded AltaVista source code to his home computer.

Chavet admitted that he had accessed the network using the login of a colleague, allegedly because he was curious to know how the project continued developing after he left the team. The case caught the attention of the media because Chavet had started to work for Microsoft. Some authors suspected that he was working in the group developing Microsoft's search engine; however, this was never confirmed by Microsoft. But apparently Microsoft was not involved. No Microsoft systems were analyzed by law enforcement authorities in the context of the case.

This anecdote is one of the few published cases where the victims found out "on their own" that source code had been stolen, that is, they found out without locating the source code on the black market. There are few published details about how AltaVista found out that the source code had been illegitimately downloaded, but there are some obvious observations:

- The access pattern to the source code was atypical: Large chunks of source code had been downloaded in a short time. If a regular software developer accesses source code in the course of day-by-day work, that developer does not download all the files at once. Instead, only the files that will be read and perhaps changed will be accessed. Then, some modified files would be uploaded and others downloaded—perhaps for the next bug fix. Rarely would a developer need a large number of files simultaneously. It would be even more rare for developers to have or take the time to read files that belong to completely different modules other than the ones they are working on.

- The download was done from outside of AltaVista, and it was done using an IP address that was not supposed to access this source code.

So, this download reveals some "unusual features". It should be possible to flag this suspicious pattern in an automatic way. Nevertheless, it took almost two years until Chavet was captured.

The suspicious usage pattern is similar to that of the Cisco attack. Cisco's intrusion detection system, however, did not flag the theft of source code. Cisco in fact never said how much source code was stolen.

4.4   INTELLECTUAL PROPERTY PROTECTION

For the most part, the best defense against information theft is a physical and/or logical one: Build some sort of software wall around the information that is to be protected, for example.

But what is to be done from a legal point of view if that wall is penetrated and some information is in fact stolen? Are there sufficient legal deterrents to minimize the possibility that information thieves will steal your information? That brings us to the topic of intellectual property protection, and intellectual property law.

There are three primary legal ways of protecting intellectual property—trade secret law, copyright law, and patent law. One attorney writing on this subject sees a chronological sequence to the emphasis placed on each of these approaches (Coles 2005). He sees trade secret approaches coming first in history (pre-1975); the emphasis, he says, then shifted to copyright (1975–1990); whereupon patent approaches became the norm (1990-the present). That does not mean, of course, that trade secret is no longer used,or that patents weren't sought prior to 1975; it simply means that there have been trends in intellectual property law usage.

In any case, these legal approaches are all very different from one another. Specifically, some of them are focused on intellectual creations rather than just basic information. In this book, we have divided information theft into two topics: the theft of data and the theft of software. These legal approaches are all applicable to pursuing cases of theft of software, since software is an intellectually creative endeavor. But they are less applicable to the theft of data. Data, for the most part, can neither be patented nor copyrighted, although it can be and often is treated as a trade secret.

Interestingly, none of these approaches are relevant when the method of software development chosen is "open source" since that movement does not believe in intellectual property ownership. Open source does have something similar to, and in fact the opposite of, copyright protection: CopyLeft protection. We will return to this subject in a bit.

An interesting dispute has arisen regarding the effect of such legal protection on creativity. Some say that this protection supports the creator in the sense that it allows profit from the creator's work, a strong motivating factor that leads to further creation. Others say the opposite: Protecting such information prevents others from being as creative as they might otherwise be if they were not fettered by such laws. The dispute is as old as innovation. In Wagner (2004), for example, we see that the same dispute was alive and well 120 years ago. Thomas Edison, still today one of the largest patent holders in the United States, had filed 1093 patents on his various discoveries. Opponents' questions ranged from the validity of the things he patented to derision of the U.S. Patent Office as "underqualified" to judge Edison's work. The then new-fangled thing called the "light bulb" raised what the article called a "swirl of controversy." Was this really an original discovery, or was Edison relying on the work of others to the extent that his contribution was minimal? Was it significant enough that issuing a patent for it really mattered? Did the patent office know enough to pass judgment on these issues?

Regardless of such disputes and their historic relevance, we will discuss intellectual property protection approaches here because they are immediately relevant to preventing dark side theft of information.

In the following sections, we spend a bit of time on each of these intellectual property protection approaches. Be aware, however, that if this is a matter of deep concern to you, there is no substitute for legal advice. Our discussion, in the context of software engineering and dark side matters, is superficial and inadequate for legal protection compared to the advice that a qualified attorney will be able to give. (It is also important to note that not just any attorney will do; intellectual property protection specialization is vital in any attorney you engage over these matters.)

4.4.1 Trade Secret Protection

What Is a Trade Secret?   For something to be considered a trade secret, the information must be secret in the first place. If it is known to the public, it is usually not considered to be "secret" anymore. Even if it is not known to the public, but it is known to most of the employees of a company, the court might deny that it was still a "secret." However, there are important exceptions: Genovese, in the prior case study of the Microsoft code theft, was sentenced to two years in prison because he sold parts of Windows source code—even if the source code was circulated on hacker message boards and was hence previously available to the public.

Generally, a trade secret is defined as business information generally not known in the trade, used in secrecy, that affords a competitive advantage. State law governs trade secret law in the United States; this definition may vary from state to state, but the following conditions are generally part of any such law.

To utilize trade secret protection, its owner must

- restrict access to the protected information,
- have users sign restrictive licenses,
- place proprietary and confidentiality notices on all materials, and
- have employees sign nondisclosure and trade secret acknowledgement agreements.

The owner of the information should be aware that if it is disclosed, trade secret protection is lost.

Source code and confidential data can be trade secrets from a legal point of view. In main stream language, however, we may think more often of trade secrets as something more narrowly defined than just data or source code. Examples of trade secrets (in main stream language) could be algorithms, details of an agreement, or the design of a new product.

A classical example of a trade secret would be a list of clients. Departing employees who take with them a business book of clients are the nightmare of all companies and a frequent topic in blogs on stolen trade secrets.

Client Lists Misappropriated by Departing Employees.   If the list of clients is very long, it can only be misappropriated by obviously illegal means: The departing employee can take media such as CDs or flash drives out of the office building, usually shortly before he or she quits the job. Other ways of sneaking the data out are e-mail or network access from computers outside of the office building. All these ways can be controlled by the company—in principle. Some bloggers suggest, for example, that employers should check the pockets of leaving employees, not allowing memory sticks and other media being to be brought out of the office building.

In principle this sounds reasonable, but we, the authors, have no experience in regards to how this policy could work in practice. If a company wants to prevent an employee from getting a memory stick out of the office building, it will need to apply similar detection methods to those applied to prevent material from being taken into or out of prisons. How should we imagine this "checking of pockets" in practice? What if, for example, 150 employees are fired on short notice?

If the list of clients is shorter, say 20 or 50 clients, it is more difficult to find convincing arguments that the list was really a "trade secret." In the auto industry, for example, there are only a small number of car manufacturers. They maintain business relations with a limited number of suppliers of components such as car batteries or bulbs. These lists of supplier companies are quite short and are likely not considered secret. Everybody in the industry knows them. Nevertheless, details of certain agreements can still be secret. This is shown in the case study of Lopez (found later in this book) where Volkswagen paid a one-billion dollar fine to General Motors in relation to espionage regarding such agreements.

Another problem surfaces if the departing employee memorizes the secret data (for example, the list of clients). Or if the employee just happens to know the clients, without making a special memorizing effort. In many cases, this "misappropriation by memory" can be prevented only if the "memory" was considered in the initial working contract. One possible solution is to forbid the employees to work for competitors for a certain time—so-called non-compete clauses (NCC).

What type of noncompete clauses are allowed depend on the legislation. California, in the United States, for example, invalidates noncompete clauses for all but equity stakeholders in businesses (California Business and Professional Code ¶16600, 16601). In Germany, the employee must be reimbursed during the time of any such restriction. If the employee does not receive at least half of his or her former average salary (including all bonuses), the clause is not valid. This mandatory legal obligation of reimbursment makes the non-competition clause quite expensive for the employer and seriously restricts their flexibility.

In other cases, when the departing employee is not reimbursed, it becomes quite complex. The non-compete clause has the effect that the employee cannot continue his profession because virtually all potential employers could be considered "competitors." How should he earn his living in this time of non-competition?

After all—to whom "belongs" the client?

Some bloggers complain that the departing employees think that somehow "the clients belong to them, not to the former employer." And in many cases, the new employer pays a new employee according to "how much business follows them."

It is hard to say to whom the clients really "belong" from a moral point of view. If you ask the clients, they would probably answer that they were not aware of "belonging" to anybody. If a sales representative has for many years carefully managed relations to "his clients," the clients might "feel" closer to the sales representative than to the anonymous organization he or she represents.

4.4.2 Copyright Protection

Copyright is a legal method used to protect copies of an original work fixed in any tangible medium of expression (such as source code listings or media of some sort).

Copyright protection, in the United States at least, is afforded by a collection of copyright laws.

To use copyright protection, the owner must

- place a copyright notice on the published version of the material,

- register with the United States Copyright Office (this must be done at least before any infringement suit is filed), and

- deposit copies of the protected material with the Library of Congress (since doing this voids trade secret protection, there is some provision for making a partial deposit).

Note that the key words for copyright protection include "original work" and "fixed in a tangible medium." The protection covers not the ideas behind what is being copyrighted, but the expression of those ideas in the media. Most books and similar writings, for example, are copyrighted. If the owner so desires, software source code can also be copyrighted. Information in the form of data would almost never be copyrighted.

4.4.3 Patent Protection

A patent is an official document granting an inventor the exclusive right to make, use, and sell an invention for a limited period of time.

Patent protection is based (in the United States) on the Constitution and enabling federal laws, but the notion of patent is worldwide. Note that patents are intended to cover inventions. It is the inventive idea that is patented, for example, whereas the representation of the idea might be copyrighted. The differences between these forms of intellectual property protection are subtle, but their impact is profound.

Patent protection is a very old form of intellectual property protection. However, its use in the software field has been fairly recent. The delay was partly because the patent process can be lengthy and laborious and costly (it frequently takes several years) and partly because it was not clear for a long time whether software products were really "inventions." Early on in the computing field, patents were thought to be relevant only to hardware, for example, but not applicable to software. Also, expertise in matters of software, a very new field, was seriously missing from the patent office people who would need to judge the patentability of a product.

Here is an example regarding the role of expertise: According to Wagner (2004), a suit was filed against Microsoft by a company named Eolas Technologies. The suit claimed that Eolas had patented some ways of doing Web page plug-ins that Microsoft had appropriated for its own products, specifically Internet Explorer. The patent office had to dig deep to come up with a judgment. But it finally disagreed, noting that the work that Eolas had patented was based on pre-existing work, having been originated by Tim Berners-Lee a decade or so before. (Note also that the patent office may have made a mistake in accepting that original patent, but its litigation processes allowed it to correct that mistake when it really mattered.)

4.4.4   Steganography

In the previous sections of this chapter, we presented methods of protecting intellectual property by using appropriate parts of the law. Here we present something rather different, something that involves hiding such material rather than physically or legally protecting it.

Steganography is a method of hiding secret data in apparently innocent files (such as in images). Here is a fictitious example: A secret message is hidden in an image. Each bit of the message is mapped to one pixel of the image. If the bit of the message is a "0," then the pixel of the image is changed to an even number; if the next bit of the message is a "1," the pixel is changed to an odd number. In this way, each pixel of the image can hide a single bit of the secret message. The result will be a slightly "blurred" image, but the changes can hardly be seen.

Real steganography uses advanced mathematics to hide the secret data—something that is beyond the scope of this book. However, for a first understanding of the principles the fictitious example suffices. There have been a few cases published where employees used steganography to actually steal (leak out) data (for example, in apparently innocent images of colleagues or social events). It is interesting, then, that this approach can be used either to protect data by hiding it or to steal data (again) by hiding it. In fact, there are stories to the effect that terrorists have used this approach to transmit secret messages.

This is not a commonly-used approach, for either purpose. It is not easy to use, it requires specific software which may be considered to be illegitimate, and only rather small amounts of data can be hidden.

4.5   OPEN VERSUS CLOSED SOURCE

Open source software is software that is freely and openly available in source code form. Closed source software, by contrast, is proprietary to the company that produced it, with efforts being made to prevent the source code from being visible outside the company.

Most of the previous discussion of intellectual property protection, as you might imagine and as we have previously stated, is irrelevant to the subject of open source. It is not secret, so trade secret protection does not and cannot apply. Its creators do not copyright it, so there is no notion of copyright protection. And, similarly, patent protection is never sought.

Interestingly, the open source community, concerned about things related to intellectual property protection, has defined something it calls the CopyLeft process. (The name is cutely chosen; if copyright is a protection offered to closed source code, then CopyLeft would be the comparable method for open source code!)

CopyLeft, according to Wikipedia, is a copyright licensing scheme in which an author surrenders some but not all rights under copyright law. Instead of allowing a work to fall completely into the public domain (where no copyright restrictions are imposed), CopyLeft allows an author to impose some, but not all, copyright restrictions on those who want to engage in activities that would otherwise be considered copyright infringement. Under CopyLeft, copyright infringement can be avoided if the would-be infringer perpetuates the same CopyLeft scheme. For this reason CopyLeft licenses are also known as "reciprocal" or "viral" licenses.

Our earlier discussion of the misappropriation of Windows and of Cisco source code opens the door to discussing the general topic of open versus closed source code security: whether open source code (such as Linux) is more or less secure than proprietary "closed source" code (such as Windows and Cisco). Here is a summary of the arguments of the both camps.

- The advocates of closed source argue that hackers may use access to the (open) source code of an operating system to search more efficiently and completely for vulnerabilities. For this reason, an operating system based on closed source should be more secure.

- The advocates of open source argue that source code being available to the public allows many experts to read, test, and validate the code. For this reason, an operating system based on open source should be more secure.

The above considerations are meant to help the reader form his or her own opinion:

In many cases, it is possible to reconstruct portions of the source code from the compiled "executables." So, the hacker can find vulnerabilities also in this "recompiled" source. This solution is possible, and it has been done. However, the process of reverse engineering is anything but perfect and the quality of the resulting source code is significantly lower than the original. Having access to the original source code provides the attacker with a whole new class of attack, especially if the hacker gains access to the source code of systems that are important for security (such as operating systems or network security).

The notion of open software may seem recent to younger members of the software profession. However, in the early days of the field (1950s–1960s), all software was free and, for the most part, open. It did not occur to anyone in the software field for perhaps a decade into its existence that there could be a market for software.

All software during that time was "bundled" with hardware; when you bought a computer you bought the software that came with it.

It took a federal antitrust lawsuit in the 1960s against IBM, the dominant computer manufacturer of the time, to create a market for software. IBM lost the antitrust case and was forced to "unbundle" software, so that the computer hardware buyer could buy their software from another source if they chose. Initially, few computer buyers chose to do so, and the market for software—and the existence of software companies—was very slow to take shape.

During that time, most computer manufacturers and/or their users had "user groups." In those user groups, software was freely shared. The SHARE organization of users of IBM mainframe computers, for example, had an elaborate catalog of software offerings available to IBM customers, and it was in fact considered an honor to have software code you had written offered (free) there! Thus the notion of free and open software is a very old one, and the notion of proprietary and closed software is, by contrast, relatively recent!

The number of vulnerabilities found in both open source and proprietary code does not seem to support the "security by obscurity" claim of closed source systems: Windows does not appear to have fewer vulnerabilities than Linux.

Sidebar: Security Through Obscurity in Crypto Systems

Crypto systems face a similar security problem to that of operating systems: If the crypto algorithm is known to the public, attackers have more efficient ways to find flaws and weak points in it. A published algorithm, on the other hand, allows for many mathematicians to study and validate the algorithm. If none of them found a flaw, the algorithm should be considered "safe."

In crypto systems, the discussion about "security through obscurity" is older and more mature than in operating systems. In 1883 Auguste Kerckhoffs expressed a principle which is now known as "Kerckhoffs' Law." This principle states that a crypto system should be secure if everything about the system—except the key—is public knowledge. This law has been restated (perhaps independently) by Claude Shannon as "the enemy knows the system." Among cryptographers, "Shannon's maxim" is widely embraced while only a few generally accepted systems use "security through obscurity."

Security Concerns ... or Simply Economic Interests? Some authors suspect that economic interests might be a stronger argument for the nondisclosure of the source versus security considerations: Closed source simply stabilizes a certain position in the market better than open source, where each competitor can read the source code and learn from it.

Studying the source code may reveal secret algorithms. In some cases, the owner of the source code can protect these algorithms by some kind of intellectual property protection approach, as discussed previously.

In conclusion of our chapter on the theft of information, we are providing you with one last example.

Google's Algorithms. Large portions of the inner workings of Google's search engine are not disclosed. The reasons may include this one: By not disclosing the algorithms, it is more difficult for other software companies to develop competitive search technology. Another reason might be that knowing details of the underlying algorithms makes it easier for tricksters to manipulate the position of their page in the search results. Notice, there are entire books on search engine optimization (SEO) that deal with the question how a few subtle details of a Web page can significantly influence the "ranking of the page" in the "organic search results." Google and the other search engines consider quite a few of these strategies illegitimate "black hat SEO". By keeping the details of the algorithms undisclosed, Google makes it more difficult for "black hats" to exploit details of the algorithm.

CHAPTER 5

ESPIONAGE

This topic is included in our book primarily because you can't exclude it. The topic is too romantic, well-publicized, and perhaps even glamorous in some highly-fictionalized cases.

We don't have a lot to say from a software project point of view. In fact, neither of us has encountered any significant amount of espionage—"spying" in the popular lingo—on the projects with which we have been involved. Perhaps that's because espionage doesn't happen very often, or perhaps it's because it does happen and the spies who do it are clever enough not to let us know they are doing it. One of us authors has worked with a lot of businesses, including banking, and the other has worked primarily in defense industries. Both are areas where one might expect espionage to happen, and we suspect that there is not very much espionage happening in the software project world.

Nevertheless, we bravely tackle the topic here, with a few case studies to describe episodes where espionage is known to have happened:

5.1 INTRODUCTION

Espionage in History, Culture, and Fiction. Spying has a long history. Spies are mentioned in the oldest parts of the bible some thirty-five hundred years ago:

When the Israelites left Egypt and arrived at the Jordan River they selected 12 spies, one leader from each ancestral tribe. The spies were to explore the Promised Land, Canaan (Moses 4: 13–14). But they came back with bad news: They reported the overwhelming military and economic strength of Canaan. The spies were so deeply impressed that they even reported erroneous "facts," that is, of giants who were allegedly living there. Moses was disappointed by the fear of the Israelites and the spies of trust in the Lord. So he decided to delay the attack for the famous 40 years in the desert.

When the Israelite army finally attacked Caanan under their leader Joshua, they sent spies to the town of Jericho (Joshua 2:1–7). Rahab, a prostitute in Jericho, helped the spies in a crucial situation: She hid them in her house when local authorities came searching. Rahab's house was built into the city wall so the spies could easily escape. In turn, the Israelites promised to spare Rahab and her family in the military action that was to come. Without Rahab's support the spies' mission would have probably failed.

The military action was a complete success. The Israelites massacred the residents of Jericho and killed "everything that is breathing"—one of the earliest reported genocides in human history. Nevertheless, they kept their promise and spared Rahab, who had marked her window with a red cord, so that her house could easily be spotted by the Israelite army. After the attack, Rahab retired from her business, she married an Israelite and became a respected woman in Israel. The New Testament contains some hints that she might have been in the line of King David's and Jesus' ancestors (Matthew 1:5).

Intelligence gathering is probably even older and was most likely used in almost all wars in human history. Most of this time, however, the broader public was not much aware of the existence of spies. This lack of awareness stems from the very nature of their work: secrecy and stealth. In the last century, a number of novels and films have been dedicated to spies, and brought awareness of this profession into the mass media.

Among the most prominent is Ian Fleming's fictional character James Bond. He is an extraordinarily skilled super-spy. During the cold war James Bond loyally served Her Majesty, the Queen of England, and finished a number of successful and impressive missions against the Soviet Union. Fleming gave James Bond the code name "007," which matches the international phone prefix for Russia. But there is a long list of other spy movies and novels. Many of them feature "gray loners" in the role of the spy—very different from the handsome, sociable, and seducing James Bond. They are frequently in the role of something like a private investigator. One of these different fictional spies is John le Carré's character George Smiley. He is a more realistic figure—an imperfect, finite human. Sometimes George Smiley is considered the "anti-Bond."

5.2 WHAT IS ESPIONAGE?

Espionage, according to the dictionary, is spying by one government on another. Such spying can take many forms; in general, it is an attempt to obtain information important to one government and from another, in some sense competing, government. Although the dictionary seems to make it clear that spying is a government activity, the term has been borrowed, over the years, to cover one company spying on another. In this context, it is called industrial espionage.

This chapter of our book will focus on both types of espionage. But, inevitably, most of our case studies will be about industrial espionage, because governments are normally reluctant to talk about governmental espionage, and it takes a particularly egregious case to rise to the level where citizens (or authors of books!) might become aware of it.

It was interesting (and, in fact, important!) to us as authors to make a clear distinction between the topics of hacking, information theft, and espionage. At first they seemed to be distinct entities, easy to discuss separately. But the more case studies we became aware of, the more the lines of demarcation began to blur.

Hacking, in the public eye at least, is about mischief-makers who want to cause harm to the systems they invade. But more recently, hackers are motivated by profit and steal information which they can then resell. In that sense, the line between hacking and information theft is obscured.

Similarly, the line between information theft and espionage is blurred. Spies are obviously seeking to steal information. Here, however, their motive is more often to help another entity—a government or an industry—than to make money themselves. But, of course, that distinction is not always the case. Some spies steal information to make a profit on it from their target entity, just like the ordinary information thief or the profit-oriented hacker.

In the end, we have made some somewhat arbitrary choices in allocating our case studies to the categories in which you will find them. There is a justification for the choices we have made, but it may not always be obvious to the reader—or among the authors!—as to what that justification is. Still, this is our book, so please forgive us these arbitrary decisions!

5.3 CASE STUDIES

In many reports on cyber attacks, we read something like this: The attack was traced back to the IP address of a server that is based in country X—e.g., China. The authors of these reports seem to conclude that the government of country X encouraged the attack or was even involved. We doubt that this conclusion is valid.

In the Cisco anecdote told in the chapter on theft of information, the attacker was an Uppsala-based Swedish citizen. The snippets of the source code appeared on a Russian server. According to all published evidence, no Russian citizens were involved, nor was the Russian government.

It is widely known that hackers have "armies" of compromised computers, the so called "zombie computers" or "botnets." The hacker has access with privileges to these computers, that is, similar to a system administrator. Some hackers control hundreds of thousands (!) of zombies and use them for illegal purposes. Each of our computers could be affected—unless you are an expert on network security. Therefore, it is easy for a hacker to host illegitimate files on a computer of institutions or innocent people—people who do not have the faintest idea that their computer is being abused for illegal purposes.

Another possibility that enables espionage is sites that offer free web hosting. Frequently, these sites have little surveillance of the uploaded content, except perhaps obviously illegal content such as child pornography and terrorism. Another possibility is the message boards visited by hackers. Anyone could post to these message boards. It does not matter in which country the server is based.

In April, 2007, during the military conflict between Russia and Estonia, servers in Estonia were attacked. It appears that some of the servers that controlled the attack were based in the United States. For political and other reasons, it is extremely unlikely that the U.S. government supported any cyber-attack against Estonia while Estonia was in a military conflict with Russia. Hence, this observation makes clear one fact: Conclusions from the geographic position of a server in relation to the responsibility of a certain government are rather doubtful. That is, "The controlling server of a certain attack was based in country X. So, there is some evidence that the government of X is somehow involved in the attack." Statements of this kind are rather doubtful.

Another viewpoint is that consumer targeted attacks are frequently related to Russian or Eastern European sites. The traces of industrial espionage, military, or government targeted attacks seem to lead to China. In some cases, there are additional indications. This was the case in the attack against the Dalai Lama: The Chinese government did political and administrative analysis ("in the real world") that can hardly be explained without illegitimate access to the Dalai Lama's e-mails.

We came across one case study that is primarily about government espionage. (Note, however, that it does cross the somewhat blurry border into the industrial espionage area.) That study is found below as Section 5.3.1. Additionally, as we have said, espionage case studies are usually about purely industrial espionage. Section 5.3.2 and subsequent sections are an interesting collection of those.

5.3.1   Sweden Versus Russia

Superficially, this is a story about the Swedish company Ericsson, an organization prominent in the electronic products area. In this case, however, there were overriding government implications. The product in question was the computer-based guidance system for Sweden's Gripen fighter plane, the primary strike fighter of Sweden, a fact that made it of interest to certain foreign powers.

As the story begins in 2002, two Ericsson employees and one former employee are taken into custody on charges of having distributed secret documents to a foreign power. Then the matter spreads: Two additional employees are suspended under similar charges. For a time, although the matter was of some concern, it appeared that the incident might not have been particularly serious. None of the employees were particularly senior and therefore they might not have accessed terribly important documents.

But what happened next entailed a serious escalation of the matter: Sweden expelled two Russian diplomats who, the government said, were *directly linked* to the case. In typical diplomatic tit-for-tat fashion, Russia then expelled two Swedish diplomats. But just as the matter seemed to be turning serious, a cloak descended. We don't know what happened next, but we do know that Sweden and Russia now have a satisfactory diplomatic relationship!

5.3.2   Shekhar Verma

The Massachusetts-based Dassault Systèmes company SolidWorks develops and markets mechanical design software solutions. Since 1996, SolidWorks has been cooperating with Mumbai-based Geometric Software Solutions Company, an organization that develops add-on software products and provides project services for 3D modeling software such as SolidWorks.

Around 2000, Geometric received the source code of SolidWorks for debugging purposes. Shekhar Verma, an employee of Geometric, left the company in June

2002 and took the source code (valued at $60 million) with him. Verma offered the code for sale to SolidWorks's competitors. One of them was fair enough to tell SolidWorks that their source code was for sale. They informed law enforcement authorities; an undercover FBI agent met Verma in a five-star hotel in New Delhi, India, pretending he wanted to buy the code for $200,000.

The cooperation between American and Indian law enforcement authorities led to the arrest of Verma. Little is known about the results of the lawsuit. In 2006, four years after the case happened, blogs appeared on the Internet to the effect that Verma was still not convicted, still free, and still working as a software developer, a circumstance that demonstrated the inefficient working of the Indian legal system.

5.3.3   Lineage III

In April 2007, the Korean newspaper *Digital Chosunilbo* reported that the game producer NCsoft might have been a victim of theft of source code regarding their new game Lineage III. The Korean police suspects seven former NCsoft employees of having demonstrated the source code to an unnamed Japanese game producer during a job interview. The police suspected that the source code might have been copied illegally during this demonstration.

Johann has worked in Romania's software industry. He has heard rumors of Romanian software developers who demonstrated source code that they developed for former employers, during job interviews, on a regular basis.

5.3.4   GM versus VW: Jose Ignacio Lopez

In 1993, Jose Ignacio Lopez, the purchasing chief of car manufacturer General Motors (GM), joined competitor Volkswagen (VW) where he took a similar position. Shortly before Lopez left GM, he extracted a lot of material from the GM purchasing database and took the print-outs with him to Volkswagen. There, he employed an assistant who keyed the data into the VW database.

GM had a log system in place that recorded all accesses to the database. Analysis of these log files revealed the unusual usage pattern of accessing large amounts of data in a short period of time. This suspicion of "illegitimate data collection" initiated further investigations by law enforcement authorities. They interviewed the assistant who keyed in the data and found the evidence necessary to file a law suit. After a lengthy legal procedure, the case was finally settled with an agreement between GM and VW in 1997: VW was ordered to pay a $100 million fine and was required to buy car parts from GM worth $1 billion.

5.3.5   British Midland Tools

British Midland Tools is an engineering company in the automotive tools industry based in Tamworth near Birmingham, Great Britain. In 2004, several staff members left British Midland Tools and joined Midland International Tooling Ltd. (MIT), a company that began to offer services similiar to those of British Midland Tools only a few weeks after the former staff members had left.

There were suspicions that the former British Midland Tools staff members had taken blueprints with them when they left and joined MIT. British Midland Tools began a legal action and obtained a search order. During the raid, the blueprints in question were found, but the address blocks were deleted. There was no obvious evidence regarding the origin of the blueprints.

The blueprints were maintained using the engineering drawing software AutoCad.

The deleted address blocks of British Midland Tools were found in the blueprints with the assistance of a consulting company that specialized on forensic computing. (But these address blocks had been replaced by the address of MIT, of course.) However, the internal data management of this specific CAD system also records information on data that has been deleted. Further analysis of MIT's system revealed two pages of the quality manual of British Midland Tools in the slack space on the hard disk—data that should not have been there.

5.3.6 Solid Oak Software

It is well-known that various world governments (for example, Iran, China, and Germany) filter Internet content to restrict certain kinds of materials (e.g., sexually explicit content) from their people. The California-based Solid Oak Software produces software for performing this filtering. Like most (closed source) companies, the way Solid Oak Software does what it does is considered proprietary, and the company jealously guards its code to make sure that it cannot be used competitively by others.

However, there is a China-based company called Jinhui Computer System Engineering that produces a similar program; such a program is being used by the Chinese government for their filtering activities. And—the plot thickens—Jinhui was accused by Solid Oak of stealing portions of its code. The portions in question have to do with a list of terms to be blocked, instructions for updating the software as new restrictions are created, and an old news bulletin that actually promotes the Solid Oak software!

Solid Oak was able to obtain a copy of the Jinhui source code after receiving an anonymous email containing the charges of theft, and researchers at the University of Michigan have conducted the analysis that led to the discovery of the apparent thefts. For their part, Jinhui denies the theft, saying "that's impossible." But a Solid Oak spokesperson is "99.99% certain" that the code in question has been stolen. The matter grew in financial importance as China's date for requiring such software on all personal computers sold in the country neared (the date for the filters to be in place was July 2009). Because the computers in question are sold only in China, the matter is one for Chinese, not American, law to resolve.

As of the writing of this book, the matter had not been resolved. Often, in cases of this kind, even if there is a resolution, it usually emerges from an out-of-court settlement and includes the provision that the terms of the settlement cannot be disclosed. Thus the resolution may never be publicly known.

5.3.7 Proctor & Gamble versus Unilever

The next example is a classic industrial espionage case that involves many aspects the public has come to expect from such cases: private investigators, dumpster diving, and a subsequent lawsuit.

This case "exploded" into public attention in 2001 when it was discovered that private investigators hired by Proctor & Gamble (P&G) had sifted through garbage outside the offices of Unilever, a prime competitor. The significance of this dumpster diving was that the two companies known to be competing in the hair shampoo market: P&G was aware that Unilever had some serious plans afoot in that area, particularly involving bidding for the Clairol hair care brand that was up for auction at the time.

What happened next? P&G won the competition for Clairol. But around the same time, P&G executives became aware of the espionage action that (they say) violated the internal ethics guidelines of the company. Did Unilever find out first and threaten to file suit, or did P&G confess to the matter and "come clean"? Eventually, both events happened, but in the murkiness of the surrounding story it is hard to be sure which came first.

P&G did respond to Unilever's threat of a lawsuit (which, according to news reports of the time, would have been for "tens of millions of dollars" in restitution) and agreed to negotiate. Unlike so many others stories of this type in our book, we know how this one came out: P&G made an out-of-court settlement worth some $10 million.

5.3.8 News Corp Versus Vivendi

This case study is about encryption, perhaps the ultimate in espionage defensive activities. As the story began in 2002, a subsidiary of Vivendi, the French pay-TV company called Canal Plus Technologies, had made allegations against NDS, a UK-based technology firm owned at the 80% level by News Corporation (News Corp).

Both Canal Plus and NDS use encryption technologies to prevent competitors or even customers from accessing their encoded programming. But the two encryption schemes are different. In the allegations, Canal Plus charged that NDS hired a team of scientists to crack its code, which the crackers then intended to circulate to hackers who would put the scheme onto a publicly-accessible website.

If you think that was complicated, what was to happen next was even more so. NDS refuted the claim, and the two companies prepared to go to court. However, before that could happen, a bigger business deal came into play: News Corp bought an Italian TV company from Canal Plus, and at that point, apparently as part of that deal, Canal Plus dropped the lawsuit.

5.3.9 Spying: Was A TI Chip Really Stolen by a French Spy?

This may well be one of the strangest espionage stories in the history of the computing field. It involves spies, lawsuits, a mysterious out-of-court settlement, and actual companies that we have all heard about.

The story was originally reported in the *Wall Street Journal* and retold in Glass (1999, pages 124–127), where the citation to the original article can be found. In that story, the companies and people involved were actually named, so we can talk specifically about who did what to whom, who was accused of doing what to whom. Additionally, we can wonder, in the end, about what happened to the whos and the whats.

The subject of the story is a computer chip. The two companies involved were Texas Instruments (TI) and the French company Machines Bull (Bull). The contention in the story, and the beginnings of the espionage story, center on who originally invented that chip: TI says it did. Back in 1974, it said, a TI engineer named Michael Cochran invented this chip, and TI began using it in a variety of applications, including automotive applications with a widespread usage. But Bull says it invented the chip.

The company said the chip was invented by a Bull employee in France named Michel Ugon. To complicate matters, Bull actually patented the chip (in 1978), whereas TI had not.

It's time for the plot to thicken. Around 1976, TI hired an engineer from France, Jean Pierre Dolait, who worked his way up at TI and eventually, by 1989, was European marketing director for semiconductors for TI, based in Nice, France. About that same time, someone mailed a package from an IBM plant in France to … well, we'd tell you to whom the package was mailed, but the label had come off and it had to be returned to the sender at IBM. And when it was returned, IBM was shocked to find that it contained highly sensitive IBM technical documents.

They called in the FBI. The subsequent FBI investigation led to the realization, at least the American companies and the FBI said, that France had spies operating in several American companies that were shipping secret materials to French contacts. And, the FBI said, the spy inside TI was Dolait. The FBI questioned him and learned enough to believe that he had been feeding information to Bull from TI for 13 years. TI immediately fired Dolait for spying.

But the plot isn't finished thickening! Time passed, and (apparently) sufficient parts of the story were forgotten. Bull found that around 1991 a chip it was using was in use at TI. Bull negotiated with TI, which didn't at first make any connection to the espionage activity, and were close to reaching a settlement when it began to dawn on TI that the widespread usage of the chip was going to lead to a huge payoff to Bull. According to the story, negotiations broke down and Bull filed suit.

Big mistake! Emboldened by the need to fight the lawsuit, TI began doing research into the questionable chip, and found that it was indeed of its own design. TI had not patented the chip at the time, it said, because it didn't want to disclose its capabilities, which would have been necessary in a patent application. Dolait, TI said, had access to the chip, and would have been the spy who stole it.

Stories involving lawsuits often get very murky by their ending, and that was certainly the case here. What usually happens—what the legal systems want to happen—is that the two parties settle the case out of court. But the murkiness comes from the fact that most such settlements preclude either party from disclosing the terms of the settlement. In other words, we know that the problem has gone away (the case was settled in 1995, just before the original *Wall Street Journal* article was published), but we don't know if anyone was really guilty of anything.

So ... was their really espionage here? And did it result in the theft of someone's computing product? We actually don't have the answers to those questions. But it's certainly true, if you read the original story and follow its implications, that all the elements of an honest-to-goodness spying case were present. The original *Wall Street Journal* article says that if the case didn't involve espionage, it was at least a case of massive "bureaucratic bumbling."

5.3.10   Conficker

The Conficker story is a highly visible one. To this day, there have been many reports in the popular and computing press about it. But it is also a very murky one. Unlike most of our other espionage case studies, it is not at all clear who is trying to do what to whom! Is it even a case of espionage? We'll let you think about that as we proceed to tell the Conficker story.

Conficker (also known as Downup, Downadup, and Kido) is a computer worm that targets Windows operation systems. It was first discovered in November 2008. Then five new versions (named Conficker A, B, C, D, and E) appeared.

Conficker applies some advanced technological features:

- The download of new versions and payload is done using peer-to-peer technology. As such, the worm does not have to access a central server. Instead, the attackers can upload a new version to any infected computer. This method makes it extremely difficult to trace back any new version to the worm's authors.

- The payload of the worm is digitally signed. This method prevents other hackers from reusing the core of Conficker and adding their own payload.

- Conficker has a sophisticated self defense: It cripples anti-virus programs and deactivates other security parameters.

Most of these technical features have been seen before: Many malware attacks use methods of auto defense one way or another. Peer-to-peer technology is not new, either: BitTorrent clients (like uTorrent) apply this method, and many people use it on a regular basis (for example, when downloading movies). Digital signatures have been applied routinely for decades.

What makes defense against Conficker more difficult is the fact that all these technologies are used together in a single worm. Conficker uses rather new and advanced versions of these technologies. The author(s) of the worm did not make any major mistake; they did not leave any gap for defense. This adds to the reasons why it is rather difficult to respond to the Conficker threat. At the time of this writing, it is not fully understood from a technical point of view. Additionally, the leading experts in computer security do not have a clear strategy on how to respond to this threat.

A number of facts make Conficker different from other computer worms. One of them is its success. The estimates for the number of infected computers range between 2 million and 12 million. The owner(s) of Conficker have system administrator privileges on these computers. The worm connects the infected computer to a so-called botnet. In this way, Conficker can control all of the millions of computers like a single system. The computing and communication power of this botnet easily outperforms the most powerful computing centers in the world. Due to its sophisticated self defense, it is anything but easy to clean an infected computer again—even if it is known that the system is infected. According to published reports, quite a number of well protected systems have been infected, including the network of an Air France base.

One of the most interesting facts about Conficker is that no one really knows who is behind the attack, who are the authors of the worm, and what they want to achieve. Botnets are not new. Organized criminals use them frequently to send spam messages or to launch distributed denial of service attacks. Conficker, however, has not done any real damage so far. It has not done anything that we would usually expect from malware such as sending spam messages or deleting files. It just spreads to as many computers as possible and installs its botnet software there.

One version of Conficker distributed some "scare-ware"—it distributed announcements from some alleged security companies, offering to clean the infected system for a fee. The announcements were phony, intending simply to gain the perpetrators access to more computers. The discovery of the scare-ware in April 2009 intensified discussions in the security community: Initial hopes were that a light could shed on the mystery of who is behind Conficker. This discussion, however, faded out because the connection between Conficker and the security company turned out to be doubtful. In sum, this distribution of scare-ware might be part of Conficker's strategy to confuse security experts. Meanwhile, many bloggers believe that the question about the authors of Conficker is still open. Some bloggers suspect organized crime might control the worm. If Conficker is really owned by organized crime, we should expect to see more attempts to take profit from it. After all, the black-market value of a botnet this large could be millions of American dollars. It is hard to imagine an organized criminal who can resist the temptation of making profits at this high of a value.

Sidebar: Rough Estimation of the Black-Market Value of Conficker's Botnet

The value of an infected computer covers a wide range. Some experts in cyber-warfare estimate the cost for infecting a large number of systems to be less than $1 per system. Spyware authors suggest systems that are infected for the first time cost more than $100. The black-market value for highly protected systems (such as in the core network of a French air base) are probably far beyond these numbers. The number of infected computers is not exactly known—most experts estimate several millions. No matter what numbers in this wide range we may choose, the black-market value of the Conficker botnet is many million dollars, perhaps even tens of million of dollars. Anyway, it is big business.

Other bloggers express the opinion that Conficker is the work of a single person or a small group of hackers. These persons might have been surprised and overwhelmed by their own success. Perhaps the hackers got scared of possible legal consequences and abandoned the worm.

Conficker's behavior differs from other malware we have seen so far. It is managed according to a new strategy. In addition, it is constructed very professionally from a technological point of view, without any major mistake that might open the door for defense. For these reasons, many bloggers suspect that government-sponsored intelligence might be involved in the development of Conficker. We have no idea which government might have sponsored the worm and for what reasons.

We, the authors, do not know who is behind Conficker. Intelligence agencies, however, might know. In a way, Conficker has an effect similar to a missile test: A country that was supposed to have no missiles suddenly launches a missile successfully. This test missile does not do any damage but falls in the ocean or in the middle of a desert. No one is hurt, nothing is destroyed. Most people don't even notice the launch of the missile. Those few who read it in the newspapers forget it after a few days. However, foreign intelligence that observes the launch on their satellite screens are on high alert.

Conficker might have a similar effect among cyber-warfare experts. If Conficker is really controlled by foreign intelligence, it is also a demonstration of power: "Look what we could do against you if we want to be bad. So, you'd better be nice to us."

Sidebar: Possible Scenarios of Large Botnets Controlled by Foreign Intelligence
Cyber-warfare is a rather new word in the long history of human conflict. So far, we have little experience with real cyber war. The following considerations are little more than science fiction:

Controlling such a large botnet could be quite attractive for an intelligence agency: The owner of the botnet has access to all data processed by the computer—all files, all e-mails, all web-surfing activities, the microphones and web cams connected to these systems, virtually everything. This data contains a lot of information for an intelligence agency: confidential economic and technical information, details about personal preferences, personal relations, perhaps even clues for possible ways to perform corruption and blackmail. And this data is available from a huge number of infected systems.

Botnets could be important in possible future cyber wars. Controlling so many computers could cause huge destruction. Controlling a huge botnet is in some ways equivalent to installing nuclear missiles. They are not in use—at the moment. Their coordinates and codes are top secret. They are just there, demonstrating power and waiting patiently for the time when their owners consider their use necessary.

5.4   CYBER WARFARE

And all of that brings us to the subject of cyber-warfare, perhaps the ultimate subject in computing espionage. Cyber-warfare is a rather new way of going to war. However, in some of the more recent military conflicts, cyber-warfare methods were applied or considered.

Iraq 2003.   In 2003 the CIA prepared plans for a cyber attack against Iraq. The plans included steps to block Saddam Hussein's bank accounts and cripple the country's financial system. In the end, these plans were canceled because the United

States was worried about high collateral damage. There was the risk that the banking systems of other countries in the Middle East might collapse or, even worse, the world's entire financial system might suffer damages. If these plans had been put into place, they would have constituted the biggest cyber sabotage ever.

Estonian Cyber War.   During the military conflict between Russia and Estonia, cyber-warfare methods were used. The attacks began on April 27, 2007 and swamped Web sites of Estonian organizations, including the site of the Estonian parliament. Eventually, the attacks were traced back to Russian botnets. The Russian government denied having anything to do with these attacks. This may or may not be true.

The botnets in question are known to be controlled by organized crime and are rented on a routine basis (such as for sending spam messages). So it is hard to say to what extent the owners of the botnets (the so-called "herders") were advised and coordinated by Russian intelligence. Some experts are of the opinion that the attack was too large to have been conducted completely without the support of government and large telecommunication companies. Others, however, think that some botnet herders with patriotic feelings conducted this attack without any government support; they did it purely based on informal peer-to-peer communication.

Estonia is by far less dependent on the Internet than other countries such as those in North America or Western Europe. This is true for both every day life and the control of important infrastructure. So the attacks were more of a nuisance and did not have a dramatic impact: The Estonian authorities had to host their sites at large providers abroad, and online communication with their citizens was made more difficult. Nothing worse happened.

Even if the impact of the cyber war in real life were rather limited, the attacks caused a lot of interest among cyberwar experts because it was one of the first examples of using the methods of cyber-warfare during a military conflict.

Impact of Cyber Warfare and Defense: Collateral Damage.   The preparations for the cyber attack against Iraq showed that any kind of cyber war carries a high risk of collateral damage. Information technology and communication resources all over the world are so tightly knit that it is hardly possible to limit the effect of cyber attacks to the systems of a certain country. Due to this risk, a cyber war might be in conflict with international laws on warfare which request that collateral damages should be minimized.

Who Is the Attacker?   The few cases of cyber-warfare and attacks carried out by government sponsored intelligence demonstrate how difficult it is to trace back the attack with some reliability. According to the best information available to us, the authors, there have been no cases so far where the attacker could be identified without doubt. There are cases in which many security experts claim that they might have some more or less convincing "guesses" about the attacker. In all these cases, however, the blamed governments denied being involved. In other cases—such as Conficker—we have not read any technically sound explanation as to who might be behind the attack. This observation makes cyber-warfare very different from classical warfare, where there is usually little doubt as to who the attacker is.

Neutral Countries.   In traditional warfare, it is a major issue if a fighting army accesses resources based in neutral countries. This access usually requires diplomatic negotiations at the highest level. When defending a cyber attack, things might evolve so fast that the negotiations might not be possible anymore. During the attack, the situation might change in a few micro seconds, and there would simply be no time for calling the ambassador and asking permission to shut down a server in that country.

Privacy and Human Rights.   The development of cyber defense is only at its beginning. Governments in North America and Western Europe claim that any defense will conform to existing privacy laws and respect human rights. Some security experts, however, doubt that an efficient defense within these frameworks of law will be possible at all. As such, human rights activists are concerned about the serious limitations on privacy that might happen in the future.

REFERENCE

Glass, Robert L. *Computing Calamities*, Prentice-Hall, 1999.

CHAPTER **6**

DISGRUNTLED EMPLOYEES AND SABOTAGE

In most of this book, we have looked at dark side material from the point of view of dark side acts: subversion, lying, hacking, etc. But as we sought material relevant to those sections of the book, we kept running into something that didn't quite fit with that categorization. There were many anecdotes and studies about something that was orthogonal to those dark side acts. That "something" was the role of the disgruntled employee in dark side activities.

6.1   INTRODUCTION AND BACKGROUND

Disgruntled employees are plentiful in the computing and software business. The acts they commit may very well be categorized as we had intended—acts of subversion, hacking, lying—but what tied them together and demanded that we pay attention to them was the "who" of their activities, not so much the "what" that we had been using all along. The "who" disgruntled employee is making huge amounts of mischief in our field.

But how much mischief? A 2008 study, reported in Chickowski (2009) said that 55% of employees stole data/information from their employers when they left due to a layoff. That report even invented a term for the activity—"layoff theft," defined as "the tendency of laid off employees to steal company information."

There was other, similarly damning, data. A study in early 2009 by Michael G. Kessler & Associates, Ltd. found that 35% of the theft of proprietary information is perpetrated by discontented employees (note that these may have been laid off but they also may still be working for the company), 28% by outside hackers, 18% by other US companies, 11% by foreign companies, and 8% by foreign governments (the remaining 10% count as "miscellaneous"). A very similar 1999 study, conducted by the Computer Security Institute and the FBI, found that 55% of respondents reported malicious acts by insiders. The well-known Gartner Group estimates that 70% of unauthorized access to information systems is committed by employees (the word "disgruntled" does not appear in this data). Yet another FBI study says 65% of security breaches are by discontented and former employees.

Note that the data cited here is for slightly different things ("employees" versus "disgruntled employees" versus "former employees" versus "insiders") but that the numbers are surprisingly similar: Somewhere around 60–70% of data theft is conducted by these employees (disgruntled, former, or otherwise). That's an astonishingly high number.

There's another piece of data in these studies that raising an even more alarming specter. Eighty-two percent of the respondents to the study reported in Chickowski (2009) said that their employers would simply not be aware that their information had been stolen. The Kessler study reported that most of these incidents go unreported; for every one that is reported, the study showed 400 went unreported!

What does all of this add up to? The Kessler study reported "losses greater than $100 million." The 1999 Computer Crime and Security Survey puts the number at $124 million, and says that it (1999) was the third straight year that such losses had exceeded $100 million. Once again, the numbers are fairly consistent. Disgruntled (and other) employees are making companies pay a huge penalty.

What do these employees steal? Another research study notes that stolen data may include customer data, contact lists, employee records, financial reports, and a variety of other forms of intellectual property. Often, the study says, the data stolen is to help the disgruntled employee get a new job or start their own business.

So far, our book has taken the point of view that the disgruntled employee is the bad guy, and his or her victim is the company from which the disgruntled employee takes the information. There is, of course, another point of view. Interestingly, there is a recent book entitled *Getting Even* that takes the position it is not the disgruntled employee who is at fault, but the dysfunctional business process that triggers the act of revenge in the disgruntled employee. A review of that book is included here. That viewpoint, incidentally, is echoed on numerous blogs that discuss these kinds of disgruntled employee acts. Occasionally, the blogger may side with the employee against the company involved. More often, blogger respondents repond to the original (at least somewhat neutral) blog and take the side of the employee against the company. ("It was their [the company's] fault" and "they deserved it" is the recurring theme of these blog responses).

Be that as it may, in the remainder of this chapter we will tend to side with those who blame the employee. We will present many of those anecdotes from the computing, popular, and academic press about the actions of these disgruntled employees. Because there are so many such anecdotes, we will classify them as follows: data issues (the employees took corporate data for a variety of reasons that will result in the subcategories to this section), software issues (the employees took software itself, not data [there are surprisingly few such stories]), and system issues (the theft rose above the level of data or software). We will then conclude this chapter with some thoughts on what to do to ward off the actions of those disgruntled employees.

Note: Late in the creation of this chapter of our book, we came across a study about sabotage on software projects. That presented us with a problem. We had not included "sabotage" (our dictionary defines it as "deliberate damage") in our list of dark side topics, and yet here it was in this newfound study, begging (as clearly a dark side subject) to be included with our material. It is interesting to note that, in some of the responses to our survey on subversion reported earlier in this book, some of our responders equated the two things, subversion and sabotage. This is not uncommon in the computing and software world. Those trying to "subvert" a project are often referred to as trying to "sabotage" it. However, our dictionary makes a clear if somewhat subtle distinction between the two. Subversion, it says, seeks to destroy authority or undermine loyalty or faith; sabotage is deliberate damage. The history of the word "sabotage" is, in fact, interesting and illuminating in connection with this definition. The term originated with factory employees who tried to damage factory machinery by throwing their wooden shoes ("sabots" in French) into it.

We reviewed the structure of our book and decided that sabotage fit best into this chapter on disgruntled employees. In fact, when we looked at what those disgruntled employees were doing, for many of them it was "sabotage"; perhaps it was an act of rationalizing on our part, but the more we thought about it the more of a link we could see here! Plus, it nicely solved the orthogonal dilemma mentioned at the beginning of this chapter. Most of our chapter material in this book is *about dark side acts*, yet this chapter on disgruntled employees is about *who committed dark side acts*. But with the inclusion of sabotage in this chapter, we can now say—with some confidence—that this chapter is about the "who" of the dark side and the "what" behinds the acts.

We begin with the discussion of dark side disgruntled employee issues below, then explore the acts of sabotage we learned about in that late-discovered study!

Sidebar: Review of the book

Getting Even: The Truth About Workplace Revenge–and How to Stop It, by Thomas M. Tripp and Robert J. Bies

We have all been in a position where someone has wronged us and we want to get even with them. This book is about the management implications of such all-too-human incidents.

The authors make the point early and throughout the book that revenge results not from inadequate or psychologically damaged employees but from dysfunctional business processes. They begin with a definition of revenge: an action in response to some perceived harm or wrongdoing by another party, which is intended to inflict damage, injury, discomfort, or punishment ... They go on to point out that there are three actors in a revenge incident: the avenger, the offender (who causes the problem), and bystanders (often, innocent).

It is interesting that there is some conflict between this definition, which is focused heavily on the people involved, and the dysfunctional business process view, which is focused even more heavily on business activities. It is as if there is a disconnect between the authors' view of revenge incidents and the definitional view.

This book grew out of many years of author research into the subject that they originally saw as "organizational justice." They see three "triggers" for revenge episodes: goal obstruction (where someone or something tries to keep the avenger from achieving some goal), breaking the rules and social norms (where someone has not played by the nominal rules of the workplace), and damage to reputation (which is self-explanatory). And they see several forms of revenge: freeze-out (isolating the offender), private confrontation (between the two primary parties), bad-mouthing (of the offender), refusal of help (for the offender), quitting (by the avenger), and poor performance appraisals of the offender (if the avenger is in a position to do so).

What can the manager do to minimize such acts? There are two key things, according to the authors: Don't provoke employees yourself, and take constructive action when there is provocation among employees. And, the authors conclude, insist on fairness and justice for all employees; don't get rid of "bad" employees, get rid of bad procedures.

Did you think, when you read this book's title, that "getting even" was about violent acts of revenge? Violence, the authors are quick to point out early in the book, is rare in acts of revenge. But the authors do note that revenge is often "sloppy" because the victim tends to assign more blame to the offender than is deserved.

The book is highly readable and chock full of anecdotes. It weighs in at 180-plus pages, just the right length for a fairly short airplane trip. The message it imparts is not a particularly profound one, but one well worth thinking about.

6.2   DISGRUNTLED EMPLOYEE DATA ISSUES

The most numerous dark side disgruntled employee incidents involve data. It is easy to imagine why. Most of us in the public, and most reporters, understand the role of data in a business's operation. The role of software products (another category we will discuss later in this chapter) is far more subtle. So, in what follows, we will discuss several cases of disgruntled employees venting their feelings by doing things to their former company's data.

6.2.1   Data Tampering

There are lots of different things that a disgruntled employee can do to his former company's data. One of the most damaging is tampering with that data. By tampering we mean modifying it, not taking it. (Others refer to this as data manipulation and even data deception [Biros, George, and Zmud 2005].) In the studies that follow, the disgruntled employees did some amazing things with that data.

Lee Chen.   According to a 2007 FBI report, Lee Chen was terminated by his Illinois-based company in 2007. Not too long thereafter, he began accessing that company's data without authorization. He "downloaded thousands of computer files, deleted customer files, changed the prices on invoices bound for customers, and tampered in other ways with the company's computer files." (During the time he was doing that, according to the FBI report, the company's network operated "significantly slower.") Chen acknowledged in his guilty plea agreement that the company was forced to spend over $10,000 to restore the integrity of its computer system.

Chen's sentencing was scheduled to happen in early 2008. We are not aware of what his sentence was, but the maximum sentence for his activities would be a 12-month imprisonment term and a fine of up to $100,000.

Wikimedia.   Yes, you read that correctly, the heading on this section is Wikimedia, not Wikipedia. In this story, a Wikipedia founder named Jimmy Wales was accused of editing pages of Wikipedia content in exchange for donations to his new company, the Wikimedia Foundation. That is, of course, a no-no. Wikipedia may have user-generated content with a minimum of controls over its content, but at the same time the spirit of the system is that postings are made to provide information, not for personal gain.

What happened in the story was this. An unfavorable bio about a person was posted on Wikipedia, and Wales—according to the story—offered to make the bio more objective in exchange for a $5000 donation. The story gained quite a bit of traction in the Wiki media, where one wag dubbed it "Donorgate." Wales denied the story, but by then it had taken on a life of its own.

But the story became more complex as time went on. First of all, the unfavorable bio was about a person who had been sued by his former employer for misappropriation of trade secrets when he left that former employer. Apparently there was indeed a $5000 donation to Wikimedia in his name, and—according to the evolving story—he subsequently rescinded his donation.

There were also a couple of incidents about Wales himself. First of all, a former colleague at Wikimedia accused him of misusing foundation funds. (But that former colleague was later termed a "disgruntled former employee" by another Wikimedia colleague.) The second incident involved a former girlfriend of Wales, who leaked purported instant messages from Wales that implied Wales had indeed used his influence to change the subject Wikipedia entry. (That episode got messier when the former girlfriend opened an auction to sell off some of Wales's clothing on eBay.)

The discussion went on for some time. Various other players jumped in and took sides on the matter. One headline about the subject of the negative bio quoted a boss of Wales at Wikimedia as "playing the disgruntled former employee card" about the bio subject. (To complicate matters, that headline, apparently erroneously [although it is hard to be sure in this story!] said the boss was a Wikipedia, not Wikimedia, employee!)

We are not aware of how this story eventually ended, but we suspect that it died with more of a whimper than a bang!

A Potpouri of Other Data Tampering Stories.   The following stories were reported in the article "San Francisco Held Cyber-Hostage?" from the July 17, 2008 issue of an online privacy digest, or in the Biron, George, Zmud *MIS Quarterly Executive*, (March 2005) reference (reference list provided in this chapter).

- In 2008, Danielle Duann, a former employee of the Life Gift Organ Donation Center in Houston, Texas, was indicted for computer hacking. Duann allegedly deleted database records used to match organs to needy patients after she was fired in November, 2005. The U.S. FBI says the deletions caused more than $70,000 in damages and had the potential to affect medical treatment.

- In 2007, Lonnie Denison pleaded guilty to intentionally sabotaging a data control center in the California Independent System Operator Corporation (CAL ISO). The Feds described Denisons' effort as an attempt to bring down the Golden State's power grid. Denison, a contractor working at CAL ISO, broke into a high security computer room and pushed an emergency electrical shut-off button for the computer room, crashing the computers that communicate with California's deregulated power market.

- In October 2003, Andrew Garcia, a former employee of monitor maker Viewsonic, was sentenced to a year in prison for deleting critical server files that were necessary for Viewsonic's Taiwan office to do work.

- In 2003, Alan Giang Tran plead guilty to one count of hacking. Tran, a former network administrator for the Inglewood, California-based Airline Coach Service and Sky Limo Company attacked his former employee's network, deleting files and changing passwords. The hack crashed the company's dispatch system, causing thousands in losses. When his house was raided by the Feds, they discovered a file folder labeled "retaliation."

- Roger Duronio, a disgruntled former UBS PaineWebber employee was sentenced to 97 months in jail for planting a time-bomb program that destroyed files on thousands of computers inside the financial giant's computer network. Duronio planted the code before his February 22, 2002 resignation, which followed repeated complaints by Duronio about his salary and bonuses. The timer for the code went off on March 4; Duronio shorted UBS's stock on the day of the time bomb, hoping to make a profit by having the rogue code drive down the company's stock price.

- Back in 1996, two credit union employees altered customer credit reports in the company's database in exchange for bribes. Their normal duties included revising erroneous reports, and they simply went beyond that responsibility in order to make money. The total amount of the fraud loss was $215,000, and, according to one report, "the risk exposure to the credit union was incalculable."

- A Charles Schwab investment specialist manipulated the accounts of his clients in order to wire himself money that belonged to the clients. The loss ran into the "thousands of dollars."

- A foreign currency trader used various approaches, including manipulating data, to make himself appear to be one of his investment bank's "star producers." In fact, his transactions were costing the bank over $600 million.

6.2.1.1 Thwarting Data Tampering   Interestingly, the Biros et al. article referenced above attempts to not only identify incidents of "data manipulation" and "data deception," but seeks ways of allowing managers to become aware of such actions. The authors' efforts were not very successful. Using three different approaches to alerting/training employees to detect such activities, Biros et al. found that the best approach allowed their subjects to identify 8 out of 20 pieces of bad (tampered) data, and the worst only about 2 of the 20.

6.2.2 Data Destruction

Some disgruntled employees don't stop at simply tampering with their employer's data—they actually destroy it! In the cases that follow, employees—who must have been really angry—systematically did away with various kinds of data. The motive was usually to cause the employer grievous harm and make ongoing business difficult for the company.

In contrast to reactions toward some of the other cases in this chapter, the reaction of bloggers to this kind of activity was almost universally negative. That was especially true when the destruction of the data harmed not just the employer, but the employer's customers. For example, in one case, the disgruntled employee destroyed medical records. Bloggers universally condemned this attack and suggested that very long prison terms (longer than the actual sentences) should be meted out for such activities.

In these cases, we often do not have a record of how the case eventually played out. But what is interesting about them, we believe, is the variety of ways in which a variety of data is vulnerable to the acts of disgruntled employees.

Joseph Patrick Nolan.   This is a peculiar case. Nolan, a 26-year-old IT worker, resigned from his job in 2007. (At that point, it appears that he was not a disgruntled employee). The company told him what he had to do to qualify for termination pay, but he failed to follow through with the paperwork (the action involved signing a form). As a result, the company did not provide that termination check.

Nolan retaliated. He wiped out the company's payroll and personnel files. He was caught and convicted. We do not have a record of what his sentence was, but we do know that the cost to the company to repair the damage was about $30,000.

Blog Site Shut Down.   In this case, we do not know the name of the disgruntled IT employee, but we do know that at some point in 2008 or 2009 he was fired for theft of company materials (he had worked for a blogging site). We also know that he was the person who had defined that company's backup procedures.

After his termination (and apparently using that backup procedure knowledge), he overwrote all of the company's backups. According to the story, the backup setup he had defined was one more commonly used for data redundancy than for data backup, which made it easier for the disgruntled employee to destroy the data.

The company reports that it was unable to recover the lost data.

Database and Boot Files.   In this 2008 story, a disgruntled former employee hacked into his former employer's e-mail system and deleted its Microsoft Exchange server database and core boot files. He also sent out spam messages containing pornography and viruses to the company's e-mail lists. He had only worked for the company for a few months before he was fired.

The prosecutor in the resulting trial urged the court to send a message to other hackers / disgruntled employees that this kind of activity would not be tolerated. In the end, the culprit was sentenced to a year and a day in prison and three months' home detention afterwards. There is no record of whether the prosecutor thought that this was a sufficient message.

Patient Data.   This is the case we referred to earlier: Customers of the former employer of the disgruntled employee were disadvantaged by his actions.

The employee, a former IT network services engineer and technical services manager for a community health center who resigned from his job after a negative performance review, attacked his former employer's system twice, a few weeks apart. The first time (in late 2005), he disabled the automatic backup database of patient information. The second time, he deleted data and software from its servers.

The judge threw the book at the disgruntled employee. He was sentenced to 63 months in prison and ordered to pay restitution of nearly a half-million dollars. (At the time, this was one of the longest sentences ever imposed for computer hacking.) Both the judge and bloggers who commented on this case thought that because the hacker had essentially endangered some patient's lives by destroying their data, the sentence was by no means excessive.

Playing the Market.   In this case, a disgruntled computer systems administrator at a brokerage house planted a logic bomb in their computer systems just before he resigned. His expectation was that the bomb would negatively effect the company's business, and because of that he purchased a sizeable put option on the company's stock. The damage done, according to the brokerage house, amounted to more than $3 million.

GTE Data Deleted.   Here, a disgruntled employee of GTE issued commands into three different network computers used by the company, causing electronic information stored on those hard disks to be deleted and prohibiting anyone from preventing that destruction of data. The company reported that the damage cost in excess of $209,000. We do not have a report on what happened to the disgruntled employee.

Lawyer Referral Agency.   The head of a lawyer referral agency resigned from her office, under duress. That made her angry, and she destroyed forms, procedures, correspondence, and historical records. She was not technically smart, however, and fortunately the agency was able to restore all of the deleted data.

6.2.3   Data Made Public

Disgruntled employees, as we have seen, can tamper with data and actually destroy data. But there is one other thing they can do with data, something that may have even more serious repercussions in the long run: They can take data that is supposed to be private and make it public.

Most enterprises have some kind of data for which they have a corporate as well as a public responsibility to keep private. As we saw in the past section, medical records are one such collection of data. Other such data includes personnel data; most of us are required to tell the companies we work for some things about ourselves that the company may need to know, but which we would rather not have broadcast to the world at large. Most people would prefer that even such seemingly innocent things as our home address and phone number are not known outside a limited circle of people.

In the cases that follow, disgruntled employees deliberately latched onto such data and either made it public or threatened to make it public. The goal of these employees was usually retribution, and sometimes the threat was even used as leverage to get the company to come to the table on some other issues. In any case, the victims of these activities were not only the companies involved, but also the individuals whose privacy cover was blown. Again, most bloggers took a dim view of these kinds of activities.

Global Crossing Development Company.   This case, from circa 2001, may be one of the most vicious and danger-filled of all the cases in this book.

The story is about a disgruntled former IT employee at the telecommunications firm Global Crossing. While he was employed at the company, he refused to provide his social security number, tried to hide the fact that he had a criminal record, and threatened the director of human resources. Subsequently, as you might imagine, he was fired.

After he was let go, he began picketing the company's offices, holding up a placard that referred to a Web site he had created. On that Web site, he displayed Global Crossing personnel data: payroll information, social security numbers, birth dates, and home addresses.

Global Crossing, seeing that legal action was no doubt in their future, began archiving various versions of the Web site and turned those archives over to the FBI. As time went by, the disgruntled employee increased the size of the Web site, escalating from the original 15 employees to more than a thousand!

The company sought a restraining order against the former employee, and the process server who delivered that restraining order was threatened. (He posted her license plate number and other personal information on his Web site, told her that his actions would get "much, much worse," and discussed the possibility that she could be stabbed with a knife, going so far later as to say "I will kill you," according to a legal summary of the case published on the Web site AltLaw.) The disgruntled employee also railed against the company's chairman and its assistant general counsel in a similar manner.

The Web site postings appeared periodically over a five-month period. According to an internal memo, the publication included data on all employees on Global Crossing's payroll as of a certain point in time. (The company currently has about 8000 employees.) An attorney for Bermuda-based Global Crossing said the company is pursuing both civil and criminal action against the former IT worker. Both the FBI and the police department in Beverly Hills, California (where the information is alleged to have been stolen) are on the case.

The legal case dragged on over an enormously long period of time, partially because the disgruntled employee kept firing his court-appointed attorneys and representing himself (AltLaw speculated that he did so in hopes of making the case eventually die of old age!). It was finally resolved in a three-week jury trial in 2007; the defendant was found guilty on eight charges (all but one of the charges against him) and was sentenced to a 46-month term in prison (this was at the top of the relevant sentencing guidelines). He was also given an additional three-year term of supervised release; he is now on that status.

One more note: the disgruntled employee also filed an astonishing number of appeals in the case, and much of the AltLaw discussion dealt with the legitimacy of those appeals (it found nearly all of them spurious).

RBC Dain Rauscher.   This case, unlike the one discussed above, opened rather slowly. The company in question, RBC Dain Rauscher (a brokerage firm with offices in Minneapolis), became aware in 2005 that someone made public information on some of its 300,000 households (presumably, customers). The company had no idea at the time who had accessed the data and made it public, nor was there any evidence that data had been misused, but the company notified those 300,000 client households via a letter that a problem brewing might be brewing.

The only clue that there might be a problem was this: Some clients (apparently 100, chosen at random) had received an anonymous letter containing names, addresses, tax identification and corporate ID numbers, and birthdates. The letter, which was filled with profanity, said it was from a former Dain Rauscher employee who had been fired and was seeking revenge. The letter stated that the former employee had access to information on "thousands" of clients and had sold the information to an unidentified buyer.

The resolution of the matter is not known to the authors.

HMO Kaiser Permanente.   This case study is about a disgruntled former employee of the very large U.S. health organization named Kaiser Permanente. What makes the story unusual is that, in this case, the disgruntled employee was a woman. (She called herself the "Diva of the Disgruntled"!) A newspaper in California, *San Jose Mercury News*, broke the story in an article, reporting that Kaiser Permanente was in the process of informing 140 of their insured patients that a former employee had posted confidential medical information on her blog. The Diva of the Disgruntled said that it was Kaiser Permanente's fault and that the company itself had included private patient information on systems diagrams posted on the Web.

Once again, we are not aware of the resolution of this 2005 case.

American Eagle Outfitters.   In this 2002 case, a disgruntled former employee of American Eagle Outfitters posted passwords and logins for the company's network on a hacker e-mail list. He also posted information on how to get into the company's network. Subsequently, he used that information himself in late 2002, hoping to disrupt the company's busy holiday season business.

In this case, we know the legal ramifications of this case; the disgruntled employee was sentenced to 18 months in prison.

AOL.   An AOL software engineer, back in 2003, stole the personal information of 92 million (!) customers and sold the data to spammers. At first, he underestimated the value of what he was selling, getting around $28,000 for it. But as he became more experienced at what he was doing, he began charging $100,000 per sale! His prison sentence was for 18–24 months.

Prudential Insurance.   This case is centered on a Prudential employee who believed himself to be underpaid. To get even, he stole information on 60,000 Prudential employees, and sold it. Furthermore, he tried to make it look like his former supervisor was involved in the theft. There is no record that we have regarding how much money he made or his eventual sentence.

6.2.4   Theft Via Data

The case studies in this chapter until this point have been focused on data as a goal. Data was tampered with, destroyed, or made public. In this (brief) section, data is the means to an end: Disgruntled employees used a company's database(s) to accomplish some other goal (but generally stealing something).

Cisco.   Note that we have encountered Cisco before in this book, but in an entirely different case from this one.

The goal in this case was profound. Two accounting employees of Cisco Systems, Geoffrey Osowski and Wilson Tang, exceeded their authorized access to the company's computers. The goal of their action was to illegally issue to themselves Cisco corporate stock in the amount of nearly $8 million!

The two were caught, and each was sentenced to 34 months in prison.

6.3   DISGRUNTLED EMPLOYEE SOFTWARE ISSUES

We have already seen many cases involving data as the goal and the means to a particular (usually illegal) disgruntled employee's end. Much less often, we see software as the goal.

In this section, we will present software cases. We suspect the reason that there are so few such cases presented under the general heading of "acts of disgruntled employees" is that most such employees know what to do with data, and but they have much less of an idea what to do with software. Software-involved nefarious activities generally involve taking a software product from one company to another, but that is not necessarily something that a disgruntled employee will do. Perfectly "gruntled" employees may also take software products. especially if they were involved in the creation of the product in the first place. But that is a vastly different kettle of fish than what disgruntled employees tend to do.

6.3.1   Software Destruction

The only cases we have come across regarding software and disgruntled employees were cases where one or more software products were destroyed.

Omega Engineering.   Timothy Lloyd, 39, spent 11 years working for Omega Engineering as a chief programmer; during that time, he designed and implemented Omega's network. At the end of that period, for reasons not stated in the case analysis, he was demoted and fired.

He decided to get even. Omega, according to the case, was a high-tech measurement and control instruments company. Lloyd constructed a "time bomb" that went off without warning on July 31, 1996, deleting most of the company's key software programs. Omega attorney Grady O'Malley called the deleted programs "the lifeblood of the company."

The loss, according to the company, was on the order of $10 million in sales and future contracts. Lloyd was caught, tried, convicted, and sentenced (in 2002, after more than one retrial) to three years in prison for the crime. He was also ordered to pay $2 million in restitution.

Microsoft (!)   We have encountered Microsoft before in our book (it is difficult to avoid multiple but different stories relating to one computing company, especially a leading one like this!) And because the company involved is so prominent, we find it surprising that this particular case didn't achieve more visibility!

Microsoft, in this case, employed another company to port various Windows applications to such alternative platforms as Unix and Linux. The other company, California-based Mainsoft, apparently had inadequate protection mechanisms for the Windows operating systems software source code that they needed to perform these porting tasks; the software source code was stolen.

The case contains no report of what its legal ramifications were.

6.4   DISGRUNTLED EMPLOYEE SYSTEM ISSUES

Disgruntled employees, as we have seen here, wreak a lot of damage on the data on the companies that they have left. Less often, we have also seen, they attack their former company through its software.

But perhaps the ultimate computing retribution comes when the disgruntled employee attacks an entire computing system. In these cases, the employees don't simply access data or software and do something prohibited with it. They actually take down computer systems.

Cox Communications.   This is a fairly straightforward system disabling story. A 38-year-old employee of Cox, William Bryant of Norcross, Georgia, was asked to resign and to leave the company forthwith. He did, but then attacked the company's computer systems, "knowingly causing the transmission of information to a computer used in interstate commerce, and as a result intentionally and without authorization causing damage to that computer." (The quotation is from the legal charges brought by Cox against Bryant. The damage was apparently a service outage for the computer that was attacked.)

The result of the 2007 legal case was that Bryant pleaded guilty to the charges and was subject to a maximum sentence of 10 years in prison, along with a $250,000 fine. It is not known what the actual sentence was.

Interestingly, blog-reader reactions to this story varied from "Cox deserved it" to "what a stupid thing for the employee to do."

Pacific Energy Resources.   In this 2009 case, the system disrupted was one where there could have been serious consequences. Fortunately for both the company, Pacific Energy Resources, and the employee, Mario Azar, what could have been an environmental disaster was only a system outage.

The system in question was one that monitored for leaks on several off-shore California oil platforms. What happened was that the employee, who had been working under a contract, did not receive a renewal for his contract; he then tampered with the leak-detection computer systems. The fortunate circumstance was that during the time of the outage, no leaks occurred, and therefore the system would not have been needed to detect any leaks.

Azar was indicted and faced a maximum ten-year term.

One report of the incident noted that "this was not the first time a hack was directed at the environment." It went on to mention two cases: There was one in Australia, where a disgruntled employee was sent to prison in 2001 for two years after he had gained unauthorized access to a state of Queensland sanitation system, causing the release of millions of gallons of raw sewage; and yet another took place in Ohio, where a worm was inserted into a network at a nuclear power plant, disabling safety monitoring for nearly five hours.

Interestingly, several bloggers defended the employee's actions, saying that the employee in question had not been paid for two months and was owed $9000 by the company. They went on to say that they knew the employee and the case personally and thought the company had done badly by him on several levels.

Be that as it may, the crime seemed far more momentous than the offenses alleged to have been committed by the company. "Hell hath no fury like a disgruntled employee" would seem to be an apt description of these kinds of vicious acts.

Akimbo Systems.   The cases in this section of our book tell an interesting story of the variety of computer systems that disgruntled employees may attack. In this case, the e-mail capability of Akimbo Systems was disabled.

Steven Barnes was fired by Akimbo in 2003. After his termination, he discovered that his login to Akimbo's system still worked; he turned the company's e-mail system computer into an open relay server capable of sending out large amounts of spam, deleted the company's Exchange database, and damaged its operating system in such a way that it would crash when it was rebooted. Akimbo said that, as one result, its computer was blacklisted by several spam blocking services.

Barnes complained, however, that his firing was at the hands of "a group of baseball-bat-wielding thugs" who had turned up at his house and confiscated both his work and personal computers.

In any case, Barnes was sentenced to a year in prison, three years on probation, and a requirement for $54,000 in restitution.

The response in the blogosphere varied enormously in this case. The reactions hinged on personal belief of the story about being fired by "thugs." Those who believed the story sympathized with Barnes and went so far as to suggest even more ways for him to get even with Akimbo (some even in ways that, the responders noted, couldn't be detected)!

City of San Francisco.   In this 2008 story, Terry Childs, a five-year employee of the IT section of the city of San Francisco, was disciplined on the job, and his employers attempted to fire him. In retaliation, Childs began to tamper with the city's network computers. Apparently, he created an access code that prevented anyone from using the computer except for himself; then he refused to turn that code over to the city! (He had turned two such codes over to the police, but as it turned out they didn't work).

The network in question handled such things as the mayor's e-mail messaging and the city's electronic court records. Headlines of the resulting stories asked "San Francisco Held Cyber-Hostage?" and described the event as "wreaking havoc."

Childs was arrested and held on $5 million bail, partly as a result of his failure to turn over the access code.

Interestingly, one of the newspaper stories about the case said that "disgruntled or fired employees have always used computers to get a dose of revenge" and went on to note that although the system in question was disabled, "no actual damage was reported."

Elite Web Hosting.   It was hard to categorize this particular case in the taxonomy of disgruntled employee actions we have provided in this book. That's because, in this case, the employee set out to destroy not just data, not just software, not even just a computing system, but in fact a whole company!

Back in 2000, a disgruntled former employee hacked into Elite Web Hosting's computer System and proceeded to send e-mail to every customer containing vulgar language. The e-mails claimed the company was moving into the porn business and that the company's owner had been siphoning off company money for personal use.

The tactic worked, almost immediately. Thirty steady customers discontinued their relationship with Elite, taking with them $5000 each in monthly income. Elite hired a computer security company to address the problem, and the company suggested that Elite strengthen its defenses against such activities. The barn door, of course, was being closed after the horse was stolen!

The case did not say what happened to the disgruntled employee.

Forbes.   A terminated and troubled employee of Forbes, one who worked in the computing department, crashed 5 of the company's 8 network servers in such a way that the data in the servers was deleted and none of it was recoverable. Forbes had to close its New York office for two days and suffered losses of more than $100,000.

Lockheed-Martin.   A Lockheed Martin employee sent 60,000 colleagues a personal e-mail message, one that requested a response. The resulting volume of e-mail traffic was enormous. The e-mail system crashed, and a Microsoft emergency response team had to be flown in to repair the damage.

(Many of the latter episodes above are taken from the article (Nelson, Sharon D. and Simek, John W. "Disgruntled Employees in Your Law Firm: the Enemy Within") which appeared in the computer forensics online newsletter *Sensei Enterprises, Inc.*, in 2005).

6.5   WHAT TO DO ABOUT DISGRUNTLED EMPLOYEE ACTS

There is no shortage of thoughts in the public and computing press and relevant blogs about what to do when disgruntled employees attack. Perhaps the most astonishingly complete collection of such thoughts can be found in an April 2006 blog by Dan Morrill; the article is entitled "Disgruntled Employees and Intellectual Property Protection":

> Disgruntled employees have a number of motivations, and usually can justify their actions by circular logic, including "the company can afford it." The ability of people to believe that the company "owes them" goes a long way in justifying the acts. As well, people's personalities will change from their standard personality, and they will trial the attack before it is fully implemented. Managers should be on the look out for alterations in behaviors, and in finding unexpected software on computing systems like the existence of hacker tools, server software, and other applications that should not be on the computers in question. As well, managers should be looking for large transfers of data out of the company network that are unexplained, or not to the usual trusted trading partners, or along known VPN links.

Morrill then went on to note a 2005 report by McAfee that was rich with specific thoughts on the subject, specifically noting the issues that companies face when trying to protect their computing systems:

> That 2005 McAfee report described some of the common issues that companies face when dealing with their own internal computing systems.
>
> - One in five workers (21%) let family and friends use company laptops and PCs to access the Internet.
> - More than half (51%) connect their own devices or gadgets to their work PC.
> - A quarter of these do so every day.
> - Around 60% admit to storing personal content on their work PC.
> - One in ten confessed to downloading content at work they shouldn't.
> - Two thirds (62%) admitted they have a very limited knowledge of IT Security.
> - More than half (51%) had no idea how to update the anti-virus protection on their company PC.
> - Five percent say they have accessed areas of their IT system they shouldn't have.
>
> As well, McAfee has also quantified a system of four major personality types that inhabit a company's security infrastructure.
>
> - **The Security Softie.** This group comprises the vast majority of employees. They have a very limited knowledge of security and put their business at

risk through using their work computer at home or letting family members surf the Internet on their work PC.

- **The Gadget Geek.** Those who come to work armed with a variety of devices/gadgets, all of which get plugged into their PC.

- **The Squatter.** Those who use the company IT resources in ways they shouldn't (i.e., by storing content or playing games).

- **The Saboteur.** A very small minority of employees. This group will maliciously hack into areas of the IT system to which they shouldn't have access or infect the network purposely from within.

Then, Morrill got down to the protection nitty-gritty. His blog described specific procedures and concepts at length:

Intellectual property protection should be in line with the estimated dollar cost should the data be lost, or otherwise accidentally disclosed or intentionally disclosed. While no solution is perfect, information security personnel rather need to set up speed bumps that will discourage all but the most dedicated internal hackers. Most people who are internet and not internet savvy or hacker savvy will attempt one or two tools, and if they do not work, then they will abandon the process. Simple controls and processes can go a long way to reducing these kinds of threats.

Personnel

- Do not use group accounts; each person should have their own account on the network

- When using service accounts passwords should be highly complex and stored in a password vault

- No person should have access to a service account, domain administration, root, enterprise administration account or otherwise without a solid check out procedure

- Do not store critical passwords in spreadsheets on a network share

- Have Human Resources policies that have clear and direct consequences including termination for releasing or otherwise compromising computer passwords or sharing user accounts

- Do background checks on all incoming employees to the company

- Do credit checks on all incoming employees to the company

- If they blog and disclose it, read what they write about with a critical eye as to what kind of employee the person would make. Is their blog full of angry statements or self aggrandizing statements? Blogs are an excellent way of discovering the personality behind the person

- Talk to their references that they provide on their resume (and be careful not to commit any HR violations)

- Trusted trading partners should also have their own accounts on the network

- Trusted trading partners should be on their own VPN, and access should be limited by IP address to what resources the trading partners need

- Monitor sharp and sudden changes of peoples personality, if uncomfortable, put the personnel on a special project that reduces the risk of losing data and reduces their permissions on the network
- Be prepared to work with law enforcement if needed
- Be prepared for news services to find out that there has been a hacking attempt and to ask questions
- Be prepared to handle questions from members of the companies, investors, investing houses, and other interested parties
- Have a fully cognizant legal person ready in case of a intellectual property or company wide event that would lead to the loss of data
- Have more than one person doing the same job, have key person insurance in the event of a loss of key personnel
- Have policies and procedures for contractors, trusted trading partners, and regular employers that clearly spell out requirements for internet access
- Have a clearly designated process for releasing data onto web sites, and other company properties that can be accessed by the general public

Technological Controls
- Use software that limits access to USB, CDRW, and DVD-RW drives on computing systems. They should only be unlocked when adequate need has been established for them
- Always test backups, conduct a quarterly emergency drill where complete loss of computing systems are effected, and how to recover from any disaster
- Log all security events on a network and use a collation engine to sort through them looking for locked passwords, escalation of privilege, and other signs that someone may be trying to figure out the security mechanisms of the network
- Watch for very large transactions off the network that would indicate an off hours or very large data transfer off the network.
- Be able to attribute events to IP, System name and IP address, login for all suspicious events on the network
- Verify all data on the network and have more than one person filling any particular technological function
- Conduct regular software inventories using a tool like SMS or other software inventory tool
- Check all contractor equipment to ensure that it meets company standards. If there is software that is not normal for the company, or their equipment has hacking tools or other tools, have them remove it.
- Develop a "VPN Jail" for all unknown systems that connect to the network when someone first connects a new system to the network.
- Keep abreast of hacker tools, and other technologies that can enhance or defeat the companies current security mechanisms

- Monitor search engines, peer to peer networks, and other networks for the existence of the companies intellectual property

These solutions do not have to be costly to implement, but do require coordination at the management level to make the process successful. As with all new policies and technological controls, feasibility studies will help the company determine which controls and processes make financial and business sense. Management and senior Management coordination are also required to make these processes and changes successful. Companies should also be evaluating their perceived risk along with actual defined risk.

Perceived risk is when the company thinks that there could be a violation of data because of inadequate controls either personnel or technological. Actual risk is when data is discovered leaving the network, or found on the internet. Management should designate a team to review all personnel and technological controls and then develop a threat scenario based on the likelihood of something happening. From that scenario, controls and technology should be reviewed that will mitigate or reduce the risks that the company deems likely to have happen. No process should be undertaken without management, and in many cases, HR and Legal review.

Thanks to Dan Morrill for providing this exceptionally complete set of thoughts on "what to do" about disgruntled employee actions on his blog. In the end, the best that a company can probably do is to follow guidelines and concepts such as these. They may or not prevent disgruntled employee damage, but they will give the company in question the satisfaction that it has tried as hard as it can!

6.6 SABOTAGE

We had no more than finished writing the preceding material on disgruntled employees when we came across an exciting piece of research on IT sabotage and espionage. As we mentioned early in this book, there is a severe shortage of research studies on dark side subjects. We seized on this late-found study and decided that it should be discussed in our book. But where, we wondered, should we include it? Among all the dark side matters we had bumped into and decided to include in our book, we had accounted for espionage (see that chapter) but not sabotage.

We considered making it a separate chapter all its own, but in the end, as we examined the case studies in this section on disgruntled employees, we decided that it would fit best here. Disgruntled employees perform many dark side acts that vary in intensity, as we have seen, but many of those acts could be considered acts of sabotage. Below you will find our discussion of this excellent study, presenting both a summary of its relevant findings and our own critique of those findings.

The CERT Study. The following material is abstracted from the study "Comparing Insider IT Sabotage and Espionage: A Model-Based Analysis" that was performed by the Carnegie Mellon University's Software Engineering Institute. We refer to this work as the "CERT study."

The CERT study is based on 30 IT sabotage cases and nine cases of espionage that were presented and discussed. Analysis of these cases resulted in the development (in the study) of models for IT sabotage and espionage. Based on those models, the researchers working within CERT derived observations and recommendations. In the context of our book, the observations are of particular interest:

Note that the usage of quotes in this section refers to the CERT study.

"Observation #1: Most saboteurs and spies had common personal predispositions that contributed to their risk of committing malicious acts."

The following personal conditions appeared again and again in the analyzed cases.

- The insider has debts perhaps due to alcohol or drug problems or because of inadequate consumer behavior. These reasons create a need for more money than the expected salary and make the insider vulnerable toward espionage and/or sabotage.
- Some people have the tendency to get very angry over small reasons,
- "An exaggerated need for ego satisfaction or to control others can overcome constraints against rule breaking."

The researchers of the CERT study group the observed personal predispositions into four categories, including the following:

- "Serious Mental Health Disorders"
- "Personality Problems"
- "Social Skills and Decision-Making Biases"
- "A History of Rule Conflicts"

"OBSERVATION #2: In most cases, stressful events, including organizational sanctions, contributed to the likelihood of insider IT sabotage and espionage."

"OBSERVATION #3: Concerning behaviors were often observable before and during insider IT sabotage and espionage."

"These behaviors included

- tardiness, truancy
- arguments with coworkers
- poor job performance
- security violations
- attack preparations"

"OBSERVATION #4: Technical actions by many insiders could have alerted the organization to planned or ongoing malicious acts." "A technical indicator is a technical event, condition, or action that indicates increased risk. For instance, saboteurs sometimes created backdoor accounts—unauthorized accounts unknown to anyone except the person who created them—to facilitate system access following termination."

In many espionage cases, the disloyal insider accesses large amounts of classified information. Frequently, the disloyal insider's technical access to the classified information was legitimate; that is, the insider did not "hack" into the database, but used his or her legitimate user account. However, the access to this specific information was not justified by the task at hand.

In the context of Observation #4, the researchers of the CERT study observed something that they called a "trust trap". A trust trap is a reinforcement loop that prevents the detection of a disloyal insider: In the beginning, the disloyal insider conceals his suspicious technical actions or remains undiscovered with a bit of good luck. Since the organization does not discover anything that should make them suspicious, they dedicate fewer resources for monitoring the disloyal insider (because he has achieved a certain level of trust). Due to the lower degree of monitoring, discovery of suspicious events are less likely, which in turn leads to growing trust. This trust trap can lead to a situation where a disloyal insider can act rather overtly without much effort of concealing his suspicious activity and still runs very little risk of being discovered.

"OBSERVATION #5 In many cases, organizations ignored or failed to detect rule violations."

"OBSERVATION #6 Lack of physical and electronic access controls facilitated both IT sabotage and espionage."

Here ends the excerpt of the CERT study. What follows is a discussion of the findings of the study in the context of this book.

Thoughts About the CERT Study.   Observations #1 and #2 from the CERT study, presented above, paint the picture of a complicated and perhaps even troubled colleague. Many of our readers have probably encountered colleagues and co-workers who match that description. Over a long period of time, these complicated colleagues are increasingly discontent with the organization and with their working conditions but—surprisingly enough—don't leave the organization. Frequently, they are isolated in their peer group, or they choose to take the role of a loner. They exhibit an increasingly provocative behavior that includes the refusal of discipline, late arrivals to the office or to meetings, lack of respect for superiors, and rule violations. From such workers we frequently hear remarks such as "they owe me a lot" However, nobody understands why anybody might owe the disgruntled employee anything.

Practical workplace experience suggests that these problems usually do not resolve themselves in time. Organizational sanctions will make things worse—the complicated colleague will have even more reason to be discontent. The lack of sanctioning of the rule violations may be even worse because it emboldens the disgruntled person: He or she will try out even more provoking behavior. Additionally, the lack of sanctioning of the rule violation may lead to a general decline of discipline on the entire team.

It is quite possible that this spiral of provoking behavior and organizational sanctions escalate to a point where the disgruntled employee acts in a really harmful way—IT sabotage.

If things cannot be settled by discussing the problem, it might be best to terminate (in a civilized way, without scandal, if possible) the worker before it is too late. It may be wise to look out for termination conditions that can furher exacerbate the already disgruntled employee. In addition, the organization should make sure that he or she has no access to technical ways to commit sabotage and/or revenge. This is what common sense suggests.

In many of the cases analyzed in the CERT study, the common sense approach failed for one reason or another. In some cases, the organization was not aware that a problem existed, or they were not aware of the severity of the problem. In other cases, the organization decided not to terminate the employee but to go on with him despite the known problems. One of the CERT case studies includes a high level CIA officer with alcohol problems. Despite repeated reports of this problem, he remained in his position. The story ends with a huge espionage scandal.

Observations #3 through #6 demonstrate that insider sabotage and espionage are rarely isolated actions "out of the blue sky." Instead, there is usually a history of suspicious technical and nontechnical behavior (such as the creation of backdoor accounts, the installation and test of malignant software, and access to large amounts of classified data that are not related to the task at hand). The suspicious behavior could have been detected by the organization if proper monitoring were in place. In the least, the organization should have become alert. Unfortunately, however, they did not find it out, they ignored it, or they did not react properly. Otherwise, the ensuing disaster could have been stopped before it was too late.

One of the anecdotes of the CERT study included such backdoor accounts. The disloyal system administrator created three additional accounts without the knowledge of the persons for whom these accounts were created (one of them was for the CFO). Later, after termination of his employment, the disloyal system administrator abused these accounts for sabotage. The creation of backdoor accounts was against the security policy of the organization in question. The authors of the CERT report conclude that proper monitoring of the administrator's activity should have discovered these rule violation and hence prevented the act of sabotage before it was too late.

Such cases of rule violation were observed quite frequently prior to sabotage and espionage. For this reason, the study gives a recommendation:

"RECOMMENDATION #4: Research policies, methods, and tools for auditing and monitoring behaviors and technical actions that are indicative of insider IT sabotage and espionage."

This recommendation is meant to reduce the risk for espionage and sabotage. It sounds plausible, but will it really reduce the risk?

The study says that whenever you encounter a malicious act you will also find suspicious technical actions prior to the malicious act (at least, in the vast majority of cases). This observation matches our (the authors) personal experience and many readers will probably confirm that there might be a grain of truth in it.

The inverse conclusion is less clear: Whenever you find suspicious technical actions you should be on alert for a malicious act in the future. This inverse conclusion is the base of Recommendation #4, which can be understood as "look carefully for suspicious technical actions."

The authors doubt that the setting of the CERT study allows for the following conclusion to be made: The existence of suspicious technical actions makes it more likely that espionage or sabotage will happen. For researchers to draw this conclusion, another research setting would be required, such as one where there are sequences of technical actions (some resulting in sabotage, others not). The researcher would need to know which of them resulted in sabotage and which did not. If it is possible to forecast the probability of sabotage based solely on these sequences of technical actions then the conclusion would be valid. Even a few suspicious technical actions make sabotage highly likely. The CERT study allows only the following conclusion to be made: If you don't find suspicious technical actions, then sabotage is very unlikely. But that's not the same.

Why is this inverse conclusion doubtful? The researchers of the CERT study knew already that sabotage had already happened in a certain case. Using this knowledge, they worked backwards and studied in detail the history of actions of the saboteur (while knowing already that he is a saboteur). They found a number of technical actions that should be called suspicious.

Perhaps such suspicious technical actions are very frequent. If you research the activities of a typical system administrator over a longer period of time—say five years—it is very likely that you will find a handful of activities that could somehow be considered suspicious. Every time the admin created an account, we have to ask why this account has been created and if there might have been disloyal motivations behind that activity. Such a detailed study would certainly lead to results that indicate some suspicious actions. (It is impossible to end up with completely empty hands.)

Let's again tell the story of the account for the CFO in a fictitious way:

An honest and loyal system administrator has no thought of sabotage. He notices that the CFO is the only top manager who does not have remote access to the corporate database. In fact, the CFO does have a kind of remote access, but this access is not compliant to protocol XY, that is, the base for the organization's VPN. For this reason, the CFO has only an unsecured remote access to the database. The loyal system administrator decides that this should be changed.

The admin expects that it is only a matter of time until he will receive "the call." Which call? The CFO calls from an important off-site meeting, and she says she has to access the database … not in half an hour but RIGHT NOW. This call can come in two years or in two days. But it is very likely that this call will come sooner or later.

The admin has a number of options. He can call the CFO and explain to her the technical problem—or at least *try* to explain it. CFOs have a tendency to not be interested in such technical things. What will happen afterward depends on the personality of the CFO, how much of a sense of humor she has. One possible outcome is that the CFO calls the supervisor of the admin and asks that in the future she is not be bothered anymore with such details. She tells the admin's boss that she had REALLY other things to do than to worry about protocol XY and something that seems to be called a VPN.

This is one possible outcome of the story. However, the admin has other options: He could just create a reliable remote access for the CFO on a rainy Friday afternoon. He tries the account a few times and waits for "the call." If he wants to make sure that the account really works "remotely" he might try it from his PC at home. So he is prepared for "the call" and everything will work out well.

Notice that this fictitious story includes quite a number of suspicious technical actions, including the creation of backdoor accounts and the ability to access classified information from a private PC. In this story, the organization maintains a detailed "security policy" that disallows these actions. This "security policy" accompanies the "Internal Guidelines for System Administration." Both documents cover a couple of hundred pages and are not easy to read—another job for a rainy Friday afternoon!

Should the organization now fire the admin? Should they dedicate significant resources to monitor his activity carefully? Probably not.

Let's continue now with this fictitious story: Due to an unexpected event the previously loyal system administrator gets very angry, leaves the company, and commits acts of sabotage using the account that he created for the CFO, once upon a time. The report of the sabotage incident will inevitably come to the following conclusion: "Suspicious technical actions happened prior to the sabotage incident. Proper monitoring within the organization should have discovered these actions. An adequate reaction to these suspicious technical actions would have prevented the sabotage." Notice, however, the report will make this statement only after it became evident that sabotage happened, that is, not in a prognostic way based solely on the sequence of actions.

If we know how the story ends, it is easy to spot suspicious technical actions and concerning non-technical behavior. However, if we don't know the result, it is much more difficult to give criteria when a sequence of actions makes it much more likely that sabotage will happen.

It is not our intention, in this section of our book devoted to thoughts on the CERT study, to cast aspersions on that work. Certainly the field of computing and software needs more such studies of dark side matters. (We noted at the outset of our book how rare such research work is, and we encourage other researchers to become engaged with it).

The point we do want to make here is that solutions to dark side matters are necessarily complex. Simplistic solutions that result in unintended consequences may be even more trouble than the problem they are working. Still, we applaud the authors of the CERT study for some thoughtful work on an important topic, and we are pleased to present their observations in this chapter of our book.

REFERENCES

Biros, George, Joey F. and Zmud, Robert W. "Inside the Fence: Sensitizing Decision Makers to the Possibility of Deception in the Data They Use", *MIS Quarterly Executive*, March, 2005.

Chickowski, Ericka, "Do Layoffs Pay?" *CIO Insight*, April, 2009.

Morrill, Dan, "Disgruntled Employees and Intellectual Property Protection," http://www.infosecwriters.com/test_resource/pdf/disgruntled_employees_DMorrill.pdf, April, 2006.

"Technical Report, CMU/SEI-2006-TR-026 ESC-TR-2006–091, CERT", Software Engineering Institute (SEI) at Carnegie Mellon University (http://www.sei.cmu.edu/reports/06tr026.pdf, http://www.infosecwriters.com/text resource/pdf/disgruntled), September, 8 2009.

CHAPTER 7

WHISTLE-BLOWING

Whistle-blowing (the act of exposing a wrongdoing in the hope of bringing it to a halt) doesn't fit neatly into our book. The previous several chapters have all been about dark side acts, that is, the kinds of actions people take when they are stepping over into the dark side. People subvert, people lie, people hack, people steal information—all of these are dark side things people do.

Whistle-blowing, on the other hand, is in some ways the opposite of these acts. Whistle-blowing is not an act of wrongdoing. Whistle-blowing, as we have said above, is the act of exposing a wrongdoing. Good guys tend to whistle blow. Bad guys have a tendency to carry out dark side acts. Whistle-blowers, in fact, may be blowing the whistle on the very kinds of dark side activities that we have been discussing in this book.

However, it is not a universal belief that whistle-blowers are invariably the good guys. Those on whom the whistle is blown may not think so at all. Whistle-blowers may make mistakes; think they have identified a dark side matter to blow the whistle on, only to find that they are wrong (see the side bar "Things are not always what they seem"). In fact, some people have identified other terms for whistle-blowers. Politicians speak of "leaks," and try to "plug" them, creating the general feeling that leaks and leakers are themselves wrong (many of those who leak may perceive of themselves as whistle-blowing!)

In recent years, and in legislative actions of the recent years, the tide has pretty much turned to favor whistle-blowing, however. Stronger and stronger laws are passed to protect whistle-blowers (we will learn more about this later in this chapter). The popular view of whistle-blowing, stimulated by movies (for example, *Erin Brockovitch*) and books about whistle-blowers that laud whistle-blowing, has turned dramatically positive. There is still concern over political leaks, but somehow politicians (and, to date, the public) have managed to see leaking as a different thing from whistle-blowing (the first as negative, the second positive!)

But at the same time, and all too often, whistle-blowers are ignored. In the recent case of the Madoff Ponzi $50 billion fraud scheme, one whistle-blower tried to notify the government agencies that would have been responsible for stopping what was going on, only to find the agencies "neither willing nor able" to act on his information. (The angered whistle-blower actually said the agency staff were "too slow, too young, and too undereducated.") After the fact, congressional investigators

The Dark Side of Software Engineering, by Johann Rost and Robert L. Glass
Copyright © 2011 IEEE Computer Society

lauded the whistle-blower, but it was all too late for the investors who lost huge sums of money.

The purpose of this chapter is to explore the issue of whistle-blowing in the context of dark side issues and software engineering. We will learn that, although there are serious studies of the causes and effects of whistle-blowing in the general and academic literature, there are very few such studies about whistle-blowing in the software engineering field literature. In fact, there are few documented instances of whistle-blowing in software, let alone case studies.

To introduce the subject in what follows, we will present a "once upon a time" story about whistle-blowing in software engineering. From there, we will move on to discuss whistle-blowing in more depth: why we see it so seldom in our field and what whistle-blowing means in the disciplines that see it more often.

Sidebar: Things Are Not Always What They Seem

When I, Johann, was a student in Germany, one of our teachers was a foreigner. He was not employed as a professor but he was in charge of teaching some lectures. The teacher had already lived quite a while in Germany, but his German language skills were still rather weak. It is difficult to say if his disappointing teaching performance stemmed from the language problems, from lack of pedagogic competence, or from the coupling of these issues. Since I was a student at that time, I was not in the position to assess his work formally. However, I suppose he must have had some credentials because the university employed him—despite his insufficient language skills.

I chose to miss his lectures and prepare myself at home for the (mandatory) exam. I know, however, that some of my fellow students openly expressed their disappointment in the class. The teacher reacted in an interesting way: He concluded that the criticism from the students came from the fact that he was a foreigner, that is, from another culture. He expressed his disappointment that Germany had not yet finished with its fascist history and that even his young students were allegedly following these malignant ideas.

All this happened quite a while ago. Afterwards, I went to Romania and started a software business. The Romanian and the German people are connected by a friendship measured in centuries: The first Romanian king was elected from the German noble family Hohenzollern. Germans are very much appreciated in Romania and I did not encounter any hostilities to foreigners or rejection due to my nationality.

Nevertheless, at the time that I had arrived in Romania, all foreigners were required to have a certain license plate on their car, one that immediately indicated their foreigner status. I was frequently stopped by the police; it was easy to spot us due to the license plate, and I had the strong suspicion that I was just stopped because we foreigners were an attractive source of bribe money. (It was widely known that the Romania of the 1990s faced problems with corruption.) It was always a good idea to have small American bank bills on hand to solve problems "between friends." (All foreigners were considered "extremely rich" in that emerging economy. At that time, the official salary for a policeman in Romania was about $50 per month. It is quite likely that a foreign manager would try to solve any "problem" with cash—an attractive solution for both sides.) For me it was simply a matter of fact: This was the reason why I was stopped at least once a week. And it also was a matter of fact for all my friends (Germans and Romanians) with whom I discussed this issue.

At that time, I was already an experienced driver. Nevertheless, I had to adapt to the practical differences of the traffic system in Romania, even though the written laws were similar. After while, I realized that I was making some minor driving "mistakes," that is, I hadn't mastered the Romanian "practice" or way of driving. But in time, I polished my driving style and the mistakes disappeared. But then—surprise, surprise—the frequent police control disappeared too.

At that point I realized the Romanian police were fighting not only the problem of corruption but also the problem of extremely undisciplined drivers. And they did it by applying time-proven methods against undisciplined drivers: Stop them, have them fill out lengthy forms, and discuss (patiently) the details of a certain crossroad—all in the Romanian language, of course. I began to undertstand that for them I was just another undisciplined driver. From this experience I learned a lesson: Things are not always what they seem. I was sure that I was being singled out because of my foreigner status, but in fact I was being singled out appropriately because I was simply not driving properly by Romanian standards.

Now, in hindsight, I have a new opinion of the anecdote of the teacher with insufficient language skills: I think he and probably most of his friends were completely sure that the real reason why he was criticized was due to the perceived fascism in Germany. He was blind to his own inabilities, as I had been to my own.

7.1   A HYPOTHETICAL SCENARIO

A Motivating Example.   Once upon a time there was a giant retail corporation (which we will call Giant Retail [GR]) that had a BIG problem. The company did a huge business with a myriad of customers, but their back office accounting systems were a terrible mess. They had to stock excess inventory to make sure they didn't run out of deliverables. Their systems couldn't remember exactly who had bought what from them or who owed how much. Customers complained; management complained; no one was happy.

The companies that encounter these kinds of problems find that there is a packaged solution for them. In the old days of computing (could we call them the "good old days"?), the in-house information systems (IS) department patched together a loose collection of programs to address these problems; nowadays there are integrated solutions that can be bought off the shelf. We will call these packaged solutions BOISEs (back office information system for the enterprise).

Once GR's upper management heard about BOISEs, there was no holding back. They ordered a BOISE from the biggest vendor of these packaged systems (BIG BOISE), listened to the sales pitch of the vendor and of the consulting company that would do the installation for them, and salivated at the size of the savings they were going to have.

But they did something else: They had indavertently sewed the seeds of a whistle-blowing experience—something far more serious. The savings the BOISE would net GR were so huge that upper management immediately factored those savings into their customer contracts. "We will sell you our products for X% less," they told their customers. "Where X is very large because we are going to see huge savings from the implementation of our new BOISE." The customers were delighted. And so was GR's upper management because their sales figures rose according to the enthusiasm of their customers.

But then something bad happened. The promised savings didn't show up at the same time as the reduced-price contracts kicked in.

The first person to notice this was Steve Straightarrow, a programmer/analyst in GR's IS division. He saw almost immediately that whatever the long-term savings of a BOISE, it was going to take awhile—say, a year or three—to accomplish. And in the meantime, the company was going to lose a substantial amount of money on each reduced-price contract they fulfilled. Not only that, but during that "awhile" period, the same old inadequate information systems were going to have to service this rapidly increasing collection of new and old customers. Problems were going to escalate dramatically.

Steve, being a peon at the bottom of the management ladder, could see this problem coming long before it was visible to the managers up at the top of that ladder. And so he did what you would expect anyone named "Straightarrow" to do: He reported the problem to his manager, whom he then thought would report it to his manager, with that process being repeated until the news would reach someone way up in the stratospheric portions of the ladder who could "Do Something About It." This was, of course, an act of whistle-blowing, but just barely, since it is the sort of action that any good employee will take when he or she sees a problem. Management, however, didn't want to hear it; the escalating problem was essentially a denial of carrying-through a top management corporate strategy. "Our reduced-price contracts are going to cause us to lose money? Nonsense!"

Steve was appalled at management's inaction. He couldn't just let the matter drop. So next he took his story to the on-site consultants who were installing the BIG BOISE package. This was, once again, an act of whistle-blowing, somewhat more substantial than his in-house activity, since it involved going outside his company. But the consultants didn't want to hear about it either. They were making a tidy sum of money on their installation contract, and they didn't want anything to perturb that income flow. So, once again, Steve's warnings were ignored.

Finally, he went to the management of the packaged software company BIG BOISE and told them his story. This was getting to be pretty serious whistle-blowing because it involved a highly visible company outside of Steve's own. What do you think happened next? Did the BIG BOISE people suggest to GR's upper management that they slow down and back away from their excessive promises and problematic contracts, or did they—once again—ignore Steve's concerns?

You get to write your own ending to this story, if you wish to. In the sections of this chapter to follow, we'll give you some clues as to what might have happened next, based on research studies into the results of whistle-blowing activities in the real world. Remember, in fact, this whistle-blowing story never really happened! We said at the outset that this was a "once upon a time" story. There is no Steve Straightarrow at GR, although there is a GR and there is a BIG BOISE. No one warned management at the real GR in time to avert the real corporate disaster that was rushing at them. GR lost so much money on those misbegotten contracts, in fact, that a short time later they had to declare bankruptcy. Lawsuits were filed (fairly ugly lawsuits) between GR and the consulting company and BIG BOISE. Eventually those lawsuits were settled—as usual—under terms that precluded anyone from knowing who was penalized and how much was money was exchanged. GR settled into that no man's land to which bankrupt companies are consigned, and there was no happy ending to this once upon a time story.

Would there have been a happy ending if there had been a Steve Straightarrow blowing the whistle and being heard? We'll never know the answer. But we can at least imagine that whistle-blower involvement would have been a better thing than the non-whistle-blowing—what actually happened in this once upon a time story.

7.2 WHISTLE-BLOWING AND SOFTWARE ENGINEERING

Let's bring the discussion back to our central issue. What is whistle-blowing? Here are some definitions. Whistle-blowing: to expose a wrongdoing in the hope of bringing it to a halt. Whistle-blower: One who reveals wrongdoing within an organization to the public or to those in positions of authority.Whistle-blowing is an under-researched topic, one which tends to attract public attention on certain spectacular occasions, but otherwise seldom is seen or described or studied. This fact is particularly true in the field of software engineering. The only research studies we came across on this topic totally ignored software engineering, as if whistle-blowing never happened there.

In fact, that may be true. Robert is also an author/editor of books on software project failures and a collector of computing and software failure stories. Nowhere in those failure stories and studies has he come across a tale of whistle-blowing. Failures happen in our field, but apparently no one blows the whistle on them. We will explore this claim in a bit more detail in the upcoming sections, telling failure stories and pointing out where whistle-blowing might have occurred (or, in a few cases, came very close to occurring). But first, we'll analyze the circumstances as to why the reports and occurrences of whistle-blowing are so absent in the software field.

By going over those failure stories and analyzing the critical moments where whistle-blowing might have occurred, it is possible to abstract-out several reasons as to why whistle-blowing never happened. Those reasons, extracted by Robert from an analysis of a few dozen failure stories found in his books [Glass, 1996, 1998] are presented below.

1. No one was willing to listen to the possibility of failure.
2. No one knew enough to be sure the whistle should be blown,
3. Potential whistle-blowers were too busy in the midst of project activities to feel they had time to blow the whistle.
4. Warning shots were fired that made potential whistle-blowers reluctant to proceed.

Each of these reasons for a failure to whistle-blow are elaborated in the following text.

No One Was Willing to Listen to the Possibility of Failure. This is perhaps the predominant reason for whistle-blowing not happening on the failing projects in question. Here are some examples.

- The Denver airport baggage handling system is one of the most visible computing/software failure stories of all time. Its story is told in [Glass, 1996, pp. 23–51]. Reports on the failure appeared on the nightly news while the contractors struggled to get a complex system to work. Eventually they failed, and the system was considerably scaled back to make it work. At one point, the contractor, BAE systems (which had built such systems successfully before), "told them [the city of Denver and its contractors] that they were going to need one more year to get the system up and running, but no one wanted to hear that." The act of BAE telling the contractors that there was insufficient time to do the job was not an act of whistle-blowing, since it was their job to do so, but it was certainly an example of key players failing to listen to what they didn't want to hear.

- CONFIG was to be the reservation system to end all reservation systems, and a consortium of leading travel-focused companies banded together to make it happen (Glass, 1998, pp. 220–254) CONFIG died amongst swirling accusations about lying, as noted earlier in this book. But there were also attempts to pass on status information early on, information that was studiously ignored. Two years before it was finally cancelled, "many sales representatives who were interviewed expressed a belief that the CONFIG project should be abandoned." And later, a key player is quoted as saying "… they certainly never wanted to hear that there were any problems." And even later, one player said, "I wrote three whistle-blowing memos to three vice presidents … I couldn't stop it. It was a sacred cow project." (Note that this is one of the few times that the term "whistle-blowing" was used in any of these failure stories).

No One Knew Enough to Be Sure the Whistle Should Be Blown. Computing and software projects can be terribly complex, and individual participants in a project may have knowledge of only one small and obscure portion of a larger system. Under those circumstances, it is difficult for anyone to be in a position to blow the whistle.

- Mitch Kapor is one of the early success stories in the microcomputing and software field. He has a track record of producing so-called "killer applications" that became huge technical, financial, and societal successes. But he eventually bent his pick in a company he called ON Technology, where he proposed to build a unique (and, as it turned out, difficult/impossible) software package that he thought would create a whole new market. (The story is told in Glass [1996, pp. 97–100].) The project staggered from one crisis to another, where no one blew the whistle because "no one even pretended to know how far behind the project was."

- One of the most spectacular computing/software failures of all time is the FoxMeyer Drug Co. project, which is a story not only of project failure but, in the end, of corporate failure as well. The story is told in (Glass, 1996, pp. 104–112) and it describes a massive enterprise resource planning (ERP) implementation that ended up destroying the company doing the ERP installation. One key player is quoted in the story as saying, "Many of the problems can be traced to the complexity of integrating the corporate information system.

What we did was relatively small." In other words, the ERP project team knew so little about the totality of what was happening that blowing a whistle in the midst of such ignorance was simply unthinkable.

Below we will discuss the Westpac Bank CS90 project in more depth. But it is worth noting here that CS90 project team members, wondering about the apparent impossibility of the tasks to which they had been assigned, finally reconciled their concerns with "maybe they know something I don't." In other words, even in the face of failure's near-certainty, it is always possible to convince yourself that you don't know enough to criticize what is going on.

Potential Whistle-Blowers Were Too Busy in the Midst of Project Activities to Feel They Had Time to Blow the Whistle.   One of the most exasperating problems of most software projects is that poor or even phony schedule estimation leaves the project team with too little time to do the job. It is characteristic of software projects (and software teams) that, in spite of knowing that a schedule is impossible to achieve, the team works flat-out to try to achieve the unachievable schedule. Terms like "Death March" and "Crunch Mode" are used (in book titles, among other places) to describe this phenomenon. Under such circumstances, it is not surprising that hardly anyone ever blows a whistle. Taking time to whistle-blow means stealing time from other, apparently more important, goals.

In the colorfully-named "Project From Hell" (Glass, 1996, pp. 97–101), a small project gets in huge trouble. The author speaks of "missing dates not by months, but by five years or more" … on a 20-person project! The author tries to get the team to use newer and presumably better technologies, but "the development manager says they aren't interested in creating more work for their overburdened staffs. Everyone has already worked incredible overtime on this project."

If there isn't time for the project team to learn how to "work smarter," there certainly isn't time for it to engage in whistle-blowing!

Warning Shots Were Fired that Made Potential Whistle-Blowers Reluctant to Proceed.   In books on computing project failure, as we mentioned before, the subject of whistle-blowing rarely comes up. For example, in the two books used as source material here, the term "whistle-blowing" only was used on a couple of occasions. We've discussed reasons that probably suffice to explain why whistle-blowing is so rare on computing projects. But there is one further reason, alarming in its implications, that is worth bringing up. Whistle-blowers on these projects knew that trouble would follow them, perhaps immediately, if they blew the whistle.

Earlier we mentioned the CONFIRM travel reservation system. In a chilling discussion of the desirability of having low-level employees speak up (they tend to be the ones who see problems coming the earliest), it was noted that "… some employees did complain about the technical problems—several of them paid for this with their jobs."

Westpac is one of Australia's leading banks. Some years ago, Westpac embarked on an ill-begotten attempt to produce their own integrated banking information system, CS90, with the expectation that it would be so avant-garde that

Westpac could sell it to other banks and make a great deal of money on it. To do that, they proposed to use concepts so advanced that most software specialists had no idea how to do them, and there was considerable animosity generated when they tried to do it anyway. The story of CS90 is told in several places; see Glass (1996: pp. 132–137) and Craddock (1999).

Craddock's version of the story is particularly interesting because he actually worked on CS90. (In fact, his article is a kind of whistle-blowing after the fact, but in his article he notes some whistle-blowing that occurred during the project itself). In one such episode, Craddock and his colleagues complained about the infeasibility of what they were being asked to do, and "... were told to 'shut up and get on with it." (Craddock also said "We were asked to believe at least six impossible things". On another occasion, Craddock had written a program to check for some program files that progress reports had indicated were complete; Craddock's program found that no such program files existed, and he was told to "destroy the program" that uncovered the misrepresentation of what was happening. We will see later in this chapter that whistle-blowing does not always produce benign results and opposition to whistle-blowers is often sufficient to deter them from their quest.

7.3   MORE CASE STUDIES AND ANECDOTES

There are, as we have said, few examples of whistle-blowing on software projects. Interestingly, there are also few research studies on the subject of whistle-blowing, whether on software projects or other kinds of activities. But that does not mean there are *no* anecdotes and case studies about whistle-blowing. There is an ever-growing literature of whistle-blowing stories, ranging from newspaper and TV items to movies (such as Julia Roberts in *Erin Brockovich* and a number of movies about whistle-blowing in the tobacco industry) to books (we will discuss some of those in what follows). Whistle-blowing has caught the public's attention in an astonishing number of ways.

Here we will report on some of those case studies found in books on the subject. Books on whistle-blowing tend to have an interesting variety of positions that they take on their chosen subject. Some simply report facts via objective case studies, some conclude that whistle-blowing has negative consequences and tend to convince the reader never to try doing it, and some by contrast see whistle-blowers as heroic "ethical resisters" who are essential to exposing corruption in government and industry. The diversity of viewpoints can be both confusing to the reader and enlightening—by reading these books, you can feel you have been exposed to all the possible viewpoints on the matter!

7.3.1   Jeffrey Wigand and Brown and Williamson Tobacco

Our first case study in this section is taken from the book (Johnson, 2003), a book that is more factual than opinionated on the subject; it is also a book that notes the United States tends to "export" the notion of whistle-blowing to other countries as a means of helping such countries minimize corruption.

This is a fairly famous case study, one involving a key player in the tobacco industry. We will reference it once again in the next section of this book.

- Jeffrey Wigand also worked for the Brown and Williamson Tobacco Corporation for four years. From 1989 to 1993, he was Vice President of Research and Development and in charge of hundreds of scientists and workers. His annual salary was about $400,000. Wigand, who had a Ph.D. in biochemistry and endocrinology from the University of Buffalo, had been frustrated when he attempted to develop a "safer" cigarette, that is, one with lower carcinogens. Wigand also experienced the company's resistance to his recommendations for changing and removing cancer-causing tobacco additives and flavoring from its cigarettes. After he confronted the CEO on these health-related matters, Wigand was unceremoniously fired.

- In 1994, Wigand became a whistle-blower. Among his many allegations, Jeffrey Wigand accused the company of using additives to manipulate nicotine delivery, editing out incriminating data from company reports, intentionally misleading the public about tobacco's addictive properties, and other serious wrongdoings. He exposed the company's questionable practices, first with the Food and Drug Administration (FDA) in the spring of 1994 and then with the U.S. Department of Justice, which was investigating the industry's efforts to make a 'fire-safe cigarette.'

- Dr. Wigand's insider testimony against the tobacco industry appeared in court documents, newspapers, and on television. The company retaliated against him with lawsuits and negative publicity. Wigand accused them of retaliating with physical threats. Eventually Wigand appeared on the television program *60 Minutes*, which, in turn, led to the making of a movie, *The Insider*, starring Russell Crowe as Wigand. The filmmaker's assumption was that *The Insider* would reach a sympathetic audience who might identify with, rather than condemn, whistle-blowing. They were right. Here we see the example that during the last three decades, whistle-blowing has become a permanent part of American vocabulary, culture, and organizational life.

7.3.2   A Longitudinal Study of Whistle-Blowing

Our second case study is taken from a different book, (Glazer and Glazer 1989). This book is based on in-depth, longitudinal studies of actual whistle-blowers conducted over a period of six years with 64 whistle-blower subjects. Most of this book's case studies are taken from the point of view of the whistle-blower him- or herself. The following case study, however, is very different: It presents a devastating picture of what happens to a whistle-blower from the viewpoint of the whistle-blower's wife.

- "Nineteen years ago, I married a man who was outgoing, secure, bold, and optimistic. Harry was self-confident, enthusiastic, and ambitious about his career. As a husband he was interested in and supportive of my activities. Later, as a father, he was involved in the lives of his five children and made every effort to spend as much time with them as possible.

- Once an outgoing person involved in the interests and activities of his family, Harry became withdrawn, spending whatever hours he could in isolation, pouring over his documents, compulsively reading and re-reading every memo dealing with his work situation. When he and I did sit down to talk to each other, he could speak of nothing but what was happening at work and what his supervisors were doing to him, the pain and suffering he was going through evident in his shoulders and strained quality of his voice.

- All of this, of course, had an effect on the rest of the family. We were afraid to approach Harry with our own needs and concerns, having come to expect his rejection and withdrawal because he no longer had time for or interest in us. One of our children was referred for psychological counseling. I found it necessary to seek work outside the home in order to escape from his oppressive presence and influence. His sleeplessness disturbed our night's rest. We all observed the profound effect of his work situation on him: The bold man became fearful and intimidated; the aggressive person become reticent and insecure; the optimist become hopeless; the relaxed and outgoing person become tense, withdrawn, and isolated; the well-rounded man become obsessive, paranoid, and neurotic. No longer was he the loving spouse and father. He was the stranger who, although living among us, was not with us.

- If his supervisors had set out with the intention of destroying his personality and ego as well as his career by subjecting him to threats, harassment, abuse, intimidation, and humiliation, they were totally successful. He who only wanted to do what was right was instead the victim of many wrongs."

7.3.3 An Even More Pessimistic View

The third case study is taken from yet another book, (Alford, 2001). This is the most pessimistic of all the books we authors have seen, speaking of whistle-blower's "broken lives" after they buck "organizational power." The most powerful case study in this particular book is a hypothetical one; it depicts a kind of worst case scenario of what can happen to a whistle-blower.

- "You work for Gigantic Defense Industries as an auditor. You complain about overcharging, first to your boss, then to the Department of Defense (DoD). You are fired, and the DoD is expected to enforce your right to your job. This process may take several years and is unlikely to be resolved in your favor, given the historical reluctance of the DoD to overturn its contractors. You have a legal right to appeal to the United States Court of Appeals. This right will cost you at least $50,000 to exercise, that is, just to get a judge to hear your case. The cost includes locating witnesses, deposing them, lawyers' fees, filing fees, and more. The case will drag on for years. Ten years is not unusual. Perhaps the court will decide in your favor, but probably not. Whistle-blowers have won only four of almost 10,000 cases to reach the federal courts under the Whistle-blower Protection Act of 1989. One whistle-blower I spoke with spent $100,000 just to get a federal judge to hear her case. 'I had my day in court, only it wasn't a day, but a few minutes. The judge said I didn't have legal standing to sue, and I was back on the street $100,000 poorer.'"

7.3.4   Academic Whistle-Blowing

There is one case study on information technology whistle-blowing that recently (as final touches to this book were being made) appeared in the press, but it is an odd story—it is not about industrial whistle-blowing, but instead academic whistle-blowing!

The scene of this story is a small Australian University, the University of New England. And the key player, the whistle-blower, is a faculty member from that university, Dr. Imre Bakor of its Mathematics, Statistics, and Computer Science program.

Here's a look at how the story unfolded, taken in part from an account that appeared in the *Software Practitioner* newsletter in September 2009 (used here with permission; see the end of the section for the full reference):

Plagiarism Runs Rampant At Australian University IT Program
A scandal is brewing at Australia's University of New England (UNE). Students in UNE's Master of Information Technology degree program have been caught plagiarizing; nearly all of (220 out of 230) master's theses over a recent period (which also included plagiarized material).

To date, although a whistle-blower has shone a light on the scandal, the university is still trying to decide what to do about the matter, One possibility is that the guilty students will be stripped of their degrees. Most of the students, according to the whistle-blower, are foreign students from the Indian sub-continent who were caught because the English in their theses was far superior to their own knowledge of English! Some of the material had been taken verbatim from such sources as *The Guardian* (a British newspaper) and a U.S. business magazine.

The IT program is not administered by UNE but rather by the Melbourne Institute of Technology (MIT, but not the US MIT!; note also that MIT is not the same as the more prestigious RMIT, the Royal Melbourne Institute of Technology), which complicates the matter of how to resolve the problem. Students in the program typically hope to use their degree as leverage for permanent residency in Australia.

The whistle-blower, Dr. Bokor, was not from the IT program itself, but instead was from UNE's own computer science program, and his whistle-blowing was initially ignored by UNE administrators. In fact, he was placed on notice that he could face academic misconduct charges, apparently on the grounds that there was a delay in his reporting the problem. But the whistle-blower contends that he identified the problem as long ago as 2006. In any case, the problem still has not been resolved.

A former UNE chancellor has said that this is "the worst case of plagiarism in Australian history."

There is a bit more to add to that newsletter account that focuses on the whistle-blower and what happened to him. Dr. Bokor had been opposed to the IT program from its inception in 2004, believing that it was a weak substitute for his own computer science program; he felt that the IT program was designed more to stimulate enrollment than to offer needed academic knowledge. (This is not unusual. Computer science and information technology programs are uneasy bedfellows in many academic institutions.) There is some reason to believe that this opposition may be one reason why his whistle-blowing efforts were ignored early on. In fact, when Dr. Bokor made his first attempts at whistle-blowing, he says, his superiors "just pooh-poohed me and told me to go away." (He goes on to say that those superiors were in fact champions of the IT program). At the same time, Dr. Bokor and a colleague were fighting a retrenchment effort, and that further confused the perceived motivation for his whistle-blowing.

Eventually, two important things happened: The university dropped its charges against Dr. Bokor and began a focused study on the facts behind the case. Given that many of the events happened in 2007, it is still somewhat alarming that no resolution of the case has yet been made! The news story, appearing in mid-2009, is symptomatic of the ongoing fact that the UNE is not at all sure how to handle the matter. (Lane, Bernard. "UNE Accused of Allowing Plagiarist to Graduate," *The Australian* (newspaper), July 29, 2009).

7.3.5 The Sum Total of Whistle-Blowing

The final book we will mention, (Dworkin, Miceli, and Near, 2008), does not contain case studies. It is instead a research-based analysis of the whistle-blowing field, attempting to define in a factual way the nature of whistle-blowing and its outcomes as reported in research studies. We will say no more about this book here; see the Appendix to Chapter 7 for the final chapter of that book. It is a chapter that assumes whistle-blowing is a good thing, from both the enterprise and the whistle-blower points of view, and discusses how to bring about more of it.

The sum total of these case studies is somewhat unsatisfying. Some of them present whistle-blowing as a desirable activity with positive outcomes, and label the whistle-blower as a heroic person. Some show whistle-blowing resulting in broken lives, and by implication something that you would be insane to try. In a sense, this mixed bag of case studies is one reason why we chose to end this chapter, not with the presentation of case studies, but with the presentation of research results. In the cold light of research, rather than in the human light of case studies, perhaps we can obtain a somewhat more objective view of whistle-blowing and its outcomes. There is very little whistle-blowing in the software field, we have already noted several times. In this case study section, we see yet another reason why that status has come about. But in the Appendix to Chapter 7, for those inclined to consider whistle-blowing on future (or even current!) software projects, we will see how it might be approached, and a more supportive view of what may result from such activity.

REFERENCES

Alford, C. Fred. *Whistle-blowers: Broken Lives and Organizational Power*, Cornell University Press, 2001.

Dworkin, Terry M., Miceli, Marcia P. and Near, Janet P. *Whistle-Blowing in Organisations*, Routledge (Taylor & Francis Group), 2008.

Glass, Robert L. *Computing Calamities*, Prentice-Hall, 1998.

Glass, Robert L. *Software Runaways*, Prentice-Hall, 1996.

Glazer, Penina M. and Glazer, Myron P. *The Whistle-blowers- Exposing Corruption in Government and Industry*, Basic Books, 1989.

Johnson, Roberta Ann, *Whistle-blowing: When It Works and Why*, Lynne Reiner Publishers, 2003.

Craddock, Chris. "Tales from the Academic Mafia, The Real Inside Story of Westpac's CS90" *The Software Practitioner*, March 1999.

PRACTICAL IMPLICATIONS OF THE RESEARCH INTO WHISTLE-BLOWING

It is self-evident that whistle-blowing can be very beneficial for societies and their members, for example, when a hazardous product is taken off the market, or when stock options are properly reported as a result of whistle-blowing. Some observers may be concerned that whistle-blowing can also be costly to organizations (e.g., by undermining the authority structure, relationships, or trust in organizations). But increasingly, research shows whistle-blowing, and appropriate response to it, can also benefit the organizations in which wrongdoing is occurring (e.g., Glomb et al. [1997]; Magley and Cortina [2002]; Miceli and Near, [1994]; Miceli et al. [2001b]). Nowhere is this point better exemplified than in the comments of one of the world's leading investors: Warren E. Buffett, chairman of the board of Berkshire Hathaway, a global investment firm with 180,000 employees, praised the company's recently installed hotline in his 2005 chairman's letter. "Berkshire would be more valuable today if I had put in a whistleblowing (hot)line decades ago," he wrote. "The issues raised are usually not of a type discoverable by audit, but relate instead to personnel and business practices." (Slovin, 2006, p. 46).

Thus, managers who wisely and ethically do not allow the negative consequences of wrongdoing to play out, and don't want lawmakers or legal authorities to further intervene in their activities, can take steps to improve conditions for whistle-blowers. These steps may encourage whistle-blowers to limit their reports to internal channels, thus reducing the risks and costs associated with external disclosure, such as bad publicity. Thus, one key purpose of this section of the book is to identify steps that such managers can take to avoid the negative effects of wrongdoing and whistle-blowing.

It is ironic that effective organizational response to whistle-blowing can produce many potential benefits, yet whistle-blowing still is an uncommon event. Unfortunately, this is not because organizational wrongdoing is also unusual, thus rendering whistle-blowing unnecessary. Instead research and media reports indicate

(This material is excerpted from the book *Whistle-Blowing in Organisations*, by Marcia P. Miceli, Janet P. Near, and Terry Morehead Dworkin, copyright 2008 by Routledge Publishers, Taylor & Francis Group. Reproduced with permission of Taylor & Francis via the Copyright Clearance Center).

(a) that most employees who perceive that wrongdoing is occurring do not act on it, primarily because they believe nothing will be done to correct the problems, and (b) that these beliefs are often well founded. These findings suggest, in many instances, that no advice we can offer in this section will make a difference. Our advice is predicated on the assumption that there is a sincere wish on the part of the top management team to encourage appropriate internal whistle-blowing, but this condition obviously is not present in certain situations. Presumably, legislators or others have more to say about encouraging reluctant wrongdoers to change or punishing those who refuse. We also offer advice to legislators, and to policy makers, potential or actual whistle-blowers, and other parties. Our focus is primarily on management and, in particular, on those managers who want to develop the important strategic strength of proactively avoiding wrongdoing and its aftermath.

Ideally, material offering advice about whistle-blowing would be thoroughly grounded in a comprehensive body of controlled research, and this research would address costs relative to the benefits of practical options. Ideally, the advice might use—but would not rely greatly on—impressions, guesses, logical deduction, or personal experiences. What seems logical or reasonable—and perhaps true in one situation—may not be consistent with what is more generally found to be true. For example, it may seem "obvious" that threatening retaliation will reduce the incidence of whistle-blowing, because threats impose a cost and suggest high risk of more costs, for example, ruining one's career. But empirical evidence strongly suggests that threatening retaliation does not discourage many whistle-blowers, and indeed may encourage some to report wrongdoing to the media or other outsiders, as in the case of tobacco industry whistle-blower Dr. Jeffrey Wigand. And, advice based on personal experiences may be contradictory. For example, one advisor may suggest that organizational systems should become more formalized, to ensure greater procedural justice and reduce the probability that issues will fall between the cracks, and to satisfy legal requirements (e.g., SOX). Another advisor may instead assert that such formalization undermines trust in the organization, that it may be perceived as "CYA" or "window dressing," and that formalization may not foster—and may even interfere with—building the kind of culture that truly rewards and sustains ethical and productive behavior. How can managers sort out such contradictions?

Some Questions Regarding Whistle-Blowing Hotlines

- Holding everything else constant, do hotlines produce more complaints than other methods, such as informally encouraging employees to report concerns to their supervisors? Are the hotline complaints valid and do they offer evidence of actual wrongdoing, or do they reflect petty concerns, efforts to embarrass someone, etc.? What is the "signal-to-noise" ratio of hotlines versus other methods? Must someone listen to and process 10 or more complaints in order to hear one valid complaint?

- What difference does it make to offer anonymous complaining as an option? Do more employees come forward, or is it harder to follow up when investigating such complaints?

- What are the characteristics of more successful hotlines versus other methods?

- Is it better and more cost effective NOT to encourage whistle-blowing, but instead to endeavor to avoid wrongdoing in the first place?

- Is there some way to quantify the benefits of correcting wrongdoing identified in hotline complaints with the cost of establishing and maintaining hotlines?

- Are there net advantages of outsourcing the hotline function (e.g., employees may feel freer from potential retaliation if reporting to a third party), and if so, do they outweigh the net advantages, if any, of in-house hotlines?

- Do industry, organizational, or employee characteristics make a difference? For example, if a hotline system has worked successfully in a relatively newer and smaller organization with highly educated, young employees, is there evidence it will be equally successful in a large, bureaucratic organization in which employee demographic (or job) characteristics vary widely?

Further, general advice without comprehensive empirical evidence backing it may not be very useful. For example, one could recommend that an organization establish a hotline to encourage valid internal complaints. But before accepting this recommendation, managers might want to know the answers to specific questions, such as those [in the list above], pertaining to hotlines.

Alternative potential sources of answers to such questions exist. Fellow managers could offer responses by describing their own experiences with hotlines or based on what they believe could happen. Interviews with or surveys of managers could aggregate these experiences or opinions, to identify and report general trends or shared views. Academics could review existing research on what drives people to blow the whistle, for example, and use reason to develop advice about hotlines. But the best answers would come from controlled research that directly examined questions like those in [above list].

Unfortunately, to our knowledge, such research is rare to nonexistent. For example, we know of no published studies that have (a) systematically varied (or even measured) employer actions, such as training or improved communications specifically designed to discourage retaliation or to correct problems identified by whistle-blowers, and (b) then measured the effects independently, for example, through before-and-after measures of complaint levels or employee perceptions. Obviously, access to data that would meet rigorous standards of experimental design is a major issue, but also, conducting this research is challenging because top academic journals demand a theoretical basis for predictions. Surveys of non-randomly-selected managers or complaint recipients about what they think would bring employees forward, or their experiences with different techniques, may be the best information that now is publicly available.

Therefore, we must rely on the other sources as described above.

We caution readers about the limitations of the advice we present here, and urge organizations and researchers to undertake more rigorous research directly examining practical questions. In the discussion that follows, we attempt to specify the source or basis for particular recommendations.

Actions that Managers can Take   There appear to be two ways to stop corruption and wrongdoing in organizations: (a) for external forces (e.g., government regulatory agencies or the free market) to exert influence over the organization to convince top management to terminate ongoing wrongdoing or avoid new wrongdoing; and (b) for internal forces within the organization to exert pressure on members not to engage in wrongdoing to start with—because dismantling an organization culture that normalizes wrongdoing, after the fact, is very difficult (Misangyi et al. in press). Cultures that normalize wrongdoing (Ashforth and Anand 2003) provide a "logic of corruption" that may be best disrupted by "institutional entrepreneurs" who attempt to reframe the culture, through "legitimating accounts" that support symbolic identities and meanings that give forth to a new, "anticorrupt logic" (Misangyi et al., in press). It strikes us, to the extent that the term can be appropriately applied to employees below the level of top management, that whistle-blowers might be one of the most important types of institutional entrepreneurs to launch such a change in the culture of the organization that supports normalization of wrongdoing. The question then is how to encourage whistle-blowing. Managers who do so may avoid the obviously intrusive external forces that would otherwise exert pressure on them to avoid new wrongdoing or terminate existing wrongdoing.

Few studies have been performed involving interviews and surveys with managers focused specifically on identifying actions to encourage whistle-blowing. They include the works by Treviño, Weaver, and colleagues (Treviño et al. 2001, 2006), and the preliminary reports (Heard and Miller 2006a, 2006b). The latter study was conducted jointly by the International Business Ethics Institute, in partnership with others, including the Ethics and Compliance Officer Association. At the time of our writing, more specific information about methodology has not been published.

In general, the results of that study and of prior empirical research support the notion that top managers should create a culture for encouraging good performance that is ethical. Preventing behavior that undermines this goal and responding appropriately to irregularities, including perceived wrongdoing, obviously must be a part of such a culture, because these actions promote self-correction and reinforcement of ethical values and standards. In fact, Weaver noted that organizations have the opportunity to create the development of moral agency among their members, thereby leading to stronger moral identity among those members: "Moral actions can reinforce moral identity, making it more central in one's overall self-concept" (Weaver 2006, p. 351). He suggested that moral behavior is the wrong dependent variable; instead we should be concerned about developing moral identity among organization members, because only a strong sense of moral identity can lead an employee to develop a schema of moral agency that will allow that person to engage in moral behavior on a consistent basis. Organizations reinforce the development of moral identity through their actions, and moral behavior, engaged in by employees, reinforces the culture of moral identity among organization members as a group. But organizations "that foster moral muteness" provide less opportunity for the development of moral identity, likely leading to less moral behavior among members (Weaver 2006, p. 352). Where moral identity is an essential intermediate variable in the whistle-blowing process is not a settled matter at this point and remains for future research. In any event, we believe that managers can best foster strong moral identity, and we hope—moral behavior—among members through creation of a positive organization culture.

The creation and maintenance of a positive culture is a long-term, comprehensive goal, and there are many systems that can support the development of that culture. These can be roughly categorized into (a) policies and human resource systems, for example, involving organizational entry, training and development, and employer financial incentives for whistle-blowers; and (b) systems to investigate and respond to concerns.

Policies and Human Resource Systems According to a *Wall Street Journal* article (Lublin 2006), experts on sexual harassment advise that employers should create a "tough" anti-retaliation policy that permits dismissing employees who retaliate. Similar policies may be appropriate for other types of wrongdoing as well, and policies to encourage whistle-blowing should go beyond protection from retaliation and punishing the whistle-blower, as has been detailed (e.g., [Heard and Miller, 2006a]). Policies can be incorporated into the materials given to employees during orientation and made available on company intranet systems. Below we discuss how organizations can support policies and "walk the walk" in action.

Organizational Entry To the extent that dispositions and other individual differences are important determinants of employee behavior, research suggests that the selection process is important. Employees can search for and select employees who possess attributes associated with observation of wrongdoing, and whistle-blowing.

Preliminary research suggests that negative affectivity is associated with observation of wrongdoing, but not necessarily with whistle-blowing. Employees with high negative affectivity more correctly may recognize wrongdoing than do people with low negative affectivity scores; if so, they would be valuable employees. However, if they tend to be overly critical, perhaps training would help to clarify organizational definitions of wrongdoing.

If dispositions such as optimism contribute to whistle-blowing, then human resources managers could take steps to ensure that optimistic applicants are included in those selected. Of course, there is another side to this argument. As suggested in the research on negative affectivity and speculation on the effects of extreme optimism, highly positive people may distort reality, for example, by not seeing wrongdoing when it is occurring (Peterson 2000]). Perhaps a middle ground, or a commitment to diversity of personalities, will be shown to be ideal.

The limited research to date suggests that proactivity is associated with whistle-blowing by employees who have observed wrongdoing. There seems to be little downside risk regarding recruiting and hiring highly proactive people, because proactive personality is associated not only with whistle-blowing within the organization, but also with other positive outcomes such as sales success (e.g., [Crant, 1995]). These findings (Miceli et al. 2001b) provide even more reason for those critical of whistle-blowing to rethink their views. Proactive people can provide a very positive resource to the organization—in sales, in prosocial organizational behavior, in problem-solving—though some managers may feel threatened by them.

After newcomers join the organization, orientation materials can be helpful. In many larger organizations, employees are provided with employee handbooks at the time of orientation. Many companies include codes of ethics and anti-retaliation policies in these handbooks (Lublin 2006). For example, Michaels Stores Inc. recently added an anti-retaliation policy to its corporate code of conduct, which middle and upper managers must sign annually. "Management primarily wanted to ensure a pleasant working environment free from all types of harassment," says a spokeswoman for the Irving, Texas, company. "The fact that it could potentially reduce legal exposure was a secondary focus" (Lublin 2006, p. B4). Lawyers may encourage employers to have employees sign a form stating that they have read and understand the whistle-blowing policies (and other policies, such as those concerning sexual harassment and retaliation).

Advice concerning the specific content of materials pertaining to whistle-blowing has been offered; for example, code standards should show how seriously the organization takes employee concerns, tells employees what to expect when raising concerns (Heard and Miller 2006a, 2006b), and, most importantly, where to take concerns. Clear procedures, actively and effectively maintained, reduce not only harassment liability but also the likelihood of punitive damages. They can also help reduce fines and penalties under the Corporate Sentencing Guidelines (U.S. Sentencing Commission 1991).

Training and Development Organizations should provide training to reduce the incidence of wrongdoing (such as discrimination, including sexual harassment) and retaliation against those who complain (Lublin 2006). For example, Cardinal Building Maintenance Inc., a commercial janitorial service, requires supervisors and managers to attend an annual five-hour class about workplace bias and harassment, and one-fourth of the course focuses on retaliation (Lublin 2006, p. B4).

Similarly, Heard and Miller (2006a) recommended training, both for employees and for managers, dedicated exclusively to raising concerns, avoiding retaliation, and recognizing when retaliation is occurring. They provided specific suggestions on the content and process of such training. For example, trainers should discuss reasons to report concerns, show how concerns will be addressed, and emphasize that speaking up produces a positive impact (Heard and Miller 2006a). Obviously, the vast body of research on training and development has identified many ways to enhance the value and transfer of training in general (e.g., Hatala and Fleming [2007]; Shapiro, King, and Quiñones [2007]), and it could be applied to whistle-blowing training as well. While all of this advice is reasonable, we know of no controlled research demonstrating the effectiveness of training regarding whistle-blowing and such research is sorely needed. Despite this dearth of research, the federal government has begun to require training about whistle-blowing. This mirrors what many states have done in the area of sexual harassment.

Employer Financial Incentives for Whistle-Blowers   Here we consider the question of whether the employer's voluntarily offering whistle-blowers financial incentives, such as a percentage of savings recovered as a result of whistle-blowing (e.g., where embezzlement is caught), a salary increase in a merit system, a one-time cash bonus (e.g., in a suggestion system), or some other financial reward for whistle-blowing, affects whistle-blowing. As for financial incentives offered by entities other than the employing organization, such as the federal and state governments in the case of fraud committed by contractors, we discuss these in the section of this chapter focusing on advice for policy makers.

Observers of wrongdoing consider the costs and benefits of acting, along with other factors. The simplest interpretation of motivation theory would suggest that valued employer rewards for internal whistle-blowing would lead to greater internal reporting, all other factors such as potential retaliation being equal or minimized. Consistent with the model, a KPMG survey showed that "workers said rewards or incentives for adhering to company standards would reinforce ethics programs" (Ridge 2000, p. A1).

However, we know of no private sector U.S. organizations that provide direct financial incentives specifically to reward whistle-blowing, other than in the case of accountants and internal auditors, for example, at the consulting firm BDO Seidman (e.g., [Rankin, 2004]). Further, the research literature generally has not examined whether financial incentives actually affected whistle-blowing. Because both financial incentives and whistle-blowers are exceedingly rare, the coexistence of low frequencies of both implies that it is possible that they do vary together, and the more financial incentives, the more whistle-blowing. Of course, without further evidence, this is simply an untested hypothesis.

One study (U.S. Merit Systems Protection Board 1981) posed a hypothetical question on a survey: employees in general (not just observers of wrongdoing or whistle-blowers) were asked whether they would be more willing to blow the whistle if they received financial rewards for reporting wrongdoing. Somewhat surprisingly, a large majority said this would not affect their behavior. On the one hand, this is consistent with the fact most whistle-blowers to date have acted without clear financial incentives. Maybe they could see important nonfinancial benefits already in the situation, are extremely selfless, or process information in ways most people might consider "emotional" rather than a rational assessment of expected costs and benefits. On the other hand, most past whistle-blowers' experiences, and the survey result, do not necessarily demonstrate that the majority of employees really are uninfluenced by financial incentives, for at least four reasons.

First, in general, psychologists and others have long debated the extent to which people's descriptions of how they would act in a given situation (when presented with a hypothetical scenario by a researcher) reflect real behavior when actually in that situation. People may want to please the researcher or respond in ways that are consistent with the image they want to have of themselves. Of course, variables such as social desirability or self-monitoring (whether biases or dispositional tendencies) may also influence actual workplace behavior (in this case, actual whistle-blowing) as well (e.g., Hewlin [2003]; Premeaux and Bedeian [2003]; Smith and Ellingson [2002]; Turnley and Bolino [2001]). But the key point is that what people say they would do is not necessarily the same as what they would actually do, and what people say would influence their behavior is not necessarily what actually influences them. More specifically, a recent meta-analysis of whistle-blowing studies showed that the predictors of whistle-blowing intentions (such as those that may be measured with a hypothetical question on a survey) are not necessarily the same as the predictors of actual whistle-blowing (Mesmer-Magnus and Viswesvaran 2005).

Second, some form of variable pay is widely used by private employers in the United States and the vast majority of these programs are individually based merit pay (salary increase) programs or bonus systems (Zall 2001). If managers did not believe or find through experience that employees could be encouraged, via pay, to behave in ways that top management wanted, why would they operate these systems, which are costly and difficult to administer? And if an employer wanted valid whistle-blowing as well as good job performance, why couldn't it use similar systems to encourage either?

Third, in the United States at least, taboos and privacy concerns often discourage employee admissions that money is valued or influential on their effort. Even CEOs are expected to say that they live for the challenge of their work first and foremost. Millionaire athletes are not worthy of respect unless they play "for the love of the game." Yet, clearly the amounts and nature of compensation influence their behavior.

Fourth, respondents may have viewed this question as asking whether they must be bribed in order to behave in a morally correct or appropriate way. The vast majority of respondents had indicated in a previous question on the same survey that they approved of the reporting of wrongdoing. Because it may be unacceptable to most people to admit that cash incentives would be necessary to do the "right" thing, it may have been easier to simply say they would make no difference. For any of these reasons, then, survey responses relative to incentives may bear little relationship to what employees actually think and do, and more research is needed to determine whether and how compensation can be structured to encourage whistle-blowing.

Systems to Encourage, Investigate, and Respond to Expression of Concerns
When a concern is voiced, managers should be certain to focus on the wrongdoing alleged in the complaint and not engage in attacks on the complainant. A full and fair investigation should be undertaken and swift corrective action taken when the complaint is well-founded. To the extent confidentiality is not at issue, positive feedback indicating how the problem has been corrected should be shared with others as well, for example, "thanks to a report from one of our associates, we were alerted to this problem and took the following actions." Where complaints are unfounded, employees can be counseled on what is lacking; for example, is the evidence unclear? Below we discuss systems that can help facilitate this general advice.

Internal Communication Channels and Hotlines   According to a KPMG survey of private and public sector employees (e.g., Grimsley [2000]), more than four-fifths of respondents would choose their supervisor or another manager as the complaint channel, if they were to report concerns (Heard and Miller, 2006b). But the same survey showed that "'people are not reporting misconduct because they are not encouraged to do so,' says Richard Girgenti, a KPMG executive" (Ridge 2000, p. A1). Thus, managers should "create a corporate culture where dialogue and feedback are regular practice—and this should extend to every level of employee throughout the organization. Such a culture can build the foundation of an open problem-solving environment, demonstrate to employees that it is safe to raise concerns, and exhibit that the organization takes retaliation seriously" (Heard and Miller 2006a, p. 2).

Heard and Miller recommended anonymous surveys to assess employee perceptions, as a first step in a two-way communication process in which employees express their views. They offered specifics about the content and analysis of the surveys, and recommended follow-up focus groups. They also recommended that multiple, effective communication channels be available, to enable employees to select the person(s) with whom they are most comfortable sharing sensitive information. Alternative channels are essential to avoiding liability in sexual harassment cases so that the victim does not have to report to the harasser; the same logic would apply here.

Consistent with this advice, researchers have found a positive correlation between increased internal whistle-blowing and having specific, identified routes for whistle-blowing, a particular person identified to receive and follow-up the information, and a strong, non-retaliatory policy encouraging whistle-blowing (Barnett, Cochran, and Taylor [1993]; Miceli and Near [1992]). Open door policies do not meet these requirements. They are also unlikely to result in compliance under the Federal Sentencing Guidelines (U.S. Sentencing Commission 1991).

The Investigation Process and Correction of Wrongdoing   The primary purpose of the investigation process is to determine whether the complaint has merit, so that appropriate actions can be taken. Organizations and their members are not well served by ignoring real wrongdoing, such as discrimination or serious unsafe working conditions. But they are also not well served by rewarding the gadfly or chronic low performer seeking to distract attention, nor by wasting time on frivolous complaints. As Perry noted, "although the authenticity of a whistle-blower's complaint may be irrelevant for the organization that chooses to ignore it or to retaliate against the whistle-blower, it is clearly relevant to the organization that wishes to respond appropriately. Responsive organizations are faced with investigating the complaint to identify whether it is authentic or inauthentic" (Perry 1991, p. 12).

Determining merit or authenticity often is easier said than done. Obviously some whistle-blowers can be mistaken, or may find objectionable certain types of behavior that are not widely defined as wrongdoing, but there have been many documented cases where valid concerns were ignored. Further, many complaint recipients perceive that only a tiny minority of complaints are valid, but other data suggest that in reality many more have substance, at least under certain circumstances. Unfortunately, the validity of complaints, and predictors and consequences of validity, have rarely been studied systematically; so, findings must be considered preliminary. But they certainly raise a critical point: Obviously, employers who perceive that complaints are frivolous are unlikely to take corrective action, and if they refuse to act on a large proportion that are valid, then even employees with valid concerns will quickly conclude that nothing will happen if they complain. This creates a vicious circle in which employees rarely report real wrongdoing, so officials take few corrective actions, to which employees react by believing nothing would be done to correct wrongdoing if it were reported, and reports drop further. The extant information suggests that organizations should examine not only the numbers of complaints filed, but also what proportion of complaints is found to be meritorious. They should look for ways to improve investigations or take other steps—such as clarifying what wrongdoing is, what evidence employees should provide, etc.— where these numbers are low.

In their study of employers' advice and practices, Heard and Miller identified two key tendencies that should be avoided: (1) "shooting the messenger," in which focus is misdirected from resolving the wrongdoing and toward punishing the whistle-blower, and (2) eliminating the "bad apples" (punishing the wrongdoers) but failing to "identify a systemic cause or rectify the actual problem" (Heard and Miller 2006a, p. 7). They offered steps for employer consideration, including:

- "Ensure responsibility for investigations is clearly delineated and effective processes are in place for conducing investigations;
- ensure investigations can take place relatively quickly;
- focus on the complaint, not the complainant;
- ensure communication gaps are closed (i.e., lack of communication between HR and the Ethics Office can have serious implications, e.g., under SOX);
- take reports of retaliation seriously and follow up on them; discipline those that commit wrongdoing;
- [and] provide feedback to the individual that reported the wrongdoing" (Heard and Miller 2006a, p. 7).

We would call particular attention to the advice on retaliation. Litigation regarding retaliation is the largest source of discrimination claims currently. As noted in a recent article appearing in *Business Week*, in 2005 and 2006, retaliation claims represented 30% of all charges individuals filed with the Equal Employment Opportunity Commission, an increase from about 20% 10 years ago. Further, a recent Supreme Court ruling clarified that excluding an employee from meetings, relocating his or her office, or other actions falling far short of firing could lead to liability (Orey 2007).

Again, because of a dearth of controlled empirical research specifically examining the effects of implementing such recommendations, we cannot offer citations in support of them. However, all seem reasonable, based on the research on how and why whistle-blowing occurs and on the importance of effectiveness in the process.

Heard and Miller (2006) emphasized that, if an anonymous survey or other assessment of employee perceptions reveals problems, it is important for organizations to rectify the problems. Once a specific incident of wrongdoing has occurred, it is not too late to realize benefits, if communications from management to employees are open. After a specific incident has been reported and wrongdoing remedied, companies can publish "scrubbed reports of actual cases to illustrate the action taken by the organization to rectify problems and punish wrongdoers" (Heard and Miller

2006a, p. 7). Implementing this recommendation would likely help counteract employees' tendency—demonstrated in controlled research—to believe nothing could or would be done if wrongdoing were reported. Consistent with this advice, research (Miceli et al. 2001b) suggests that encouraging reporting and immediate correction about which employees are informed may also have desirable effects almost as good as those resulting from preventing wrongdoing in the first place. These benefits go beyond reducing tangible costs to the organization associated with wrongdoing itself (e.g., adverse publicity, damaged reputation, lawsuits); managers who prevent or correct wrongdoing may engender positive feelings and favorable consequences among employees.

Monitoring and Following Up   Implementing programs and actions intended to encourage whistle-blowing is not sufficient; managers need to monitor the success of the programs and make changes where needed. For example, in the case of sexual harassment, the *Wall Street Journal* recommends that a thorough follow-up be conducted several months after the initial intervention to ensure that retaliation does not occur (Lublin 2006). Similarly, Heard and Miller recommend steps for maintaining effective communication, for example, by reminding employees about the available channels (Heard and Miller 2006a). Periodic republication also reduces legal liability and is required under certain federal laws.

Advice to Whistle-Blowers and Potential

Whistle-Blowers.   Prevailing legal arguments, both in U.S. law (Miceli and Near 1992) and British law (Callahan et al. [2004]; Vinten [1994]), suggest that "whistle-blowing is warranted if the whistle-blower believes, in good faith, that the wrongdoing has implications for public policy; that is, some portion of society is endangered by the organization's actions" (Near and Miceli 1996, p. 508). Further, ethicists have indicated that one condition necessary for the justification of whistle-blowing is that "the whistle-blower has acted after a careful analysis of the danger: (a) how serious is the moral violation; (b) how immediate is the moral violation; (c) is the moral violation one that can be specified?" (Bowie 1982, p. 143). Clearly such prescriptions depend on the accuracy of the potential whistle-blower's observation of the facts surrounding the wrongdoing [Near & Miceli, 1996], and they imply that the nature of the wrongdoing is critical. They may also depend on the process used by the whistle-blower (e.g., taking steps to embarrass a perceived wrongdoer or interfere with legitimate work processes, rather than focusing on solving the problem) (Miceli and Near 1997).

Therefore, it is not surprising that many experts who work with whistle-blowers (e.g., Devine [1997]) emphasize the importance of having sound evidence and following good process. This process should be informed by the relevant law (to enable the whistle-blower to retain the maximum protection available) and the literature on distributive, procedural, and interactional justice (e.g., Miceli and Near [1997]). For example, it is important for whistle-blowers to know that large rewards under the False Claims Act are not available unless the information is useful and novel, and leads to a conviction. Unfortunately, because there is little research on specific tactics and their relative effectiveness, we cannot be as specific here as we would like to be.

Advice to Policy Makers In some sense, given the risks and costs, the perception on the part of many complaint recipients that few cases have merit, and the limited direct rewards for whistle-blowing, it is remarkable that anyone ever chooses to challenge organizational wrongdoing. The legal protections for employees do not guarantee protection from retaliation. Further, research strongly suggests that legal changes focused on encouraging organizations to change the wrongdoing, and punishing organizations that ignore whistle-blowers, would have greater impact.

Preliminary research on corporate response to legal changes showed few changes, at least early on. A survey of human resource executives from Fortune 1000 firms (Near and Dworkin 1998) asked whether their firms changed their whistle-blowing policies in response to changes in new state statutes (see also Dworkin, Near, and Callahan [1995]). The authors expected that firms might have created internal channels for whistle-blowing in response to the new legislation, but very few firms indicated that they had created their policies in responses to legal changes. For most, this meant reliance on an open door policy as their primary mechanism for internal whistle-blowing. Unfortunately, most employees do not see such policies as effective or protective, and they have not been used successfully to encourage internal reporting of wrongdoing (Keenan 1990).

These studies, of course, predated passage of SOX. Moberly has charged that, prior to this event, legislative attempts designed to encourage whistle-blowing in order to reduce retaliation fit what hetermed the "anti-retaliation model" and were largely unsuccessful because the laws focused only on discouraging retaliation against whistle-blowers and not on encouraging whistle-blowing behavior (Moberly 2006). He argued instead for the structural model, exemplified by SOX, which both: (a) provides incentives for whistle-blowers by showing them clearly that whistle-blowing is not disloyal to the firm but supports it, and (b) provides clear, safe, and effective channels for whistle-blowing by providing that the complaint recipient should be an independent member of the audit committee of the board of directors. As he noted, prior to the most recent wave of scandals in the late 1990s, several legislative attempts in both the anti-retaliation model and the structural model were unsuccessful, because they were not implemented properly.

Most companies have established hotlines as an intermediary recipient between the whistle-blower and the audit committee, and this may reduce the effectiveness of the model. Some commentators recommend that the organization have a designated recipient inside the company, such as an ombudsperson in addition to a hotline.

Success is possible only if the legislative models prohibit retaliation against whistle-blowers, provide sufficient incentive to persuade whistle-blowers that coming forward is in the best interests of society and the firm, and create effective channels for reporting the wrongdoing, anonymously or otherwise, to safe complaint recipients outside the chain of command in the firm and at the top of the firm (i.e., the audit committee). Once firms recognize the potential of SOX and other structural methods to root out wrongdoing early and provide channels for its internal reporting, so lawsuits may be avoided and problems rectified quickly, they will be better able to use these structures to improve their overall effectiveness and reduce costs.

Laws that require whistle-blowing procedures and encourage whistle-blowing may also have the effect of making whistle-blowing more acceptable and positive. There is some evidence that private employers have changed their policies over time, in part because employees and citizens demand it. For example, a survey by the Ethics Resource Center found that 79% of employers have a written ethics standard, up from 60% in 1994 (Grimsley 2000). We believe that employers will be more likely to take such actions in the future, because of pressures from individual employees who are increasingly responding to legislative changes aimed directly at potential whistle-blowers. For example, SOX, governing public companies (e.g., those listed on exchanges), requires some additional actions focused on effectiveness in correcting wrongdoing rather than preventing retaliation, for example, requiring that corporate lawyers report misconduct to top management and, if there is no response, to the board (Dwyer et al. 2002). Future research should examine whether this is sufficient incentive to organizations to take responsive action.

The literature on sexual harassment law can serve as an example for how whistle-blowing law and corporate practice (e.g., training) could be improved (e.g., Dwyer et al. [2002]). Over the past 20 to 25 years, U.S. Supreme Court decisions have provided more incentives and penalties for employers, and surveys indicated that there is much greater awareness and disapproval of sexual harassment in varying forms than previously (e.g., Erdreich, Slavet, and Amador [1995]). Thus, one effect of oversight of employers seems to be that employees show greater awareness of wrongdoing and their legal rights in the workplace. In fact, a new law applies to federal agencies and requires them to pay for settlements and judgments against them in discrimination and whistle-blower cases out of their agency budgets, and thus "will hit agencies in their pocketbooks" (Barr 2002, p. B2). Further, agencies are required to file reports with Congress and the attorney general on data such as the number of complaints filed against them by employees, the disposition of these cases, the total monetary awards charged against the agency, and the number of agency employees disciplined for wrongdoing involving discrimination or harassment (Barr 2002). There are potential financial incentives for citizens who save the federal government money by informing it of fraud by contractors or other activity (e.g., Zingales [2004]). As noted previously, the False Claims Act, dating to the Civil War, allows whistle-blowers to collect up to 30% of the damages (Callahan and Dworkin [1992]; Seagull [1995]). In 1986, the False Claims Act was revised, such that whistle-blowers were more likely to receive a reward (Callahan and Dworkin 1992). Prior to 1986, about six false claims for government funds had been reported per year by whistle-blowers. Since 1986, the number has jumped substantially, with more than 3000 qui tam cases filed by 2004 (Phillips and Cohen 2004). False Claims Act recoveries have exceeded $17 billion, with nearly $1 billion recovered in the first quarter of 2006 (Taxpayers Against Fraud Education Fund 2006) and it has produced awards as high as $77 million (Haddad and Barrett 2002). Also, changes in the IRS reward structure have led to more reporting.

Recent studies indicate that SOX has not been effective in encouraging whistle-blowing; indeed, it has been reduced since the law's passage. Several commentators have urged that SOX be amended to include rewards in order to make it more effective and have discussed various ways to create a reward fund. Whether it is possible to encourage private sector employers to offer financial incentives has not been determined.

If potential whistle-blowers are motivated to act by financial rewards, then private employers may be more likely to protect themselves—as well as to help other members of society—by changing their policies and procedures to prevent wrongdoing in the first place and to terminate it when informed by their employees that wrongdoing is ongoing. We believe that these changes in the legal environment eventually will have an important impact on encouraging employees who observe wrongdoing to blow the whistle. The type of wrongdoing (specifically wrongdoing that results in fraud against the federal government) will probably become an important predictor of whether employees who observe wrongdoing decide to blow the whistle.

Conclusion   Throughout this chapter, we have attempted to provide concrete suggestions to the parties involved in the whistle-blowing process. Unfortunately, research has not developed to the point where we can offer specific, unequivocal evidence in support of all of these suggestions.

REFERENCES

Ashforth, B. E., and Anand, V. "The normalization of corruption in organizations." In R. M. Kramer and B. M. Staw (Eds.): *Research in Organizational Behavior* (Vol. 25, pp. 1–52). Amsterdam: Elsevier, 2003.

Barnett, T., Cochran, D. S., and Taylor, G. S. The internal disclosure policies of private-sector employers: An initial look at their relationship to employee whistleblowing. *Journal of Business Ethics*, 12, 127–136, 1993.

Barr, S. "Making agencies pay the price of discrimination, retaliation." *Washington Post*. May 16, 2002: p. B2.

Bowie, N. *Business Ethics*. Englewood Cliffs, NJ: Prentice-Hall, 1982.

Callahan, E. S., and Dworkin, T. M. "Do good and get rich: Financial incentives for whistle-blowing and the False Claims Act." *Villanova Law Review*. 1992: 37, 273–336.

Callahan, E. S., Dworkin, T. M., and Lewis, D. Whistle-blowing: Australian, U.K., and U.S. approaches to disclosure in the public interest. *Virginia Journal of International Law*. 2004: 44, 879–912.

Crant, J. M. The Proactive Personality Scale and objective job performance among real estate agents. *Journal of Applied Psychology*. 1995: 80(4), 532–537.

Devine, T. "What to expect: Classic responses to whistle-blowing." In: *Courage Without Martyrdom: The Whistleblower's Survival Guide* (1997, pp. 27–48). Washington, D.C.: Government Accountability Project and Fund for Constitutional Government.

Dworkin, T. M., Near, J. P., and Callahan, E. S. Governmental and social influences on corporate responsibility. Paper presented at the International Association of Business and Society, Vienna, Austria, 1995.

Dwyer, P., Carney, D., Borrus, A., Woellert, L., and Palmeri, C. Year of the whistleblower: The personal costs are high, but a new law protects truth-tellers as never before. *Business Week*. December 16, 2002; p. 106.

Erdreich, B. L., Slavet, B. S., and Amador, A. C. Sexual harassment in the federal workplace: Trends, progress, continuing challenges (Report of the Merit Systems Protection Board) 1995. Washington, D.C.: U.S. Government Printing Office.

Glomb, T. M., Richman, W. L., Hulin, C. L., Drasgow, F., Schneider, K. T., and Fitzgerald, L. F. Ambient sexual harassment: An integrated model of antecedents and consequences. *Organizational Behavior and Human Decision Processes.* 1997: 71(3), 309–328.

Grimsley, K. D. Office wrongdoing common. *Washington Post.* June 14, 2000, p. E02.

Haddad, C., and Barrett, A. A whistle-blower rocks an industry. *Business Week.* June 24, 2002, pps. 126–130.

Hatala, J.-P., and Fleming, P. R. Making transfer climate visible: Utilizing social network analysis to facilitate the transfer of training. *Human Resource Development Review.* 2007: 6(1), pps. 33–63.

Heard, E., and Miller, W. Creating an open and non-retaliatory workplace. *International Business Ethics Review.* 2006a, Summer, pp. 1–7.

Heard, E., and Miller, W. Effective code standards on raising concerns and retaliation. *International Business Ethics Review.* 2006b, Summer, pp. 1–11.

Hewlin, P. F. And the award for best actor goes to …: Facades of conformity in organizational settings. *Academy of Management Review.* 2003: 28(4), 633.

Keenan, J. P. Upper-level managers and whistleblowing: Determinants of perceptions of company encouragement and information about where to blow the whistle. *Journal of Business and Psychology.* 1990: 5, 223–235.

Lublin, J. S. Theory and practice: Retaliation over harassment claims takes focus. *Wall Street Journal.* April 16, 1007, p. B4.

Magley, V. J., and Cortina, L. M. Retaliation against military personnel who blow the whistle on sexual harassment. Paper presented at the annual meeting of the Society for Industrial and Organizational Psychology, Toronto, Ontario, Canada. (2002, April).

Mesmer-Magnus, J. R., and Viswesvaran, C. Whistleblowing in organizations: An examination of correlates of whistleblowing intentions, actions, and retaliation. *Journal of Business Ethics.* 2005: 62, 277–297.

Miceli, M. P., and Near, J. P. *Blowing the whistle: The Organizational and Legal Implications for Companies and Employees.* 1992. New York: Lexington.

Miceli, M. P., and Near, J. P. Listening to your whistle-blowers can be profitable! *Academy of Management Executive.* 1994a: 8(3), 65–72.

Miceli, M. P., and Near, J. P. Whistle-blowing as antisocial behavior. In R. Giacalone and J. Greenberg (Eds.), *Antisocial Behavior in Organizations* 1997. Thousand Oaks, CA: Sage Publications, pp. 130–149.

Miceli, M. P., Van Scotter, J. R., Near, J. P., and Rehg, M. T. Individual differences and whistle-blowing. Paper presented at the 61st Annual Meeting of the Academy of Management, Best Paper Proceedings, Washington, D.C., 2001b.

Misangyi, V. F., Weaver, G. R., and Elms, H. (in press). Ending corruption: The interplay between institutional logics, resources, and institutional entrepreneurs. Academy of Management Review.

Moberly, R. E. (2006). Sarbanes-Oxley's structural model to encourage corporate whistleblowers. *Brigham Young University Law Review,* 2006(5), 1107–1180.

Near, J. P., and Dworkin, T. M. Responses to legislative changes: Corporate whistleblowing policies. *Journal of Business Ethics,* 1998: 17, 1551–1561.

Near, J. P., and Miceli, M. P. Whistle-blowing: Myth and reality. *Journal of Management,* 1996: 22(3), 507–526.

Orey, M. Fear firing: How the threat of litigation is making companies skittish about axing problem workers. *Business Week,* 52+ (online), April 23, 2007.

Perry, J. L. The organizational consequences of whistleblowing. Unpublished manuscript, Bloomington, IN, 1991.

Peterson, C. The future of optimism. *American Psychologist,* 2000: 55, 44–55.

Phillips, J. R., and Cohen, M. L. *False Claims Act: History of the law,* 2004. Retrieved from http://www. phillipsandcohen.com/CM/FalseClaimsAct/hist_f.asp.

Premeaux, S. F., and Bedeian, A. G. Breaking the silence: The moderating effects of self-monitoring in predicting speaking up in the workplace. *Journal of Management Studies*, 2003: 40(6), 1537.

Rankin, K. (2004, November 22). P.C.A.O.B. wants auditors to blow the whistle. WebCPA.com. Retrieved March 29, 2007 from http://www.webcpa.com/article.cfm?articleid=8921.

Ridge, P. S. Ethics programs aren't stemming employee misconduct, a study indicates. *Wall Street Journal*. May 11, 2000, p. A1.

Seagull, L. M. Whistleblowing and corruption control: The GE case. *Crime, Law, and Social Change*. 1995: 22(4), 381–390.

Shapiro, J. R., King, E. B., and Quiñones, M. A. Expectations of obese trainees: How stigmatized trainee characteristics influence training effectiveness. *Journal of Applied Psychology*. 2007: 92(1), 239.

Slovin, D. Blowing the whistle. *Internal Auditor*, 2006: 45–49.

Smith, D. B., and Ellingson, J. E. Substance versus style: A new look at social desirability in motivating contexts. *Journal of Applied Psychology*, 2002: 87(2), 211–209.

Taxpayers Against Fraud Education Fund. False Claims Act recoveries top $17 billion since 1986, $1 billion in first 3 months of FY 2006. Retrieved January 24, 2007, from http://66.98.181.12/whistle77.htm.

Treviño, L. K., and Weaver, G. R. Organizational justice and ethics program "follow-through": Influences on employees' harmful and helpful behavior. *Business Ethics Quarterly*, 2001: 11(4), 651–671.

Treviño, L. K., Weaver, G. R., and Reynolds, S. J. Behavioral ethics in organizations: A review. *Journal of Management*, 2006: 32(6), 951–990.

Turnley, W. H., and Bolino, M. C. Achieving desired images while avoiding undesired images: Exploring the role of self-monitoring in impression management. *Journal of Applied Psychology*, 2001: 86(2), 351.

United States Sentencing Commission. Sentencing Guidelines. Chapter 8 1991.

U.S. Merit Systems Protection Board. *Whistle-blowing and the federal employee*. 1981. Washington, D.C.: U.S. Government Printing Office.

Vinten, G. Whistleblowing–fact and fiction: An introductory discussion. In G. Vinten (Ed.), *Whistleblowing: Subversion or corporate citizenship* (pp. 1–20). 1994. New York: St. Martin's Press.

Weaver, G. R. Virtue in organizations: Moral identity as a foundation for moral agency. *Organization Studies*. 2006: 27, 341–368.

Zall, M. Pluses and minuses of variable pay. Retrieved January 12, 2007, from http://pubs.acs.org/sub-scribe/journals/tcaw/10/i09/html/09work.html.

Zingales, L. Want to stop corporate fraud? Pay off those whistle-blowers. *Washington Post*. January 18, 2004, p. B02.

PART 2

VIEWPOINTS ON DARK SIDE ISSUES

This section of our dark side book is a step outside the box. Here, we present the views on dark side matters of several well-known computing and software figures.

INTRODUCTION

The topic of the dark side in computing and software engineering, as we have been saying throughout our book, is an unusual one. Not many writers have chosen to write about it. Not many researchers have chosen to study it. Most practitioners have experienced it in one guise or another, but except for talk around the water cooler or the printer, not much is said about it in the more official channels of practice.

Because of that, we felt the need to sound out some other computing folks on their own experiences and expectations about the topic. We were curious, to be honest, that with all the formal silence on the matter, how many of these well-known computing folk would choose to say anything it.

We contacted a few dozen people whose names and reputations we knew and were gratified that a fair percentage of them chose to say something for our book. This is the section of the book where we share those viewpoints with you.

Our inquiry was pretty broad. In essence, we asked them to "say anything you want on this topic as long as it is at least somewhat relevant." What follows is our contact inquiry, and then the resulting viewpoint writings.

> A colleague and I are putting together a book to be called *The Dark Side of Software Engineering*, under contract to IEEE Computer Society Press. It will include a chapter called "Viewpoints," in which we hope to include essays from people like you on anything that appeals to you related to our subject matter.
>
> To explain what we mean by the "dark side" and why we chose to write about it, I am attaching a draft of the Introduction section to the book. It also contains some personal anecdotes about the topic; we hope all of this stimu-

lates your writing juices into wanting to say something in viewpoints. Essays could be something similar to

- personal anecdote(s), and lessons learned derived from them
- facts and/or data on dark side matters, and/or
- opinions and/or beliefs about dark side matters.

In other words, almost anything (relevant!) goes.

There are no length constraints—short is OK, but a few pages would also be OK. (Plus we'll want to print a short (one paragraph or so) bio for each contributor). Deadline would be in the next couple of months (the manuscript is due to IEEE by the end of the year).

Let me know if you would like to write something.

The responses to this inquiry were fascinating. In the end, we classified them into two categories: Opinions, Predictions, and Beliefs (Chapter 8), and Personal Anecdotes (Chapter 9). If you've been paying close attention here, you'll notice one category that's missing. In our original inquiry to potential viewpoints authors, we had a third category: Facts and/or Data. Not one of our responders had anything to say in that category! That's not surprising, of course, because we've been saying—and thinking—all along that there was very little research in these dark side fields, and the absence of that category in our viewpoint responses was simply one more manifestation of that.

Be that as it may, we find these viewpoint opinions and anecdotes fascinating, and we hope you will, too!

CHAPTER 8

OPINIONS, PREDICTIONS, AND BELIEFS

We were particularly pleased in putting together this viewpoints material to get some of our contributors to express beliefs about the matters of the dark side. Of course, we could have expected some of our contributors to say something such as "dark side is bad, light side is good" (or something comparable), but we wanted something more than that.

And we got it! In the opinions material that follows, we find things ranging from an astonishingly complete discussion of a topic that we have seen no one else discuss—automated crime—to some more (at least comparatively) light-hearted discussions of beliefs, like "pretending," the evils of "business-speak," and software folk as "pathological code-hackers." It is interesting that most of our viewpoints contributors chose to tell personal anecdotes (which we will see in this chapter) rather than express beliefs and opinions (or even predictions!), but we are very happy with those who chose to be more opinionated on the matter!

Welcome, in what follows, to the world of expert opinions on matters dark side.

8.1

AUTOMATED CRIME

Donn B. Parker
CISSP (Retired)

We must anticipate a new type of high tech crime that involves the computer as both a tool and a target of attack. I call this new cybercrime "Automated Crime." It is a complete crime, packaged in one or more computer programs, that can be executed entirely in the time-scale of computers, in only a few milliseconds and before any victim could blink an eye. There is no human interruption or interaction needed after starting the crime program, and no human recognition of its existence is possible until it is finished and disappears. When the perpetrator executes the program, it automatically commits the crime and removes all evidence (including itself) before the victim can react. Expert software developers could package an automated crime and pass it on to any number of potential perpetrators. Without needing any technical capabilities, perpetrators could then execute the crime in their computers to attack any number of victims' computers without the developers' or even the perpetrators' further involvement. Anybody could possess or own a copy of the crime application software and distribute it through the Internet, for example, to be executed in the victims' computers at any time. It could be designed so that the perpetrator would not know the victim, what crime occurred, what method was used, or what the results would be.

Based on 30 years of study and interviews with more than two hundred computer criminals, I define cybercrime more liberally than most researchers do, as being any crime in which the perpetrator uses some special knowledge or tool of information technology. The computer plays the role of object, symbol, tool, or subject in cybercrime. It may be the object of attack, such as in sabotage or theft of computers. It may be a symbol for intimidation or deception or a tool to perpetrate a crime in some other environment. And it may be the subject of a crime when it creates a unique environment in which a crime occurs or creates a specific form of information that is the target of a crime. Automated crime is a new form of cybercrime that could play any or all four roles.

We have automated business processes; why not automate the crime that attacks those processes? The next major cyberspace disaster could be automated crime. It seems to be developing incrementally as hacker software tools evolve and become more sophisticated. It goes far beyond today's blended computer viruses, worms, and Trojan horse attacks. Because automated crime may lead to full-scale information warfare, perhaps I should remain quiet about it, hoping that it will not

---

The Dark Side of Software Engineering, by Johann Rost and Robert L. Glass
Copyright © 2011 IEEE Computer Society

come to pass. But I believe that it is probably better to warn the potential victims and defenders of this new escalation, even if doing so alerts their enemies to a possible new line of attack. In any event, I do not provide enough details here to constitute a recipe for automated crime.

Automated crime would be complete—from the selection of a victim to the perpetration of the misdeed and the covering of the perpetrator's tracks—all packaged in a single computer program or suite of programs. Malicious technologists can now package well-conceived crimes and give or sell them to others. By doing this, they would be introducing the concept of possessing, selling, buying, giving away, or acquiring potentially perfect crimes for the first time in criminal history. Crimes could be copyrighted or patented just like automated business processes. Innocent or not-so-innocent users could download them as freeware through the Internet or might ultimately even be able to purchase them in software stores for $39.95, from a shelf containing four-color, shrink-wrapped crime-in-a-box products. One might be labeled *Accounts Payable Fraud;* another *Payroll Checks Fraud*; and another, *Quickmail Espionage*. You may be legally able to possess a crime. No law would be broken until you anonymously launch one from your computer, but who is to catch you after it totally erases itself and all evidence of where it came from, and the ill-gotten gain?

A perpetrator of an automated crime who has acquired one of these software packages may have only the collection of information, script, and programs directly needed for the crime under his or her temporary control. He may never actually permanently possess or know any of their contents or other resources that might be used in the crime. Victims would not necessarily suffer any disclosure or unauthorized observation of their information. Therefore, no confidentiality of their programs, data, or victims may have been violated, yet security has been violated, and an offense has been perpetrated. This is a possession and use issue, and not necessarily a confidentiality issue. It is a good example of where we must recognize a more fine-grained concept of information security than merely confidentiality, integrity, and availability (CIA) to be able to anticipate and deal with the threat of automated crime. This more fine-grained approach must include the concept of possession to be protected in information security, so that confidentiality and possession safeguards together and separately may correctly deal with protecting information in hand, under control, and as knowledge. This means that information security must protect victims from the loss of in-hand possession of copies of their information as well as from violations of privacy. Security must deal with the possession in the form of control over information, and it must deal with confidential knowledge as a separate issue. These subtle but important differences are needed to understand and fight automated crime within the scope and definition of information security.

Example of Automated Crime.   Here is an example of a hypothetical automated crime. While browsing the Internet, you encounter the offer of a freeware program called GetRich. You copy and load it into your computer and execute it just out of curiosity. (It might even be loaded into your computer and executed without your even knowing about it.) The first and only screen displayed to you says, "GETRICH. How much money do you want?" You decide to play the game and key in $34,000. "Where do you want it?" glows out at you from the screen. You enter your name and the name and the Internet address of your bank. After you hit the "start key," follow the instruction, then "press any key to begin," the screen disappears, and nothing more happens. You forget about it until the next day, when you discover that your bank account balance is $34,000 greater than it was yesterday. (Or it might be a lesser amount because the developer of the crime has figured out how to get his cut along the way.) What a strange coincidence. You try to look for the GetRich program but find that it is gone from your computer. When you attempt to download the program again, in an attempt to find out what happened, you discover that it is no longer available from the Internet source. You check with your bank and find that there is no record of the source of a transfer of funds into your account. End of story, at least from the perpetrator's perspective.

Now consider this automated crime event from the victim's perspective. A small company in Hong Kong is one of the thousands of customers using a well-known commercial accounts-payable software package in their online computer. The head accountant comes into work one morning and discovers an out-of-balance debit suspense item of $34,000 in the double-entry bookkeeping system. He looks at the transaction log. Nothing there. He looks at the audit log. Nothing there either. He looks at the payments register. Nothing. He gets desperate and looks for debits in the receivables. Nothing. He calls his bank and is told that a funds transfer was ordered and made to a Caribbean offshore bank, and that is all they know. Two people in different parts of the world who don't know one another, and never will, were associated for only three milliseconds through a phantom computer program that doesn't exist anymore. They are ships passing in the night. End of story.

Here is what happened: It involves a former computer programmer employee of a commercial software company that provides a popular accounts payable system using electronic data interchange (EDI) for making payments. He developed a set of programs to steal money by duplicating payments that are then diverted indirectly to the perpetrator's address, and he teamed up with a hacker who is an expert in computer attacks and the Internet to develop an automated crime.

The programs start by scanning IP addresses for Internet-connected host computers with root control vulnerabilities and that also use the accounts payable package. A computer is found, and the automated crime programs probe and discover a vulnerability that allows them to assume root control. The attack programs are automatically sent to the selected computer and proceed to modify the accounts payable package temporarily and execute it. Duplicates of recent payments and suppression of the duplicate payments prevention control are made in the victim's system. This causes funds to be transferred by EDI from the victim's bank, with the payee name and address changed to the address of a Caribbean offshore private bank, and a numbered account that had been inserted by the software developer when he first designed the automated crime. The programs separately send instructions to the private bank to forward the money to the perpetrator's account in his bank. Each transfer, from perpetrator to victim and private bank to the perpetrator's bank, passes through commercial ISP anonymizers that hide sources and destinations of messages. The programs then erase the logged entries of the transactions in the victim's computer, erase the attacking programs, and restore the correct code in the victim's computer. This seems to be close to achieving the perfect crime. The victim could easily conclude that the event was accidental and couldn't be reversed. I have prudently omitted some of the critical details here, but an expert consultant on anonymous and secret use of offshore private banks assures me that what I have described here is workable.

Tools that could Evolve into Automated Crimes.   I started developing the concept of fully automated cybercrimes when I became aware of the development of hacker tools and valuable security vulnerability testing software. For example, packet-switched networks such as the Internet are highly vulnerable to so-called "sniffers," which might become parts of automated crimes. Since information destined for an Internet host computer node flows through many other, possibly hostile nodes of a network, hackers insert these software sniffers into Internet nodes and can monitor all of the passing traffic. A sniffer searches each packet of data passing by for desirable information to capture, such as passwords from the initial packets of logon processes in other nodes. In some cases, hackers hide sniffers in others' software, making the software a form of Trojan horse. Other malicious hackers subvert existing utility programs in victims' computers on networks to convert them into sniffers. They can then acquire key information that has been stored by the utility in the victims' computer systems. The Internet is currently suffering from many such attacks in which hackers have collected tens of thousands of passwords. Many kinds of malicious hacker attacks are conducted through the insertion and execution of computer programs, such as viruses and worms, in others' computers. A perpetrator may use a computer to gain control of another computer to use in the attack on a third computer, such as in recent distributed denial-of-service attacks. He may also engage in network weaving by chaining several computers together in this fashion.

The ultimate objective of the worm program, a precursor to automated crimes, used by a convicted computer science student in his 1988 attack on the Internet was to engage in automated hacking by placing copies of his program in 6000 computers. He could have then used the computers of his victims to search for, guess, or otherwise capture passwords as long as the worm resided in them. The program was quite complex and had a fatal flaw that caused it to run wild and duplicate itself repeatedly in all of the attacked computers until they became saturated and slowed to a standstill. The losses included millions of dollars used to pay expert technologists to eradicate the worm copies and restore the availability, authenticity, and integrity of the violated systems.

Legitimate utility programs that are useful for malicious hacker attacks are readily available for sale or free of charge from legitimate sources. For example, the ComSec bulletin board system (BBS), serving more than two thousand computer security specialists worldwide, has offered the Setspass computer program that can be used to change supervisor passwords if an attacker has physical access to a local area network (LAN) operating system server. Another service provides Getser, which gathers the serial numbers of all servers currently logged on to a network.

Tempsup creates a temporary supervisor-equivalent user IDs, Xsend can cause a denial-of-service attack by saturating users with broadcasted messages, Hack.exe allows masquerading of any logged-on user, and Netcrack does an alphanumeric password search if a system allows unlimited logon attempts. Legitimate security specialists use the latter tool to test their employers' systems for weak passwords. ISS System Security Scanner is a good system configuration scanner. SATAN is another important tool that could be the basis for developing automated crime. I describe its possible use in a more detailed exposition in the next section.

Anatomy of An Automated Crime. A fully automated crime could involve eight steps carried out by a script, program, or suite of programs executed automatically in sequence without human intervention or interaction:

1. Purchasing an automated crime.
2. Scanning or searching to find host computers containing the desired assets to attack.
3. Finding the vulnerability in the selected system or systems in preparation for the attack.
4. Using that vulnerability to gain control, resources, and authority.
5. Setting up any other necessary conditions external to the victim systems.
6. Engaging in an abusive activity.
7. Converting that activity to some form of gain for the perpetrator and/or loss to the victim.
8. Eliminating evidence and avoiding possible negative consequences of the criminal activity.

The first step is acquiring the automated crime malware. The malware market and sales are well developed. Web sites in Russia, for example, sell malware for prices stated in WMZ—a form of electronic currency supported by Moscow- based WM Transfer Ltd's WebMoney online payment system.

The computer program engaging in steps two and three of scanning and finding may be one such as SATAN which is an acronym for "Security Administrators' Tool for Analyzing Networks." It is freeware, released to the world on April 5, 1995 through the Internet, and designed to scan computers, probe for vulnerabilities, and report security weaknesses in network computers that run UNIX operating systems. SATAN probes for fifteen well-known vulnerabilities that may be present in UNIX systems and reports this information back to the person running the SATAN program through the Internet. The source code is readily available and could be easily modified to extend SATAN's capabilities to probe for new vulnerabilities and take advantage of the vulnerabilities that are discovered rather than reporting them.

Therefore, SATAN, as well as other such tools, could be the basis or first step for developing a completely automated crime. In ordinary computer crime, social engineering or other types of intelligence gathering often must be performed to have enough information to engage successfully in the computer crime. SATAN could replace some or all of this first stage of intelligence gathering. Some of the SATAN probes require superuser privileges for testing; therefore, some automated crime may require beginning with root or administrative authority, obtained in step four as I previously indicated.

Since SATAN can scan and probe many computer systems throughout a network automatically without interruption, it casn fulfill the second step in automated crime, identifying and selecting targets automatically for the criminal activity, even before finding the vulnerability. The documentation for SATAN identifies a "break-in" scanning level called "All Out," which was to be implemented in a future release. This would accomplish steps four and five of using the identified vulnerability in the automated crime. The most insidious aspect of SATAN is the ease with which it may be used, thus extending the possibilities of highly sophisticated automated crime to a much larger potential population of "newbie" perpetrators who may have little technological capability. SATAN's ready availability increases the likelihood of this kind of extension and usage. SATAN currently lets the user explore the security aspects of a targeted computer system, or literally hundreds of targeted computer systems, for the users to make intelligent decisions regarding the vulnerabilities. The decisions themselves can be programmed and appended to SATAN and made a part of a larger suite of programs to engage in a complete crime.

A security probe in SATAN contacts the target host system using a TCP/IP-based protocol, such as simple mail transport protocol (SMTP); file transfer protocol (FTP); or remote procedure call (RPC). The target system, mistakenly identifying that the SATAN probe is from another trusted computer making a service request, responds by returning whatever data suits the service request. IP spoofing to impersonate another computer can be used to make the target computer assume that it is communicating with another trusted computer system, where it would have privileged access and communication. Some preliminary social engineering may be required to obtain this information.

A computer program to engage in a criminal act to accomplish steps four and five could then be immediately executed on a privileged basis, or its execution could be delayed using a Trojan horse logic bomb technique to engage in a further crime at a later time. This program or part of the program could engage in fraud, espionage, sabotage, stealing, extortion, or a host of other criminal activities.

Sabotage, stealing, or espionage may be the easiest types of crimes. Fraud would probably be the most complex and difficult, requiring significant detailed knowledge of the target system. However, an act against a popular commercial software package would facilitate a wide choice of victims that use that package. I have listed all of the possible ways in which information loss may occur in steps five and six of an automated crime in the list on page 255. I consider this to be a nearly exhaustive list. Security defenders should consider all of these loss actions in any security architecture design and selection of controls to deal with automated crime. It is not possible to predict what unknown perpetrators will do to a specific victim. In some cases, they are likely to include multiple crimes within a single automated crime package.

The seventh step of the automated crime is conversion to criminal gain. The results from step five would be automatically converted so that the perpetrator may remove all of the gains from the system, or systems, in which the crime occurred. This could include causing a loss to the victim during the crime. The gain could be merely the satisfaction of successful sabotage with no removal or conversion of information. In a financial system fraud, the conversion could constitute the establishment of a line of credit; in a banking system, it could consist of the transfer of funds from one bank's computer to the perpetrator's account in another bank's computer. We may consider the conversion to be completed when the funds are transferred and credited to the account in the other bank system. On the other hand, if the transferring bank considered the transaction to be fraudulent soon enough, it is possible that the bank could reverse the transaction. Therefore, irreversibility could become a desirable criminal objective in conversion to gain. Considering various banking rules in different countries, it may be necessary to remove stolen money as cash from a bank, in order to achieve irreversibility of a cybercrime.

The last step in an automated crime of erasing evidence may not be necessary if the crime is a hit and run situation where the criminal does not care whether his or her identity and actions have been discovered. However, if the perpetrator requires that the crime, after being executed possibly within a few milliseconds, is to remain covert and the perpetrator is to remain anonymous, then the last act—avoiding detection and identity, at least long enough to remain free of any suspicion—is a necessary step. In addition, this step could include the elimination of evidence so that later prosecution or litigation would be less likely, or if prosecution occurred, would be a sufficiently weak case for the perpetrator to be exonerated.

Eliminating evidence of the crime and all copies of it within a computer system, or network of computer systems, may be a formidable task. Consider all of the possibilities of backups, shadow copies, audit logs, uncleared computer buffers, discarded printer paper, printer drums, and data remaining in unassigned disk sectors, as well as what computer operators may see or record. However, the elimination or modification of any of this evidence could be done as a part of the continuous crime.

As I have indicted, hackers could build entirely automated crimes, beginning with the automatic selection of victims, by enhancing available tools. They would progress to discover vulnerabilities that would allow them to gain root access to the victims' computers, perpetrate criminal acts, convert the acts to criminal gains, and conclude with erasure of all evidence of the crimes. An expert could package an automated crime and test it endlessly to demonstrate that it works correctly and perfectly. Ordinary crimes can be planned, even extensively, but with only one real execution and not necessarily exactly as planned since circumstances, involving real people that are unpredictable, will change. Computers, on the other hand, are designed to be predictable and are less likely to change. An automated crime can execute any number of times under exactly the same circumstances in each instance in a predictable victim computer. It can do this because many different victim computers operate with the same operating system and application that would be the objects of the attack in the design of the automated crime.

Inadequacy of the Law.   The developer could limit an automated crime to anticipate and avoid specific criminal laws, rules of evidence, and legal precedence. The US Computer Fraud and Abuse Act was modified in 1996 to make passing viruses a crime, and the same act may criminalize transmitting any automated crime.

Article §1030, (a), (5). (A) states: "Whoever knowingly causes the transmission of a program, information, code, or command, and as a result of such conduct, intentionally causes damage without authorization, to a protected computer, shall be punished ..." This may mean that creating an automated crime is not a crime, and transmitting it to others would also not be a crime, since no harm results from the act of giving it to a possibly unknown perpetrator. Only the perpetrator would be committing a crime by executing the automated crime package. The crime could possibly achieve perfect-crime status by design and testing to be certain that it could not be detected, or if detected, it could remain unsolved and still be a perfect crime. Even if it were solved but not prosecuted, or if prosecuted but resulting in the exoneration of the perpetrator, the crime would be successful, if not perfect. The crime can be designed to require specified characteristics, input, or actions of the perpetrator. It could also be designed by law enforcement agents to be used for entrapment to ensure that, unknown to the perpetrator; he or she would be apprehended and likely would be convicted. Imagine the sting potential (and danger of entrapment of the perpetrators) for law enforcement purposes.

Security Against Automated Crime.   This kind of automated crime is going to require a new and far more sophisticated level of information security. In particular, we may have to develop security computer programs (agents) that will automatically engage in the battle of avoiding, deterring, preventing, detecting, mitigating, recovering from, and engaging in retribution against such attacks, possibly without the time for human intervention. Anti-virus, intrusion detection, and intrusion prevention programs will be seen as only initial and crude types of automated security. The security program or suite of programs must also operate in computer time without human intervention, avoid doing any unnecessary harm, and possibly start and finish before any human could be aware that any problem and its prevention has occurred. Legally acceptable evidence must also be recorded and preserved by the security program for later human analysis and action, such as prosecution. The security program itself must also be protected from unanticipated detection and compromise by the perpetrator of the automated crime.

Automated crime may require new automated security programs if we are to deal with crimes that happen before human real-time intervention can occur. Using SATAN as an example of one step in an automated crime brings to mind the possibility of using the freeware Courtney (Lawrence Livermore Laboratories) or Gabriel (Los Altos Technologies, Los Altos, California) that are used to detect the probing from SATAN in a victim's computer. In addition, sophisticated rule-based detection systems may be used. Examples are DIDS, developed by Trident Data Systems for the U.S. Air Force, the New Intrusion Detection Expert System (NIDES), and most recently Emerald, developed by SRI International for the U.S. Government, as well as other tools capable of analyzing audit trail records for unusual activities. NIDES uses both rule-based and statistic-based real-time detection techniques in computer time speed.

Each of the eight steps that I identified in an automated crime can also be identified as steps in the security process as well. The initial finding of a victim system must be addressed first in automated security. Disguising or maintaining a low profile of a computer system or the software in it would be an important control at this stage. The security against automated crime requires preventing and detecting the placement of hackers' programs into victim's computers, or preventing the malicious modification of existing programs. Computer and network owners can do this by using monitoring and detecting software, firewalling computers to protect perimeters of networks, and using security agent software that pokes around looking for trouble within systems. Firewalls consist of ordinary desktop computers serving as network gateway computers that filter all incoming and outgoing messages. Commercial security firewalls are now popular, especially for connection to public networks such as the Internet. Network owners can also insert filtering software directly into network servers, hubs, switches, and routers to limit passing of harmful information possibly identified by signature. Firewalls and filters can limit the placement of active malicious programs that could modify or become resident among accepted programs in networked computers. They can further restrict communications according to times, addresses, sources, and destinations.

The next step of thwarting probes that identify system vulnerabilities could be done using programs such as Courtney or Gabriel. When this probing is detected, it should result in termination of the attack, and alarms would then result in ending the automated crime activity followed by human intervention. However, sophisticated attack methods will soon be attempting to overcome this type of detection by programs. If automated crime developers anticipate such specific programs, they will divert them from their ultimate purpose by increasingly sophisticated attack programs. Surely there will be new versions of SATAN that are transparent to known detection programs, and new detection programs that will, in turn, overcome the current versions of SATAN, as we have experienced with the computer virus and antivirus one-upsmanship competition.

The next step in automated security efforts will be to avoid or stop the perpetrators' computer programs from taking advantage of the vulnerabilities discovered and acquiring unauthorized privilege. Eliminating and avoiding the vulnerabilities and limiting privilege before any attacks would be the most desirable approach; however, not all vulnerabilities can be eliminated. Therefore, at least detection of known types of attacks should be programmed into the automated security programs.

Setting up external conditions and the criminal act are the next steps. They must also be avoided, or prevented if not avoidable. Automated security should detect the act if it can not prevent or mitigate it to minimize loss. Internal application controls that are commonly found in application systems to accomplish these functions would be too numerous to mention here. One important exception is that they could be derived from a convenient and useful framework called the Clark-Wilson Integrity Model. This model of well-formed transaction systems is described in a paper, "A Comparison of Commercial and Military Computer Security Policies," by D. D. Clark and D. R. Wilson.

Unpredictability.   Creating controlled unpredictability or uncertainties in systems is another powerful means of protection that we have not fully exploited. I have noted a common fear among two hundred computer criminals that I have interviewed: they universally feared unpredictable circumstances, environments, and events during their crimes. If one unpredictable situation arises, they may end up in prison. Criminals find that computers are ideal targets, because they are so predictable in all of these ways. Automated crime requires predictable or, at least, deducible program codes to attack in victims' computers, and criminals can test them endlessly during development of their programs to optimize their attacks. That is why the second step for developers of automated crimes is to find and use computers that have a recognizable operating system and application software. We could exploit this requirement for predictable systems for cybercrime attacks by periodically changing code in our systems but preserving its function. However, significant research and development would be required, for example, to create compilers that would compile source programs into polymorphic object programs, different after each compilation but performing the same function. We could also possibly make them dynamically self-changing so that they would be different before or after each execution. In addition, we would need tools to maintain and trouble-shoot the dynamic code, and we would have to protect the tools from theft and study by the automated crime developers.

There are other less challenging means of protection as well. Irreversible conversion to criminal gain, as described in step eight, is an important but little addressed subject in security. It is important because it provides indications about where designers must place controls relative to the information or assets subject to abuse. The logical location in a system at which the criminal gain irreversibly leaves the system would be the last place for controls to be to stop the conversion to gain process. This may be at a printer that prints checks, at an ATM where cash is withdrawn, where an account is debited or credited, in a loan officer's desk computer, or in a retail store where goods are delivered on credit to a perpetrator or an accomplice.

Finally, we must preserve the evidence of automated crime and protect it from attacks by the perpetrator's automated system in step seven in our automated security efforts. Record-only backups and audit logs protected by encryption are important safeguards for these purposes. Attempting to physically remove evidence from the system such as by printing or removing removable disks will probably not be effective in an automated attack since the automated crime would likely destroy all such evidence before victims could physically save it.

Concluding Remarks   Automated crimes will go far beyond being computer viruses. They could become total, perfect crimes, unless we devise automated security to resist, detect, mitigate, and recover from each packaged crime that we know about or could anticipate. We must have an adequate information security foundation model to anticipate such events. Preserving confidentiality, integrity, and availability (CIA) would do little to stop automated crime. The reason that I was able to envision automated crime was that I conceived of the possession of information (in this case, automated crime code) as being different from knowing information. I then applied this finer-grained view of security to conceive of a perpetrator possessing and executing an automated-crime program without knowing its contents and how it functions.

The key to being aware of these important fine points is to understand the characteristics of information and all its forms and understand that losses go far beyond merely loss of confidentiality, integrity, and availability from destruction, disclosure, use, and modification. I continue to insist that information security must preserve availability and utility, integrity and authenticity, and confidentiality and possession from all of the many losses I identify in my book, *Fighting Computer Crime, a New Framework for Protecting Information* (John Wiley and Sons 1998).

We must anticipate increasingly sophisticated automated crime, and ingenious hackers that package easy-to-use computer program tools that adapt and extend into fully automated criminal tools for less skilled perpetrators to use. The only viable response to fully automated crime is fully automated information security that takes place at the computer time-scale speeds of the crime, before victims could be aware that a crime has started and security efforts have stopped it. Law enforcement investigators must be aware of the possibilities and engage in intelligence efforts to find and stop the skilled criminals that are at the root of the problem. This is our challenge for the very near future.

The Complete List of Threats to Information

Threats to Availability and Usefulness

- Destroy, damage, or contaminate
- Deny, prolong, accelerate, or delay use or entry
- Move or misplace
- Convert or obscure

Threats to Integrity and Authenticity

- Insert, use, or produce false or harmful data
- Modify, replace, remove, append, aggregate, separate, or reorder
- Misrepresent or repudiate (reject as untrue)
- Misuse or fail to use as required

Threats to Confidentiality and Possession

- Locate
- Disclose, observe, or monitor and acquire
- Copy
- Take away or control
- Claim ownership or custodianship
- Infer

Exposure to Threats

Endanger by exposure to any of the other losses

Failure to engage in or allow any of the other losses to occur when instructed to do so

INFORMATION SOURCES

Vijayan, Jaikumar. Malware for sale. Computer and Internet Security Insight. *Computerworld*. April 10, 2007. http://www.techworld.com/security/features/index.cfm?featureid=3293).

Clark, D.D. and Wilson, D.R. IEEE Computer Society *Proceedings of the 1987 Symposium on Security and Privacy*. Oakland, California, April 1987, pps. 184–194).

O'Reilly, F. Protecting Networks with SATAN, May 1998, http://oreilly.com/catalog/9781565924253/#top).

Parker, Donn B., *Fighting Crime: A New Framework for Protecting Information*, New York: Wiley, 1998.

BIOGRAPHY

Donn B. Parker, a retired senior information security consultant, spent 30 of his 50 years in the computer field at SRI International researching and consulting on information security and against computer crime and abuse. He is the founder of the International Information Integrity Institute at SRI.

He has written six books on computer crime, ethics, and information security management. His first book was *Crime by Computer*, (Scribner, 1976) (For that book he interviewed more than 200 computer crime perpetrators worldwide). He is also the author of *Criminal Justice Resource Manual on Computer Crime*, available from the U.S. National Institute of Justice, and coauthor of *Ethical Conflicts in Computer Science, Technology, and Business* (QED Information Sciences, 1990). His last book was *Fighting Computer Crime: A New Framework for Protecting Information* (1998).

He was awarded the 1992 Information Systems Security Association Individual Achievement Award, the 1994 National Computer System Security Award from the U.S. Government Departments of Defense and Commerce, the Aerospace Computer Security Associates 1994 Distinguished Lecturer Award, and the MIS Training Institute Infosecurity News 1996 Lifetime Achievement Award. The Information Security Magazine profiled him as one of the five top Infosecurity Pioneers (1998). The Information Systems Security Association inducted him into its Hall of Fame in 2000, and he was inducted into the SRI International Hall of Fame in 2002. In 2003, the International Information Systems Security Certification Consortium (ISC) presented him with a lifetime achievement award. Donn can be contacted via e-mail: donnlorna@aol.com

8.2

LET'S PLAY MAKE BELIEVE

Karl E. Wiegers
Process Impact

Years ago I had a friend, Dave, with a diesel Volkswagen Rabbit. Back then, diesel fuel was not as readily available as it is today. One day, Dave pulled into a truck stop to fill up and saw a sign that said "50 Gallon Minimum." Dave stopped at the pump with his Rabbit and its 10-gallon tank and told the attendant, "Let's give it a shot." Dave was pretending that he could meet the 50 gallon minimum, hoping that by the time the attendant figured out he couldn't, Dave would have the fuel he needed and could hit the road.

We do a lot of pretending in the software world, too. It's not exactly lying. It's more a matter of imagining—or hoping—that things are going better than they really are. Sometimes a team pretends they can accomplish some objective within the imposed constraints when there is absolutely no way this can be done—and everybody knows it. Other times, people pretend they've finished a task when it really is only partially complete, or that a milestone has been reached when its terminus still lies just over the horizon.

Pretending, especially when all the participants know they're pretending, does a disservice to all affected stakeholders. It can lead people to reject the objectivity of data and progress tracking as they imagine that whatever they are pretending is in fact true. It leads to playing games, as team members manipulate "the system" to try to look good. Pretending can result in undelivered products, unfulfilled expectations, and unhappy stakeholders in an unhealthy culture of mistrust and deception.

An Iron Pentagon. I saw a striking example of pretending when I taught a project management class at a state government agency some years ago. Project management books often describe the so-called "triple constraint" or "iron triangle." The idea is that projects have imposed constraints of scope, cost, and time (or scope, resources, and schedule, depending on what source you read.) The three sides of the triangle are related, such that changing one constraint affects one or both of the others. The idea is correct, but the simplistic triangle is, simply, wrong.

Instead of a triangle, I consider five interrelated project dimensions: schedule, staff, cost, quality, and scope (Wiegers 1996). Quality obviously must be incorporated, as it's possible to work very fast and do a crappy job, but that certainly isn't any project team's goal. I also find it valuable to split "resources" into the separate dimensions of the project's budget and the staff available to work on the project. The project manager can trade these two dimensions off against each other. Sometimes a project team has plenty of money but a headcount freeze. Then they have to spend the money in other ways, such as subcontracting work or acquiring training and tools to increase productivity.

On any given project, one or more of these dimensions will likely be *constraints* with zero flexibility for the project manager. Other dimensions may be key project success *drivers*, with important targets that might have little flexibility. But the project manager can succeed only if at least one dimension is a *degree of freedom*. Such dimensions provide some flexibility the manager can balance against the other, more constrained dimensions when project conditions change or estimates turn out to be optimistic.

I described this five-dimension concept in the project management class I was presenting to this state government agency. One student in the class told me that all five of those dimensions were constraints on her project. Senior management had dictated a firm delivery deadline (schedule) for a fixed feature set (scope). The project manager had a fixed team size (staff) with no hope of hiring more people. No additional funding was available beyond the original allocation. Quality was said to be paramount and defects were unacceptable. Yet the project team had committed to this project, pretending that somehow they would be able to pull it off within the bounds of these highly restrictive constraints.

In my view, they couldn't. I explained to this student that the project would almost certainly fail to meet its objectives within the imposed constraints. Even if all their requirements and estimates were perfect (which is extremely unlikely), the project manager had no latitude for responding to change requests, unexpected events, or risks that strike the project. It is naïvely unrealistic for project managers, team members, senior management, or customers to expect that a project will go exactly as planned with no deviations or surprises. The project manager *must* have one or more degrees of freedom among these five dimensions. Everybody knows this truth, at least implicitly. But the project stakeholders still pretended that this overconstrained project was feasible.

The Budget Treadmill.   In another class I taught at a government agency in the same state, I was told that all projects absolutely needed to be completed by June 30 of a particular year. The reason for this was that the state has a biennial funding cycle and their fiscal year begins on July 1. So on every other June 30, all project teams would deliver whatever they had accomplished so far and declare victory. Unfortunately, often not all of the features had been implemented, the software was full of defects, and it wasn't usable by anyone for its intended purpose. Then, on July 1, the project team invariably was able to get more money and time allocated so they could complete the project.

That is, the team pretended that the project was done on June 30 even though everyone involved knew it wasn't. In this way managers could claim they had completed their projects on time and on budget, even though none of them really had. The projects just picked up again in the next funding cycle wherever they left off.

Apparently, everyone in the organization was aware of this real-but-not-quite-real budget cycle pretending. Perhaps even the customers knew not to trust the IT department to deliver its products by the promised June 30 date.

This type of pretending is a form of gamesmanship in which members of the organization find a way to manipulate the established system to avoid being harmed by the system. This pretending has become deeply ingrained in this state government's culture. Such dysfunctional behavior leads to artificial estimates, meaningless metrics, empty promises, and unfulfilled expectations.

An alternative and more realistic strategy would be to acknowledge that schedule and budget are constraints, therefore making scope a degree of freedom. Instead of pretending that a miracle will take place, acknowledge the realistic possibility that not *all* of the desired functionality will be delivered by the end of the biennial funding cycle. Make plans and commitments that realistically consider what functionality can be delivered at the desired quality level by that time. Plan a staged release with rigorous requirements prioritization to deliver the maximum customer value by the end of the funding cycle, with the expectation (or at least hope) that more resources will become available in the following cycle to complete the project. This way, even if higher priority projects consume the resources next time, customers will have received a workable, if less-than-ideal, product.

REFERENCE

Wiegers, Karl E. *Creating a Software Engineering Culture*. New York: Dorset House Publishing, 1996.

BIOGRAPHY

Karl Wiegers is Principal Consultant with Process Impact, a software process consulting and education company in Portland, Oregon. His interests include requirements engineering, peer reviews, process improvement, project management, risk management, and metrics. Previously, he spent 18 years at Eastman Kodak Company as a research scientist, software developer, software manager, and software process and quality improvement leader. Karl received a Ph.D. in organic chemistry from the University of Illinois.

Karl's most recent book is *Practical Project Initiation: A Handbook with Tools* (Microsoft Press, 2007). He's also the author of the books *Software Requirements, More About Software Requirements, Peer Reviews in Software: A Practical Guide*, and *Creating a Software Engineering Culture*. Karl has written more than 170 articles on software development and management, chemistry, and military history. Karl has served on the Editorial Board for *IEEE Software* magazine and as a contributing editor for *Software Development* magazine. You can reach Karl at http://www.processimpact.com.

8.3

DARK, LIGHT, OR JUST
ANOTHER SHADE OF GREY?

Les Hatton

Oakwood Computing Assoc., Ltd.

At the risk of repeating the central premise of this book, this short contribution, like all the others, is not about software failures, but about collective and individual personality traits of the people involved in software. In other words, it is about people, and all the wonderful and terrible things they get up to.

For the last twenty years or so, I have worked in forensic engineering. After an earlier career as a computational scientist, I thought that it would be important to study software project and system failures in the hope that the enormous waste of money which resulted could be mitigated in some way by improved methods of implementation. Twenty years later, I am in a good position to contribute to this book. As far as I can see, at the bottom of every great software project failure, when you have sifted through the engineering elements and carefully balanced their contribution, the same lesson always results: Software systems almost invariably fail for human reasons and not for engineering reasons, because software development is no different from many other areas of human endeavour. It should be but it isn't. Humans do stupid things and continue to do stupid things because there is nothing to really stop them.

I think the problems with software really started about 25 years ago when a terrible thing happened—because of the inability of software researchers to develop concepts of quantifiable engineering (the presence of measurement usually prevents some of the dafter excesses), software was quickly subordinated by business gurus into a branch of management. It was about that time that large accountancy companies (you will remember some of the leading culprits), suddenly got into the software business, rightly sensing a killing and implementing what became known rather misleadingly as business "improvement" systems. They didn't really have a clue about software but they felt they knew about management, so it was a small step to rebadge themselves as improving business data flows and processes using software. After all, it seemed that anybody higher up the evolutionary ladder than a newt could develop software. Add to this a similar level of ignorance of software amongst middle- and upper-managers in most organizations, and the result was like throwing germs into a Petrie dish. Business opportunities exploded, the $3000 a day "consultant" with two years of experience emerged, and the real age of software project

The Dark Side of Software Engineering, by Johann Rost and Robert L. Glass
Copyright © 2011 IEEE Computer Society

failures started. (After 35 years of developing systems, I still do not know how anybody could ever spend a billion dollars on software. What on earth do they do? Of course, this may also account for the fact that I still have to work.)

I have many unpleasant memories of this period, including having one of these companies flying over several so-called "hot shots" from various countries to attempt to discredit my research in front of their customer, after I drew attention to significant deficiencies in its systems (which were safety-related). Thank goodness for peer-reviewed published research, which they had not troubled to do, or, apparently, read. Sadly, I'm not sure this would be enough today, in an era when Internet-lubricated digital media has demonstrated more than adequately that truth can be overcome by spin if you repeat it often enough.

As a result of this subordination, software development entered a dark age, from which it may find it difficult to emerge. The language of software projects changed from engineering descriptions into the endlessly changing but always vacuous landscape of business-speak. Instead of users, we were engaged as stake-holders. (I think of myself nowadays as a stakeholder in the same sense as the legendary actor Peter Cushing in a vampire film.) Instead of engineering compe-tence, we now have gravitas as in the following Laws of Gravitas:

- "Blame sticks to the last one out of the door."
- "Bull**** attracts more bull****."
- "Bull**** rises to the top."

I'm sure you can add your own.

Instead of learning something, we now are mentored into self-awareness and personal growth. Removing my finger temporarily from the recesses of my throat, instead of trying to improve engineering skills (mathematics is no longer a require-ment in many CS courses and significant numbers of our graduates are very poor indeed at programming as a result), we talk of improving their management skills, as if the art of actually programming a system has become supremely irrelevant compared with talking banal generalities about them. Instead of prototyping some-thing to understand its feasibility and scalability, we indulge in fatuous risk assess-ments (assessing the unassessable), to be submitted to a management class who wouldn't recognize an equation, or indeed, an argument based on the scientific method, even if presented in a golden bowl surrounded by rose petals.

You will be familiar with the resulting inevitable stages of these grandiose and idiotic schemes, which go something like this:

1. Think of a hopelessly ambitious project, such as providing instant digital access to millions of complex, rapidly time-variant, heterogeneous medical records from anywhere, completely securely, by anybody with little or no training.
2. Ask as few potential users as possible.
3. Add a multibillion dollar price tag and a suitably long time scale, so that you can escape long before the faeces hits the fan.
4. Subcontract it to the cheapest bidder.

5. Make sure you have no technical expertise in the area whatsoever, so that you don't hold things up with tedious questions about reality.

6. Launch at a media event with a catchy title.

7. Make sure you have a good marketing budget to repeatedly tell people everything is fine.

8. Time your exit carefully.

That is the real dark side and tragedy of software development. In and amongst the great achievements—the World Wide Web and, perhaps most importantly of all, open source—we have allowed it to be hijacked by ignorance so that it can sustain self-delusion, hubris, wild over-ambition and sometimes breathtaking incompetence, just as in the normal business world.

No wonder the credit-crunched, media-spun ordinary person in the street is almost as suspicious about the role of computers in their lives as they are about bankers and politicians. I do regret that I wasted twenty years finding it, but thank goodness for open source. There is hope.

BIOGRAPHY

Les Hatton is managing director of Oakwood Computing Associates Ltd., and holds the Chair of Forensic Software Engineering at the Kingston University, London. He received a number of international prizes for geophysics in the 1970s and 1980s before becoming interested in software reliability and switching careers in the 1990s. Although he has spent most of his working life in industry, he was formerly a Professor of Geophysics at the University of Delft, the Netherlands, and prior to that, an Industrial Fellow in Geophysics at Wolfson College Oxford.

He has published many technical papers, and is the author of the 1995 book *Safer C*. He has designed, implemented, and/or managed the production of several government and commercial IT systems, including the world's first portable seismic data processing package, SKS.

His primary interests in computing science are forensic engineering, information security, legal liability, and the theory of large systems evolution. In mathematics, he is active in signal processing, medical image processing, sports biomechanics, and modeling the effects of high frequency sound on marine mammals.

He is the guitarist and harmonica player with the Juniper Hill Blues Band. Les can be contacted via http://www.leshatton.org/.

8.4

RATIONAL SOFTWARE DEVELOPERS AS PATHOLOGICAL CODE HACKERS

Norman Fenton
Professor of Computer Science
Queen Mary University of London
CEO, Agena Ltd.

I have been involved in developing software systems—both for commercial and research reasons—for 25 years, with the last 15 years mostly at the managerial, rather than hands-on programming, level. I am CEO of a company that develops niche software solutions for risk assessment and our products have thousands of users worldwide. I have also spent much time (for example, as an expert witness) independently evaluating major software systems and the way they were produced. On top of that, I have been teaching practical project-based software engineering courses at British Universities to large cohorts of students every year since 1986. The dark side of software engineering that I am reporting here is based primarily on my own experience of either working with, or observing, developers on a range of software projects (including safety-critical ones). Although the experience is personal, it is fairly extensive in that I have observed several thousands of software developers over that time. Although many of these were at least to some extent under my own supervision and/or training, most were not; so the kind of systematic 'failings' I am reporting on cannot be attributed solely to my own deficiencies as a software engineering trainer and leader.

My thesis is that most software developers, including those who genuinely understand the benefits of good software engineering practice, are pathological code hackers. The extent of the problem—and the extent to which it is sometimes covered up—provides a worrying case of the dark side of software engineering.

Let's be clear first that there are some software developers (including ones who call themselves software engineers) who are proud to be labelled as "hackers." They let it be known to their colleagues that they are scornful of either the need to produce any kind of design or documentation, or even the need to pay any attention

---

to such documentation when produced by others. They feel that anything that gets in the way of coding right away is a bureaucratic irritant.

There are also plenty of "software engineers" who, although privately sharing the same view as the self-proclaimed hackers, would publicly deny any such accusation outright and point, as evidence, to the courses and qualifications they have on design methods. But anybody who has ever managed software engineers can easily recognize such 'private' hackers from the lack of design and documentation associated with their work.

My example of the dark side of software engineering does not relate to either the self-proclaimed or secret hackers. Rather, it relates to the software developers who are, in normal circumstances, totally committed to (and understand the value of) basic software engineering practices but who, when it comes to the crunch, ignore absolutely everything that is not writing code. In other words, there are genuine "software engineers" who are pathological hackers. They hack not because they feel it is the best way to get things done, but because they are irrationally drawn to the act of coding, much like a reforming drug addict craves a fix. My concern is that, based on my own fairly extensive experience of either working with, or observing, developers on a range of software projects (including safety-critical ones), most genuine software engineers ignore even the most basic examples of good process as soon as any kind of pressure is applied on a project.

Before backing up my thesis with some examples, I need to clarify the scope of software engineering practices I am referring to. I am *not* including the heavy-weight specification and design methods that dominate so much of the standard software engineering literature, and I am certainly not including anything as sophisticated as formal methods, verification, or metrics-based quality assurance and testing methods. I am not including those because I do not believe that there is any kind of consensus or evidence base supporting the effectiveness of such methods on anything other than very highly specialised projects. Moreover, despite their dominance of the software engineering literature, such methods have barely made a pin-prick on actual commercial practice. What I *am* including are the basic processes that characterize any engineering discipline and which are considered crucial even for the most agile software development projects: *planning*, *designing*, and *unit testing*. So, for example, even in a three-month extreme programming Java development project, I would expect to see a brief written plan, and something like a high-level class diagram produced before coding starts. During coding, I would expect JUnit tests to be written for at least the most important methods. I would also expect any project involving more than one developer to use some basic configuration and version control, and a simple method of tracking defects. Those are the kind of very humble 'software engineering' processes I am talking about. The total effort required for these humble 'non-coding' and up-front activities might be four days for a three-month project. Apart from the self-proclaimed hackers discussed above, I don't know of any software developer who does not accept that such an investment will very quickly produce a return in terms of ultimately decreased coding time, as well as improved quality and maintainability of the final code. Yet, in such examples (and I have seen many), even those activities are normally ignored by rational software developers who see a three-month deadline as an excuse to start writing code on day one and to ignore the other basic quality control practices completely.

By refusing to think about and document the most basic design ideas, even experienced developers end up with poor code that directly contradicts their own principles of good design. I can never forget the example of a highly experienced commercial software developer, Jack, who actually gave invited lectures on the importance of separating the GUI components of a system from the underlying application; he truly understood the devastating potential ramifications of not separating these at the design stage. At the time, Jack was chief software engineer on a project that involved developing a complex set of mathematical models and functions together with a GUI to shield end users from the underlying complexity. This was a major project, lasting several years, and involving Jack and a number of other programmers. The first few increments were excellent. But the company eventually needed to make some changes to the GUI and also needed to build some new applications that used the underlying mathematical models and functions. It was at this point that it was discovered that not only had Jack failed to produce an upfront architectural design for the system, but he had bundled all the coding together in such a way that the GUI and underlying application were totally inseparable. In fact, the code was so intrinsically linked that, a) even the most trivial changes to the GUI required a total understanding of ALL the application programming (even though the latter in terms of functionality was completely independent), and b) it was impossible to create separate API calls to the underlying application programming functions because these were all completely dependent on the GUI. So how did this happen? Jack had started doing a proper separation of the logic and knew this required some upfront (non coding) design preparation; but, he was so excited about the prospect of developing the GUI that, without revealing it to the rest of the team, he started writing GUI code and hardwiring in some of the application stuff to demonstrate it was working. In other words, the instinct to hack code was pathological. After a few weeks of doing this he presented it as a fait accompli 'design' to the rest of the team, who were forced to start writing the mathematical stuff as part of the GUI. None of this was known to senior management, who had been pleased to see regular progress.

My experience of reviewing software on major safety critical projects suggests that, alarmingly, things are not much different there either. I have been shocked to find that on such projects (involving typically over a hundred developers), very experienced programmers routinely ignored even the most basic requirements of configuration/version control and defect tracking, despite the very sophisticated and easy-to-use systems that were in place to make this more or less automatic. For example, some catastrophic errors were found to be the result of nothing other than code conflicts due to programmers bypassing normal version control. When questioned, the programmers knew the potential ramifications but, under the pressure of tight, impending deadlines, could not resist the temptation to cut corners even though it saved them just a matter of minutes. That is pathological behavior, and I know it happens to the best of us (I've been guilty myself). On a safety-critical project that had the most stringent mandated documentation requirements for specification and design, enormous sections of code (covering hundreds of thousands of lines) that proved to be highly problematic and error-prone turned out to have been written without any attempt at proper specification or design at all. How did this happen, and in particular, how did such code get through the mandated documentation standard which, for example, required UML class diagrams and sequence diagrams? It was simple: instead of producing such documentation up front before coding, and updating it as the code evolved, the UML tool enabled developers to press a button to "reverse engineer" a full set of UML diagrams that they could pass off as having been produced first. Even though deep down they knew it would be harmful in the long run to ignore the careful up-front design, they felt the pressure was such that anything other than coding was non-productive.

All of the pathological hacking behavior I've observed in commercial projects is repeated and validated on a grand scale on the software engineering group projects I run every year at the University. Every year, despite my emphasis on the need for following the minimal good practice described above, most of that goes out of the window (even from the best students) as soon as the pressure is on; every year in their reviews they say (perfectly honestly) that if only they had followed the practices better they *know* they would have produced something better. Again they admit to pathological behavior and I can empathize with them. Even though you *know* you are going to lose in the long run by focusing only on the coding, you simply cannot resist.

From an empirical perspective, what my experiences have shown is that even where "real" software engineering practice is applied it, its use may be exaggerated. The safety-critical project I mentioned above may have produced volumes of UML, but it is clear that UML was not actually *used* on the project. Sadly, my experience suggests that 40 years of software engineering research has largely been ignored by practitioners. If the guys who really do know about this stuff and appreciate its worth only pay lip service to it, then maybe the self-proclaimed hackers just happen to be more honest than the rest of us.

BIOGRAPHY

Norman Fenton is Professor of Computing at Queen Mary University of London, and also CEO of Agena, a company that specializes in risk assessment software for critical systems. Norman has been involved in both the research and practice of software engineering for 25 years, but his recent research has focused on causal models (Bayesian nets) for risk assessment. In addition to extensive work on causal models for software defect prediction, this work covers a wide range of application domains such as legal reasoning (he has been an expert witness in major criminal and civil cases), medical trials, vehicle reliability, embedded software, transport systems, and financial services. In support of these applications, Agena has been building Bayesian net-based decision support systems for a range of major clients.

CHAPTER 9

PERSONAL ANECDOTES

In the beginning, in our quest for viewpoints material from well-known computing and software authors for this book, we asked potential contributors to provide relevant material that discussed

- personal anecdotes, and lessons learned derived from them
- facts and/or data on dark side matters, and
- opinions and/or beliefs about dark side matters.

You have already seen, in earlier chapters on viewpoints, that absolutely no one provided us with anything in that second category, facts and/or data. We weren't surprised by this turn of events because we already knew that research into dark side matters in software and computing is nearly nonexistent; it would have been a surprise if our viewpoints request had turned up some studies we hadn't previously been aware of. So we were not surprised, but we *were* disappointed. It would have been nice if something new and interesting and informative had come out of the woodwork at this point to supplement our previous work.

You have also seen that we did get some fascinating contributions in that opinions and beliefs category, and that material constituted the material in the book section you just finished reading.

Now for category three (listed first above), those personal anecdotes and lessons learned. To be honest, we love anecdotal material. Oh, we know that academics frown on it, saying things such as "you can prove anything with anecdotal evidence." But if you take anecdotes in the spirit in which they are intended—interesting storytelling relevant to the topic at hand—they can make a topic come alive and dance on paper in ways that no other form of presentation can!

So we are presenting you with a plethora of dark side anecdotes. We were very pleased to find that most of our dark-side viewpoint contributors preferred to present us with a personal anecdote. We won't try to summarize those anecdotes in any way for you here—after all, you can prove anything with anecdotal evidence, and we don't want tot get caught in that trap! Just take the stories that follows as some great examples of computing storytelling.

9.1

AN OFFICER AND A GENTLEMAN CONFRONTS THE DARK SIDE

Grady Booch
IBM Thomas J. Watson Research Center

In 1977, I was declared an officer and a gentleman by act of Congress, having just graduated from the United States Air Force Academy with a bachelor's degree in computer science. I'm no longer an officer—although hopefully still a gentleman—but in my very first assignment as a second lieutenant, I encountered the dark side of software engineering.

By way of context, I need to explain that integrity was a concept that was central to my Academy experience. USAFA enforced an honor code that stated "we will not lie, cheat, or steal, nor tolerate anyone among us who does," and by enforced, I mean that as a cadet we took that code deadly seriously. Cheating on a test was obvious grounds for dismissal, but even fudging about when you signed back on to campus after leave was deemed an ethical breach. Now, attending a service academy is not exactly your typical undergraduate experience (I should also mention that, for all but my senior year, USAFA was a male-only institution), but for the cadets, the code was an important element in shaping us as war-fighters.

After graduation, I didn't become a pilot—I knew that I'd always fly a desk because my eyesight was not 20/20—and indeed I'd planned for that, as I knew that USAFA would offer me an excellent foundation in computer science and I'd be able to work on some infinitely cool software-intensive systems. My first assignment bore that out: I was directed to Vandenberg Air Force Base in central California, attached to what was then called the Space and Missile Test Center (SAMTEC) where I served first as a project engineer for a new telemetry system, and then as program manger for a new range safety display system (called, in the spirit of blindingly obvious military acronym-ese, RSDS).

This met my test for infinitely cool. Here I was, a twenty-something with a multimillion-dollar budget that pushed the edge of what we imagined we could do in the space program—namely, to build a system that, in real time, fused sensor data from dozens of radars around the globe and presented it up, using one of the earliest color vector displays from Evans and Sutherland. And yes, just like in the movies, there was a big red button that the range safety officer would push if the bird went off mission. This was a complex distributed system, long before the protocols we now take for granted were ever in place.

A brief aside: I got my first e-mail address in 1979, on what was then the ARPANET which, at the time, had only about two hundred nodes in the entire network, and thus had a printed directory of every e-mail address in the world. So yes, this was a wickedly fun time that was ahead of its time.

As was typical for these sorts for things, the Air Force outsourced the development work: in the project office, we set the specification and then went out for bid, planning then to manage the effort from vision to deployment.

And this is where I had a startling collision with the dark side.

The specs were out in the wild; we had received responses from all the bidders, and were going through our selection process. One day, I received a call from one of the bidders—not unusual; we would often have to field technical questions for it's not like our specifications exhibited the perfect clarity as they do in contemporary systems (yes, I'm being sarcastic)—yet this call was a bit different. After the usual pleasantries and questions, the bidder made mention that they had expected their stock to rise (red flag number one) and that I should consider investing (red flag number two), and by the way, if as a lieutenant I didn't have the funds to do so, he'd find a way to help me (red flag number three, with all sorts of loud klaxons going off in my head).

I was stunned, having never imagined anyone so blatantly trying to bribe an officer, especially given how USAFA's honor code was a part of me. I had been conditioned to expect the best from my colleagues—that they would always act in an ethical manner, especially those folks involved in pure technology that was clearly free from moral consideration. Even while he was talking, I began to enumerate the dozens of federal laws this bidder had violated. After I got off that call, I immediately created a memo (remember, this is in pre-e-mail days) and then called my security officer, who calmly took my report.

And then we planned a sting operation to nail this malfeasant.

I scheduled a callback with the bidder, only this time the call was wiretapped and recorded, and he indeed again made an incredibly clumsy attempt to bribe me, which was more than enough to hoist this man by his own petard.

I understand that he spent some time in a federal prison, and no, his company didn't win the bid.

To frame this in contemporary language, here we had a classic outsourcing deal, tainted by an unethical bidder who, so hungry to win, resorted to an incredible breach of ethics. For me, this was quite an introduction to the dark side of software engineering.

In college, I'd learned all about the craft of software development and, over the years, have honed my craft. But, this early experience shaped my understanding of the human element of developing complex systems. Over the years, I have witnessed death marches rising from incompetency, design decisions made out of emotion or avarice, posturing by CEOs, project managers, and code warriors out of fear or for political gain or as a means of petty revenge, and even an outright ethical breach of a profoundly stupid bidder.

As I consider what separates us from take the vision of a software-intensive system and then turning that into raw, running, naked code, I recognize that some things, such as the laws of physics, are fundamental constraints, while others, such as how we design a particular algorithm or architect a system of systems, are classical problems of systems engineering. And yet, what this experience tells me—and other more subtle ones over the years confirm—is that engineering software-intensive systems is ultimately a human activity, and thus subject to all the drama associated with the human experience. For me, the dark side of software engineering springs not from the technology itself, but rather from the very human ways we architect our systems, architect our organizations, and attend to the moral and ethical dimensions of how we use the technology we create.

BIOGRAPHY

Grady Booch has served as Chief Scientist of Rational Software Corporation since its founding in 1981, and through its acquisition by IBM in 2003. He now is part of the IBM Thomas J. Watson Research Center, serving as Chief Scientist for Software Engineering, where he continues his work on the *Handbook of Software Architecture* and also leads several projects in software engineering. Grady is one of the original authors of the unified modeling language (UML). He is the author of six best-selling books, including the *UML Users Guide* and the seminal *Object-Oriented Analysis and Design with Applications*. He writes a regular column on architecture for *IEEE Software*.

Grady is a member of the ACM, the American Association for the Advancement of Science, Computer Professionals for Social Responsibility, as well as a senior member of the IEEE. He is an IBM Fellow, an ACM Fellow, a World Technology Network Fellow, a Software Development Forum Visionary, and a recipient of Dr. Dobb's Excellence in Programming award, as well as three Jolt Awards.

Grady received his Bachelor of Science from the United States Air Force Academy in 1977, and his Master of Science in electrical engineering from the University of California at Santa Barbara in 1979.

9.2

LESS CARROT AND MORE STICK

June Verner
Visiting Professor LERO
(Irish Software Engineering Centre)

The particular project that is the subject of this discussion has been described elsewhere by the author in some detail. Those papers discuss quite different aspects of the project, namely effort and schedule estimation in a fourth-generation development, and a general consideration of using prototyping and incremental development ([Verner and Tate 1988], [Tate and Verner 1990]). One aspect not discussed before was the very negative attitude of some of the users to the proposed implementation and how this was overcome.

The application was a computerized administrative system for the New Zealand Correspondence School, which at that time had some 40,000 students. It was designed to support these groups of people:

- teachers in dealing with students (from preschool to adults), including student work packages, progress, examinations, and any special needs;

- deans in monitoring the status of the special circumstances that qualify a student for Correspondence School education; and

- management in monitoring the needs and performance of the students and the service levels of the school and allocating resources accordingly.

Few of the clerical staff, teachers, or the management had used computers before, and most had little experience of the administrative use of computers. Their attitudes included scepticism of what computers could do for them, and, on the part of many teachers, an instinctive distrust of the "big brother" image of computers. There was also concern that managers would be able to more closely monitor their work. Right from the start it was made very clear to all that the introduction of a computerized system to replace the current manual system would result in no redundancies; that those clerical staff no longer required would be retrained, if they wished, for other positions within the organization. The majority of the teachers believed that a new computerized system would take away most of the interesting parts of their jobs and leave them to focus on the more boring aspects of their work. In addition, the many sections within the school organized their work differently and each of the sections believed that their way was the "only" way. The CEO was keen that the work should be standardized, and that a module in one area required the same amount of effort by students and teachers as that from another area. This would give him much better insight into staff and student workloads, and he would be able to put in place measures to compare staff workloads and productivity. The CEO was aware that there was significant opposition to the system by the users. There was no suggestion that the users would actively sabotage the system, but just a belief that they were very distrustful of a new system, would not want to use it when it was implemented, and would not be cooperative in the requirements elicitation process. The developers needed the cooperation of quite a large number of the users to gather requirements for the system.

The developers worked in the same building as the users and were in more or less continual contact with them, both formally and informally, particularly at lunch and tea breaks. The CEO, who had quite a powerful personality, was heavily committed to the system and was fully aware of the negative attitude of the majority of users. He made it quite clear that he was prepared to support the development team with more than just lip service, and made his support of them very public. He was very frequently seen having lunch and coffee with the development team in the staff lunch room. It very quickly became apparent to all that if any staff did not cooperate with the development team, the CEO would probably hear about it pretty promptly. This resolved the problem of cooperation as regards to the system requirements and the desired functionality. However, it did not deal with the actual use of the system.

Within the organization, there was a dean who had some awareness that computerization could result in substantial benefits to her group and she was very enthusiastic about the system. The project manager decided to work closely with her, and to implement the system in increments with her group's enrollments making up the first increment. The increments were at two levels. New systems were introduced by section within the school and, for each section, by chronological subsystem within the school year. Her group (adults) was offset from the rest of the school, with enrollment starting two months before the bulk of other enrollments. Thus adult enrollments would be the first minor increment, followed by adult student work processing (despatch, receipt, marking, and return), other groups would then follow, such as secondary enrollment, secondary student work processing, and so on. Only the adult and part of the secondary section would be computerized in the first year; most or all of the remaining school sections, primary, pre-school, institutions, special needs, and the rest of the secondary section, following in the second year.

The adult group were the first to use the system and all senior members of the group were provided with terminals linked to the main computer. With the help of the dean it became known quite quickly that the system was providing significant benefits to the staff who had access to the system and that it was minimizing many of the time-consuming aspects of their job. Before long, having a terminal on your desk was perceived to be a status symbol, and others began to want a terminal, too. Soon, if you didn't have a terminal on your desk, then you weren't important.

Following the successful computerization of the first two sections, the others followed rather more easily, though care had to be taken not to become too complacent about user acceptance. As users became more aware of the comprehensiveness of the database information and all its interrelationships, their use of and reliance on the system grew. The user acceptance, sometimes rather reluctantly given, eventually produced a strong commitment to the system. The extent of user involvement was indicated by a large and continuing growth in user report requests following the first year. In less than five years, the whole system was so successful that the hardware had to be upgraded as the initial hardware was outgrown.

Lessons learned for us were: 1) the importance of the no-redundancy policy, 2) the importance of strong and visible senior management commitment and sponsorship, and 3) that reluctant users can be enticed to use a system if it is very carefully sold, and it provides them with enough benefit.

REFERENCES

Tate, G. and Verner J. M. "Case study of risk management, incremental development and evolutionary prototyping." *Information and Software Technology.* (32)3: April 1990, pp. 207–214.

Verner J. M., and Tate G. "Estimating size and effort in fourth-generation development." *IEEE Software.* (5)4: July 1988, pp 15–22.

BIOGRAPHY

Dr. June Verner is a visiting professor of Software Engineering at LERO, The Irish Software Engineering Centre, Limerick, Ireland. She has a Ph.D. in software engineering from Massey University, New Zealand and has worked in academia and industry for the past 25 years in New Zealand, the United Kingdom, Australia, Hong Kong, Ireland, and the United States. She has published more than 100 research papers, mainly in empirical software engineering and project management, and is on the editorial board of the *Journal of Systems and Software*, *Information and Software Technology* and the *Software Quality Journal*. Dr. Verner was program cochair for the IEEE International Conference on Global Software Engineering 2009 and IEEE Empirical Software Engineering Symposium 2005.

9.3

"THEM AND US": DISPATCHES FROM THE VIRTUAL SOFTWARE TEAM TRENCHES

Valentine Casey
Software Systems Research Centre,
Bournemouth University

This essay outlines some of the experiences gained and the lessons learned while establishing and operating virtual software development and maintenance teams by an Irish-based company, Software Future Technologies (a pseudonym), who were partnered with a large U.S. financial organization, Stock Exchange Trading Inc. (also a pseudonym). Stock Exchange Trading Inc. had been in operation for more than forty years and was a market leader in their field. As a result of their sustained success and expanding market share, they had an on-going requirement for the development and maintenance of bespoke financial software. Until this juncture, all development and maintenance activities had successfully been undertaken in-house. Having reviewed their operation, they identified that their in-house IT strategy had become too expensive and could not be sustained. The solution was to find an efficient alternative, which would leverage the experience of their existing IT department, while maintaining the level of quality and support required at a cost effective price.

Initially, a number of local and near shore outsourcing strategies were considered, but were rejected due to cost. It was then recognized that Stock Exchange Trading Inc. would have to look further afield for a cost cost-effective solution. They had previously successfully outsourced their Y2K legacy code renovation to an Irish-based company, Software Future Technologies. The possibility of exploring and expanding this relationship was identified. After extensive negotiations between the management of both organizations, a four-year contract was agreed to and signed. This resulted in a partnership between Stock Exchange Trading with Irish-based Software Future Technologies to undertake the development and maintenance of all its software applications. The establishment and operation of virtual teams was jointly determined as the most effective strategy for achieving this goal.

Software Future Technologies, was owned by a U.S. multinational, and operated as an independent profit center, and was wholly Irish-managed. In global software development (GSD) terms, Ireland as a location, while being geographically off-shore, is often considered near-shore, due to its linguistic and cultural similarities to the United States. As both organizations had previously successfully collaborated, the establishment of virtual software teams was initially considered a straightforward and simple task.

A common sense approach was employed by both organizations, based on their limited experience of outsourcing, for the establishment of the virtual teams. It was decided that four separate cross-site teams would be established. Each team would consist of 20 cross-site members; tasks would be shared among team members regardless of location. Each cross-site team would operate as a separate unit and take responsibility for different development and maintenance projects. It was decided that a U.S.-based project manager would manage each team.

Forty staff members were selected from the existing IT personnel at each location based on their technical ability and levels of experience. Stock Exchange Trading Inc. had a well-defined and documented process and it was agreed that this would provide the basis for the operation of the virtual teams. Initially, very little modification was made to the process to facilitate a virtual working environment. Conference calls and e-mail were selected as the main methods of communication. It was also agreed that direct telephone calls would take place between remote team members when required. To familiarize Irish team members with the U.S. organization's process and documentation, a basic orientation course was developed and undertaken. The focus of this course was process-centric and ignored such issues as cross-site cultural differences and possible communication problems. The U.S.-based team members were not offered virtual team orientation or any other type of relevant training.

Once the Irish team members had undertaken basic orientation, there was an unexpected demand, which required the Irish team members to spend 6 to 12 months working on-site in the U.S. organization on what would become their virtual teams. This was an unplanned emergency strategy and arose due to the need for Stock Exchange Trading Inc. to develop software for a number of new projects within a short timeframe. At that juncture, the infrastructure for the virtual teams had not been established. This resulted in moving the Irish team members to work on site with their U.S.-based colleagues on a temporary basis. This proved to be a good opportunity as it allowed the Irish team members to meet, work, and develop professional relationships with their U.S.-based colleagues and management. This was initially successful and was considered at the time an excellent base on which to build the virtual teams. However, this experience did not prevent the breakdown of those relationships when the full impact of operating in a virtual environment was encountered.

Given the near-shore cultural status ascribed to Ireland, it was of interest to note how both groups worked together in their respective teams. There were clear cultural differences between the U.S. and Irish team members. This was reflected in their behavior, the way work was carried out, and their attitude to authority and process. These differences became apparent to both groups, but did not result in any problems being encountered while they were collocated in the U.S. This experience had its benefits as it allowed them to develop a limited understanding and appreciation of each other's culture and provided first hand experience of working together.

While both groups worked very effectively when they were collocated, future problems were postponed rather than prevented.

On completion of the urgent projects, the Irish team members returned home. At that stage, the infrastructure was in place and the virtual teams were established. Initially, everything seemed to be going well, but soon problems arose. This resulted in working relationships breaking down between the Irish- and U.S.-based staff. Rather than working as a team, they actively obstructed each other and looked for every opportunity to hinder each other's progress. This directly impacted productivity and resulted in increased project time and costs which seriously threatened the success of the virtual team strategy.

Following an investigation, it became clear people who worked together very successfully while collocated were now actively obstructing and blaming each other for all the problems that arose during their projects. It was obvious that team members were aligned by geographical location and there was a very clear "them and us" culture in place. This was an unexpected outcome, given the level of harmony achieved in the earlier collocated projects. Questions had to be asked: How had this happened? How could it be addressed? How could it be stopped from reoccurring?

The misuse of e-mail was identified as a major contributing factor to the conflict, alienation, mistrust, and lack of cooperation between team members across the sites. While e-mail was used to communicate, it was also used as a weapon to publicly attack remote team members. The practice of copying senior management on minor problems, which were caused by team members at the other location, was widespread. Both groups were equally guilty of employing this tactic. This activity had the desired effect of highlighting a problem, but it alienated the individual it was directed toward. It also had a negative impact on fellow team members at that location, who saw it as an attack on their group as a whole. This situation was further compounded by management in both organizations reacting to these e-mails and getting involved with minor issues that the relevant team leader should have addressed. It was noted that management in their response normally took the side of individuals where they were located. This further alienated and added to the mistrust felt by people at the other location. It was clear that the "them and us" culture was not just restricted to team members. It was also prevalent between some levels of management in both organizations. As a result, the projects were negatively impacted.

This issue had to be addressed and a documented e-mail procedure was the solution. Clear guidelines were agreed upon, stating when, how, and to whom problems should be highlighted. This procedure was clearly outlined to team members at both locations. All minor issues were to be raised directly with the team leader and only with those directly involved. If and when it was necessary, it was the responsibility of the team leader to inform the relevant project manager of issues that could not be addressed within the team. If the project manager was unable to resolve the matter, it was their responsibility to raise the issue with senior management at both locations, who would formulate a joint response. It was noted that following the change in procedure very few minor issues were raised with the project managers and none had to go to senior management for resolution.

Having addressed the immediate manifestation of the problem, it was important to determine why it had arisen in the first place. An explanation of why the virtual team members in both locations had reached this situation and why they were still not cooperating needed to be discovered. It was recognized that a number of factors were involved. Distance and the lack of the opportunity for informal communication played a part. A five-hour time zone difference between sites meant the opportunity for direct contact was limited to three hours a day. No informal method of communication was available at the time.

Surprisingly, given their previous experience of working together, cultural differences came into play. While the Irish and U.S. culture appeared similar, distance highlighted their dissimilarity. The Irish attitude to authority and respect required that it must be earned rather then imposed. This manifested itself in the Irish tendency toward frankness, to question procedures, their use of humor and work ethic. These attitudes were construed by the U.S. staff as confrontational in the virtual team environment. The U.S.-based team members' belief in their technical superiority, their view that the Irish team members were working for them, not with them, and their sole ownership of the process were seen as naïve and arrogant by the Irish staff. Again, this problem only arose when working in the virtual team environment. These conflicting perceptions added to the mistrust and alienation felt by both groups and needed to be addressed.

The process while effective for single-site development and maintenance proved inadequate for a virtual team environment. It was seen as being imposed and the sole property of the staff of Stock Exchange Trading Inc. Team members based in Software Future Technologies, while having relevant suggestions for process improvement, were not consulted and any suggestions they made were ignored. This added to the alienation being experienced by the Irish staff. To address the process issue, the need for establishing common goals, objectives, and rewards were identified. The process had to be totally re-engineered to incorporate these issues. A common vocabulary, with clear definitions of artifacts, deliverables, and milestones, was jointly formulated. These were incorporated into the development of a shared and agreed process, which specifically addressed the needs of the virtual environment in which it operated. The input of staff at both locations was encouraged and valued, and this was clearly communicated to all the parties involved.

These measures helped to facilitate team cooperation and build trust and relationships. While these addressed some of the problems experienced, they did not fully explain the underlying cause. How had teams that worked effectively when they were collocated for up to a year deteriorate into opposing groups? This question needed to be answered; after extensive interviews, motivation was identified as a major contributing factor. While the majority of the teams were collocated in the U.S., the American team members did not understand the full implications of the virtual team strategy. Once the virtual teams were established, the full impact on their day-to-day work, promotion, and future employment prospects became clear. Management reinforced these negative aspects by utilizing the strategy to justify maintaining salaries at their current levels. They also stressed the additional cost of U.S.-based staff, and the need for them to be more productive and value-adding to justify the extra expense. The effect was unmotivated people who directed their hostility toward their fellow team members in Ireland, who they saw as a threat to their careers. This manifested itself in a lack of cooperation, alienation, and outright obstruction when and where the opportunity arose. This was met with a similar negative reaction from the Irish side, which felt that if this were how the Americans worked, it would be more effective to move the whole operation to Ireland. These attitudes were identified as a major contributing factor to the problems experienced and were compounded by the other issues outlined.

Once it was realized these were the problems, the only effective strategy available was to make it clear to staff at both locations—if utilizing virtual teams was not an option, the only feasible economic alternative was outsourcing the whole operation to the Far East or Eastern Europe. The options had to be made clear,: Work as a team regardless of location or find new positions elsewhere. This was a drastic approach, but the seriousness of the situation warranted it and there was no alternative if the virtual team strategy was to continue. The management of Stock Exchange Trading Inc. were made aware that their "motivation strategy" was totally counter productive and rather than negatively focusing on cost they should highlight how the use of virtual teams provided a secure future for everyone involved. This, along with the other measures outlined, helped to establish a productive working relationship between sites, and facilitated the completion of projects on time and within budget for the lifetime of the contract,

BIOGRAPHY

Dr. Valentine Casey has over 20 years experience in the software industry and his industrial roles have included software engineer, team leader, project manager, and software quality manager. He has also provided consulting services, focusing on distributed software development, software process improvement, and software testing to the financial and telecom sectors. He is an SEI-trained CMM assessor and holds a Ph.D. in computer science and an M.Sc in software re-engineering from the University of Limerick. He also has a B.Sc. in economics and management from London University. He has managed globally distributed projects and virtual software teams and carried out research in the area of distributed software development for the last 10 years, initially at the University of Limerick (where he pioneered this work) and then as a researcher with LERO, the Irish Software Engineering Research Centre. Currently, he is a researcher and lecturer at Bournemouth University (United Kingdom), where he is the global software development research area leader. He can be reached via e-mail: vcasey@bournemouth.ac.uk.

9.4

WHAT IS IT TO LIE ON A SOFTWARE PROJECT?

Robert N. Britcher, retired from IBM

Apparently, lying is common on software projects. Robert Glass's survey indicates that 86% of those asked replied that they had seen lying on "perhaps 50% of projects."

I have my own soul to wrestle with. In 1988, while leading the technical proposal for the FAA's advanced automation system (AAS), I condoned and polished IBM's position that we could develop 1.5 million lines in the programming language Ada in 18 months. Some high percentage of reuse was estimated to assuage any anxiety that might arise. I don't recall the exact estimate.

In retrospect, several million lines of Ada *were* developed, but over 60 months—most of it revisions, or written to fix the thousands of software defects. Of course, no one asserted that the estimated 1.5 million lines of Ada would not be revisions. Nor was it stated that these would be 1.5 million lines of code verified as correct. If anyone were to ask, many tens of thousands of those lines, perhaps a few hundred thousand, had already been written during the design competition, as prototype code. As Ada was relatively new, there were few studies available to undermine our standards for counting.

As it turned out, the AAS project was terminated after 10 years (1984–1994) because the business case—geographically combining and relocating the U.S. ground control facilities to save millions per annum in operations cost—was never a serious possibility, although Congress had bought the idea. Ongoing difficulties were described as "challenges." Credit was given, and progress payments were made, for PowerPoint slides. Requirements creep overcame any doubts that the project might some day end. In other words, the project was masterminded and carried out not unlike hundreds of others. But, on my salary during that time, I bought a house and two automobiles. In the end, a very large, awfully good thing happened. Domestic air traffic control emerged largely untouched. The system has proven to be as safe as ever, perhaps *because* the AAS failed.

One might ask, then, what is it to lie in this environment?

I look at the truth this way: First, it requires some form of trust and cooperation. This must have emerged in man some millions of years ago when several hunters had to work together to bring down a wildebeest and then rely on one another

The Dark Side of Software Engineering, by Johann Rost and Robert L. Glass
Copyright © 2011 IEEE Computer Society

to share it. One can imagine how long humans would have survived if, time after time, Johnny convinced Jim to take the point, risking life and limb, and then, after the kill, Johnny and his friends shut Jim out on the food? It may not be that truth is ontologically necessary, but it has proven to be biologically necessary.

Second, from a practical point of view, truth relies on natural language and groups. (Not that we don't lie to ourselves privately—with appropriate consequences.) Natural languages are not formal languages like Ada, or predicate calculus. They are immensely flexible, as to be vague, and the vagueness increases with each passing idiom and slogan. One need not work in the military-industrial complex to acquire the knack of avoiding [speaking about] facts.

Third, there are many external and internal influences that weigh in on our subjective lives. As members of families, churches, schools, nations, and corporations, most of us are awash in attitudes and opinions. Truth has a strong cultural bias.

These are three of some environmental factors in recognizing and telling the truth. They encapsulate another set, the attributes of truth. Logicians reckon these to be the *context* of a fact or a statement, its *truth value* (can it be validly assessed as true or false, or is it neither or meaningless), its *meaning (what in the real world is being represented, symbolically)*, and—I would add one more—*meaningfulness*. The last appeals to me because the environmental constituents, evolution, language, subjectivity, are not simply of reason; they are charged with emotional content. Humans are not like Mr. Spock.

Now, let me analyze the AAS case of a manager reporting that his team's software was on schedule for delivery to the laboratory, fully aware that his team had violated the standard (contractual) practice of inspecting and unit-testing 100% of the code.

First, there is trust and cooperation: Is little Davey operating in a field of trust, on a project in which Congress has been misled? Cooperation. The rules of cooperation on large government projects are quite clear. Good news is passed on to the next authority up the line, who is getting paid even more money to tackle even greater risks. One cannot expect the first-line manager to be pessimistic or sound pessimistic when there are risk-reduction margins and reserves he or she does not know of. Little Davey did the best under the circumstances; everyone worked hard, and the people are experts.

Language. The jargon of corporations, governments, and technology in general are perfectly suited to evade the truth. We said we were going to write 50,000 lines of code this quarter and we did it—and we tested it. Surely the aggregate was tested in the software integration lab when the shakedown scenarios were run. Not stated is that the shakedown scenarios consisted *not* of propositions such as "$p \wedge q \wedge yF(y)$ iff $y \rightarrow x \wedge z$ ....", but, rather, something like "$-p \rightarrow$ abort".

Subjective influences: To this, we can add the insane drive of the manager who was told by his father that if he did not make the position of second line manager in five years, like his father did, don't come home again!

Now, as to the attributes of truth. First, the context. On AAS, promises had been made, gifts exchanged—lots of them. Expectations ran perpetually high. Enter little Davey to report on Build 1. The project manager, a vice president, is seated at the head of the table, his direct reports at his side. Lying in this context is a little like 85-year-old Aunt May making her entrance in the sitting room after spending the better part of the afternoon preening herself. "Oh, Aunt May, you look lovely!" "I love your dress," etc. It's quite appropriate.

The truth value is easily evaluated: the *proposition* ("We are done.") is neither true or false (using bivariate logic) because the term "done" is undefined. Meaning? Everyone in the room knows the jargon and the code words. "Done," undefined as it is, still has *some* meaning. In this case, it means, "We made it, but there is still work to be done." Enough of the report (the statements, the assertions, the propositions) is true, including how much OT was put in and the splendid performance of the team and the code compiles, et al. Any breach of the truth discovered later will merit only a cool glance or a few raised eyebrows at the ensuing banquet.

As for meaningfulness, everyone will be satisfied to not know with any certainty that little Davey hedged on his commitments. For the manager, his optimistic report of the pseudo-facts means that he will likely be rewarded. In 2009, the stakes would be even higher: he might not lose his job. Weighed against the $3.5 billion contract, to do what can wait or should never be, his livelihood and his family's health and welfare are decisive in this case. He must tell the truth as he sees it—and did.

BIOGRAPHY

Robert N. Britcher teaches a number of courses in the systems engineering program at the Johns Hopkins University Whiting School of Engineering, including software systems management. He is retired from IBM, where he worked on government systems, including air traffic control, satellite imagery, automated publishing, military digital networking, and submarine messaging. He is the author of *The Limits of Software*, (Addison-Wesley, 1999). He lives in Gaithersburg, Maryland, and can be reached at rbritcher501@comcast.net.

9.5

"MERCILESS CONTROL INSTRUMENT" AND THE MYSTERIOUS MISSING FAX

A. H. (anonymous)

In my project management lecture, I tell my students anecdotes from my professional experience in software development projects. I want them to be prepared for the mean world outside. They always are shocked because stories about subversive stakeholders destroy their illusion that in "real" software projects, all stakeholders work together constructively towards joint success. The students (in their work life) expect team play which even exceeds the chaos they experience during their studies, such as when some fellow students do not contribute their part to the team project. Somehow, they believe that after the end of their hectic studies, they will go to work in the morning and know exactly what they will do during the day and have the time budget for it. (I suppose this illusion helps them to get through their studies.) Consequently, the idea of deliberate project sabotage irritates them a lot.

In what follows, I'll tell you two of these anecdotes and two of my tricks. I hope that my enemies won't read this.

One of the software projects, for which I was the project manager, took place in the midst of storms of internal tension on the customers' side. Knowing this was helpful to react successfully against the tricks of one of the subversive stakeholders.

The project's objective was to replace the current back office software because, over the years, the number of users and the data volume had increased and the technology had reached its limits. The system's performance had become very low. So, it was decided to introduce a better-performing technology and to have a standard product customized to their needs. The company had a central department and ten subsidiaries in the whole country. It was this central department that decided to invest in the new technology and that defined most of the requirements. The employees from the subsidiaries were invited to add their own requirements. However, seeing the software and learning about its abilities enforced their suspicion that the central department wanted this product in order to have more control over the subsidiaries, their way of working, and their data. The product produced a host of reports about all kinds of data and about the work done in the subsidiaries. Being call center

The Dark Side of Software Engineering, by Johann Rost and Robert L. Glass
Copyright © 2011 IEEE Computer Society

software rather than back office software, it was by default allowed to read other users' task lists and calendars. The future users were told that they should use this system for managing all their meetings, tasks, and calendars.

The central department did not take the employees' worries seriously. At first, I tried to keep out of this discussion because it was their internal problem to decide about their software requirements.

One day, when I was having lunch with the project manager on the customer side, he told me ("by the way") that he had heard that the works council believed that the main objective of changing to the new software was to better monitor the employees. I took this very seriously because in Germany the works council has the veto right, i.e., if they object to the rollout of new software, it cannot be used. So, they are success-critical stakeholders for the project. I asked for names and phone numbers of these persons in order to contact them and to talk to them about their concerns. However, I was told that I should not take them too seriously, they were just making a lot of unnecessary fuss. As I knew that this person tends to underestimate risks, I decided to keep my eyes open and to prepare for problems from the direction of the works council.

For a while, nothing happened. The project continued. But one day, I had occasion to talk to someone whom I could ask about the rumors concerning the works council. Yes, in fact, there would be a meeting of the works council's IT group, where they would discuss and decide whether the new software could be used or whether it would be turned down. Among trade unions, you must know, this software has the reputation of being a merciless control instrument. So, I thought it was possible that they might turn the software down completely, without giving us occasion to customize it to their wants. And even if they did not manage to end the project completely, they could delay it considerably. I knew that the IT group met only once a month.

This second person I talked to gave me names and phone numbers of the persons I should contact. My plan was to treat them as important stakeholders, to ask them for their requirements, and to implement them as far as possible, even if it would be us who paid the bill. At any price, I wanted this project to succeed, because it was important for my own career and also my company had a strategic interest in rollout and in maintaining this software—it was an important customer and this project was intended to serve as a reference project in the future.

For several weeks, I tried to get these persons on the phone, but did not manage to. They did not answer my emails and never called back, although this had been promised. At my first call, I had learned some of their concerns, but later, I did not get any further information about what they thought, wanted, might need, or planned. Then, I heard that the critical meeting would be soon. We were already in the final phase of the project, near to going live. I wondered whether they scheduled this meeting so late because the later they met, the more probable it was that it would be too late for us to react to their concerns. If during this meeting questions would have stayed open, the subsequent meeting would have been after the planned delivery date.

I tried to get help from the project manager on the customer side, and from my own department manager, but both said that the works council would not dare to turn down the project at such a late point in time. They called the rumors "nonsense." I still took the warnings seriously. Therefore, I spent some time (my evenings, by the way, because I did not really have a time budget for these activities) to gather the information that I knew they would want, and the information that I guessed they might want to see. I did some research about the product's possibilities for controlling employees. In fact, being call center software, it could turn every user into a completely transparent user. However, as the software was also envisioned for the back office, and as German laws are strict about protecting employees, each of these functionalities could be deactivated. Some, we as developers could deactivate; some, however, could only be deactivated by each user individually. I documented the results of my research in two documents. The first one was intended for the works council to show them where control was possible, and I also included screenshots that showed that in fact we had deactivated them already. The second one was a short user handbook of about ten pages about "What to do to get started." It guided the users through their first session and explained how to configure the client software. It emphasized the importance of the ability to deactivate certain functionalities in order to guarantee privacy of the task list and calendar. This document was to be given to each new user, together with the user name and password.

The expected date of the critical meeting approached and, the week before, I intensified my efforts to get someone on the phone that could tell me what I could do to help them make the right decision in the meeting. Finally, at two o'clock on Friday afternoon, I was told that someone would call me back after a meeting that was currently taking place. They asked me how long I would be in the office. I said that time doesn't matter. I would stay as long as necessary until someone called me. (Grin!) Finally, I got a callback at four o'clock. The discussion sounded very cooperative. The person told me their concerns, and I summarized what I had found out about the software and the possibilities for protecting user privacy. I asked them what information they needed and how I could help them. I got an answer and started writing. And wrote. And wrote. And wrote. Finally, I ended up with a very long write-up of information that they wanted, some of it probably (completely) irrelevant, but difficult to provide. I knew that the meeting would be Tuesday, so I asked when they need the information. Their reply was Monday morning at eight in the morning because they would need time to read it. I told them "OK, You will get it tomorrow, at the latest." Silence on the other end.

"Well," I was told, "We need all of this information, not just pieces of it." It was obvious that they had not expected that I could answer all these questions in time. He even asked me whether I always worked so late on Friday evening. (I believe that they expected that I always went home at 4.)

I promised: "It is OK, you will get it all. I have noted it down. Don't worry." (By the way: I like doing this. To misinterpret the concerns of subversive stakeholders and of enemies in a way that insinuates their goodwill is a way to irritate them a lot.)

On first thought, I saw that I already had gathered half of that information and the rest could be gathered within some hours. I was willing to work the whole weekend through to manage this, if necessary.

After the phone call, I walked through the offices to find out whether there was someone left from the project team to help me. I found someone—a student working on a master's thesis, but familiar with the project. He agreed to stay until six o'clock in the evening, so I gave him some tasks he could do easily with the knowledge he had. The rest was mine.

Some time during the night between Friday and Saturday, I sent all the material to the email address of the works council, and also to some other people who could be witnesses that I sent it completely and in time.

The whole thing was worth all those evening hours. The works council saw that we were cooperative, taking their concerns seriously, and had already taken measures to protect the employees. They had gotten all the information they had demanded, completely.

In the end, they did not object to the rollout. So, we could meet the project deadline and go live. Of course, my boss afterwards (as so often, when I invested time in risk management) told me, grinning, that reality proved that all my hysterical concerns had been baseless. In the end, everything had gone well, so all my efforts had been for nothing. Of course, this may be true, but when I look at how things went, I believe that it is not the case. Of course, I cannot prove that the works council really planned to boycott the software and consequently our ("my") project, but my gut feeling tells me that I was did the right thing.

What I learned from this: Have lunch with the customers, listen to warnings and take them seriously, be prepared, and be cooperative. When stakeholders behave in a subversive way, there is a good possibility that they might give up when you react well.

A second anecdote stems from another project. Our company was merging with another and we were expected to work together with them. We subcontracted them to do a part of a project because they were specialists for this kind of technology. We believed that they had been working on it for weeks, but no news came from them. I kept asking for their status by email. I also tried to call the responsible person but the phone was never answered. As I did not really believe that he was never in his office, I played the mobile phone trick. It always works. (Grin!) Sometimes, one gets the feeling that when someone recognizes a phone number on the phone's display, he plays the dead man. So, after some time, I use my mobile phone to call. They don't know my mobile number, as I do not use it often. And when he then answers the phone, not knowing that it is me, I have him. (By the way: Only in extreme cases do I do this—I never use the mobile phone immediately after having tried with the fixed line phone, because by doing this, I communicate that I know what he is playing at. Usually, I avoid unmasking them so brutishly.)

"Well," he said. "In fact, we have not being doing anything. We are still waiting for your fax." It was the fax with the official task assignment. They had told us that they needed something in written form, otherwise they would do nothing.

"Well," I said. "These things can happen. I will send the fax again in some minutes. Could you please contact me if you do not get it?"

I sent the fax. No one called me to tell me that the fax had not arrived, so I assumed they got it and were working *now*, finally. Time passed. I did not get him on the phone ever again. But I knew that his organization was moving, by chance moving to the new building in our backyard. So, I observed their move, went to the inauguration party, and the next day called again with the mobile. I got him on the phone. I welcomed him as a new neighbor, and I asked how they were advancing with our joint project.

"How," He said, "could we work on it? You have again not sent the fax."

I: "But if you have not got it, why did you not contact me and tell me?" (An unnecessary question, I know.)

He said something about "other things to do." I talked about the importance of the delivery of their work package and the going-live deadline, and I mentioned that if they did not start working tomorrow, we must delay the going-live.

"OK," I said. "I will send the fax again. Then, I will call. And if you do not tell me that you got the fax and if I cannot get you on the phone, I will make a photocopy, walk over, and bring it to your office. What is your room number?"

He cleared his throat and said: "I do not think that is necessary. Let's hope that the fax arrives this time."

Guess what happened. He did get the fax. And they had no excuse any more for not working. That was just in time. When talking to a colleague about this, I mused whether I would have driven down to the place where their offices had been before, about one hour away.

I would have, I concluded.

BIOGRAPHY

A. H. has 14 years of working experience, half of it in software development as a requirements engineer, project manager, and consultant, the other half as a scientist.

9.6

FOREST OF ARDEN

David Alan Grier
Professor, George Washington University

They say he is already in the Forest of Arden,
and a many merry men with him;
and there they live like the old Robin Hood of England.

Only for the briefest of times do we live in the Forest of Arden, that idyllic Shakespearean place where we are free from the demands of family, politics, and society. It is the world of academic leisure, where inhabitants are free to hunt, and to sing, and to test those qualities that attract members of the opposite sex. The Bard warns us that Arden contains "tongues in trees, books in the running brooks, and sermons in stones," but reassures us that ultimately there is "good in everything."

For eight swift college months, I lived the computerized Arden. For that short time, I was entrusted with a key to the machine room, the place where our school's time-sharing system was housed. Six of us held this responsibility and we were the little band that stood safely aloof from the regulations of the college. We knew that the machine was not widely used and so we were able to explore how this wonderful technology worked.

We spent evening after evening looking for the sermons in stone; the little lessons that we would learn by making the machine do something new. Our first challenge was to print the Japanese Yen sign, ¥, on one of the older terminals. The terminal clearly had the ability to print that symbol, as its physical print head displayed the ¥ directly below the #. Our explorations took us through the elements of ASCII code until we found the right number to place in the right part of memory.

Such tasks had a song all their own, an attraction that pulled us to them. We learned how to use the line printer as a typewriter, how to draw a picture on a TV screen, how to make the system lights flash in a syncopated rhythm. As far as we could see, there was indeed good in everything, as every little challenge taught us something new. We were loath to think that any sermon in stone would carry the sting of disproval or a lesson that would be taught by infringing on the claims of others.

I had an early hint that the computer room might not be as sheltered as I had thought but I dismissed it as a lesson that didn't apply to my technical work. One night, the captain of the woman's ski team was struggling with some computer

The Dark Side of Software Engineering, by Johann Rost and Robert L. Glass
Copyright © 2011 IEEE Computer Society

problem, noted that I seemed to have command of the machine, and asked for assistance. For an hour, we sat hunched over the terminal and in that time, I misread every signal that she sent out. I failed to imagine that every action, every word, every scent might be connected to something outside of the computer lab.

I went to my room in the hot sweat of infatuation and woke the next morning to the cold dawn of reality. Only then did I realize that her gentle smell meant that she had recently showered after a workout, that her rapt attention indicated that she was in a hurry to get somewhere else, and that her effusive gratitude meant that she did not have to ask her boyfriend for assistance.

The embarrassing pain of the encounter quickly faded, as other tasks soon commanded my energies. The six of us, the merry men who held the keys to the machine, decided that we would construct a simple interactive chat system. As we discussed it, I conceived a simple way to implement the system that used a common disk fail. At some time in my explorations, I had discovered a way to have two different programs read and write a common disk file. I had not seen this technique discussed in any of the computer manuals and had concluded that it was either a legitimate idea that was not being disseminated by the manufacturer or a novel idea that I had discovered. In neither case did I conceive that it would interact with any activity beyond the two programs that were engaged in the correspondence.

I don't recall how long it took me to write the system. I can't imagine that it took me longer than a day or two, as I had little patience for large programs at the time. I had it working one Friday night and was happily exchanging comments with a friend across the room when the program stopped dead. I tried to revive it but failed. As I tried a second time, I realized that all the programs had stopped. After a few moments, I used my key to the machine room and found the computer ablaze in signal lamps. The machine itself was no longer operating.

Twice I tried to reboot it and failed. I had been carefully taught how to bring the machine to a complete halt and restart the operating system but I was unable to make these procedures work that night. After an hour of frustration, I called the director of the center, who came over and worked on the machine. After 10 or 15 minutes, he made some comment about corruption on the disk and started a special routine that repaired the file structure.

I don't know if he ever knew what I had been doing but from his comments I soon realized what had happened. My technique of reading and writing a single file circumvented basic routines in the operating system. At some point, my two programs tried to write at the time but their commands were shuffled together by the time-sharing system. As a result, the file had been adjusted in way that caused the operating system to note an inconsistency between the size of the file and the record that described the file.

My program had inflicted no permanent damage but it had made a claim upon the computer director, a claim that I had not foreseen. Prior to this, I assumed that my experiments were fine because they dwelt in a world that I commanded. Nothing that I had done had touched on any asset that was claimed by others, or so I thought. Certainly the ¥ symbol was mine to control, but beyond it, the remaining parts of the computer system were also claimed by other users. The disk was under the responsibility of the computer director, even though he was not using it at the time.

No matter what Shakespeare may have said, stones really do not contain sermons. They hold the messages that we project onto them. While we would like to think that there is good in everything, the good claimed by one may conflict good identified by another. We believed that we were living in a forest where we were untouched by outsiders and our actions held no consequences for others. As a result, we pursued knowledge of the computer machine with an aggressive drive. None of this knowledge was completely forbidden but some of it skirted the fences of Arden and lodged in the gardens of our neighbors.

Mine was not the only program to bring the system to a halt that year, though perhaps it was the most dramatic. At the end of the year, the director reclaimed the machine room keys from us. Though he never rebuked us, he hinted that giving six college students free run of the machine had been a mistake. We returned the following year with a clear understanding that we had to follow the rules that applied to everyone else and acknowledge the claims that others made on the machine. The forest of Arden was gone and our little band of merry men was returned to the city, where we had to follow the rules. Yet once in a while, usually while tackling a big problem, we would remember that we had learned some fundamental lesson from the trees and brooks and stones of Arden.

BIOGRAPHY

David Alan Grier is the author of *Too Soon to Tell* and *When Computers Were Human*, and writes "The Known World" column for *IEEE Computer*. He is an associate professor of international science and technology policy at the George Washington University. He studied mathematics at Middlebury College, and received a Ph.D. in Statistics at the University of Washington. He was introduced to computers by his father, who was a project manager and director of consumer relations for Burroughs Computer Corporation. As a result, the younger Grier has spent most of his career working with this technology. He began working as a computer designer and then for more than a decade, he worked as a programmer. He now writes on the subject of software and the people who work with it.

9.7

HARD-HEADED HARDWARE HIT MAN

Will Tracz
Fellow, Lockheed Martin

Picture this: You are just out of grad school, working for a large tech company, getting to do all kinds of neat things that some of the more senior programmers had never heard of (though they are really smart), impressing your peers (and leaving your managers wondering what you are talking about), when you are asked to attend a meeting with your manager and your manager's manager.

The topic is a rather "aggressive" schedule that you, a rather junior programmer, have just given (and have been delivering on, repeatedly, for similar projects). It seems a hardware manager, whom your project is now supporting, is questioning the plausibility of such a budget, and would rather have one of his hardware guys cobble an ad hoc translator together, rather than risk this "formal grammar" software approach you have been using.

What was unusual about this meeting was the fear in my manager's eyes when we walked into the hardware project manager's office. I didn't have a clue; I thought I was just along for the ride, but soon the conversation turned to the topic of my project, my budget, and my schedule. Well, the hardware manager pounded his fist on his desk and said, emphatically, that this schedule is "questionable" (only he used a single syllable word instead of "questionable").

I looked at my two managers in amazement, as they were obviously stunned into silence by this other manager's bullying use of the expletive. I, sitting in a side chair, spoke up and said, "If you think you can do it better than I can, than you don't know what you're talking about. You can go try, but you will fail."

The manager looked at me, smiled, and said, "OK, you do it." As we walked out the office, my two managers took me aside and said, "We can't believe it! No one talks back to him like that." I said, "Well, I did, and he was wrong."

I never had any trouble with my estimates after that. The moral of the story? Well, there are lots of them, mostly having to do with managers who either don't always know what they are talking about, or have a certain attitude that needs adjustment. The problem is, you may not always have the opportunity to adjust it yourself, so let your work speak for itself, and let technology do the work for you.

Will What's-His-Name (a Not-So-Serious Bio)   Almost nothing is known about this person. Records of his childhood, education, and professional accomplishments were either ill-kept or have been lost in fires of mysterious origins.

Here is what we do know: Tracz is a native-born son of American parents and plays several musical instruments, although none very well, according to his wife.

He took an abnormally long time (23 years to be precise) getting the usual degrees from a couple of East Coast and West Coast institutions of higher learning, whose mascots are portrayed as lions, trees, fruits, or knights, in various shades of red, purple, orange, blue, and white.

Parts of his time were spent dwelling in the bowels of what was the IBM Federal System Division's Owego, New York, laboratory until it was rudely sold to some other company that got four times the amount they paid for it three years later … after cutting company benefits by two-thirds.

He belongs to the customary societies and organizations and edits several of their publications where he indulges in promoting a revolutionary seamless evolutionary paradigm shift toward the synergistic coordination and management of intellectual effort for the common man on even days of the week.

His interests include a run-of-the-mill selection of the current "hot" topics that seem to change based on funding cycles of various program managers and magic quadrant contents.

He has some technical publications and music videos, including a book with cartoons in it, so that even managers can get something out of it, and a song, last performed live at Pleasure Island, Disney World Village, Florida, to raise money for the "Save the Year 2000 Fund."

Finally, he claims an average number of ordinary jobs for experience. He has been a jackhammer operator, professional rock musician and recording artist, college professor, lifeguard, and sit-down comedian.

BIOGRAPHY

Dr. Will Tracz is a Lockheed Martin Fellow and principal software engineer/application architect for the Global Combat Support System-AF (GCSS-AF) application integration department at Lockheed Martin IS&S in Endicott, New York, responsible for investigating innovative applications of and evaluating technology for the GCSS-AF Architecture Integration Framework. Dr. Tracz is the cochair of Lockheed Martin's Corporate Advanced Software Technology Focus Group.

Dr. Tracz is a member of the RIT Software Engineering Advisory Board, the Software Engineering Institute Technical Advisory Group on Engineering and Methods, and an IEEE TCSE Executive Committee Member at Large. In addition, he is the editor of the *ACM SIGSOFT Software Engineering Notes*, past chairman of the International Conference on Software Engineering, sponsored by IEEE and ACM, and the author of more than 100 technical reports and books on software engineering, software architectures, and software reuse.

9.8

A LIGHTHEARTED ANECDOTE

Eugene Farmer
retired software executive

Digging a Hole in the Software Fortress … (Well, as Long as the Bad Guys Don't Know).   Roscoe Leroy was the technical rep who installed this massive new programming environment at that major defense contractor site. In the early days of computing, rows of fridge-size cabinets lined up in a computer room, with the then-traditional elevated floor carrying air conditioning, and miles and miles of wiring. The best approach for computer security in those days was to completely isolate the computer room from the outside world, make it a "black area."

But, things went wrong with a new code generator a few months after the site had become operational and was in full swing, developing some big defense program. So, Roscoe was called back to investigate. He indeed found that some patterns of source code would generate the wrong machine code sequence, and he wanted to report this back to his own development team, in a far-away country, overseas.

He was not allowed to take the culprit source code out of the black area in the form of a disk, or a tape, or a printout. He tried hard to take notes on papers, and every day, tried in his office, outside of the black area, to reproduce the defect with tiny programs, but this did not work. He offered to completely sanitize the programs; he even wrote some code to change all identifiers, removed large chunks of the code, and tried to create what he would call a "minimal faulty program," but the minimal faulty programs were still a couple of thousands of lines of code.

The security folks would not budge an inch from their position: "Not a line of our highly sensitive code can go out of this large cold computer room. Period."

On another hand, a small army of developers, in the second security circle around the computer room, were starting to breathe heavily on the neck of Roscoe Leroy: Could they fix the compilers? How do we avoid these bugs? They had to start integration and more serious testing.

One night, Roscoe had an idea. He had noticed that there were several phone lines going in/out of the computer room, not connected to anything, just wires that had been left after the last overhaul of the place. He went to the local Radio Shack and bought two small 1200 baud modems. He snuck one of the modems inside the computer room, under the pretense of doing his routine maintenance, and connected one of the computers to the modem, the modem to the phone line. A couple of days later, he finished the job at the other end, connecting his support computer, outside of the black area, to it.

The Dark Side of Software Engineering, by Johann Rost and Robert L. Glass
Copyright © 2011 IEEE Computer Society

Now he was in full business. A few more hacks, and he was soon able to transfer his minimal faulty programs outside of the black area onto his more-or-less private machine. And from there, overseas to the development team, who were thrilled to have something substantial to debug, and test their fixes. Some five months later, and 30 "minimal faulty programs" later, the compiler was declared "stable" with no known serious defect. Roscoe Leroy was transferred to the support of another major customer. Before leaving the defense contractor's plant, he discreetly disconnected his modems, and lost them somewhere under the raised floor, among coils of wiring.

Hey, as long as he was the only one to know, what could be wrong?

Easter Eggs on an Air Force Base … (Top Brass is not Amused!).   Roscoe Leroy's colleague in development in this large multinational telecommunication enterprise was this nerd, Kristof, who (since he had no life) would stay late and polish lots of code. In these early days, most people used the services of a small army of "key punch" ladies to enter their code. This was just after punch cards had been abandoned, and nobody wanted to lay them off. But Kristof insisted on entering his own code: He could type pretty fast, and he loved to try out things in the code.

One day, Roscoe is called by the Air Force to come and investigate the strange behavior of the telephone switch on two different Air Force bases. The defect is very elusive: Suddenly a phone rings, and when you pick up, there is just a busy tone, and another phone rings, and so on. Not really a danger, but very irritating. The Air Force had a special variant of the code, not the standard release. Roscoe checks the configuration installed on their switches, gets the code on a disk (in those days, a disk was the size of car wheel!), drives to the Air Force base, and sets up to track the problem: install some probes, activate all the logging and tracing features … and wait, chatting with the officers of service. After some 36 hours, finally the problem occurs. Roscoe gets a dump of the memory, and starts tracing down the source of the bug, under the amused eye of the Air Force officer on duty to keep an eye on him. These were painstaking jobs, and Roscoe was not successful: The source code he had was obviously not corresponding to what was running on this switch. He went back to his lab and searched for changes in the configuration management system. After an hour, he found that Kristof had done a succession of last-minute changes in the main code base that he inadvertently propagated to the Air Force code variant, before (a week later) removing his changes.

Roscoe confronted Kristof the next day: What was this urgent fix about? Kristof turned red in the face. He was working on some kind of practical joke that he wanted to deploy in our own facility, but it did not work as expected, and he removed it—an "Easter egg" of some sort (before we had heard of the term). Was he aware that this had leaked in the Air Force branch? No, he had no clue.

Roscoe and two technicians returned to the Air Force base the next day with a clean executable—some of it was in PROMs for the dozens of interface boards, which meant lots of work to upgrade the system.

This was followed by a rather disagreeable meeting with the Air Force hierarchy, as someone had leaked to them that this strange, erratic bug was actually some practical joke a civilian had planted in the system, bored on a cold and snowy weekend.

Big Brother is Watching You … (Or, How to Save a lot on Long Distance Calls with Little Effort). Roscoe Leroy's team had finished writing the billing system for the PBX (private telephone switch). Though this billing system was intended for hotels and hospitals, and other companies who parcel-out long distance cost to individual stations, departments, and divisions, they decided to put it in service in their own facility, which had never had any such accounting system, before going for a real beta test with real customers. They installed this on a Friday afternoon, just before a long weekend.

Some people in that facility, in marketing or sales or at some senior level, were able to call freely around the country. Returning to the plant on Tuesday morning, Roscoe found a rather long list of "toll" calls, about 200, starting Saturday morning, from a single station, and going on and on until later Sunday afternoon.

He suspected first that something had gone wrong. He mentioned this to his group lead, Eugene Farmer, and showed him the raw listing; Farmer was quickly able to identify the owner of the station, and he asked him whether he had spent the weekend making calls. The culprit first denied it, unaware of this new billing system, but then Eugene confronted him with numbers dialed, timing etc., all in the same region of the country, a picturesque place with lots of small hotels and B&Bs. Finally, the employee confessed. The total amount, according to the new billing system, was several hundred dollars' worth.

Though there was no direct consequence to this specific employee, the story quickly made the rounds at the cafeteria, in this facility, and then across the whole company. It had an interesting effect, as Roscoe learned from someone in accounting three months later: They noticed a drop of about 50% of long distance charges in the next billing cycle. It took almost a year for the billing level to regain its original level of the month they first installed the billing system (which had long since been removed).

Taking a Million Line of Code with Him … (And Selling it, Piece by Piece). Irina got a call from Roscoe Leroy, asking her for help to find a contractor to write a new driver for some new fancy device—delicate work, done in assembly, with lots of hard, real-time constraints. Irina had little time, but lots of connections, indirectly through her brother-in-law, Paul, who was working in another firm.

Paul knew someone, indirectly again, who had done this kind of work, and was looking for contracting opportunities. The message went back in steps to Roscoe, who had never heard of that person, but asked naïvely: Could he show us some piece of code he has written, plus a résumé, or a list of past clients and references?

The message went back via the same route, and two days later, Roscoe had in front of him the resume of Robert G., and a piece of code that he—Roscoe!—had written three years earlier, with two teammates. It was neatly formatted, especially the block of comments at the beginning of the module, stating it was authored by Robert G.

Roscoe was really shocked, and a quick search showed that a Robert G. had been laid off a year earlier from another division, after some repeated disagreements with his management and conflicts with his teammates.

Roscoe involved human resources from this point. They decided that they had too little evidence yet of malfeasance, so they went a little bit further: Via Roscoe, they indicated that they were willing to offer him a contract, but wanted more work to be done, and asked for more samples of code. Robert complied, and more code appeared, also traceable to the large telephone switch, only slightly modified— mostly comments were rewritten and variables renamed. The police at this stage were involved: Robert G. had left the company, taking with him a copy of the whole software base, neatly organized on three dozen floppy disks, short of a million line of code, and he was reselling it around in small chunks.

At this point, the legal department took the affair in hand, and Roscoe was not involved anymore. He heard that Robert's defense involved some mumbling about inalterable rights of the programmers over their creation.

BIOGRAPHY

Eugene Farmer is a retired software industry executive. Starting in life as a professional mining engineer, he rapidly fell in the software pot in the early 1970s, especially after he bought his first microcomputer, an Altair 8800. Software development proved to be, after all, where all the fun and the money was in those days. Farmer was mostly involved in large-scale development in the area of defense, aerospace, and telecommunications. He led numerous teams around the world, and, in particular, one talented software developer called Roscoe Leroy followed him around on a few challenging projects.

CONCLUSIONS

It is time to draw to a close our excursion through the never-never land of the dark side of software and computing. We hope that our trip has entertained and enlightened you along the way. And we hope the experience of being exposed to the dark side of computing practices hasn't been too depressing!

Perhaps we should share our own perceptions of what this trip has been like and about. First of all, although there are dark side matters on a fair number of computing projects, they do not overwhelm us. We frequently made reference, especially early in the book, to the topic of software project failure, and we noted that although some claim there is a "software crisis" based on the number of such failures, we take a much more positive view regarding failure; there would not be a successful "era of computing" if there were not huge numbers of successful software projects.

Similarly, we have an upbeat view of these dark side matters. Our view is based to some extent on data. In the introduction to this book, and scattered through its chapters, we have seen data that shows dark side matters running from uncommon to somewhat common. In other words, the data shows that our field is not besieged by dark side issues.

And then there is our personal belief. We tend to be upbeat people. One of us, in fact, has a personal view that people are essentially good: "85% of people are 85% good." That is, most of us have a small dark side streak (that's the second 15% [100%–85%]) in the expression), and a few of us are really bad apples (that's the first 15%). And, he concludes, he can live with that belief. Bad apples and dark side matters are going to occur, but sufficiently uncommonly, according to this belief, that one can still perceive the world as a relatively good place to be. (We are pleased to note, as an aside here, that the software engineering field in particular and the professional fields in general are moving to a more upbeat view of such matters. For example, we laud the recent (2008) publication of a book called *Moral Markets*, which speaks of the power of "values" to steer business marketplaces into more and more positive moral directions. The "greed is good" era, we believe, is diminishing if not disappearing. So much for whether the content of the book is depressing. We're not depressed by it, and we hope you aren't either!

Where else have we been on this excursion? Well, we saw several interesting things:

1. The topic of the dark side is rarely discussed as such in either the popular press or the literature of the field. When it is discussed, it is typically in another

---

The Dark Side of Software Engineering, by Johann Rost and Robert L. Glass
Copyright © 2011 IEEE Computer Society

guise, such as "ethics" or "management issues," and even then dark side matters do not shine cleanly through. What we have shared together in this excursion has been, perhaps surprisingly, a somewhat-unique experience.

2. This topic is also oddly defined. Dictionaries say things about related matters, such as "dark" and "darksome," but they are silent on the expression "dark side." But that's very surprising, considering that feeding "dark side" into Google or Amazon produces astonishingly high relevant hit numbers. The topic may be undefined, this tells us, but everyone knows what it is!

3. There are several ways to talk about such matters. We started out with a couple of surveys for subdivisions of the dark side topic that are rarely discussed anywhere—subversion and lying—and produced some unique and original findings that we are particularly proud of. But as we pursued the matter further, we found a number of other related topics—hacking, theft of information, espionage, disgruntled employees and sabotage, and whistle-blowing—where the topic is covered often and case studies are plentiful, where we did not feel the need to conduct a survey, and where the relevant press coverage of these matters gave us a rich lore of material to draw from. So this book is, in a sense, a strange mixture of original research findings and anecdotal material from that rich lore.

4. Although you may wish, and we might wish, to draw some general conclusions about these dark side matters, we found it nearly impossible to do so. There is a strong "it depends" factor in discussing these dark side topics. Lying happens very frequently on software projects, for example, while subversion is relatively rare. Disgruntled employees cause mischief more often than one might think, but more high-profile crimes like sabotage and espionage seldom happen. Interestingly, whistle-blowing almost never happens on software projects. We discuss each of these "it depends" matters in considerable length in the book.

5. These topics in a very real sense are "strange bedfellows." Some of them are clearly focused on matters related to software projects, but some of them are related to software engineering peripherally at best. For example, although hackers may (or may not) have software engineering skills, the effect of their work is almost never at the software project level. Theft of information, as another example (coupled with its closely-related topic "disgruntled employees"), may be performed on software projects and be focused on software products, but much more often it is focused on a company's data, far removed from any software project significance. And espionage is usually focused on a higher level target than simply a software project (although in industrial espionage, software projects are in fact a possible target).

6. In item 4, above, we spoke of the frustrated wish to draw general conclusions about these topics. In order to hold any meaningful discussions about dark side matters, in fact, we found it necessary to disaggregate the topic into those seven constituent elements that make up the bulk of our book. Here, we managed to draw some interesting subtopic conclusions about the disaggregated elements of dark side matters. But even here, there was frustration. With

respect to the causes and effects of hacking, for example, experts who have studied the issue in depth find it difficult to draw any supportable conclusions about the matter. The phrase "it depends" kept cropping up annoyingly frequently.

7. Furthermore, our disaggregated topics tangle annoyingly. We tried to draw a crisp distinction, for example, between hacking and theft of information and disgruntled employees. But, we kept finding, disgruntled employees sometimes used hacking approaches to steal information! To keep our book organization meaningful, we had to make sometimes-arbitrary choices as to which case study or anecdote went into which section of the book.

8. The organization of the book proved frustrating in another way. Most of the topics we originally studied were about dark side acts (where we define "act" as an activity conducted by someone). Subversion is an act. Lying is an act. Hacking is an act. Theft of information is an act. Espionage is an act. Whistle-blowing is an act. But "disgruntled employee" is not an act. The other topics are about the dark side's "what," but the disgruntled topic is about the dark side's "who." We wrestled with this problem for awhile, but eventually concluded that there was such a plethora of stories of what disgruntled employees did, that we would include the topic even though it was orthogonal to our book's organization. And, in addition, we came across an interesting study about IT sabotage, which we chose to link to our topic of disgruntled employees (thus adding an "act/what" dimension to our "who" discussion.

9. We had a similar problem with "whistle-blowing." As public opinion has changed over the years, whistle-blowing has come to be seen as a positive thing. Political leaks may still be seen as negative, but whistle-blowing is done by the good guys, we the public normally believe. But the problem this causes us is that whistle-blowing is not a dark side act, and therefore—once again—it doesn't fit crisply into our book's organization. But, we finally decided, since whistle-blowing usually happens as a response to some other kind of dark side activity, we could justify its inclusion here.

10. We are surprised and pleased with our viewpoints sections. This began as a gleam in the eye of Johann, and evolved into what we now think is one of the most interesting chapters of the book. Most of our contributors are people whose names you may recognize, and whose contributions to the book are fascinating, often at a personal and/or deeply felt level. It was gratifying to find that so many of our peers and colleagues were interested enough in what we were doing that they sent us along some material. We hope that you will be equally surprised and pleased!

The sum total of all of that is that we found the topic "the dark side of software engineering" both an appealing and a frustrating subject. We are pleased, however, that we engaged it, and we hope that you—our readers—are too!

Oh, and by the way, the two authors of this book still haven't met in person. Isn't the electronic era wonderful?!

INDEX

The Dark Side of Software Engineering, by Johann Rost and Robert L. Glass
Copyright © 2011 IEEE Computer Society

Printed and bound by CPI Group (UK) Ltd, Croydon, CR0 4YY

27/10/2024

14580257-0004